PACKAGE HOLIDAY LAW
CASES AND MATERIALS

PACKAGE HOLIDAY LAW: CASES AND MATERIALS

Alan Saggerson
BCL MA (Oxon) Barrister
Bencher of Lincoln's Inn
A Recorder

© Alan Saggerson 2008

Published by
XPL
99 Hatfield Road,
St Albans, UK
AL1 4JL

www.xplpublishing.com

ISBN 978 1 85811 378 4

Printed and bound in the UK.

Contents

Table of Cases

Table of Statutes

Table of Regulations and Directives

Introduction

This book attempts to gather together a range of cases and a few materials relevant to those engaged in package holiday litigation. The attempt is complicated (as with any publication of this type) by many assorted problems, not so much about what to put in, but what to leave out. No doubt another compiler would have made many of these decisions differently. Once it has been decided to include a case there is the further problem concerning the extent to which the decision should be edited. These editing decisions may well have been made differently by others. Just so that the reader is fully informed about the nature of the difficulties encountered in producing this collection, a yet further issue arises about where to *put* the materials chosen within the framework of chapter headings. Many cases deal with several distinct legal issues. Should the decisions reproduced be split between the various relevant chapters or should the case be consigned to the chapter considered most suitable? The latter course has been adopted here. This has the advantage of enabling the reader to look at the case as a whole rather than flitting from one chapter to another for relevant chunks. However, the disadvantage that some gem may be hidden away in the "wrong" chapter is admitted. It is hoped that the index will help.

The selection offered here *does* include a number of cases which are merely illustrative on their *facts* and readers will no doubt be acutely conscious that these decisions are fact sensitive. As such they may offer some useful indicators but will seldom, if ever, be determinative of another case.

Nonetheless such a compilation as this is considered particularly worthwhile for holiday cases because, with several important exceptions, the decisions are not reported elsewhere or at least not in an easily accessible form. One reason for this is that many decisions of some importance under the *Package Travel, Package Holidays and Package Tours Regulations 1992* are decisions of the County Court. It is because of this that an important health warning in the shape of the *Practice Direction (Citation of Authorities) 2001* must be given. Practitioners will be aware of paragraphs 6.1 and 6.2(iv) of that *Practice Direction* which limits the citation of County Court cases to certain restricted categories. By way of reminder the *Practice Direction* is reproduced in full at the end of this Introduction.

All this brings us to an additional observation. Care must be taken to distinguish between those cases where the judgment has been reproduced in full (and where this has been done the judgment has been taken from a transcript or official report) and those where the decision has been edited (usually in examples where the case concerned a number of distinct issues but is being used to illustrate a specific point). It will be obvious from the context where editing has occurred. Case decisions reproduced from sources such as *Current Law* are often cryptic and unauthenticated to the extent that they are reports filed by those involved in the case reported.

A section has been included on *Damages.* This comprises a small number of old, principled "warhorses" and a number of quantum reports. The selection of the latter is a particularly personal one – there are many other such reports in the books – and anyone who has been involved in the assessment of damages will know that no two cases are ever truly alike.

Detailed commentary has been avoided. Each chapter begins with a short outline of what is in store, but no more. There are now several text books dealing with holiday, travel and transport law each of which provides detailed commentary and discussion. For this reason it was considered unnecessary to include a large amount of explanatory text particularly as the whole point of the present book is to focus on the content of the decisions themselves.

I am very grateful to those who have supplied me with information about and in some instances, transcripts of otherwise unreported decisions, in particular Matthew Chapman, Ian Miller, Sarah Prager and Jack Harding at 1 Chancery Lane (formerly No. 1 Serjeants' Inn). I am equally grateful to those who have given their kind permission to reproduce decisions reported elsewhere and of course the transcribers of the unreported decisions. The editorial decisions made are, however, entirely my own as are such errors as you will undoubtedly find as you proceed.

Alan Saggerson
1 Chancery Lane
London
WC2A 1LF
February 2008

Practice Direction on the Citation of Authorities

Introduction

1. In recent years, there has been a substantial growth in the number of readily available reports of judgments in this and other jurisdictions, such reports being available either in published reports or in transcript form. Widespread knowledge of the work and decisions of the courts is to be welcomed. At the same time, however, the current weight of available material causes problems both for advocates and for courts in properly limiting the nature and amount of material that is used in the preparation and argument of subsequent cases.

2. The latter issue is a matter of rapidly increasing importance. Recent and continuing efforts to increase the efficiency, and thus reduce the cost, of litigation, whilst maintaining the interests of justice, will be threatened if courts are burdened with a weight of inappropriate and unnecessary authority, and if advocates are uncertain as to the extent to which it is necessary to deploy authorities in the argument of any given case.

3. With a view to limiting the citation of previous authority to cases that are relevant and useful to the court, this Practice Direction lays down a number of rules as to what material may be cited, and the manner in which that cited material should be handled by advocates. These rules are in large part such as many courts already follow in pursuit of their general discretion in the management of litigation. However, it is now desirable to promote uniformity of practice by the same rules being followed by all courts.

4. It will remain the duty of advocates to draw the attention of the court to any authority not cited by an opponent which is adverse to the case being advanced.

5. This Direction applies to all courts apart from criminal courts, including within the latter category the Court of Appeal (Criminal Division) Categories of judgments that may only be cited if they fulfil specified requirements

6.1 A judgment falling into one of the categories referred to in paragraph 6.2 below may not in future be cited before any court unless it clearly indicates that it purports to establish a new principle or to extend the present law. In respect of judgments delivered after the date of this Direction, that indication must take the form of an express statement to that effect. In respect of judgments delivered before the date of this Direction that indication must be present in or clearly deducible from the language used in the judgment.

6.2 Paragraph 6.1 applies to the following categories of judgment:
Applications attended by one party only
Applications for permission to appeal
Decisions on applications that only decide that the application is arguable
County Court cases, unless
(a) cited in order to illustrate the conventional measure of damages in a personal   injury   case;   or
(b) cited in a County Court in order to demonstrate current authority at that level on an issue in respect of which no decision at a higher level of authority is available.

6.3 These categories will be kept under review, such review to include consideration of adding to the categories. Citation of other categories of judgment.

7.1 Courts will in future pay particular attention, when it is sought to cite other categories of judgment, to any indication given by the court delivering the judgment that it was seen by that court as only applying decided law to the facts of the particular case; or otherwise as not extending or adding to the existing law.

7.2 Advocates who seek to cite a judgment that contains indications of the type referred to in paragraph 7.1 will be required to justify their decision to cite the case.

Methods of citation.
8.1 Advocates will in future be required to state, in respect of each authority that they wish to cite, the proposition of law that the authority demonstrates, and the parts of the judgment that support that proposition. If it is sought to cite more than one authority in support of a given proposition, advocates must state the reason for taking that course.

8.2 The demonstration referred to in paragraph 8.1 will be required to be contained in any skeleton argument and in any appellant's or respondent's notice in respect of each authority referred to in that skeleton or notice.

8.3 Any bundle or list of authorities prepared for the use of any court must in future bear a certification by the advocate responsible for arguing the case that the requirements of this paragraph have been complied with in respect of each authority included.

8.4 The statements referred to in paragraph 8.1 should not materially add to the length of submissions or of skeleton arguments, but should be sufficient to demonstrate, in the context of the advocate's argument, the relevance of the authority or authorities to that argument and that the citation is necessary for a proper presentation of that argument. Authorities decided in other jurisdictions.

9.1 Cases decided in other jurisdictions can, if properly used, be a valuable source of law in this jurisdiction. At the same time, however, such authority should not be cited without proper consideration of whether it does indeed add to the existing body of law.

9.2 In future therefore, any advocate who seeks to cite an authority from another jurisdiction must
i.   comply, in respect of that authority, with the rules set out in paragraph 8 above;
ii.   indicate in respect of each authority what that authority adds that is not to be found in authority in this jurisdiction; or, if there is said to be justification for adding to domestic authority, what that justification is;
iii. certify that there is no authority in this jurisdiction that precludes the acceptance by the court of the proposition that the foreign authority is said to establish.

9.3 For the avoidance of doubt, paragraphs 9.1 and 9.2 do not apply to cases decided in either the European Court of Justice or the organs of the European Convention of Human Rights. Because of the status in English law of such authority, as provided by, respectively, section 3 of the European Communities Act 1972 and section 2(1) of the Human Rights Act 1998, such cases are covered by the earlier paragraphs of this Direction.

The Lord Chief Justice of England and Wales 9th Day of April 2001

SECTION 1

PACKAGE HOLIDAY CONTRACTS

Section 1

PACKAGE HOLIDAY CONTRACTS

Cases in this Section

Wong Mee Wan (administratrix of the estate of Ho Shui Yee) v Kwan Kin Travel Services Limited [1996] 1 WLR 38 (6 November 1995)

PRIVY COUNCIL

LORD SLYNN OF HADLEY: On 4th August 1988 Miss Ho Shui Yee a resident of Hong Kong, was drowned whilst on holiday in the People's Republic of China. Her mother the present appellant brought proceedings in the High Court of Hong Kong against Kwan Kin Travel Services Company whose registered office is in Hong Kong China Travel Services Company and Pak Tang Lake Travel Services Company both of which carry on business in China.

In outline the facts found by the trial judge were these. Miss Ho and two school friends contracted to take a package tour to Pak Tang Lake offered by the first defendant. They left Hong Kong as part of a group of 24 persons first by ferry and then by coach. They were accompanied by a tour leader employed by the first defendant (a Miss Chan). At the border they were delayed for various reasons but on leaving the border they were accompanied by a Mr Ho an employee of the second defendant who said that he was their tour guide. The coach took them to the Shanghai Guest House where they were to spend the first night. Because of the delays which had occurred Mr Ho told them that they should leave their luggage at the guest house quickly so that they could go to visit the Ethnic Village at the lake. When they got to the pier at the lake they were told by Mr Ho that the coach and ferry had already gone and that there was no alternative for the group but to cross the lake in a speedboat. Since the speedboat took only eight persons three trips were involved the return trip across the lake taking about fifteen minutes. Mayo J had no hesitation in accepting that the group had no practical alternative but to take the speedboat across the lake and he rejected the written evidence of Mr Ho that the whole idea of going by speedboat had been suggested by members of the group and that it was outside the arrangements for the package tour. The learned judge said:

> " ... there can be no doubt in my mind that the journey on the speedboat was an integral part of the guided tour provided by the 1st Defendant."

The speedboat driven by an employee of the third defendant made the first two trips successfully. When it returned from taking the second group of eight people that employee refused to do the third trip. A " volunteer" another employee of the third defendant was found to drive the boat on the third trip. Miss Ho her two friends and Mr Ho the guide were part of the third group. It seems that the boat went very fast perhaps racing another speedboat. It hit a fishing junk which because of the angle of the boat to the water the driver probably never saw. The occupants were thrown into the water. Two were drowned one of whom was Miss Ho; the others including Mr Ho managed to get onto the junk and were taken to safety.

Mayo J did not consider that the first defendant " undertook sufficient measures to ensure that members of their guided tours were adequately protected while they were in China" and in particular:-

> " I do not consider that any adequate measures were taken to ensure that a safe system of operation was provided for the operation of the speedboat on the Lake which I have found to be an integral part of the Tour."

He ruled that the first defendant did owe Miss Ho:-

> " a primary and contractual duty to take reasonable care for her safety which included taking satisfactory measures to ensure that if speedboats were used on the tour they would be operated by persons of reasonable competence and experience."

He further found:

> " There was no evidence that any attempt was made to ensure that the speedboat which was being used as part of the Transportation was operated in a safe manner or that a safe system of operation was adhered to."

In the Court of Appeal there was no dispute that Miss Ho's death was caused by the negligent driving of the speedboat by an employee of the third defendant and that Mr Ho on behalf of the second defendant was negligent in not preventing the speedboat from being driven by someone who was not seen to be reasonably competent and qualified to do so. Whilst accepting that the first defendant did more than merely put its clients in touch with the companies in China the Court found that the first defendant did not hold out the second and third defendants and their employees as being its employees. Nor did it owe a primary contractual duty to Miss Ho in respect of what happened. Penlington JA said that it:

> " ... must have been clear to all members of the tours that it could not provide all those services itself but would delegate to other companies in China its duty to provide the bulk of them. . . .It would in my view impose an intolerable burden if the firm which put the tour package together was to be held liable for the negligence of a transport operator in another country on the basis of a breach of a non-delegable primary contractual duty."

He added that the first defendant could not reasonably have anticipated that the third defendant would use a speedboat driven by an inexperienced and negligent employee; nor could Miss Ho have expected and relied on the first defendant to make sure that the speedboat was safe, providing the package tour " would include seeing that the transportation which it was aware would be used was supplied by reputable organisations" . That the Court of Appeal accepted was done.

The issue is thus whether in this particular contract the first defendant undertook no more than that they would arrange for services to be provided by others as their agents (where the law would imply a term into the contract that they would use reasonable care and skill in selecting those other persons) or whether they themselves undertook to supply the services when subject to any exemption clause there would be implied into the contract a term that they would as suppliers carry out the services with reasonable care and skill ...

There are of course many contracts under which a person agrees to supply services when he may arrange for his obligations to be performed by others and where it is indeed contemplated that he will do so. As Cockburn CJ said in *British Wagon Co. v Lea* (1880) 5 Q.B.D. 149 at pp 153-4

> " Much work is contracted for which it is known can only be executed by means of sub-contracts; much is contracted for as to which it is indifferent to the party for whom it is to be done whether it is done by the immediate

party to the contract or by someone on his behalf. In all these cases the *maxim Qui facit per alium facit per se* applies."

The fact that the supplier of services may under the contract arrange for some or all of them to be performed by others does not absolve the supplier from his contractual obligation. He may be liable if the service is performed without the exercise of due rare and skill on the part of the sub-contractor just as he would be liable if the sub-contractor failed to provide the service or failed to provide it in accordance with the terms of the contract. The obligation undertaken is thus if the person undertaking to supply the services performs them himself that he will do so with reasonable skill and care and that if where the contract permits him to do so he arranges for others to supply the services that they will be supplied with reasonable skill and care (see *Chitty on Contracts* (1994) 27th edition pages 987-988 paras. 19-046 and 19-047).

The distinction between the two categories of case - where the party agrees merely as agents to arrange for services to be provided and where he undertakes to supply the services - is drawn in *Craven v Strand Holidays (Canada) Limited* (1982) 40 O.R. (2d) 186. There the plaintiffs claimed damages for personal injury when a bus in which they were travelling in Colombia overturned due to the negligence of the driver. The driver was not the employee of the defendant but the bus trip had been arranged as part of a package tour sold by the defendant to the plaintiffs. The Court of Appeal held that there was no implied term that the plaintiffs would be carried safely (a claim in respect of which would in any event be excluded by the exemption clause in the contract) and that the defendant would be liable only if it had been negligent in the selection of the bus operator. Lacourciere JA said (at page 190):

> " If a person agrees to perform some work or services he cannot escape contractual liability by delegating the performance to another.... But if the contract is only to provide or arrange for the performance of services then he has fulfilled his contract if he has exercised due care in the selection of a competent contractor. He is not responsible if that contractor is negligent in the performance of the annual work or service for the performance is not part of his contract."

It is thus clear that the fact that it is known that another person will or may perform the services or part of them does not mean that the contract is one of agency. In each case it has to be asked as a matter of construction into which category the contract falls. This may not always be easy.

These questions have arisen in three English cases concerned with the provision of package tours. In *Jarvis v Swans Tours Limited* [1973] QB 233 the Court of Appeal held that travel agents had on the terms of their brochure made it clear that what they were contracting to provide was not merely air travel hotel accommodation or meals of a certain standard. " They went further than that. They assured and undertook to provide a holiday of a certain quality." Edmund Davies LJ at page 239 said:

> " If in such circumstances travel agents fail to provide a holiday of the contracted quality they are liable in damages."

That was so although plainly some of the services were not to be provided by the defendants themselves.

In *Wilson v Best Travel Limited* [1993] 1 All E.R. 353 Phillips J held that for the purposes of section 13 of the Supply of Goods and Services Act 1982 which implied into a contract for the supply of service a term " that the supplier will carry out the service with reasonable care and skill" the duty of care owed by a tour operator to its customers was a duty " to exercise reasonable care to exclude from the accommodation offered any hotel the characteristics of which were such that guests could not spend a holiday there in reasonable safety" . The duty was thus recognised but the judge held at page 358 that the standards set were those applicable in the country in question unless " the absence of [a feature which will be found in an English hotel] might lead a reasonable holiday-maker to decline to take a holiday at the hotel in question" . In that case local standards had been complied with.

Their Lordships have been referred to the unreported decision of Hodgson J of 18th November 1981 in *Wall v Silver Wing Surface Arrangements Limited (trading as Enterprise Holidays)* a decision not cited to the trial judge or to the Court of Appeal. That was a case where the plaintiffs were injured when they had to jump from a hotel bedroom because a means of escape otherwise available had been barred by the locking of a gate which was normally open. It had been open when the defendant's representative had visited the hotel. The plaintiffs claimed damages initially on the basis of an implied term in their contract with the package tour operator that the plaintiffs would be reasonably safe in using the hotel alternatively by late amendment they claimed in tort.

Hodgson J rejected the argument that such a term had to be implied:

> " If an officious bystander had suggested either to the tour operator or I think to most customers that the tour operator would be liable for any default on the part of any of these people both would to put it mildly have been astonished."

Having reviewed a number of authorities he concluded that:

> " Before the court will impose obligations as a matter of general law upon parties to a contract, there must be some element of necessity present."

He thought that it would be wholly unreasonable to saddle a tour operator with an obligation to ensure the safety of all the components of a package over none of which he had any control at all. He rejected a claim based on the implied term alleged and whilst accepting that a tour operator could be liable in negligence he found that the duty of care owed by the package tour operator to its customers in that case had been fulfilled. It must be said at once that the implied term alleged in that case is not the one relied on here. Whether it is " wholly unreasonable" to impose an obligation that the services will be performed with reasonable skill and care their Lordships discuss subsequently in this judgment.

The Court of Appeal thought in the present case that it would impose an intolerable burden if the firm which put the package tour together was to be held liable for the negligence of a transport operator in another country on the basis of a breach of non-delegable primary contractual duty. This reflects what was said by Mr Justice Hodgson in the passage to which reference has been made. Penlington JA... read the first defendant's contract as being " to provide a reasonable package tour and that would include seeing that the transportation which it was aware would be used was supplied by reputable organisations" . He added " that in my opinion does not make them liable for the irresponsible action of the second and third defendants in allowing a speedboat to be driven by an apparently unqualified and as it turned out negligent driver when the appellant was not aware that speedboats might be used at all during the tour" .

On the basis of the authorities to which reference has been made the question is into which of the two categories referred to he present contract falls.

The first defendant's brochure which is accepted to contain the contractual terms between Miss Ho and the first defendant describes the itinerary for the three days. It is necessary to refer only to parts of it.

> " First day: Hong Kong - Zhu Hai - Pat Teng Lake
>
> On that day we will firstly gather at the China Hong Kong Ferry Pier or the concourse the 3rd Floor of the Macau Ferry Wharf with the receipt of our company you can receive the steamer ticket.... We will board the deluxe double jet hydrofoil ... Upon arrival there our staff will handle the customs formalities for (you). After getting through the customs we will board the deluxe coach to Pat Teng Lake Holiday Village at Zhu Hai City....
>
> Second day: Pat Teng Lake Holiday Village-
>
> Chong Shan Hop Spring - Pearl
>
> Amusement Park - Chui Hang
>
> Village - Shi Qi Fu Wah Hotel
>
> After breakfast accompanied by the tourist guide we will visit the rustic and beautiful Holiday Village ... Following that we will go to Chong Shan Hot Spring for lunch by coach. After lunch we will go to Pearl Amusement Park, ... Then we will get on the coach at the designated time ... when we will go back to Fu Wah Hotel ... We will have supper at the restaurant in the hotel.... We will then live in Fu Wah Hotel at Shi Qi ..."

The price was said to include:

> " 1. Transportation as specified in itinerary.
>
> 2. Breakfast lunch and dinner for each day as specified in itinerary.
>
> 3. Sightseeing as specified in itinerary.
>
> 4. Accommodation as specified in itinerary."

The receipt stated:

> " Our company provides second class seat in Fai Tat Ferry for the departure and return journeys."

It was clearly always the first defendant's intention that parts of the package tour would be carried out by others and in particular in their respective spheres by the second and third defendants. Miss Ho and her colleagues may have appreciated that someone other than the first defendant would carry out some parts of the tour. That does not however conclude the question. It still has to be considered whether the first defendant was in reality doing no more than " arranging" the tour so that they undertook no liability for any default by those providing the goods and services or at the most a liability to take reasonable care in the selection of those who provided the services. In the present case there are in the terms of the brochure which are treated as part of the contractual arrangements no clear statements that the first defendant was doing no more than arranging the tour as agent for the travellers.

The heading of the brochure " Kwan Kin Travel Tours everything more comprehensively and thoughtfully worked out" gives some indication that it is the first defendant who has undertaken the task of supplying the package tours. Throughout the detailed itinerary it is always " we" who will do things - board the bus go for lunch live in the hotel. Their Lordships do not think that " we" is to be read simply as referring to the customers i.e. in an attempt to lay the foundation for a friendly atmosphere on the tours. " We" includes the company offering the tour and integrates the company into each stage of the tour. At Zhu Hai it is " our staff" who will handle the customs formalities for you. There is nothing to indicate that " the tourist guide" who is accompanying the group to the Village is other than an employee of the first defendant and in paragraph 7 it is the " escorts of our company who may request a member to leave the tour. The price - an all in price - includes " Transportation as specified in the itinerary and the learned trial judge accepted that the trip across the lake fell within that description. Meals sight seeing and accommodation all are set out in the first defendant's itinerary. It is the first defendant who has the right to change the means of transport provided for in the itinerary.

Taking the contract as a whole their Lordships consider that the first defendant here undertook to provide and not merely to arrange all the services included in the programme even if some activities were to be carried out by others. The first defendant's obligation under the contract that the services would be provided with reasonable skill and care remains even if some of the services were to be rendered by others and even if tortious liability may exist on the part of those others. It has not been suggested that Miss Ho was in contractual relations with the others.

In their Lordships' view it was an implied term of the contract that those services would be carried out with reasonable skill and care. That term does not mean to use the words of Hodgson J that the first defendant undertook an obligation to " ensure the safety of all the components of the package" . The plaintiff's claim does not amount to an implied term that her daughter would be reasonably safe. It is a term simply that reasonable skill and care would be used in rendering the services to be provided under the contract. The trip across the lake was clearly not carried out with reasonable skill and care in that no steps were taken to see that the driver of the speedboat was of reasonable competence and experience and the first defendant is liable for such breach of contract as found by the learned trial judge.

Their Lordships of course appreciate the desire of the Court of Appeal to avoid imposing a burden which is "intolerable" on package tour operators. It must, however be borne in mind that the tour operator has the opportunity to seek to protect himself against claims made against him in respect of services performed by others by negotiating suitable contractual terms with those who are to perform those services. He may also provide for insurance cover. He may include an appropriate exemption clause in his contract with the traveller. It also has to be borne in mind in considering what is " tolerable" or reasonable between the parties that a traveller in the position of Miss Ho could have no influence on the terms negotiated by the tour operator with third parties and if injured by their lack of care would if having no right against the package tour operator be obliged to pursue a claim in a foreign country. The difficulty involved in doing so does not need to be elaborated. In considering what is or is not tolerable as between traveller and tour operator it is of some relevance to note the Package Travels Package Holidays and Package Tours Regulations 1992 (S.I. 1992 No. 3288) made pursuant to Council Directive 90/314/EEC. The organiser or retailer of the package tour:-

> " 15(1)...is liable to the consumer for the proper performance of the obligations under the contract irrespective of whether such obligations are to be performed by that other party or by other suppliers of services but this shall not affect any remedy or right of action which that other party may have against those other suppliers of services.
>
> 15(2). The other party to the contract is liable to the consumer for any damage caused to him by the failure to perform the contract or the improper performance of the contract"

These terms do not of course apply to the present contract but they do throw some light on the contention that an unreasonable burden would be imposed if the contract were held to contain a term that reasonable skill and care would be used. Their Lordships are satisfied that in the present case such a term was to be implied in respect of the services provided and to quote Cockburn CJ whether the work " is...done by the immediate party to the contract or by someone on his behalf" . Their Lordships accordingly conclude that if the tour operator agrees that services will be supplied whether by him or others on his behalf to imply a term that those services will be carried out with reasonable skill and care is not imposing on the tour operator a burden which is intolerable as the Court of Appeal thought. Nor is it wholly unreasonable as Hodgson J thought in *Wall v Silver Wing Surface Arrangements.*

Accordingly their Lordships will humbly advise Her Majesty that the appeal should be allowed and the judgment of Mayo J restored.

Watson and Another v First Choice Holidays and Flights Ltd and Aparta Hotels Caledonia SA, unreported, 13 July 2000 (Deputy High Court Judge James Goudie QC)

MR GOUDIE QC: This is an action for damages for serious personal injuries and consequential loss sustained by the claimant as a result of an accident which occurred on 4th July 1995 in Tenerife. Tenerife of course is part of the Kingdom of Spain. The claimant was in Tenerife on holiday. He was aged 19 at the time. He was in a self-catering flat, in a block of flats called Xanadu, part of a resort development at Playa Las Americas.

In the early hours of 4th July the claimant, another young man, Ian Barnshaw, and two young women went to Caladonia Park, another block of flats in Playa Las Americas. All four were on holiday. The two women had invited the claimant and Mr Barnshaw to their flat. At the reception area the staff refused to allow the men to enter. An altercation developed and the security guard at the block of flats chased the claimant and Mr Barnshaw off the premises. Instead of leaving by the same way that they had come, the men left by an exit leading to an area bounded by a wall, slightly less than 14 inches high. Both men jumped the wall without seeing what was on the other side. They fell more than 65 feet to the Tarmac road below. Both unsurprisingly suffered grave injuries.

The first defendants are an English company who are in the business of supplying holidays. The claimant had a contract with them. I do not have to consider whether he could sue them in Spain as a co-defendant with the second defendant or otherwise, although it is clear that the claimant could sue the second defendant in Spain, and Article 5(1) of the Brussels Convention provides:

> " In matters relating to a contract, a person domiciled in a contracting State may in another Contracting State be sued in the courts for the place of the performance of the obligation in question."

The second defendants are a Spanish company. The claimant had no contract with them. They owned and ran the resort. The claim against them is in tort. The Contracts (Rights of Third Parties) Act 1999 was of course not in force at the material time.

The present proceedings were issued against the first defendant on 2nd July 1998. It has made no application to set aside the proceedings against it. Indeed it served a defence on 8th January 1999. Liability is put in issue. Contributory negligence is alleged. Then in March 1999 the proceedings were amended in order to add the second defendant. The proceedings have since been re-amended.

The second defendants were served in Spain in October 1999.

They challenged the jurisdiction of the English court by an application dated 5th November 1999. The second defendant's application was heard by Master Eyre on 17th April 2000 and dismissed. On 15th May permission to appeal was granted by the learned Master himself.

Also in July 1998 Mr Barnshaw brought proceedings. He sued the second defendant alone. He brought his proceedings in Spain. He blamed the security guard. The Spanish Court held that the hotel was responsible for the security guard, even though at the time of the accident the security service was contracted out to another company. The proceedings in Spain were described as extra contractual. They were based on an Article of the Spanish Civil Code which provides for a liability for negligence. The Spanish court ruled that there were three elements for liability. First:

> " Something outside the standards of care and proportion established by legal provisions and socially accepted."

Secondly, harm, and thirdly, a causal link.

On 3rd February 2000 Mr Barnshaw's claim was dismissed. The Spanish court held that the fall suffered by Mr Barnshaw was due entirely to his own negligence. The effective cause of his injuries was jumping over the wall and the action of the security guard was causally irrelevant. There was also a subsidiary point about signage and lighting.

The second's defendant's application in these proceedings is based on Schedule 1 to the Civil Jurisdiction and Judgments Act 1982 and the Brussels Convention to which I have already referred.

Section 3 of the Civil Jurisdiction and Judgments Act 1982 provides by subsection (1):

> " Any question as to the meaning or effect of any provision of the Brussels Conventions shall, if not referred to the European Court in accordance with the 1971 Protocol, be determined in accordance with the principles laid down by and any relevant decision of the European Court."

The United Kingdom and Spain are both Contracting States within the meaning of the Brussels Convention. Accordingly the primary rule is that the second defendant, as a Spanish domiciled party, should be sued in the courts of Spain. That is Article 2.

The courts of other Contracting States have jurisdiction only in one or more of three circumstances. Firstly, if the courts of the other Contracting State have exclusive jurisdiction under Article 16. Secondly, if the courts of the other Contracting State has special jurisdiction under Articles 5 to 6(a). Thirdly, if there has been prorogation of jurisdiction under Article 17. There are no issues of prorogation of jurisdiction or exclusive jurisdiction in this case. Accordingly the English courts have jurisdiction over the second defendant only if they have special jurisdiction.

Special jurisdictions include under Article 5(3), in matters relating to tort, the courts for the place where the harmful event occurred. However, the claimant contends that the English court has special jurisdiction under Article 6(1). It is common ground for the purposes of this application that the application must succeed unless the claimant can indeed rely on Article 6(1).

Article 6(1) provides:

> " A person domiciled in a Contracting State may also be sued where he is one of a number of defendants in the courts for the place where any one of them is domiciled."

The second defendant is one of two defendants and the other, the first defendant, is domiciled in England. On the face of Article 6(1), the second defendant is a proper party to the English proceedings.

The second defendant submits nonetheless that the English court does not have jurisdiction under Article 6(1) on each of three grounds. First, they submit that the claimant has not shown a good arguable case against the first defendant. I reject that submission. The contract is governed by English law. The Package Travel Package Holidays and Package Tours Regulations 1992 pursuant to Council Directive 90/314/EEC on package travel, package holidays and package tours, apply to the first defendant.

Regulation 15 provides, under the general heading "Liability of other party to the contract" for proper performance of obligations under contract. By paragraph 1:

> " The other party to the contract is liable to the consumer for the proper performance of the obligations under the contract irrespective of whether such obligations are to be performed by that other party or by other suppliers of services.

This shall not affect any remedy or right of action which that other party may have against those other suppliers of services."

Subparagraph (2) provides:

> " The other party to the contract is liable to the consumer for any damage caused to him by the failure to perform the contract, or the improper performance of the contract unless the failure or the improper performance is due neither to any fault of that other party nor to that of another supplier of services because
>
> (a) the failures which occur in the performance of the contract are attributable to the consumer;
>
> (b) such failures are attributable to a third party unconnected with the provisions of the services contracted for and are unforeseeable or unavoidable; or
>
> (c) such failures are due to
>
> > (i) unusual and unforeseeable circumstances beyond the control of the party by whom this exception is pleaded, the consequences of which could not have been avoided even if all due care had been exercised; or
> >
> > (ii) an event which the party to the contract or the supplier services, even with all due care could not foresee or forestall."

Paragraph 5 of Regulation 15 provides:

> " Without prejudice to paragraph 3 and paragraph 4 [to which I need not refer] liability under paragraphs 1 and 2 cannot be excluded by any contractual term."

Regulation 2(1) defines contract. It means the agreement linking the consumer to the organiser or to the retailer or to both as the case may be.

A claim against the defendant based on the Regulations would be a claim in contract, not a claim in tort for breach of statutory duty, (emphasis added) but the case against the first defendant does not plead as against the first defendant the Regulations which are referred to rather in the first defendant's defence.

Also as against the first defendant, the claimant might seek to rely upon a case, not cited to me, the decision of the Privy Council in *Wong Mee Wan v Kwan Kin Travel Services Ltd* [1996] 1 WLR 38.

It is not however apparent that the claimant could formulate a good arguable case against the first defendant in tort.

Certainly he has not done so. In my judgment the position therefore in summary is that the plaintiff does not have a good arguable, or indeed any case, against the first defendant in tort, but does have a good arguable case against the first defendant in contract.

Spencer v Cosmos Air Holidays Ltd, 24 November 1989, (1989) *The Times* December 6

Court of Appeal (Civil Division)

FARQUHARSON LJ: In the Summer of 1986 the appellant, who was then 18 years of age, wished to have a holiday in Spain with her two girlfriends, Susan Walker and Jacqueline Flemming. Accordingly she made a booking with the respondent, who carried on the business of tour operator and travel organiser, by signing a booking form in the name of herself and her two friends. The contract was for the respondent to arrange an air flight for the three girls from Manchester to Spain and to provide accommodation for them for 14 nights at the hotel Rosamar Park in Lloret de Mar at a price of £266 per person. The booking form contained words to the effect that the appellant had read and accepted the " Cosmos Fair Trading Bond" which was contained in a brochure published by the respondent containing details of the holidays they provided.

The Fair Trading Bond makes it clear that the respondent was not a travel agent but was acting as a principal. The document contained information setting out the price guarantees given by the respondent; the arrangements which would be made if the holiday had to be cancelled by either party; details of holiday insurance, and so on. At the foot of the page, under the heading "Liability", appeared the following disclaimer:

> " We are travel and holiday organisers only. We do not control or operate any airline neither do we own or control any shipping company, coach or coach company, hotel, transport or any other facility or service mentioned in this brochure. We take care in selecting all the ingredients in your holiday, but because we only select and inspect them and have no control in the running of them, we cannot be responsible for any injury, death, loss or damage which is caused by any negligence of the management or employees of an independent contractor arising outside our normal selection and inspection process. "

The money representing the costs of the holidays was duly paid. The appellant and her friends left Manchester on 28th July 1986 and began the holiday in Lloret de Mar. Unhappily on 6th August of that year they were instructed by a representative of the management of the hotel to leave. As accommodation was difficult to come by the girls spent the next two nights sleeping on the beach. On the third day following their expulsion from the hotel a representative of the respondent managed to get a room for them at another less pleasing resort called Malgrat, which was some 15 miles from Lloret. There they completed their holiday.

Subsequently the appellant brought these proceedings claiming that the respondent had broken its contract by failing to provide her and her friends with the accommodation they had paid for to their great misery, distress and humiliation. The reasons why the girls were turned out of the hotel were set out in the defence filed by the respondent. It was alleged that they were intoxicated on their arrival in Spain and remained so through their holiday, with the result that they were abusive to others and disruptive in their behaviour; that they assaulted the hotel security guard; that they allowed drunken men into their room, and that they were shouting and screaming late at night heedless of the management's warnings. In short, they were thoroughly objectionable and upset the other guests.

It was agreed on the pleadings that the contract between the parties contained an implied term that the plaintiff and her friends would not conduct themselves in a manner which would cause discomfort or make themselves objectionable to other guests and/or the hotel staff. If the complaints of their conduct were true, then plainly the appellant and her friends would have been in breach of that implied term. When the trial of the action took place the only evidence of their alleged misconduct was contained in a letter from the Manageress of the hotel tendered under the Civil Evidence Act 1968 – a letter which had been written the day following the expulsion. It was in these terms – addressed by the Manageress to a representative of the respondent:

> " We are writing to inform you that last night Misses Spencer x" – those were the three girls of course – " were expelled from our Hotel Rosamar Park for assaulting one of our night security guards. Though the act of aggression was more than sufficient reason to expel the girls it was not the only reason. They were a problem from the very first day they arrived on account of their moral and civil behaviour. From the first day their behaviour was scandalous, together with other clients who were also expelled, around the corridors of the hotel, the terraces and the lounges. They were warned repeatedly that if they did not behave in a proper manner they would be expelled. These were warnings were laughed at from beginning to end. "

The appellant stoutly denies that she or her companions were guilty of this misbehaviour.

It is agreed on both sides that if the girls were guilty of the conduct alleged, then the appellant's claim should be dismissed; that is because the obligation of the respondent under the contract was, *inter alia*, to provide accommodation at this hotel. If the appellant and her friends through their own misconduct put themselves in a position where they cannot avail themselves of this accommodation then the obligation of the respondent is *pro tanto* discharged. It was therefore vital that the learned judge should have made a finding one way or the other whether the girls had so misbehaved. Unfortunately, he did not do so and, in my judgment, the case will now have to go back for these findings to be made. Whether the judge decides the issue on the strength of the evidence he has heard or hears further evidence will be a matter for him.

Counsel for the respondent, Mr Aldous, submits that if the judge finds that the girls had not in fact been guilty of the conduct alleged, the respondent is still entitled to judgment in this action. Indeed, the judge's decision was based, or partly based, on the matters which counsel is now submitting. As the case is presently before this court – even though it must be remitted for the reasons already given – we have, with the consent of both parties, heard argument on these further issues.

To develop them I turn to the judgment, which is in the form of an agreed note approved by the judge, in which the learned judge said this:

" The rights of the Hotel Manager go further than an actually proved case of misbehaviour. If the Manager receives apparently reliable reports that a guest has misbehaved then I think it very likely that the Manager is entitled to eject that guest. In this case it seems probable that the Management of the hotel had good reason to believe that certain guests misbehaved and therefore could no longer stay in the hotel. I think it is also probable that the Management believed that it was the Plaintiff and friends. In those circumstances would they, the Management, be liable to the Plaintiff? Only if they made no serious effort to investigate the matter i.e. they had come to a negligent conclusion.

Could the Defendants really be in a worse position than that of the Management? I doubt it. In this contract there is an exclusion clause in the brochure. Regarding the possibility that someone misbehaved – and I am quite satisfied that someone did – it is possible that the Management made a mistake in identifying those responsible.

In view of the possibility of the mistaken identity I ought to find:

(i)   *that the hotel would be liable;*

(ii)   *that therefore the Defendant should also be liable for breach of contract.*

In the absence of any exclusion clause, the Defendants might be responsible. I do not feel that the authorities on this point are sufficient to enable me to say yes or no to that. But having regard to the exclusion clause I take the view that because of the possibility that the Defendants might be held liable for a breach of contract over which they had no control, this is not only a reasonable clause but also the sort of clause that anyone in the travel business could be expected to put in the contract. I find that the inclusion of this clause in the brochure is wholly reasonable and that the Defendants are entitled to rely upon it. The Management may have been negligent, but even if they had been, I cannot see that these Defendants should be made responsible. "

[The Respondent] has adopted this line of reasoning by submitting that in a contract of this kind – that is, for the provision of holiday accommodation in an hotel – there is to be implied a term that where there has in fact been serious misconduct in the hotel which disturbed other guests, and the management of the hotel come to the conclusion, on reasonable grounds, that a particular guest is responsible, then the management is entitled to evict that guest even though he or she has not in fact misbehaved at all. He has argued that such a term is to be implied on the basis of giving the agreement business efficacy, as set out in the doctrine of *The Moorcock* (1889) 14 PD at page 64. A more modern statement of the law familiar to all lawyers is to be found in the observations of Mackinnon LJ in *Shirley v Southern Foundries* [1939] 2 KB 206, where at page 227 he said:

" Prima facie that which in any contract is left to be implied and need not be expressed is something so obvious that it goes without saying. So that if while the parties were making their bargain an officious bystander were to

suggest some express provision for it in their agreement they would testily suppress him with a common 'of course'".

Counsel has submitted here that if an intending holiday-maker when making a booking was told that if the hotel staff, on reasonable grounds, though he or she was guilty of serious misbehaviour where such had been taking place in the hotel they would evict the guest even though the belief was wrong, the intending holiday-maker would evict the guest even though the belief was wrong, the intending holiday-maker would readily accept that as a term of the contract to give it business efficacy. Counsel submits that any guest would agree to such term on the basis of his or her own comfort. Quite apart from the fact that the court has not been referred to any authority which supports this proposition, I would reject it. The chance of any holiday-maker accepting the inclusion of such a term seems to me to be quite unrealistic. He is not so much likely to say " *Of course*" to the suggestion as " *No fear*" . Accordingly, I would hold that no such term is to be implied, and that if the judge finds that the appellant has not been proved to have misbehaved in the manner alleged she is entitled to succeed on her claim.

I use the phrase " has not been proved" because, on the pleadings, it is clear that the burden of establishing her misbehaviour lies on the respondent. It was the respondent's task under the contract to provide the accommodation agreed upon. It is admitted on the pleadings that for three days at all events that accommodation was not provided. The respondent nevertheless says it is not in breach of contract because of th3e girls' misconduct. If a party admits that it has not fulfilled its part of the contract because of the misbehaviour of the other party, then it must prove that misbehaviour. Prima facie the respondent here is in breach of contract, so it is for the respondent to justify its non-provision of accommodation.

It will have been seen from the citation I have given from the judgment that the learned judge made no finding as to whether the respondent was negligent, or the hotel management was negligent, in concluding that the girls were guilty of serious misbehaviour, basing his decision rather on the fact that even if the hotel management was negligent, the respondent was protected by the exclusion clause set out at the beginning of this judgment. As I have held that no such implied term as to the inaccurate belief of the management can form part of this contract, a consideration of that clause does not now arise. I will therefore content myself with observing that it is designed to protect the respondent from vicarious responsibility for the negligent acts of the hotel management and staff. As the contractual obligation of the respondent is to arrange suitable holiday accommodation and not to run the hotel, I would for my part have thought that in tort no such vicarious liability would arise at common law, even without the clauses in the agreement.

The submission in the present case is that it protects the respondents from responsibility for a negligent enquiry on the part of the hotel staff when investigating the conduct of one of its guests. I doubt whether this amounts to " injury, death, loss or damage" contemplated by the terms of the clause. It is not therefore necessary to consider whether it is ineffective by reason of the Unfair Contract Terms Act 1977.

Finally, we have been asked to consider the award of damages which was fixed by the judge at the request of the parties. The learned judge came to the conclusion that the appropriate sum, if the appellant's claim was made out, would be £2,000. By a cross notice of appeal the respondent seeks to challenge that figure as being too high. It is appropriate, of course, that the judge should take into account the standard of the holiday which was to be expected from the money that was paid; principally to the fact that the girls were turned out of the hotel and, in the premises, turned out wrongly, and forced to sleep on the beach for two nights; and that this experience would have exposed them to distress and unhappiness as a result. But even allowing for all those features – which I do not in any way discount or under-value – I would for my part have thought that the award of damages fixed by the learned judge was still too high. I would accordingly reduce that award to a figure of £1,000 and accordingly allow both the appeal and the cross appeal.

MUSTILL LJ: I would approach the issues in this case by asking a series of questions and suggesting answers to them.

The first question is this. What is the nature of the plaintiff's cause of action? This is pleaded as a cause of action in contract, which is indeed the only way the claim could have been pleaded. The plaintiff's complaint is that she did not receive the benefit of the accommodation which the defendant had undertaken that she should receive.

The second question asks: What is the relationship between the plaintiff and the defendant? In the past some tour operators have tried to engineer for themselves the position of travel agents, doing no more than assemble for the customer a package of contracts made through the operator's agency direct between the customer and the various airlines, hoteliers, coach operators, and so on, with the operator incurring no liability beyond a duty to ensure that the arrangements are carefully made in accordance with the customer's instructions. It is quite clear that no such relationship existed here. A reading of the brochure leaves no room for doubt that the defendant personally undertook to secure, subject to specified exceptions, that accommodation in the stated hotel and for the stated period of time, together with transportation, was provided for the plaintiff.

The third question enquires whether it would be a defence to a claim by a customer to be compensated for damage resulting from a failure to provide hotel accommodation that the hotel proprietor had justifiably excluded the customer on the ground of unacceptably disruptive conduct? And, if so, why? I would answer this question in the affirmative. In the course of argument it was suggested that the conclusion should be reached through the medium of an implied term. For my part, I would prefer the more direct route and say that the plaintiff could not complain of a non-performance by the defendant that she herself had brought about. Whatever rationale is preferred, the answer must be the same, and counsel for the plaintiff has not sought to argue the contrary.

The fourth question is this: Upon whom lies the burden of proof in relation to the disruptive conduct upon which the defendant has sought to justify her expulsion from the room? To my mind it is absolutely clear that the burden rests with the defendant. It was their obligation to see that 14 days' accommodation was provided. A failure to perform that obligation is admitted on the pleadings. If the defendants wish to exonerate themselves from liability for this non-performance they must allege and prove the facts necessary to excuse them.

The fifth question takes this shape: Would the position be different if the hotel proprietor had excluded the customer in the bona fide and reasonable but nevertheless mistaken belief that the customer had been guilty of unacceptably disruptive behaviour? The contract already contains a most elaborate set of express provisions regulating the rights of the parties in the event that untoward happenings occur. Can a term be implied in addition relieving the defendant from liability in a situation such as I have posited? The test of an implied term is that it must be necessary to give business efficacy to the contract. I would have thought it not reasonable to imply a term depriving the customer of all remedy when excluded from the benefit of services paid for on grounds which were without substance. At any rate it seems to me absolutely clear that the implication of such a term is not necessary in order to make the contract work.

The outcome of these answers is the conclusion that the plaintiff has a valid claim for damages, subject only to the effect, if any, of the clause headed " Liability" . This leads to the sixth question, namely: Whether the language of the clause is such as to exempt the defendant from liability in a case such as the present? I consider that the answer is " No" . The reason is not that because of inept drafting the clause misses its mark, but because, in my judgment, the clause does not even set out to exclude claims in contract for failure to provide the services comprised in the holiday. The circumstances in which a prima facie claim raises where the holiday is either completely missed or is unacceptably modified are set out in the various elaborate provisions of the Fair Trading Bond – provisions which, as it seems to me, assume that the liability clause does not bear on such a situation. That clause is, to my mind, plainly intended to deal with a situation where the performance of a part of the services has been sub-contracted to a third party and where, through the negligence of the third party, the customer has suffered loss or damage, whether through personal injury or otherwise, and proceeds against the tour operator in tort. In such a case the clause aims to exclude any vicarious liability of the tour operator for the sub-contractor's wrongful act unless the operator is personally at fault. But here we are not concerned with a cause of action in tort, and the fact that the failure of performance resulted from a blunder by the hotel management does not make this the kind of claim in negligence with which the clause was intended to deal.

This opinion makes it unnecessary to express any concluded view on the validity of the liability clause in the light of the Unfair Contract Terms Act 1977. As at present advised, it seems to me that the clause is perfectly reasonable if it is understood in the sense which I have just suggested, and, indeed, may do no more than reproduce the position which exists at common law. But I would personally take a great deal of persuading that it would be reasonable if it meant that even though the defendant deprive a customer of the whole or part of the contractual services, as a result of a mistake by a sub-contractor the customer is to have no recourse in law. However, as I say, it is unnecessary in the event to state a conclusion upon this point.

Where does this leave the present appeal? The judgment of the County Court plainly cannot stand. Equally plainly we cannot substitute a verdict for the plaintiff because, as her counsel very properly accepts, if it were shown that she had misbehaved in the way alleged, she would have no claim, and the learned judge has not found one way or another whether she did misbehave. So there must be a re-trial.

There remains the cross-appeal on damages. The parties have very sensibly agreed that we should decide this, even though liability remains to be established, for otherwise the matter might have to return to this court after the re-trial. I agree with my Lord's opinion that the damages awarded were too high, and I also agree that we should substitute the figure which he has indicated.

I too, therefore, would allow both the appeal and the cross-appeal.

Williams v Travel Promotions Ltd (t/a Voyages Jules Verne) [1998] EWCA Civ 295 (19 February 1998)
Court of Appeal (Civil Division)

SIR BRIAN NEILL: This is an appeal by Mr Peter David Williams from the order dated 17th February 1997 of His Honour Judge Byrt Q.C., sitting in the Mayor's and City of London Court, whereby he dismissed the appellant's application to set aside the judgment of District Judge Samuels given in County Court arbitration proceedings on 10th June 1996.

The respondent to the appeal is a company called Travel Promotions Limited, which trades under the name Voyages Jules Verne.

In August 1994 the appellant saw a brochure of Jules Verne and booked a holiday tour with the company to go to the Victoria Falls in Zimbabwe. The tour was due to begin on 26th December 1994 and to return to England on 4th January 1995. It involved flying into and out of Livingstone Airport in Zambia and then crossing the border into Zimbabwe, where the people on the tour were going to stay. It offered two alternative hotels: the Sprayview Hotel and the Victoria Falls Hotel. The appellant chose the Sprayview Hotel.

A few days before Mr Williams was due to fly out with his tour he received a letter from Jules Verne (undated, but I believe sent on 17th December 1994) which was in these terms: " Ref: The Flight of Angels [the name of the tour] - 26 December 1994

> " We are writing to advise you that in order to avoid the early morning return transfer to Livingstone Airport on 4th January, and on the recommendation of previous passengers, we have been able to secure a small allocation of rooms at the Intercontinental Hotel in Livingstone located close to the Falls in Zambia for the night of 3rd January 1995. You are advised that we were unable to secure rooms for the entire group, so have made a priority for those passengers who have pre-booked the optional day tour of Livingstone.

> " On the 3rd January we will transfer you to the Intercontinental Hotel shortly after lunch for an overnight stay. On the 4th January you will be transferred to the nearby airport for the return flight to London Heathrow Airport.

> " We feel sure that this slight change to the arrangements will certainly enhance the itinerary and trust you will enjoy this unique opportunity of experiencing the Falls from the Zambia side. "

The appellant went on the tour, and for the next few days all went well. But on 3rd January, the day before he was due to return, he had to transfer, as had been suggested in the letter, to the Intercontinental Hotel in Zambia. The move took place during the afternoon and this caused the appellant, as he would say, very considerable inconvenience and annoyance.

After he had returned to England Mr Williams corresponded with the tour company, and he and 16 others of the party made complaints about this move on the afternoon of 3rd January. He did not receive any satisfactory answer, however, and so eventually, on 30th October 1995, he issued proceedings. In his particulars of claim he set out the loss suffered, which he put at £148.20, to which he added a sum by way of interest.

The circumstances of the move on 3rd January of which he was complaining were set out in paragraph 4 of his particulars of claim as follows:

> " The circumstances of this move were such that the effect of it was to cause the loss to the plaintiff not only of one half day of his holiday at Victoria Falls outright, but also of using the full day as he wished, without any significant, or any, benefit to him. The plaintiff was put to inconvenience and trouble in consequence of the move, including that of additional packing and unpacking; of re-registration; and in being provided with only a continental breakfast on the morning of 4 January 1995, whereas a full cooked breakfast would have been provided at the Sprayview Hotel. Further, the effect of the move was to render the plaintiff captive to the expensive restaurant of the Intercontinental Hotel, causing the plaintiff to incur additional cost in respect of his evening meal on 3 January 1995."

The tour operators, the defendants, served a defence on 8th December, relying on the conditions in the brochure. Before I turn to them, however, I should make a brief reference to the further and better particulars of the defence, which was served subsequently on 19th February 1996, in which the defendants set out their account of the events of 3rd January. They said:

> " The plaintiff was not accommodated in the Sprayview Hotel, Victoria Falls, Zimbabwe with effect from the afternoon of the 3rd January 1995 but was instead accommodated in the Intercontinental Hotel, Livingstone, Zambia. This was because the defendant had discovered by experience gained from earlier tours that it was preferable to make a border crossing between Zimbabwe and Zambia in the afternoon of the final day of the tour rather than in the evening of the final day of the tour. This resulted in a saving of time and caused less inconvenience to the plaintiff. The plaintiff was upgraded from the two star Sprayview Hotel to the five star Intercontinental Hotel."

They then referred to the booking conditions and said that the change of hotel was a " minor change" only and that they had reserved their right under the conditions to make changes.

I should now turn to the conditions, which lie at the very centre of this case. The relevant conditions were under the heading "Changes to the Scheduled Programme" .

> " *The tours scheduled in this brochure are planned many months in advance and sometimes changes may be necessary. Travel Promotions Ltd reserve the right to make changes. Your rights depend on the type of change. Alterations are either 'significant' or 'minor'. Travel Promotions Ltd has the right to make 'minor' changes at any time. We will, if practicable, advise you or your travel agent of any 'minor' change before your departure but we are not obliged to do so or pay you compensation. The arrangements featured in this brochure are by their very nature complex with services*

from many different airlines, hotels and ground transportation companies. Due to demand for flights, hotels and accommodation, over which even Travel Promotions has no control, it is not always possible to guarantee particular departure domestic flights, the aircraft type and/or the hotels featured on a particular departure date, or the precise itinerary. We therefore have to reserve the right to change any flight or hotel listed and, if necessary, even to modify the itinerary itself without prior notice. We will make every effort to provide as much advance notification as possible, but we feel it is only fair to warn you of possible variations. No compensation is payable in such circumstances, nor does it confer the right of cancellation. In practice only a few departures are likely to be affected but it must be accepted when booking that the possibility of change without prior notice exists.

" Also please note that many areas over a long period have experienced lower than average rainfall. This may result in the local authorities imposing restrictions on the use of water or associated facilities.

" A 'significant' change is a change to a departure date from the UK (but not a change to flight routes) or a change to flight timings of more than 12 hours, or a change to a lower standard of accommodation. In the event of a 'significant' change Travel Promotions Ltd will tell you or your travel agent as soon as practically possible before your departure. You are hereby informed that you then have the right to: (a) accept the alternative; or (b) purchase another holiday from Travel Promotions Ltd and if it is more expensive you will have to pay the difference, but if it is cheaper Travel Promotions Ltd will refund you the difference; or (c) cancel your holiday and obtain a full refund of all payments made to Travel Promotions Ltd, except the insurance premium. "

The matter came before the County Court under the small claims procedure, which is intended to deal with cases where no complex issues of fact or law arise (and so perhaps was not suitable for this case). That is how it came before the district judge. He heard the case, as I have already noted, in June 1996. There is a short record of his judgment. It is an agreed record, except for one particular point. It seems that the hearing began at something like noon on the date in question. It lasted over its allotted hour and did not conclude until about 1.20 p.m. Most of the hearing was taken up, so we are told, with argument on questions of law, but it was dealt with, as these arbitrations are meant to be dealt with, informally and without evidence being given on oath. Indeed, it now emerges that no evidence as such was ever given.

The judge, having heard the case for an hour and twenty minutes, said this, according to the agreed record:

" I have heard some horror stories about holidays, but this is not one of them. I am looking at a booking form signed by the plaintiff. It states 'I accept the Booking Conditions as set out in the Conditions of Passage.' Mr Williams told me, very frankly, that he read the Booking Conditions in detail. The Booking Conditions contain a term..." [He then read the clause which I have recently recited.] [I find as a fact that] this is not a significant alteration. It relates to a change of hotel for one half day. It is not unusual *for these things to happen. It had an unfortunate effect on the plaintiff, but I cannot understand why the plaintiff decided to bring this action [as the clause in the Booking Conditions is quite clear]: I cannot see that the clause is unreasonable [within the meaning of the Unfair Contract Terms Act]..."*

He may or may not (and this is a matter in dispute which I do not propose to say anything about) have been referred to the Package Travel Regulations. He continued:

" The claim must fail. There will be no award as to costs. The action is hereby dismissed."

The applicant then applied to set the judgment aside... It came before His Honour Judge Byrt on 17th February 1997. We have a note of the judge's judgment, and in effect his decision was as follows: that the question of whether the changes which had been made were necessary or significant were questions of fact for the district judge; that the defendants were not in breach of the Unfair Contract Terms Act; and that the Package Travel Regulations 1992, particularly regulation 15, to which he had been referred, were not relevant at all. He recorded the fact that it had not been argued before him that the decision of the district judge had been perverse. Accordingly, he dismissed the application to set the district judge's order aside and refused leave to appeal. But last July another division of this court gave leave to appeal.

A number of matters are raised in the notice of appeal, and I mean no discourtesy to Mr Williams in saying that I am not going to refer to all of them. But his principal arguments were these. First, he submitted that regulation 15 of the Package Travel Regulations 1992 applied, and that the effect of its application was that any deviation from the holiday as specified in the brochure meant that there had been an improper performance of the contract and, accordingly, that that improper performance could not be excused, except in one of the circumstances which are set out in the Regulations themselves.

The only other paragraph of regulation 15 to which I need make reference is paragraph (5), which provides:

" (5) Without prejudice to paragraph (3) and paragraph (4) above, liability under paragraphs (1) and (2) above [it was particularly (2) that Mr Williams relied upon] cannot be excluded by any contractual term."

So Mr Williams' first submission was that these conditions could not excuse the defendants in any event because there had been an improper performance of the contract and the reason for it did not fall within any of the specific circumstances provided for in paragraph (2) of regulation 15.

[Mr. Williams'] argument was that, if any change were made, it had to be shown to be necessary. For that purpose, he relied on what he said was the proper construction of the conditions as a whole, on the opening words and the other references to " necessary" or " if necessary" which occurred in the conditions. He submitted, therefore, that here there was no evidence of necessity; it could not possibly be said that what had happened had been necessary.

Thirdly, he said that any change which took place in the provision of accommodation at hotels had to be shown to be due to overbooking. He referred again to the terms of the conditions, which he said showed that overbooking was the only reason which could excuse a change of hotel.

Submissions (were made) to us on behalf of the respondents to the appeal, the tour operators. Dealing with matters in the same order as I have dealt with the submissions of Mr Williams, [it was] said, first, that regulation 15 of the 1992 Regulations applied to the non-performance or the improper performance of the contract. To see what that meant, one had therefore to look at the terms of the contract, and if the contract, properly construed, entitled the tour operators to make changes, as they have here, then there was no improper performance of the contract and one did not become involved with the 1992 Regulations at all.

Secondly, the word " necessary" , although it occurred in the conditions, did not, if one read the conditions as a whole, require the respondent to show that minor changes had to be shown to be necessary. That was an incorrect way of construing the conditions.

Thirdly, even if it had to be shown that a minor change was necessary, the word " necessary" had to be construed in its context. It was a word with a very wide range of meanings, and in this context it really meant, without putting it into very precise terms, something like, " changes which were reasonably required in the interests of delivering the service," or perhaps, " reasonably required for the proper performance of the contract."

Next, the changes mentioned in the conditions in the context of overbooking were merely illustrative of changes which might have to be made in the way in which the tour was conducted on any particular occasion.

So much then for the arguments. I have come to the conclusion that it is not necessary in this case to reach a conclusion about the scope or precise meaning of the Package Travel Regulations 1992 ... I think this case depends very much on the actual wording of the conditions which the respondents inserted in their brochure. To my mind, Mr Williams is correct in saying that the changes which are contemplated in the brochure and in the conditions are changes which are necessary.

The word " necessary" occurs in the opening sentence of the relevant conditions. The reader is invited to understand that sometimes changes may be necessary. It might have been very sensible for the respondents to have included in their brochure some different form of words, which made it clear to the reader that they had a wider discretion which would entitle them to make such changes as were reasonably required for the better performance of the contract. But they have chosen - and the language is theirs - to use the word " necessary" . It seems to me, therefore, that it has not been demonstrated, on the material before the district judge or indeed before us, that the important change which was made was a necessary change.

But Mr Williams had a further point, to which I have already referred, that, so far as a change of hotels was concerned, the only changes which would fall within the conditions and which could be necessary changes were changes which came about by reason of overbooking. It is not suggested, and could not be suggested, that this change, whatever the precise reason for it may have been, was due to overbooking. I do not think, if one reads the references to hotels in these conditions, that the words which are used are merely illustrative. It seems to me that readers would understand that they would be sent to the hotels they had chosen from the alternatives which had been given to them in the brochure and to which they had contracted to go in the booking form. It seems to me that to change a hotel, so that somebody has to move from one hotel to another, unless it is caused by overbooking, is something which is not contemplated within the changes to which these conditions apply. I therefore consider that, whatever evidence there might have been as to whether in fact the change was necessary, it was not necessary within the meaning of these conditions, which were limited to changes which were brought about by overbooking.

... on the issue of liability I consider that, on these conditions as presently drafted, the plaintiff is entitled to succeed.

LORD JUSTICE SCHIEMANN: I agree with the judgment that has just been delivered.

The respondent pointed out that there were all sorts of circumstances in which it would be sensible to allow ... clients to change the pre-existing arrangements, and I can see that there might well be. But this court, and, for that matter, the arbitrator, had to distinguish between what would be a sensible clause and what this particular clause provides.

We have to look at this particular clause. I quite understand that there are problems of drafting which face travel operators, who now have to contend with consumer protection legislation of one sort or another, which I do not doubt they find difficult to live with. They are to some extent between a rock and a hard place, in the sense that, if they give themselves all the liberty that they would wish to change the arrangements, then it may be found that the appropriate condition is too wide to survive the consumer protection legislation. If, on the other hand, they are prepared to tie themselves down, then there is always a case which is outside the particular words that they have chosen.

One must also bear in mind the difference between the pre-contractual and the post-contractual situation. I fully understand that it must be a difficult problem for travel operators who get out their brochures in the autumn to be sure that they can deliver the following summer that which is advertised in their brochure. These operators do draw that distinction in their brochure. One sees that, so far as the pre-contractual situation is concerned, they provide as follows:

> " Travel Promotions Ltd reserve the right to change any of the services or facilities or prices described in this brochure at any time before a contract is made between you and Travel Promotions Ltd."

That could not be wider, but it would be very difficult of course to have any meaningful contract which had that term as part of the contract. That is the difficulty that they have.

My Lord has read the relevant condition. As it seems to me, the definition of a " significant change" in the conditions is so tight that it is correct that one should give the whole clause a construction which allows the word " necessary" to have its strict meaning, so as to give some remedy where the change is " minor" , as that term is used in these particular conditions, but is nonetheless of considerable importance to the traveller concerned; and one can see, for instance, that the circumstances of the present case provide a good example. According to the conditions, requiring someone to move in a seven-day holiday to a different hotel of the same quality in the middle of the penultimate day does not amount to a significant change.

Like my Lord, I think the word " necessary" applies to any change. It will be seen, when one looks at that clause, that the right to change a hotel listed is contained in a sentence which starts off, " We therefore...." That sentence follows a previous sentence which talks about, " Due to demand for... hotels... over which even Travel Promotions has no control, it is not always possible to guarantee a particular... hotel...." In my judgment, there is force in the contention that, on these particular conditions, so far as changes of hotel in the middle of a holiday are concerned, in circumstances where one excludes force majeure, it is not envisaged that that should be done without the consent of the client concerned.

So, like my Lord, I would allow this appeal on the basis that the arbitrator misconstrued the clause which he was seeking to construe.

Akehurst and Others v *Thomson Holidays Limited & Britannia Airways PLC [The Gerona Air Crash]*, unreported, 6 May 2003, Cardiff County Court (HHJ Graham)

1. On 14th September 1999, Britannia Airways Ltd (" Britannia") Flight BY225A left Cardiff International Airport bound for Gerona in Spain. Aboard were holiday makers, each of whom had purchased a package holiday from Thomson Holidays Limited (" Thomson"). The Britannia flight formed part of the package holiday.

2. The following facts are agreed for the purposes of the issues with which this Judgment is concerned.

3. The Britannia aircraft reached the Gerona area at around 21:20 hours (local time). Flight conditions were turbulent and there was a thunder storm and rain. When the runway was initially sighted by the pilot, the aircraft was not adequately aligned with the runway and a change in wind direction favoured the reciprocal runway. A " missed approach" manoeuvre was therefore carried out. On the second approach the commander of the aircraft made a decision to land at the decision height of 251 feet (altitude 720 feet) but at some point thereafter lost outside visual references. Two automatic audio cautions of excessive sink rate were given by the Ground Proximity Warning System.

4. The aircraft then hit the runway very hard at a 2 degree nose down attitude and at an air speed of 141 knots, bouncing and touching down again around 140 metres further on. The aircraft's nose landing gear collapsed as a result of the failure of its supporting structure and the right engine nacelle and parts of the forward fuselage then contacted the runway surface. The aircraft tracked along the runway close to the centre line for 630 metres before veering to the right and departing from the paved surface at a point about two-thirds of the way (1,556 metres) down the runway.

5. From that point, the aircraft ran approximately 343 metres across flat grassland beside the runway before running diagonally over a substantial earth mound adjacent to the airport boundary, becoming semi airborne as a result.

6. At the far side of the mound, a number of medium sized trees were struck and severed, predominantly by the right wing, and the right engine nacelle struck the boundary fence. The aircraft yawed considerably to the right, then passed through the fence and re-landed in a field, with both main landing gears collapsing.

7. The aircraft then slid a further 244 metres across the field before coming to rest, with the fuselage almost structurally severed at two points, the nose landing gear and both engines detached and the underside of the left wing torque box split open near the wing root. Inside the aircraft there was

considerable floor and seat disruption in the area of the breaks in the fuselage.

8.   When it came to rest, the aircraft had travelled some 1,730 metres from the point of first structural contact on the runway and the three almost severed parts of the fuselage had rolled to the left by between 8 and 16 degrees.

9.   Difficulty was experienced in opening some of the cabin doors and three of the eight available exits could not be opened at all. The airport authorities did not at first realise that there had been a crash and then could not locate the aircraft, with the passengers having to wait for 20 to 30 minutes for assistance to arrive.

10.   Mr Akehurst and the other claimants were passengers on the aircraft. Their claims are in respect of varying degrees of physical and/or psychological injury and losses suffered by them as a result of the way in which the aircraft landed. They have brought claims against Thomson and, separately, against Britannia. The same injury, loss and damage is claimed against each defendant. The two actions have been consolidated. A Group Litigation Order has been made.

11.   Britannia has admitted that the crash was an " accident" for which it is liable to the claimants under Article 17 of the Warsaw Convention as incorporated into the law of England and Wales and given the force thereof by Schedule 1 of the Carriage by Air Act 1961 (" the Warsaw Convention") in respect of such " bodily injury" which the claimants, or any of them, have suffered as a result of the crash and for any consequential loss or damage flowing from that injury. The Warsaw Convention provides the exclusive cause of action and sole remedy that the claimants have against Britannia in respect of the crash. In *Morris v CLM Royal Dutch Airlines* [2002] 2 AC 628, the House of Lords held that:

> " For the purposes of Article 17, " bodily injury" means physical injury to the body and, accordingly, the Warsaw Convention does not permit recovery for any psychiatric condition (unless it is consequent upon physical injury or is proved to be an expression of a physical injury to the brain, central nervous system or any other component of the body caused by the accident in question) or for any pure emotional upset (such as fear, distress, grief or mental anguish)."

12.   Several of the claimants contend that they have suffered psychological injuries such as post traumatic stress disorder which have also resulted in significant loss and damage. In the light of the decision in *Morris*, they have no right of recovery against Britannia in relation to such purely psychological injuries and their consequences.

13. It is, however, the claimants' case that they are entitled to look to Thomson for compensation in respect of such injuries by virtue of the terms of their contracts with Thomson.

14. It is agreed for the purposes of the trial of the Issues that the contracts between Thomson and the various claimants were in materially identical terms. Thomson agreed to organise and arrange a package holiday to Spain in respect of each of the claimants, and each of the contracts provided, amongst other things, for the flight from Cardiff to Gerona. Each of the contracts was contained in/or evidenced by:

    (1) a Thomson Holidays invoice setting out the price and details of each claimant's holiday (including details of the Flight from Cardiff to Gerona on 14th September 1999);

    (2) the Thomson Fair Trading Charter (" The Charter") which was printed in the April/October 1999 Thomson Summer Sum Brochure, from which each of the claimants booked his or her holiday (" the Brochure").

15. At all material times Britannia has been and is a licensed commercial passenger airline. Each passenger was provided with a passenger ticket for the air travel.

16. On 31st July 2002, by consent, the court ordered the trial of the following Preliminary Issues agreed between the claimants and Thomson.

    (1) Were the Conditions of Contract of Britannia incorporated in Thomson's Brochure and Charter and thereby incorporated in each of the contracts made between Thomson and the claimants (" the contracts")?

    (2) Were the contracts subject to the provisions contained in Article 17 of the Warsaw Convention of 1929 as amended at The Hague in 1955?

    (3) Is Regulation 15 of the Package Travel, Package Holidays and Package Tours Regulations 1992 to be construed such that the claimants' rights under Regulation 15 against Thomson are limited to those rights which the claimants also have against Britannia?

    (4) Whether by reason of the happening of the crash as set out in those parts of paragraph 8 of the group particulars of claim which have been admitted by the defendant (the facts now contained in the Agreed Statement of Facts and set out above) the Flight was not provided to a reasonable standard and/or improperly performed, even if it is assumed that Britannia did use all reasonable skill and care in its conduct of the Flight.

17. During the hearing before me, Mr Jeffrey Gruder QC and Mr Nathan Pillow, who appeared for the claimants and Mr Robert Lawson, who appeared for Thomson, agreed that Issue 2 stands or falls with Issue 1. Thomson does not contend that it was the " carrier" of the claimants in respect of the Flight within the meaning of the Warsaw Convention. It accepts that the contracts would not be subject to the provisions of Article 17 unless that Article was incorporated into them via its Charter and Britannia's Conditions of Carriage.

18. Furthermore, Mr Gruder stated that on further consideration he and Mr Pillow had concluded that Regulation 15 cannot take the claimants any further than the contracts themselves. If the claimants succeed on Issue 1, then, obviously, they have no need to rely on Regulation 15 as a separate basis for liability. If they fail on Issue 1, Mr Gruder accepts that Regulation 15 is of no separate avail to them. Mr Lawson addressed submissions to me in relation to Issue 3 and appeared to be reluctant for it not to be pursued. As I understood him, the matter raised may be of some general importance to the package travel and holiday industry. However, as I indicated to Mr Lawson, in the light of what Mr Gruder said, Issue 3 no longer requires determination for the purposes of these proceedings. I do not propose to address it.

19. Consequently, I have to address only Issue 1 and Issue 4.

The Contract Documents

20. On the reverse of the Thomson Holiday invoice, attention being drawn to it upon the face of the document, appeared the following message:

> " We are pleased to state overleaf that the details of the confirmed holiday contract which you have already made with us, which is, together with the details of the charges and the balance of the holiday costs shown, subject to the particular Thomson fair Trading Charter [referred to in the Judgment as " The Charter"] or booking conditions which are printed or referred to in the brochure in which your holiday is described, to which we have not accepted or agreed any deletion, amendment or addition.....
>
> For details of airlines and aircraft planned to operate on your holiday, see the appropriate Thomson brochure...."

21. In relation to air travel, the Brochure referred to Britannia as " holiday airline of the year 1998" and " the UK's number one holiday airline" . It stated that " 98 per cent of Thomson flights are with award winning Britannia Airways" .

22. The relevant terms of The Charter are these. There is a general introductory statement:

" For 24 years, since it first appeared in 1975, the Thomson Fair Trading Charter has been a vital part of your holiday with us. It sets out the Thomson promise and is designed to protect your interests; it means you'll always get a fair deal when you book your holiday with us. You know you can trust Thomson and the Fair Trading Charter is how we prove it."

23.   The Charter itself is in two parts. The first headed " Our commitment to you – the Thomson promise" – and the second headed " Your commitment to us" . Paragraphs 108 make up the first part and paragraphs 9-16 the second part of The Charter.

24.   The relevant paragraphs of the first part are:

" 6. Our responsibility for your holiday.

We will arrange for you to have the services which make up the holiday that you choose and that we confirm. These services will be provided either directly by us or by independent suppliers contracted by us.

We are responsible for making sure that each part of the holiday you book with us is provided to a reasonable standard and as described in this brochure or in any amendments to it. If any part of your holiday is not provided as described and this spoils your holidays, we will pay you appropriate compensation. (see the " important note" in section 4). Also, if you buy a local excursion or tour through a uniformed Thomson representative, we will pay you reasonable compensation if it is not as advertised on the Thomson notice board or in the information book or Thomson resort guide.

We have taken all reasonable care to make sure that all the services which make up the holidays advertised in this brochure are provided by efficient, safe and reputable businesses and that they following the local and national laws and regulations of the country where they are provided. This also applies to excursions you buy through your Thomson representative."

25.   " 7.   Personal injury.

This section covers injury, illness or death while you are using the services that we have arranged for you.

We have no direct control over the way our suppliers provide their services. But everyone employed or contracted by us or by our suppliers is expected to carry out their duties properly. If they do not carry out their duties properly or at all and that fault results in your injury, illness or death, we may make a payment to you. We will not make any payment if your injury, illness or death was caused by an event or circumstances which that person could not have predicted or avoided even if they had taken all necessary and due care. We will not make any payment if your illness, injury or death was your own fault. If we do make a payment, it will be similar to one you would receive under English law in an English court.

26.   " 9.   Your Holiday Contract.

When you ask your travel agent or Thomson direct to confirm your holiday booking, you must sign a booking form to say that you accept this Charter. Your contract with us is made on the terms of this Charter, under English law and under control of the English courts alone."

27.   " 16.   The Conditions of your Ticket.

When you travel by air or on water, the transport company's " Conditions of Carriage" will apply to your journey. You can ask the travel agent booking your holiday to get you a copy of any conditions that apply to your journey if he/she has not already got them."

Issue 1

28.   Thomson's contention is that:

(1)   clause 16 of The Charter had the effect of incorporating Britannia's Conditions of Carriage, including its clause 16.1, into The Charter and thereby into each of the contracts; and

(2)   the combined effect of The Charter and Britannia's Conditions of Carriage is that it was a term of each of the contracts that any international carriage by air forming part of the holiday package would be subject to the rules and limitations contained in the Warsaw Convention and compensation by Thomson relating to that carriage by air would be limited accordingly.

(3)   The effect is that in respect of carriage by air forming part of the package, Thomson thereby excluded itself from any liability other than for death, wounding or " bodily injury" as a result of an " accident"   in the course of that carriage by air (and any consequential loss flowing therefrom).

29.   The Claimants dispute this. Their position is:

(1)   Clause 16 of The Charter is clear. It does not (and did not even purport or attempt to) suggest that terms from Britannia's

Conditions of Carriage were incorporated into and formed part of the entirely separate contracts between each of the claimants and Thomson. at most, it gave notice that contracts with third party carriers would be subject to different terms from the terms of the contracts with Thomson. It was perfectly open to Thomson, but Thomson signally failed, expressly to include the exclusions and limitations arising from the Warsaw Convention as terms of the claimants' holiday contracts with Thomson.

(2) The exclusion of liability contended for by Thomson is inconsistent with the express terms of the contracts, as admitted by them, and so cannot be incorporated by reference as Thomson claims.

(3) If there is any ambiguity in relation to the meaning of clause 16 of The Charter, this must be resolved against Thomson (i) as profferer and (ii) by reason of Regulation 6 of the Unfair Terms in Consumer Contracts Regulations 1994.

(4) Thomson was obliged by virtue of Regulation 9 of the Package Travel, Package Holidays and Package Tours Regulations 1992 to ensure that all of the terms of the contracts were communicated and supplied in writing to the claimants. Thomson has failed to do this and cannot now rely on terms such as those contained in Britannia's Conditions of Carriage.

30. The parties are agreed that what is involved is an exercise of contractual construction. The applicable principles of construction are agreed. It is agreed further that any ambiguity must be resolved against Thomson and in favour of the claimants both under the *contra proferentem* rule and Regulation 6.

31. The agreed principles of construction are that in construing the words used in clause 16 of The Charter, the court must attempt to ascertain " the meaning which the document would convey to a reasonable person having all the background knowledge which would reasonably have been available to the parties in the situation in which they were at the time of the contract" (*Investors Compensation Scheme Ltd v West Bromwich Building Society* [1998] 1 WLR 896 per Lord Hoffmann). It is irrelevant what Thomson subjectively wanted or believed clause 16.2 to achieve: what matters is whether the objective bystander would have understood clause 16 as incorporating all of Britannia's conditions of carriage into the claimants' contractual relationships with Thomson. Moreover, the exercise of construction must take into account the whole of The Charter: clause 16 must be construed in the context of all of the other provisions of that contract.

32. As I indicated at the conclusion of the hearing, I am very grateful to counsel for their very full, careful and helpful submissions. My conclusion is that Britannia's Conditions of Carriage were not incorporated into the contracts

between the claimants and Thomson. Hence I answer Issue 1: " No" . It follows from what I have said about Issue 2, that it is to be answered in the same way. I set out my reasons.

33.   Firstly, no objective bystander would understand The Charter in the way contended for by Thomson. Mr Lawson contends that clause 16 is no different from the other obligations which the consumer undertakes as part of its commitment to Thomson. By it the consumer is taken to agree that the conditions of the ticket provided to him by Thomson as part of his holiday are the transport company's " Conditions of Carriage" which are to apply to " your journey" . It is to be noted, Mr. Lawson submits, that the application of the conditions is " your journey" and not to " your carriage by that transport company" . Given the foregoing, the journey being referred to can only be the journey that Thomson has agreed to provide to the consumer, and accept responsibility for, as part of " his holiday" . Furthermore, in the full context of that part of The Charter in which it sits, the objective observer would not understand the clause as simply being a notification to the consumer of the existence of terms that will govern the relationship between the consumer and the air carrier. He would understand it as clearly stating that it is part of the agreement between the consumer and Thomson (i.e. a commitment of the consumer to Thomson) that the air carrier's " Conditions of Carriage" will apply to the journey Thomson has agreed to provide the consumer with, and accept responsibility for, as part of " his holiday" : namely that Thomson was providing that journey on those conditions.

34.   Furthermore, Mr Lawson submits, the wording of clause 16.1 of Britannia's Conditions of Carriage is entirely consistent with this. Its reference to " carriage" can only mean carriage by air by Britannia. An objective observer would understand this clause to say that carriage by air by Britannia was " subject to the rules and limitations relating to liability established by [the Warsaw Convention] ..." and the effect of this, in combination with clause 16 of The Charter, to be that the carriage by air arranged by Thomson would be subject to the rules and limitations relating to liability established by the Warsaw Convention. The objective observer would not find this surprising. Given the universality of the Warsaw Convention (the terms of which cannot be excluded by contract), he would not expect a tour operator to assume a greater liability in respect of carriage by air that he arranges than the carrier itself would have.

35.   Mr Lawson continues that the proper construction of the effect of clause 16 of The Charter and of clause 16.1 of Britannia's Conditions of Carriage is entirely consistent with clause 6 of The Charter. This is because they are directed towards entirely different purposes. Clause 6 deals with the services that Thomson accepts responsibility for providing and the standard applicable to their provision, whereas clause 16 (and clause 16.1 of Britannia's Conditions of Carriage) provides for the terms upon which some of those services (namely carriage by air or on water) are to be provided. In other words, Thomson is responsible for making sure that air travel " is

provided to a reasonable standard" (not that it " is of a reasonable standard") but still subject to the carrier's condition.

36.   Mr Lawson accepts that the effect of clause 16 of The Charter and of clause 16.1 of Britannia's Conditions of Carriage is to qualify the scope of clause 7 of The Charter, so as to exempt Thomson from liability for any psychiatric condition or pure emotional upset. However, this does not mean that the interpretation for which he contends is impugned. This is because:

(1)   the applicability of the transport company's Conditions of Carriage is expressly and clearly stated in The Charter;

(2)   clause 7 does not say that it covers " injury, illness or death" to the exclusion of all other terms contained in The Charter; and

(3)   the commitments made by Thomson and by the consumer in The Charter must be read together and assumed to be intended to be consistent with each other.

If the objective observer were to consider the commitments made by Thomson in clause 7 in parallel with the consumer's commitment in clause 16, he would view Thomson's commitment in clause 7 as being subject to the consumer's acceptance of the applicability of the air carrier's Conditions of Carriage in respect of any part of " the journey" involving carriage by air, as contained in clause 16.

37.   These contentions appear to me to be unsustainable. The objective observer would first read The Charter as a whole. First, he would note Thomson's clear commitments to the consumer.

(a)   The Thomson Promise designed to protect his interests; the assurance that he can trust Thomson; and that The Charter is how Thompson prove that.

(b)   Thomson's responsibility to make sure that each part of the holiday is provided to a reasonable standard and the clear commitment to pay appropriate compensation if any part is not provided as described and that spoils the holiday.

(c)   The commitment under clause 7 to make payments for injury, illness or death (not limited to " bodily injury" or limited in any other way), in particular the obligation to pay up to about £85,000 per person for transport by air with an airline licensed in a European Community Member State and compensation above that amount (without limit) if the airline fails to prove that it took all measures to avoid " your injury or death" or it was impossible for it to take such measures. Britannia is of course an airline licensed in a European Community Member State.

38.   I agree with Mr Gruder and Mr Pillow that the two clauses (clauses 6 and 7) are the only provisions in The Charter which refer to and purport to govern the compensation payable by Thomson in the event of something going wrong with part of the package holiday. There is not the slightest suggestion in either clause that Thomson's agreement to pay compensation in the event of injury is in any way restricted or limited by reference to a third party's Conditions of Carriage. Still less is there any suggestion that the third party's Conditions themselves include or refer to the Warsaw Convention and therefore contain restrictions on the type of injury that is covered.

39.   The objective bystander would move on in his perusal of The Charter to the consumer's commitment to Thomson. He would find entirely unremarkable and wholly understandable his obligations to pay for his holiday; to make extra payments in the event of a change in booking or cancellation; to follow a set procedure for complaints; not to behave disruptively; and not to share the accommodation provided. These are all commonplace obligations he would expect to see.

40.   Coming to clause 16, the objective bystander would have some difficulty, I consider, in understanding how the application of the transport company's Conditions of Carriage to his journey could form part of his commitment to Thomson. Certainly, he would see nothing to flag up to him that the benefits so clearly conferred upon him by clauses 6 and 7 were now in any way at all being cut down, much less that all liability for even the most serious psychological injuries was being excluded. He would still have in mind that the company providing the services was holding itself out as a company to be trusted, proclaiming its provision of a fair deal and its protection of the consumer's interests. No objective bystander would expect such a company to confer benefits in the clearest terms without any reservation in one part of its Fair Trading Charter and then to cut them down in a different part of The Charter. He would expect the limitations to be set out in the clauses conferring the benefits. If they were to be set out elsewhere in he document, he would expect such limitations to be set out in the clearest terms and that the consumer's attention would be specifically drawn to them. No objective bystander would consider to be fair dealing the construction for which Thomson now contends and no objective bystander would read the document in such a way.

41.   If he went on to concentrate on the words of clause 16 itself in the same way in which he might read the small print in a contract, the objective bystander would still not understand its terms to import all the unspecified limitations and exclusions of liability of the transport company's conditions of carriage into the fair deal between Thomson and the holiday maker. It is of course true that Thomson provides the ticket, but the ticket contains or evidences the contract of carriage as between the carrier and the holiday maker. Thomson is not a party to that contract. It is also of course true that Thomson arranges the journey as part of the holiday, but clause 16 days only that the transport company's Conditions of Carriage " will apply to your journey" not that those conditions are to be incorporated or included

in The Charter or are to have effect as if they were terms of the contract between Thomson and the holiday maker. As Mr Gruder points out, similarly the Conditions of Carriage referred to are expressly said to be the " transport company's" . It is not suggested that they relate to or govern rights and obligations *vis-à-vis* Thomson in any way. No mention is made of how, if at all, such conditions relate to Thomson's own terms and conditions.

42.   In my view, clause 16 would be understood by the objective bystander as notice that in relation to travel by air or on water the relationship between the consumer and the carrier is governed by the carrier's conditions of carriage. Those conditions may contain limitations and exclusions and, as against the carrier, the consumer will be bound by such limitations and exclusions. That does not affect at all the relationship between Thomson and the consumer. If Thomson decides to confer benefits or accept liability in certain eventualities in its contract with the consumer whereas the carrier chooses not to confer such benefits or limits or excludes its liability, that is a matter for Thomson. Equally, the carrier may have provisions for compensation where Thomson has none or more advantageous provisions, for example in relation to baggage. A Fair Trading Charter would draw attention to such possibilities.

43.   I do not agree with Mr Lawson that the objective observer would not expect a tour operator to assume a greater liability in respect of carriage by air that he arranges than the carrier itself would have. On the contrary, in my view a reputable tour operator holding itself out in the terms in which Thomson does might well do that. Clause 16 makes no reference to the Warsaw Convention. Furthermore, it is not limited to travel by air but specifically includes travel on water. The carrier's conditions of carriage for travel on water might exclude all liability of any kind, or the legal system of the country concerned might make the recovery of compensation extremely difficult or impossible. The customer of a reputable travel company might well expect protection in such circumstances. Thomson, in The Charter, even provide cover up to £5,000 for injury, illness or death not connected with the arrangements made by them. Certainly, in my view no objective observer would regard clause 16 as being capable of removing altogether the benefits conferred by clauses 6 and 7, which is a possible effect of Mr Lawson's contentions.

44.   For the sake of completeness, I add that I find the argument that clause 7 does not say that it covers " injury, illness or death" to the exclusion of all other terms contained in The Charter to be disingenuous. Certainly it does not say that. What is important, however, is that it does not say what it ought to say (if such was Thomson's intention) that " injury" means " bodily injury" and that psychiatric damage or emotional upset are excluded. Further, I do agree that the applicability of the transport company's Conditions of Carriage is expressly and clearly stated in The Charter. But applicability to what? The only answer which does not involve violence to the words used and is not artificial and a highly strained reading of the whole document is applicability to the relationship between the

holiday maker and the carrier in relation to the journey. Yet further, as Mr Gruder points out, the particular conditions of carriage in this case (Britannia's conditions) refer to " carriage hereunder" being subject of the Warsaw Convention. In other words, carriage by Britannia under its conditions was subject to the Warsaw Convention. That condition is to apply to the consumer's journey. The result is, as Mr Gruder says, that Thomson are telling the claimants that their journey by air with Britannia will be under Britannia's Conditions of Carriage. That in no way suggests that Thomson's liability under The Charter is also subject to – and cut down to a great extent by – the Warsaw Convention. Such an interpretation would do violence to the express words of clause 16.1 of Britannia's conditions, referring to " carriage hereunder" : carriage under Britannia's conditio9ns is self-evidently undertaken by Britannia, not Thomson. Britannia's conditions are hence irrelevant to Thomson's liability under The Charter.

45.   As a general proposition, I agree with Mr Lawson that the commitments made by Thomson and by the consumer in The Charter must be read together and assumed to be intended to be consistent with each other. On what I find to be the correct construction, the commitments can be read together and are consistent with each other.

46.   The second reason for my conclusion is that, on Thomson's case, Clause 16 would operate as an exemption clause entirely excluding Thomson's liability for psychiatric injury, regardless of the seriousness of such injury and notwithstanding the benefits expressly conferred by clauses 6 and 7. An exemption clause must be expressed clearly and without ambiguity or it will be ineffective. Such a clause needs to be construed strictly. Any doubt or ambiguity is to be resolved against the party seeking to rely upon the exemption clause and in favour of the other party. as in the case of any other written document, in situations of ambiguity the words of the document are to be construed more strongly against the party who made the document and who seeks to rely on them. Although the party receiving the document knows it contains conditions, if the particular condition relied on is one which is a particularly onerous or unusual term, the party tendering the document must show that the term has been brought fairly and reasonably to the other's attention.

47.   As an exemption clause purporting to contain an onerous term cutting down in significant measure benefits previously expressly and specifically conferred in the document in which it is contained, clause 16 falls foul of all these principles and rules of construction.

      (a)   It was not brought to the claimants' attention at all that Thomson sought to impose such a limitation.

      (b)   If relied upon as an exemption clause, clause 16 is, at best from Thomson's viewpoint, ambiguous. I have reached a conclusion as to its proper construction. If that conclusion is incorrect, the competing contentions as to its proper construction are themselves testimony to its ambiguity.

(c)   If Thomson intended to limit its liability, the limitation should have been spelled out clearly. The limitation should have been contained in the clauses explicitly setting out Thomson's commitment to make compensation payments. Since it was not, all the greater was the obligation to Thomson to be clear and explicit in clause 16. Thomson could and should have made the wording of the clause relied upon clear so that the holiday maker knew what the terms of the contract would be before he entered into it. Thomson should have spelled out that it intended to exclude liability for psychiatric injury and that its liability was to be the same as, or not to exceed, the liability of an air carrier under the Warsaw Convention.

(d)   As The Charter stands, clause 4 enabled Thomson to change the flight arrangements at any time. Though Britannia is apparently used for 98 per cent of Thomson holidays, Thomson from choice or necessity could change to another carrier whose conditions of carriage might be materially different. It could be that the carrier had not been selected at the time the holiday was bought. In the present case, Britannia remained the carrier. But there is nothing in clause 16 to alert the holiday maker or objective bystander that the conditions of carriage include significant limitations as to liability, taking away in substantial measure rights earlier clearly conferred. There is not even a reference anywhere in The Charter to the Warsaw Convention, though there is a reference to the Athens Convention.

(e)   Even on the basis of Thomson's contentions, the exclusion of liability is brought in only obliquely. Nothing in The Charter directly states or even directly suggests that Thomson is itself relying on limitations or exclusions themselves wholly unspecified and not even mentioned anywhere in The Charter.

(f)   The very considerable doubts and ambiguities which arise on the basis of Thomson's contentions as to whether clause 16 operates as an effective exemption clause and what its words are to be taken to mean are to be resolved against Thomson. This provides further support for what I conclude to be the proper construction of the contract.

48.   These considerations are so overwhelming that I consider there is no need for reliance also upon Regulation 6 of the Unfair Terms in Consumer Contracts Regulations 1994. ......

49.   Thirdly, I accept Mr Gruder's further submission that the express words of The Charter (clause 7) plainly and unequivocally cover all personal injuries

and illnesses – physical and psychiatric – without any qualification whatsoever. The meaning of " personal injury" is entirely different from, and is to be contrasted with, expressions such as " physical injury" or " bodily injury" . That was the effect of the decision of the House of Lords in *Morris*. The phrase " personal injury" clearly includes " bodily injury" and also psychiatric injury. Similarly the word " illness" obviously includes psychiatric illnesses, such as clinical depression or post traumatic stress disorder as well as illnesses which affect the body such as measles or mumps.

50.   Thomson seeks to incorporate the terms of the Warsaw Convention with its limitation to " bodily injury" . What is sought to be incorporated is hence in direct conflict with specific clauses in the agreement itself. If clauses are incorporated by reference into a written agreement, and those clauses conflict with the clauses of the agreement, then, in the ordinary way, the clauses of the written agreement will prevail. .....

....

53.   Finally, I consider that Thomson breached Regulation 9 of The Package Travel, Package Holidays and Package Tours Regulations 1992 and must be and is precluded from taking advantage of its own wrong, as the claimants contend.

54.   The material parts of Regulation 9 are:

     (1)   The other party to the contract shall ensure that –

          (b)   subject to paragraph (2) below, all the terms of the contract are set out in writing or such other form as is comprehensible and accessible to the consumer before the contract is made; and

          (c)   a written copy of these terms is supplied to the consumer.

     (2)   Not material in the present case.

     (3)   It is an implied condition... of the contract that the other party to the contract complies with the provisions of paragraph (1)."

....

Issue 4

60.   This Issue is to be determined upon the assumption that Britannia did use all reasonable skill and care in its conduct of the Flight.

61.   The claimants' case is that Thomson's obligations were strict, in the sense that Thomson are liable to the claimants for failing to provide a Flight to a

reasonable standard, even if Britannia did use all reasonable kill and care in performing it. Mr Gruder's submissions are:

(a) The test of provision " to a reasonable standard" relates to the objective quality of the service actually provided, not to the degree of care that was taken in providing it. f care that was taken in providing it.

(b) This objective " and hence strict" test is amply reinforced by the words which follow in clause 6 of The Charter. Thomson go on to promise in the same sentence that they will pay compensation if any part of the holiday is not " as described in the Brochure" . This can only be a strict objective requirement and is agreed to be such by Mr. Lawson.

(c) It is obvious from the Agreed Statement of Facts that the Flight was not provided to a " reasonable standard" on any analysis. Certainly, it would be surprising to conclude that a flight which crash landed in the appalling circumstances of this case, with the aircraft coming to rest in a field outside the airport altogether, was provided to a " reasonable standard" .

62. Mr Gruder invites the Court to deal with the question whether the Flight was in fact provided " as described in the Brochure" . He says that although this question is not specifically included in the Preliminary Issues, it would clearly greatly assist the resolution of this litigation if the Court could dispose of this issue at this early stage. It raises exactly the same issues of principle as Issue 4. The claimants' case is that:

(a) The Flight was not described in the Brochure as a flight from a UK airport " to Gerona" . At a minimum, it was described as a flight from a UK airport to Gerona Airport. It is agreed that the Flight did not in fact conclude at Gerona Airport; the plane came to rest in a field some 244 metres outside the airport perimeter.

(b) Any " flight from a UK airport to Gerona" would involve a normal (or at least a safe) landing during which the aircraft's wheels landed on the runway and taxi ways and did not detach altogether, leaving the aircraft in a field half kilometre away from the runway. It cannot be said that the Flight in this case was a flight in any conventional or natural meaning of the word – and so it was not a " flight to Gerona" as described in the Brochure.

(c) Finally, Thomson expressly described the Flight in its Brochure as: " the best holiday flight available" . The Flight clearly did not live up to its description.

63. In relation to whether the Flight was additionally or alternatively " improperly performed" , the claimants submit that:

(a)   the same interpretation applies as applies to provision " to a reasonable standard" ;

(b)   the obligation to provide the Flight " properly" was similarly objective; and it follows from the foregoing submissions that Thomson's obligation to provide a Flight to a " reasonable standard" was clearly " improperly performed" in the circumstances set out in the Agreed Statement of Facts.

64.   On behalf of Thomson, it is submitted that if Britannia did use all reasonable skill and care, then the Flight was provided to a reasonable standard and was properly performed notwithstanding that the crash occurred. This is said to be clear from the decision of the Court of Appeal in *Hone v Going Place Leisure Travel Ltd* (A2/200/3594), 14th June 2001).

65.   Mr Lawson's submissions are:

(a)   Just because there is an absolute obligation to provide something does not mean that it is an absolute obligation to ensure that it will in fact be safe and/or to ensure that its use will be free from the risk of injury.

(b)   there is no real distinction between a promise that something will be performed with reasonable skill and care and one that it will be provided to a reasonable standard. This is because the provision of services to a reasonable standard must mean to a reasonable standard of skill and care. That this is so in the context of The Charter can be seen by reading clauses 6 and 7. These clauses must be intended to be read together and to be consistent with each other. By the former, Thomson accepts responsibility for providing all services making up the consumer's holiday " to a reasonable standard" . Under the latter, payment by Thomson of compensation is made contingent upon suppliers " not carrying out their duties properly" , i.e. upon " improper performance" . The combined intent of the two clauses is therefore that the service is provided to a " reasonable standard" when the supplier has performed his duties properly, i.e. with reasonable skill and care.

(c)   it is accepted that the requirement to provide services " as described in this Brochure" is a strict requirement, imposing an absolute obligation. However, this has no impact on the matter in hand because it is an entirely separate obligation and has no bearing on what is meant by " reasonable standard" , as is evidenced by t5he fact that it has no comparator in clause 7. In any event, there is no breach of this further obligation. It is common ground that the Brochure provided that each of the claimants was to be flown from various UK airports (including Cardiff) to Gerona. This was done. The alleged description of the Flight as " the best holiday flight available" results from a selective quotation from the relevant passage. The complete sentence reads:

> " Britannia Airways has been voted Holiday Airline of the Year for eight years, which is the travel industry's acknowledgment of their dedication to ensuring that your flight is the best holiday flight available."

It is difficult to see how this sentence could give rise to any liability in the present case.

" Was the flight provided to a reasonable standard?"

66.   In *Hone*, the Court of Appeal held that the starting point must be the contract. Longmore LJ continued (para 12):

> " In the absence of any contrary intention, the normal implication will be that the service contracted for will be rendered with reasonable skill and care. Of course, absolute obligations may be assumed. If the brochure or advertisement, on which the consumer relies, promises a swimming pool, it will be a term of the contract that a swimming pool will be provided. But, in the absence of express wording, there would not be an absolute obligation, for example, to ensure that the holiday maker catches no infection whilst swimming in the swimming pool. The obligation assumed will be that reasonable skill and care will be taken to ensure that the pool is free from infection. A similar term will be implied in relation to transportation in the absence of any express wording *via* that reasonable skill and care will be exercised. A travel agent or tour operator does not usually, for example, promise that the pilot of the aeroplane will not have a heart attack."

Considering Regulation 15(2) [of the Package Travel, Package Holidays and Package Tours Regulations 1992] Longmore LJ said (para 15):

> " [It] " provides for the other party to the contract to be liable for any damage caused to the consumer by failure to perform the contract or by the improper performance of the contract. The present case .... can only be a case of improper performance. It is only possible to determine whether it is a case of improper performance by reference to the terms of the contract which is being performed. To my mind, Regulation 15(2) does not give the answer to the question, " What is improper performance?" rather it is a requirement of the application of Regulation 15(2) that there should be improper performance. That can only be determined by reference to the terms of the contract. There may be absolute

obligations, e.g. as to the existence of a swimming pool or any other matter, but, in the absence of the assumption of an absolute obligation, the implication will be that reasonable skill and care will be used in the rendering of the relevant service. There will thus be no improper performance of the air carriage unless there is an absence of reasonable skill and care in the provision of that service."

67.   The question for me in the present case is whether Thomson did assume an absolute obligation by virtue of the terms of The Charter in respect of the Flight. A question of construction, in my view, again arises. My conclusion is that Thomson did not assume an absolute obligation.

....

68.   In my view, an objective bystander would understand " a flight provided to a reasonable standard" to mean that the aircraft would be of a size and type, with equipment and fittings, reasonably appropriate to the nature and length of the journey and the type and cost of the holiday; maintained with reasonable care; and operated by properly trained and competent staff who would exercise reasonable care in performing their duties.

....

71.   In my view, to conclude that Thomson assumed an absolute obligation, the objective bystander would require to see phrases such as " safely transport by air" or " carry by air safely to ... from ..." As Longmore LJ said in *Hone* (para 16):

> " Mr Dean submits that there was improper performance because the parties expected that the air carriage would be safely executed. That would only be the position if there were a term of the contract that the air carriage would be safely executed. For my part, I do not consider that there was any such absolute term. In the absence of an express agreement, the implication was that the air carriage would be performed with skill and care" .

72.   My answer to the question raised is:

" No" .

" As described in the Brochure"

73.   It is accepted by Mr Lawson that there was an absolute obligation that each part of the holiday would be provided as described in the Brochure. I agree.

74.   I also agree with Mr Lawson that this obligation is a separate obligation from the obligation to provide a flight to a reasonable standard. The Brochure provided that each of the claimants was to be flown from various UK airports (including Cardiff) to Gerona. ...... The claimants are contending that the description in the Brochure imposed an absolute obligation on Thomson to transport them *safely* from a UK airport to Gerona Airport. I see nothing in the description imposing such an obligation. If the obligation was to provide a flight to Gerona Airport rather than to Gerona, then there was a breach: the aircraft came to rest 244 metres from Gerona Airport. But the loss and damage flowing from that breach would only be such loss and damage (if any, which is very unlikely) resulting from the aircraft coming to rest outside the airport perimeter rather than within it. It may at first blush appear to be a hard conclusion to say that the absolute obligation was discharged in circumstances where the aeroplane crash landed outside the airport perimeter. But the conclusion results from the way in which the claimants put their case. They assert that Thomson are liable to compensate them for their injuries and losses (even in the absence of any fault whatsoever) simply by reason of the description of the Flight in the Brochure. That is not sustainable. In the absence of express words that the Flight would be safely executed 9and there were no such words) the contracted obligation was to provide a Flight and no more, it being implied that the Flight would be executed with reasonable skill and care. I do not think that the description of Britannia as Holiday Airline of the Year etc. assists the claimants at all. Even the best regulated human enterprises sometimes come to grief. In the absence of clear express words or unavoidable implication of absolute liability, the redress of a person adversely affected depends on proof of negligence.

....

" Improperly performed"

76.   The claimants' contention is that the same interpretation applies to the issue of whether the obligation to provide the Flight was " improperly performed" as to " provided to a reasonable standard" and " as described in the Brochure" . The question is what, if anything, The Charter provides as " proper" for the performance of a Flight. The submission continues that Thomson agreed that each part of the holiday " including the Flight" would be provided to a " reasonable standard" , an objective – and hence strict – obligation. The obligation on Thomson to provide the Flight " properly" was therefore similarly objective. It follows that Thomson's obligation to provide a Flight " of a reasonable standard" was clearly " improperly performed" in the circumstances set out in the Agreed Statement of Facts.

77.   The arguments are the same as those that I have already rejected. As was said in *Hone* (para 15): " ....In the absence of the assumption of an absolute obligation, the implication will be that reasonable skill and care will be used in the rendering of the relevant service" . The argument of the claimants' comes to this: any airline which agrees to provide a flight to a

reasonable standard thereby becomes an insurer of the passengers against all possible perils and eventualities. I do not accept that. The proper performance of the obligation to provide a flight to a reasonable standard requires the use of reasonable skill and care and is satisfied if reasonable skill and care is taken.

78.   I understood Mr Gruder to agree at the close of his oral submission in reply that clause 7 is fault based, payment thereunder being conditional upon fault being established. Subject only to one matter which I wish to raise, that seems to me to be plainly correct. In my view, subject to this one matter, to recover compensation from Thomson under clause 7 for their personal injuries (including psychiatric injury) and losses, the claimants have to show fault on the part of Britannia resulting in the injury suffered.

The Scope of the Package Holiday Contract

Jones v Sunworld Ltd (now incorporated in JMC Holidays Ltd) [2003] EWHC 591 (QB) (24 March 2003)
Field J.

1. This is an action for damages arising out of the accidental death by drowning of Mr John Jones on 4 August 1998. The claimant is Mrs. Liza Jones who married Mr Jones on 1 August 1998, just three days before the accident. Mrs. Jones sues for damages for nervous shock and post traumatic stress disorder and also under the Fatal Accidents Act 1976. On 13 February 2003 Holland J ordered that the question of liability be tried separately from the question of quantum. The issue I have to decide therefore is whether the defendant is liable to the claimant for the death of her husband.

The circumstances of Mr Jones's death

2. On 3 August 1998 Mr Jones and Mrs. Jones flew out to the Maldives where they were to spend two weeks on honeymoon. Their destination was Fun Island which is near the equator in the south-eastern comer of South Male Atoll. Like many of the other islands in the Maldives, Fun Island is surrounded by a lagoon protected on the outer perimeter by a coral reef. The island is a narrow strip of land about 800 metres long running along a south west/north east axis. The surrounding lagoon is therefore to the east and to the west of the island. There is no swimming pool. Guests are accommodated in 42 wooden chalets which have between 2 to 4 bedrooms. It takes about 10 minutes to walk around the entire island.

3. Mr and Mrs. Jones did not go into the lagoon on the day of their arrival but at about 3.00 pm the next day they went for a walk round the island and walked into the lagoon on the eastern side. In her witness statement Mrs. Jones says that they got to about 50 yards from the shore. The sea-bed shelved gently and they were still able to wade. The water was just below her chest (she is 5ft 9in) and between her husband's chest level and his navel (he was about 5ft 1in). Her statement goes on:

> " Suddenly, it felt like we were both stepping off a steep step as the sea-bed just dropped away. I remember that as I dropped down I was completely submerged. I managed to get back onto what felt like a shelf or certainly a step up, but I felt as if there was something pulling me back into the water. It was definitely a hole I had gone down. This all happened very quickly, but I estimate that it was about 10-12 feet deep. I got the distinct impression that I was being pulled down and that I had sunk as if gravity was pulling me down. It was extremely difficult to get back out of the hole.
>
> I noticed that John had not got out of the hole so I tried to pull him out of the hole. There was nobody around to help. Even though I did take hold of him once, the pull of the water forced him out of my arms.
>
> I screamed for help whilst I was still in the water. I remember a man was sitting on the beach with his wife and they were also two nurses that were on the beach. I was screaming and trying to get people to help. They came

to try and rescue John from the water. John was unconscious and they tried for about 15 minutes to revive him by giving mouth to mouth resuscitation. They were unable to save him. The nurses stayed whereas the other people in the crowd that had gathered left."

4. Claire Shingler was the defendant's representative in the Maldives. She was based in Male, the capital. Upon hearing of Mr Jones's death she travelled to Fun Island, arriving at about 7.45pm that evening. She accompanied Mrs. Jones to Male and shared a room with her on Paradise island to keep her company. Mrs. Jones spoke constantly about what had happened. She told Ms Shingler that she and her husband had been wading in the water which only came up to the waist when all of a sudden there was a deep drop in the water where the depth dropped dramatically to about 10 ft. Mr Jones stepped out into the deep area and began to panic and went straight under.

5. The day after the accident Mrs. Jones made a statement to the Maldivian police in which she said, inter alia:

> " [M]y husband and I were wading in the shallow waters in the lagoon. The depth of the water was about 1.5 metres. At about 1645 hrs, we came to a sudden drop in the sea-bed, and being unaware of it, we walked into deep waters."

6. The defendant does not accept that the pool in which Mr Jones drowned shelved down as steeply as described by Mrs Jones. Generally speaking the water in the lagoon is shallow with the sea-bed gently shelving downwards towards the house reef. However, there are three particular areas in the eastern lagoon which are deeper than elsewhere. These areas are easily discernible from the shore because they are a much deeper blue than the rest of the lagoon.

18. I find on the evidence that Mr Jones drowned in the pool identified ... (and) at the time its maximum depth was between 6 ft 6 in and 8 ft. Although I am of the view that the gradient was steeper in August 1998 than it was found to be in March 2002, I am not persuaded that the gradient was a precipitous drop. Instead I find that the sides were such that within a pace or two Mr Jones found himself unexpectedly in water up to around his chin and that his increased buoyancy at this depth unsteadied him and caused him to panic so that he failed to swim to shallower water but instead drowned.

20. I ... find that Mr Jones could swim but that he was not a very good swimmer.

21. The claimant submits that the pool in which Mr Jones drowned was a hazard and that the defendant was under an implied contractual duty to use reasonable care and skill to warn her and her husband about it. If an appropriate warning had been given (the submission goes) Mr Jones would not have been surprised upon encountering deep water and therefore would not have panicked but would have been able to swim into his depth. In the event that the failure to warn was a failure on the part of resort rather than on the part of the defendant, the claimant relies on regulation 15 of the Package Travel, Package Holidays and Package Tours Regulations 1992 (" the Package Holiday Regulations").

22. Mr and Mrs. Jones decided to spend their honeymoon on Fun Island having visited a travel agent where they studied a brochure issued by Sunworld Limited ("Sunworld"). They chose 14 days on Fun Island on a fill board basis ... the defendant accepts that the contract entered into by Sunworld with Mr and Mrs. Jones was a contract for the supply of services and that by s 13 of the Supply of Goods and Services Act 1982 the defendant was under a duty to carry out the services it provided with reasonable care and skill. The result, contended (for) was that the services provided by the defendant extended to taking steps to ensure that the accommodation at Fun Island was such that guests could stay there with reasonable safety in the context of any applicable local standards and its own internal assessment of what safety checks should be carried out.

23. By "accommodation", [the defendant] meant the rooms, bars, restaurants and grounds of the resort. ... the service of taking reasonable steps to ensure the reasonable safety of the guests did not extend to the safety of the lagoon, since the lagoon was not within the package sold and purchased under the contract. [It was] submitted that what was in the package is to be derived from a passage in the brochure which appeared under the heading "Holiday Information":

> "WHAT THE PRICE INCLUDES
>
> * Accommodation. Prices are shown within the price panel for each property....
>
> * Meals. If you book full board you will be provided with breakfast, lunch and dinner...
>
> * Services of a Sunworld representative or appointed local representative.
>
> * Return flights: Price panels show a basic holiday price with a nil flight supplement ...
>
> * Air Passenger Duty, most airport taxes (see Local departure taxes, below) and security charges levied at the time of going to press.
>
> * In-flight meals appropriate to the airline, time of flight and destination.
>
> * Free luggage allowance usually 20 kgs (44 lbs) per person...
>
> * Transport between destination and holiday property."

No mention is made here of the lagoon. It follows, argued [the defendant] that the lagoon was outside the package.

24. [The Defendant] also relied on the evidence of Mr John De Vial who is the Managing Director of a consultancy company which advises and provides other services to the travel industry and who was a Director of the Federation of Tour Operators ("FTO") and Chairman of the FTO's Health and Safety Committee from 1998 to 2002. Mr De Vial acknowledged that whether a beach or a lagoon was within a holiday package was ultimately dependent on the wording of the brochure and the terms and conditions referred to therein but said that the practice of the tour operators industry was to regard beaches and the sea as outside the package, even where it was foreseeable that purchasers of the package would spend the great bulk of their time on one particular beach. Accordingly, whilst tour operators carry out

safety assessments (" audits") of the hotels, including swimming pools, which feature in their packages, they do not do carry out such audits of nearby amenities such as beaches, although the practice is to pass on to customers any relevant information that the operator may have, such as information about dangerous tides or currents.

25. ... the claimant argued that whatever might be the general practice, on the facts of the instant case the lagoon was within the package so that the defendant was under an obligation to use reasonable care and skill to warn Mr and Mrs. Jones about dangers in the lagoon. ... that the lagoon was mentioned in the brochure as an attractive feature of the location. Thus in the Maldives section of the brochure appear these words:

> " Each individual coral island is tiny, many are uninhabited and all are beautiful, providing their own unique version of paradiso Superb turquoise lagoons sit inside coral reefs like halos, surrounding perfect, soft white-sand beaches, the whoe [whole] being enclosed by the deep-aquamarine waters of the Indian Ocean. The clarity of the sea has to be seen to be believed as does the indescribably beautiful underwater world which will be, literally on your doorstep. Even if you have never ventured beneath the sea's surface before, we can guarantee that its warmth and the spectacular vistas it has in store will be enough to tempt even the most basic novice....You will have already read that each of the islands is very small: consequently there is room only for one hotel per island and that island is also your 'resort'"

And when describing Fun Island the brochure says this underneath a picture of the island and the lagoon:

> " Just imagine, a long narrow island paradise with two neighbouring islands (which you can reach at low tide!)...Ringed by fine sand...this coral paradise offers a good selection of watersports and entertainments ...beach volleyball and football available ... watersports on the beach; diving school."

26. ... the lagoon (together with the island) was leased by the resort owners; there was no swimming pool and the climate was very hot; and the lagoon was separated from the open sea by the house reef.

27. In my judgement, having regard to all the evidence before me, the lagoon was included in the package in the same sense as was the " accommodation" ... It is true that the lagoon is a natural phenomenon but it was an integral part of the resort over which the resort's owners had legal control by virtue of a lease from the Maldivian Government. It was virtually inconceivable that a holiday maker would stay on Fun Island and not go into the lagoon to enjoy the coolness and clarity of the water. In my opinion it would be wholly artificial to draw a line in the sand along the water's edge and say that the landward area was within the resort and hence within the package but the lagoon, marked off as it was from the open sea by the house reef, was not part of the resort and was therefore outside the package.

28. It does not follow from this finding that the defendant was obliged to assess the safety of the lagoon in the same manner as it assessed (and was obliged to assess) the safety of the buildings and paved areas on the island which could relatively easily be inspected for such things as fire safety and other risks to physical harm. Given the nature and size of the lagoon, I do not think that the defendant was under an

obligation to survey it to discover features that might have a bearing on its safety. Instead, I find that the defendant was obliged to undertake a visual inspection of the lagoon, to enquire of the resort's management if they were aware of any particular features of the lagoon that might have a bearing on safety and to inspect the records kept by the resort of any accidents reported to have occurred in the lagoon.

29. There is no evidence that the defendant carried out any of these steps. Whether the defendant's failure to take the steps they should have done renders them liable to the claimant depends on what would they would have learned if the steps had been taken. There was abundant evidence that whether observed from the beach or in the water, the water in the pools was a much deeper blue than the surrounding water, thereby indicating quite plainly the existence of areas of water considerably deeper than elsewhere in the lagoon. It follows, in my view, that a visual inspection of the lagoon would undoubtedly have revealed the existence of the pools. If the defendant had enquired of the resort management about these areas of deeper water the description they would have been given would have been substantially the same as that given in evidence ... In my judgement that description coupled with what the defendant would have seen for itself would have obliged the defendant to make its own assessment of the pools from a safety point of view. It ought therefore to have acquainted itself with the physical characteristics of the pool in which Mr Jones drowned, which were that it shelved in a way that meant that a person entering it could find himself after a further pace or two in water that had risen from between his chest and his navel to about his chin or slightly above.

30. Were the physical characteristics of the pool such that the defendant should have warned Mr and Mrs Jones of its existence?

31. [It was] submitted that Mr and Mrs. Jones were given the impression that they could wade wherever they went in the lagoon and would therefore in the absence of a warning be liable to be surprised and induced to panic if they suddenly found themselves in deep water. Mrs. Jones's evidence (was) that when she and Mr Jones read in the brochure the words: " Just imagine, a long narrow island paradise with two neighbouring islands (which you can reach at low tide!)" Mr Jones said that the two of them might do that (i.e. walk across to a neighbouring island). He also relied on the evidence that people walked in the lagoon and would be observed by other guests doing so.

32. I reject the submission that the defendant gave the impression that guests could wade anywhere in the lagoon. The brochure went on to say: " Ringed by fine sand.... this coral paradise offers a good selection of watersports and entertainments ... beach volleyball and football available... watersports on the beach; diving school." In my view the availability of water sports suggests that the lagoon may well have places where someone would be out of his depth and unable to wade. Further, the words " a long narrow island paradise with two neighbouring islands (which you can reach at low tide!)" by themselves do not give the impression that one can walk anywhere in the lagoon. Rather, they denote no more than it was possible to walk between Fun Island and the neighbouring islands at low tide.

33. In addition, there was pinned up on a notice board at the Fun Island resort a notice that included the words:

" SAFETY

Due to the strong current that is sometimes prevalent between the islands we strongly advise you not to try & cross to reach the islands on the other side of Fun Island by swimming."

In my opinion this notice would raise a real doubt in the mind of a reasonable guest staying on Fun Island about the depth of the water between the islands. I find therefore that a reasonable guest who had read the brochure and the notice would have concluded that it was at the very least doubtful that it was possible to walk between the islands, and he would not have concluded that it was possible to walk anywhere in the lagoon.

34. Moreover, the existence of pools of deep water in the eastern lagoon was clearly discernible from the shore and from within the lagoon on account of the pools' deep blue colour. It is ... plain from the colour photographs of the island and the lagoon ... It was suggested on behalf of Mrs. Jones that confusion could result from the presence of other areas of a deeper colour caused by passing clouds and the presence of patches of underwater sea grass but I do not accept this suggestion. The clarity of the water in the lagoon is outstanding. In my judgement, no one is at all likely to confuse the effect of sea grass and passing clouds on the colour of the water with the deep blue that signifies the presence of the pools.

35. In my opinion, adult holiday makers like Mr and Mrs. Jones must be taken to know that the sea-bed is not even and that there is nothing unusual about changes in depth. They accordingly must be taken to appreciate that the sea is capable of springing surprises such as the pool in which Mr Jones died, a pool of calm, clear warm water which did not drop vertically but which shelved down in a way that meant that a person entering it could find himself after a further pace or two in water that had risen from between his chest and his navel to about his chin or slightly above. As (a witness) said when he was describing the time when he and his wife found themselves suddenly in deep water, he was not expecting it, but on the other hand it was not unexpected.

36. I also think it significant that in the 10 years that preceded Mr Jones's death no guest had reported to the management any difficulty about any of the pools and that, although the resort has had 75,000 visitors, there have only been two other deaths connected with the sea: one where the deceased was snorkling and apparently died from natural causes; the other where an elderly lady died a week after returning to Europe having been found unconscious on the reef a long way from Fun Island.

37. After anxious consideration, I find that the circumstances were such that even if the defendant had made itself aware of the characteristics of the pool, those characteristics were not such that it would have been under a duty to warn. Mr and Mrs. Jones about the pool's existence.

38. Since I have held that the defendant was under a duty to become acquainted with the characteristics of the pool, the defendant and the resort owners stand on the same footing so far as knowledge is concerned. It follows that the claimant's case is not assisted by regulation 15.

The claimant's case under regulation 4

39. Regulation 4 of the Package Holiday Regulations provides:

> " (1) No organiser or retailer shall supply to a consumer any descriptive matter concerning a package, the price of a package or any other conditions applying to the contract which contains any misleading information.
>
> (2) If an organiser or retailer is in breach of paragraph (1) he shall be liable to compensate the consumer for any loss which the consumer suffers in consequence."

40. The claimant contends that the brochure was misleading because those parts of the brochure set out in paragraph 25 above gave the impression that it was safe to walk in the lagoon, and it was not. For the reasons given in paragraphs 32 and 33 above I find that the brochure does not give that impression. The claim under regulation 4 accordingly fails.

41. Mr Jones's death was a tragic and shocking accident. However, for the reasons I have given, the claimant has failed to establish that the defendant is liable to her for her husband's death.

Moran v *First Choice Holidays and Flights Ltd*, Nicola Davies QC, Deputy Judge of the QBD

JUDGMENT

1. This claim is brought by Cynthia Moran, the claimant, for damages for injuries and loss resulting from an accident which occurred on 3rd July 2001 when she was a pillion passenger on a quad bike driven by her husband on a holiday excursion in the Dominican Republic. It is alleged that the excursion was provided and operated by First Choice Holidays and Flights Ltd (First Choice), the defendant, and further alleged that it is in breach of contract and/or negligent in providing a defective quad bike which was the cause of the accident. The hearing dealt only with the issue of liability.

2. The claimant originally joined her husband, John Moran, as second defendant alleging negligence in his driving of the bike. That claim has been discontinued. The defendant, First Choice, has instituted Part 20 proceedings against Mr. Moran based upon his negligence.

3. The contractual claim is brought upon the basis that First Choice, the defendant, was either the principal to the excursion contract or liable as an agent for an undisclosed principal, in this case the provider of the excursion Dominican Quad Bikes Adventure. The defendant denies that it was a principal to the excursion contract. Its case is that it sold the excursion as an agent for a disclosed principal. Further, in respect of the accident itself it is contended that there was no causative defect in the bike nor is there evidence of lack of reasonable care on the part of the providers of the bike.

4. Issues

In his opening Mr Pusey, counsel for the claimant, identified the issues agreed between the parties:

i) What was the cause of the quad bike accident?

ii) Was the defendant acting as principal to excursion contract or as undisclosed agent for a principal to the contract?

iii) Was the defendant acting as disclosed agent for the providers of the excursion?

iv) A subsidiary issue: did Mr. Moran's driving contribute to the accident?

Facts

5. The claimant and her husband were on a holiday provided by the defendant in the Dominican Republic from 24 June to 8 July 2001. On arrival at their hotel a welcome pack was provided giving information regarding excursions available through the defendant. At a welcome meeting the following day Rachel, a tour representative employed by the defendant, gave more

information about excursions. The claimant and her husband booked and paid for the jeep safari excursion. The excursion took place. Later in the holiday they booked an excursion called 'Crazy Quads' through Rachel. It was paid for by travellers cheques. The claimant states that they received a white piece of paper, presumably a booking confirmation or receipt. She recalls that the paper was torn out of a book and there was a carbon copy which Rachel retained.

6.   On 3rd July the claimant and her husband were collected from their hotel and taken to the compound where the quad bikes were stored. Some instructions were given, crash helmets were provided and bikes were allocated. A convoy of bikes set off. Ahead of the claimant at the front of the convoy was a bike driven by an employee of the quad bike company. He led the way and dictated the speed of travel. The claimant's bike was about twenty yards behind the leader, behind her were bikes driven by tourists or members of the quad bike company.

7.   Mr Moran as the driver of the bike gave his account of the journey. He had ridden motor bikes some twenty to thirty years ago but had no recent experience. The bikes left the compound and in so doing Mr Moran negotiated a left turn without any difficulty. Thereafter Mr Moran had to turn right onto the main road. As he did so the bike did not appear to react, the result being that Mr Moran had to take a 'long wide sweep' to get back onto the road. The road gave way to a dirt track and at one point Mr Moran stopped the bike in order to obtain goggles because of the dust. About thirty minutes into the journey the bike was approaching a clump of grass in the middle of the track. Mr Moran turned the handlebars to the left to go round the grass, he then turned the handlebars to the right but the wheels did not turn. He grabbed hold of the clutch and pulled it in, he took his thumb off the throttle but it remained in position and the machine kept revving. Mr Moran tried the brake using the foot brake and hand brake but the brakes would not work. The bike went off the edge of the track, down a ledge and dropped some thirteen to fourteen feet. Mr and Mrs Moran were thrown from the bike and sustained injury.

8.   Mr Moran said that the first difficulty with the right turn he attributed to his not being used to the bike. During the remainder of the journey he had driven over a terrain which was dusty, containing stones and indentures but he did not have to negotiate any other significant manoeuvres. In stopping for goggles he had encountered no problems. The convoy was at all times travelling at a moderate speed. In short an unremarkable journey over relatively straightforward terrain save for one incident involving a right turn.

9.   The claimant's account of the journey was similar to that of her husband. Mrs Moran had been aware of the problem when the bike first attempted to turn right and had commented upon it but at the time it did not cause her much concern. No other witnesses were called on behalf of the claimant or the defendant to give first-hand oral evidence of the accident.

10.   During the course of the defence case counsel on behalf of the defendant made application pursuant to CPR r 32.1 to admit into evidence two

hearsay statements. In each case no notice of hearsay had been served pursuant to CPR r 33.2. The first statement dated 3rd July 2001 was made by Osins Polanco General Manager of the Dominican Quad Bike Adventure. The application was allowed. The statement began with the words 'Tour Report' and the following two paragraphs read:

> " Testimony of the two guides leading the tour
>
> Departure
>
> We left the hotel at 1.30pm, after having given to the clients all the necessary instructions to drive the motors. There were in total 4 people in two four wheels motors, beside the two guides in two motors, one in front to direct the clients and the other one at the back with the second couple.
>
> The tour was normal as always, but after 30 minutes when we have been at the sugar cane fields (driving very slow), the accident happened. The client lost the control over the motor and then he fell together with his motor into a hole. We went immediately to help him and he said, " I lost the control over the motor" . We called an ambulance and took them to the clinic."

11. The statement identifies neither guide. No information was provided as to the taking of this statement nor as to any other detail regarding the testimony of the guides. When challenged by counsel on behalf of the defendant as to his alleged statement immediately after the accident Mr Moran said he had spoken to no one. He had injured his wrist but his primary concern was for his wife who was crying and lying on her back. He said he would not have referred to the bike as a motor. Having seen and heard Mr Moran I accept what he says.

12. In giving evidence to the Court the claimant and her husband did so with moderation and impressed as witnesses of truth. I accept their evidence that at the start of the journey there was a problem with a right turn, thereafter no significant manoeuvre was attempted until the clump of grass had to be negotiated. For a second time a right turn was attempted and problems immediately ensued involving the wheels, throttle and brakes. I am satisfied that the cause of this problem was a defect in the bike.

Maintenance of the Quad Bike

13. Alison Ventura was the defendant's senior quality co-ordinator in the Dominican Republic at the time of the claimant's accident. It was her evidence that the excursion was operated by Dominican Quad Bike Adventure not by First Choice. The defendant's local agent in the Dominican Republic, Barcelo Viajes, had an agreement with the bike company for the provision of the excursion. Ms Ventura said that in order to carry out safety checks she went on this particular excursion twice and

visited the company's base ten to fifteen times to ensure the bikes were kept in good condition and to spot check guides and their knowledge. No oral evidence was called on behalf of the quad bike company nor were any records of maintenance or inspection disclosed. In addition to the hearsay statement of Mr Polanco a statement from Alfredo Vasquez, company mechanic of the bike company was, admitted into evidence pursuant to CPR r 32. The statement dated 27 October 2001 deals with the general system of maintenance of quad bikes. Daily checks of brakes, weekly general checks and monthly changes of oil are performed. No information was provided as to any history of specific checks upon the bike driven by Mr. Moran. The absence of any documentation to support the frequency and nature of the checks in general and upon the particular bike in question considerably limits the evidential value of this statement..

14.   Of some significance is the fact that following the accident an inspection of the bike is alleged to have been carried out. Alison Ventura was 'ninety nine per cent sure' that an inspection was carried out by the agents but it was not done immediately. She did not arrange for an inspection to take place even though she visited Mrs Moran in hospital two days after the accident and was by then aware that the claimant had 'broken her back'. As far as Ms Ventura is aware documents do exist relating to the inspection and are held by the booking agents Barcelo Viajes. No such documents have been disclosed, no explanation was proffered to the court for the absence of such documents.

15.   One single piece of information was before the court as to the post accident state of the bike. It was in the hearsay statement of Mr Polanco and read 'The motor is in perfect conditions after the accident. It proves the good conditions and its care.' Given the fact that the bike had fallen off the track, down a ledge and landed on the ground it is a statement which has to be viewed with a degree of caution.

16.   These proceedings were instituted in 2003. The hearsay statements provided by the bike company are dated 2001. The defendant has had ample opportunity to provide evidence, oral and documented, as to the pre-accident maintenance and post-accident inspection of the bike. It has failed to provide such evidence and to proffer any adequate explanation for its absence. There is no cogent evidence before the court as to the age or condition of the bike before the accident and an absence of any reliable evidence as to its post accident state.

17.   This lack of evidence must reflect upon the adequacy of any system which it is contended was operated by the bike company. It fails to provide any sound evidential basis upon which this court could make a finding that the bike in question was regularly and competently inspected and maintained. The absence of any post-accident inspection report simply serves to emphasise the dearth of any satisfactory evidence relating to the condition of the bike. In short there is no satisfactory evidence to rebut the claimant's assertion that a defect was present.

First Choice - Principal, Undisclosed Agent or Disclosed Agent

18.   It is agreed that the claim does not arise out of the original package holiday contract. The contract for the provision of the quad bike was a separate and later transaction. The factual position pleaded by the defendant was that Dominican Quad Bikes Adventure was the operator of the excursion and the principal to the contract with the claimant (paragraph 3 of the Defence of the First Defendant).

19.   The evidence of the claimant and her husband was that they at all times believed the contract was made with First Choice. In support of their belief they rely upon three matters:

1)   documentation provided by the defendant;

2)   the manner in which the earlier safari excursion was dealt with and performed;

3)   the fact that they could have bought a cheaper quad bike excursion but did not do so because of the defendant's guarantee of insurance and, for Mr Moran, the safety checks.

20.   The relevant documentation comprises:

a)   Welcome Pack

b)   Booking Form (used for the safari expedition).

c)   A document which the defendant alleges is a copy of the receipt/booking confirmation provided to the claimant and her husband for the quad bike trip.

a)   Welcome Pack

The two logos at the head of this document are 'First Choice' and 'Unijet'. It begins with the words: 'On behalf of First Choice and Unijet, it is a pleasure to welcome you to the Dominican Republic'. A further paragraph states:

> 'Tours and Trips - First Choice and Unijet offer an exciting selection of trips to suit everybody from relaxing aboard a catamaran to discovering the wild countryside on a jeep safari. All our excursions are fully insured and regularly checked to ensure that they meet our safety standards. First Choice cannot be held responsible for any excursion not supplied by First Choice as they probably will not meet our stringent insurance and safety requirements, at First Choice your safety and enjoyment are our first priority.'

There is no reference within this document to the fact that excursions which are 'supplied' by First Choice are operated or provided by another company.

b)   Booking Form

The logos on the front of this form are: First Choice, Barcelo Viajes and Outback Jungle Safari. Also on the front of the form are the following statements:

> " All tours operated by First Choice are working with the Cristal Hygiene program this ensures that they comply with stringent health and hygiene checks, they are also monitored very closely to ensure that they pass a rigorous safety tes (sic) on a regular basis. This allows you to relax and enjoy the holiday that you booked knowing tha (sic) every possible precaution has been taken.
>
> There are several 'Pirate' companies operating excursions in the Dominican Republic, these companies are not used by British tour operators because they do not reach the quality, safety and hygiene standards that we as your tour operator demand.
>
> We cannot accept any responsibility for illness, injury or death caused as a result of participating in a pirate excursion."

There is no mention in this document of Dominican Quad Bike Adventure although there is the logo of the booking agent, Barcelo Viajes. The document is written in precisely the same spirit as the welcome pack - book for tours operated by First Choice and it will provide safe tours for which they will accept responsibility in the event of a tour not meeting its rigorous standards and injury resulting.

It is unsurprising that provided with this documentation the claimant and her husband believed that First Choice was supplying the excursion and with it the relevant safety checks and insurance.

c)   Receipt/Booking Confirmation

This document was disclosed by the defendant. It purports to be a copy of the voucher given to the claimant and her husband by Rachel upon their booking the quad bike tour. The original of the document has not been produced. Rachel was not called as a witness. At the top of the document is the logo of Barcelo Viajes and Turaria which is part of Barcelo Viajes. The information entered upon the document is correct save for the hotel room number of the claimant. In the box headed 'Clients signature' no signature appears but a smiley face has been drawn. On the line headed 'date' appear a series of numbers which make little or no sense. There is no reference to Dominican Quad Bike Adventure.

21.   The claimant and her husband agree that a booking confirmation or receipt was provided. They say it was on white paper, there were no logos and it was about half the size of the document produced to the court. Taking the

defendant's case at its highest, namely the presence of the Barcelo Viajes logo at the top of the document, I do not regard this as sufficient to displace the impression created by the defendant in its welcome pack and the front of its booking form that the excursion was supplied by First Choice. I have deliberately taken this high point but am bound to state that the provenance of this document is unsatisfactory.

22.   The documentation supplied by defendant left Mr and Mrs Moran with the justifiable impression that the excursion contract was being made with their tour operator, First Choice. Nowhere in the documents is there any reference to Dominican Quad Bike Adventure and the presence of an unexplained Barcelo Viajes logo on the booking form takes the issue little further. I am satisfied that in respect of the quad bike excursion First Choice did not disclose that it was acting for its pleaded agent namely Dominican Quad Bike Adventure.

23.   Even if I had doubts as to the evidence provided by the documentation the unchallenged evidence of the claimant and her husband was that booking and performance of the safari excursion pointed to the defendant providing the excursion. The Moran's belief that the defendant was the supplier of the excursion was the basis of their refusal to book a cheaper quad bike tour no doubt from one of those operators described by the defendant as " pirate" .

24.   Counsel for the defendant referred me to the case of *Derbyshire and First Choice Holidays and Flights*, a decision of His Honour Judge Karsten QC at the Central London County Court. This type of case has to turn upon its own facts. In the reported case the facts were clearly different both as to the documentation provided by the tour company with its identification of the providers of ski equipment and the actual knowledge possessed by the claimant of the existence of the suppliers of ski boots which were causative of his injuries. The particular facts of the reported case do not assist in the determination of this claim but I am grateful to counsel for providing the authority.

The negligence of Mr Moran

25.   Counsel on behalf of the defendant approached this issue with caution and realism. There is no suggestion that Mr Moran was driving at an excessive speed or in any way that could be described as reckless. At best the suggestion appeared to be that Mr. Moran's lack of familiarity with the quad bike caused him to confuse one or more levers or modes of control. Mr. Moran denied the suggestion.

26.   Having found that the precipitating cause of the accident was a defect in the bike, the first manifestation of which was an inability to turn the bike right Mr. Moran was presented with a situation in which he could do little to avert the accident which followed. I dismiss the Part 20 Claim.

Issues - Conclusions

27.   I am satisfied that the cause of the accident was a defect in the quad bike which Mr. Moran was driving as part of a tour excursion.

28.   As to the excursion contract the defendant was at all times the undisclosed agent for the local principal Dominican Tour Bike Adventure who provide the quad bike and as such is liable for its undisclosed principal.

29.   The defendant has produced no satisfactory evidence to demonstrate that the defective bike had been regularly and competently maintained prior to the accident and was thus free from defect. It has also failed to provide any post accident inspection evidence to negative the allegation of a defect.

30.   The claimant succeeds in her claim based upon the failure of the defendant to exercise reasonable skill and care in the provision and performance of the excursion. The claim is made out both in terms of breach of the contract and breach of the duty of care.

31.   The defendant has not made out its claim in negligence against Mr. Moran.

32.   Accordingly there is judgment for the claimant upon her claim against the defendant. The defendant's Part 20 claim against Mr. Moran is dismissed.

Gallagher v *Airtours Plc*, unreported, 17 October 2000, Barrow in
Furness County Court (HHJ Appleton)

This is a claim by Maureen Gallagher against Airtours arising in the following
circumstances. On 2nd February 1997 she booked a skiing holiday, through the
Lunpoly Travel Agency in Barrow with Airtours. The holiday comprised return
flights from Manchester to Geneva, self-catering accommodation for seven nights
between 29th March and 15th April in Flain in the French Alps at a cost of £305.93.
The claimant took this holiday with a friend, a Mrs Sinton, who has not been a
witness in this case.

The transport from Geneva Airport to the resort, made as part of the holiday
arrangements, was a coach. During this journey she was offered and purchased a
skiing package through the Airtours courier on the bus. This cost her approximately
£200. She was given vouchers and told to exchange these for skiing lessons. She paid
cash on the bus. The lessons were with Ecole du ski Francais.

Unfortunately, on the fourth day of the skiing holiday she had a very nasty accident
whilst skiing. The injuries she sustained were capable of being described as quite
frightening. Anybody who has read the details of the injuries, including myself, has
the very greatest sympathy with her for the horrible injuries she suffered.

This action is for damages for personal injuries she hopes to recover from the
defendants Airtours. ... The circumstances of the claim, as described in the particulars
of claim, provide a very convenient chronology and statement of what occurred to
her. It referred to her purchase on the coach of the ski pack. That comprised a week's
ski hire, a ski pass, skiing lessons and boots. That was confirmed in cross-
examination. She had selected the package she wanted from whatever it was that was
in the envelope that the rep gave her on the coach. Unfortunately, a duplicate of that
has not found its way into the trial bundle. At all events, she was familiar with this
setup because she had had earlier skiing holidays. She had already had one skiing
holiday in 1997, so this was going to be her second; and, in all it was her sixth trip to
ski slopes. [The Claimant] said:

> " My travel companion purchased the same package. I was given vouchers
> for exchange at BSF [that is abbreviation of the French skiing school]. It
> contained details of lessons/info pack from BSF"

As part of the cross-examination, learned counsel for the defendant put to the
claimant that part of the point of the skiing holiday is to refresh and brush up in the
first day or two to the level that one had attained on the last skiing holiday, and then
to push forward the frontiers of one's skiing ability. She accepted that she would
expect the tutors to challenge her to get better; in other words to give her slightly
more demanding things to do each time. She acknowledged that there would have
been earlier examples in her skiing career when she had been challenged. She accepted
that it would be designed to improve her skiing abilities, technique and experience.

Then she comes to the day of the accident. It was on this day that a fresh instructor came.

> " By comparison with the French girl his English was poor, he smiled and
> nodded a lot and was very pleasant. But we simply could not communicate

effectively because he did not have the vocabulary. As a consequence there was very little explanation as to what we were to do or how to execute it."

[The evidence was]:

> " On the fourth day, Wednesday 2ʳᵈ April, the group had gone off piste without being given notice by the new ski instructor. We had been off piste for five or ten minutes when the instructor asked the group to go down a slope, make a banking turn to the right and come to a halt. It seemed as though we were heading into a hollow shaped like bowl ... Before we set off he explained, that's for certain, who went first. It was part of a long ski off piste. We stopped to do an exercise. There was a channel to ski round and a mound to your right. There was no track at all, but the path was obvious. Everyone apart from the claimant completed this run successfully. The run itself, the reality of it, was not its steepness, but it was very icy and hard to control in speed."

... So I have to put into the balance of my findings as to what was going on the fact that up to this particular run nobody in the group – and bear in mind Mr. Hartley was there with his wife and 12-year-old son – had made any reservations or complaint of uncertainty or problem known to Anthony, not one of them in the group.

... as Mr Hartley pointed out:

> " The instructor asked the group to go down a slope, make a banking turn to the right and come to a halt."

Mr Hartley goes on to say that he felt it was a dangerous manoeuvre, but if everybody else was going to do it he was going to try as well. He succeeded.

But following him was Maureen Gallagher, the claimant, and he recounts:

> " I looked back at her" ... " attempting the manoeuvre. She wasn't able to making the banking turn and instead went straight in over the crest of the bowl."

What actually happened to [the Claimant], unfortunately, is best described by reference to the diagrams ... [there is] a bird's eye view showing that they were going to descend – and it was not a steep slope – clockwise starting at about 4 o'clock and ending up at about 11 o'clock is the best description I can give. The second diagram shows that on the outer edge of the turn (rather like the banking on an old-fashioned Brooklands-style motor racing track) there was, as it were, a jump due to the presence of a rock outcrop. Because she was unable to make the turn sufficiently tightly she went over that outcrop and suffered the nasty injuries...

Pausing there, that has given the narrative of what occurred. The only evidence I have heard in this court from witnesses who have attended court has been the evidence in chief and cross-examination of both the claimant and her witness, Mr Hartley. The only evidence the defendants have relied on is the Civil Evidence Act statement of Mr Famzoulla (?) to which I have already made reference.

Somebody somewhere, however, must have aspired to a level of expertise about skiing and an expertise that has been denied to me in trying this case. In the last twelve/eighteen months I have noticed that sporting accidents have at least played some part in my otherwise usual diet of slipping, tripping and falling, and people colliding with each other in motorcars. I have, for example, tried a number of accidents arising out of horse riding as a sport and football. I have already tried a skiing accident case. That involved bindings not being set correctly when they were supplied to the skier.

The short point I am making is this. I have no expert evidence to advise or help me as to whether or not the activities of Mr Terrian (?) on that day did, in the eyes of a properly qualified professional, fall below the standard of care to be exercised by a reasonably prudent ski instructor of the variety of which he was. The burden of proof lies on the party who brings the action. It is plain from what I am going to be referring to in my judgment that there is no such expert evidence. It is a complete mistake to think that the court possesses any expertise in this field whatsoever. I am a judge. It is my job to apply the law to the cases that are brought before me. It is a basic principle that a claimant bears the burden of proof in a civil action. The standard of proof is the balance of probabilities. It is unfortunate if a claimant comes to court without the requisite evidence. [Counsel for the Claimant] has sought to persuade me that the matter was so obvious that the case was proved. But, with respect to him, I beg to differ.

The particulars of negligence alleged against Mr Terrian (?) are to be found at paragraph 20 of the particulars of claim. ... I will go through them. It will illustrate that a mistake was made unfortunately in the preparation of the claimant's case.

20(a):

" Failed adequately to assess the claimant's skiing ability prior to Anthony taking the group off piste."

In my judgment the claimant has failed to discharge the burden of proof in that regard. Moreover, in fact when it was pleaded, it is right up to even the time of this accident that she had made no complaint whatsoever that she was in the wrong group or that she was being asked to do anything she could not do or was unhappy about doing. So whoever was responsible for plucking that allegation at (a) out of the air has overlooked the requirement that it requires evidence to back it up. There is none, and it fails.

(b):

" Failed at any time to warn the claimant's group that that was what he proposed to do."

That was to take the group off piste. It had happened the day before. In so far as there any failure to warn about what they were about to do, Mr Hartley's evidence disproves this allegation. In fact his evidence in chief, I rather think, does that at paragraph 6. He says that they had gone off piste without being given notice, but nobody seems to have objected at the stage when he stopped them and said, " Right we are now going to go down this slope, making a banking turn to the right and come to a halt" . Nobody complained. (b), in my judgment, fails also.

(c):

" Concluded the claimant was an expert off piste skier when there was no sufficient basis to do so."

There is not, in my judgment, a shred of evidence that suggests that either Terrian or anybody else thought any such thing.

(d):

" Failed to give any indication of the difficulty given the terrain and snow conditions of this chosen off piste route."

Again, with respect, this is perhaps the hallmark of amateurish consideration of this matter, because the particular part of this run that is being complained about was this run referred to by Mr Hartley at paragraph 6 of his witness statement. I have already found as a fact that he stopped the entire group. He explained to them. Nobody complained to him of what they had done already in the morning or that anybody was in any way unhappy, and everybody got on with it, and everybody bar the claimant, who certainly had her accident, but everybody else had negotiated it without any problem.

(e) Here again, regrettably, another example of a lack of attention to detail in preparing the case:

" Failed prior to taking the group to the top of the steep bank to give the less confident skiers in the group, including the claimant, the opportunity to take an easier route."

I would, for my own part, require the evidence of an expert to explain that that would be an appropriate thing to do. But in any event, on the facts of the case, nobody up to the time that this run started made any complaint at all to Terrian (?) that they were not happy. Therefore again (e) seems a mistaken piece of criticism and I ask rhetorically: what steep bank?

I do not know where the learned pleader got the idea of the steep bank when he formulated (e), but it simply is not borne out on the evidence.

(f), as learned counsel for the defendant has submitted, adds nothing. In my judgment, rightly so.

(g):

" Instructed the group to perform a right-turn manoeuvre in a position which he knew.....was particularly dangerous by reason of the steepness of the slope."

I have already dealt with the steepness of the slope. It does not make sense. In the light of the evidence that I have heard in this court, of the run itself, " the feature of it was not its steepness" . For the learned pleader to keep on about steepness in the absence of any evidence to prove or to establish that seems to me something of a mistake. I am not impressed that there is any merit in that allegation either.

(h):

" In so instructing the group, instructed the claimant to perform a manoeuvre which was far beyond her ability."

Nothing that occurred so far had given her sufficient impetus to complain to Terrian (?) that she was out of her depth. What I do not have is any expert evidence that explains to me in terms that I could understand what technical skiing merit there is in allegation (h). It is correct she did not perform this manoeuvre, but I cannot close my eyes to the fact that everybody else, including Mr Hartley's 12-year-old son, performed it satisfactorily. If there was some defect in her technique which a reasonably competent instructor should have known about through having observed her then for that allegation, devised by counsel, to succeed it requires more than simply the evidence of the claimant and her witness, Mr Hartley, to convince me that that is the case. So that fails too.

The same is true of (i). It is part of the nature of mountains, whether they are covered in snow or not, that they are formed by a variety of geological features ... This particular mountain side does not proceed down in either a steep or a gentle slope, but it has flatter areas interspersed with steep drops, called terracing, probably wrongly by me, but it describes what has happened. She has unfortunately gone over the edge of a terrace. But without more from a skiing expert (i) is a meaningless assertion to make, as I say, without proper evidence to bring it home that there was a danger to which he negligently exposed her.

(j) relies on [the instructor] not being qualified. He was. Again I have no expert evidence to indicate the level of qualification, but what I do have at the other end of the scale is a recognition of the likelihood that, if somebody in the shape of Terrain (?) or his organisation was behaving in a criminal fashion in his treatment of clients on a ski slope, it would have been in the industry's best interests to have him pursued relentlessly and no doubt in the first place by the local gendarmerie about this accident. But there is nothing of that sort in this case at all.

I am driven to the conclusion that, enthusiastic as the claimant's solicitors and counsel may have been that they were expert about behaviour on the ski slope, a number of the allegations that I have been through are ill thought out. The others do not have evidence to prove them. I regret to say that, if the claimant did somewhere have a case, unfortunately it has not been supported by evidence sufficient to convince me in this court.

That disposes, regrettably, of really the main aspect of the case, because it seems to be common ground that the other two possible routes in which she might find success do depend upon there being negligence by the ski instructor. Both learned counsel have taken me through from their respective standpoints of what I can refer to as the contractual liability or the contractual claim aspect of the matter. [Counsel] for the claimant very candidly and with commendable frankness, indicated in the course of his submissions that he regarded the case on contractual liability as being rather better than that on the regulations. So out of deference to that approach, I will refer very briefly to the argument. It essentially comes to this. ...there is something called a Fair Trading Agreement. This is headed " Fair Trading Agreement" :

" Your contract is with Airtours Plc ... Below are terms and conditions of your agreement. When you make a booking and we accept a legally binding contract is made. "

So under 5 we see *" Our Responsibility"* :

" We accept liability for the proper performance of the holiday sold to you. We contract accommodation and other arrangements through suppliers who we have taken reasonable care to ensure are reputable ....

We further accept liability for claims for personal injury arising as the result of proven negligent acts or omissions of our suppliers, whilst acting within the scope or in the course of their employment or contract. We cannot accept liability in the following circumstances. (b) if the failure is the fault of someone else not connected with the provision of the services which make up the holiday which we have confirmed to you. "

The question is whether in the make up of this contract the ski pack was within the description or definition of the holiday " sold to you" .

Let us look now at other features of the holiday brochure. ... we see under the heading " Ski packs" – amongst the obvious essentials *" on a ski holiday are boots, skis, lift passes and ski school. All of these are bookable in the resort."*

... in the right-hand column are ski pack prices in a separate box. It says: *" Book in resort"* . It gives various prices. There is, incidently, no price given at all for the cost of six days' tuition.

Turning on and getting to the small print, at page 131 one sees there is a panel headed: *" What is included in the price"* . One reads:

" Accommodation, meal arrangements as booked. Service of our holiday service executive, VAT, guarantee prices, return flight from UK including in-flight refreshment, hotel services executive familiar with the airport, transport to your accommodation and back at the end of your holidays, airport taxes. "

" What are the extras? "

" Ski packs as detailed on resort pages" .

So this is an extra. There is a separate panel for ski packs:

" These are additional to the holiday price and only some may be prebooked in the UK. "

So the contract which the claimant acquired from Airtours is the contract that I have described by reference to the brochure and the price which she paid. What she was getting was that described... for £229 ...   " *Full fare paying passenger inclusive of return flight, accommodation and airport taxes* ". It included those items specified in the panel " *What is included in the price* ". It made it perfectly clear what are the extras not included in the price, and that is the ski pack.

Returning to the Fair Trading Agreement, the responsibility accepted in clause 5 is this:

" *We accept liability for the proper performance of the holiday sold to you.* "

The holiday which was sold to the claimant did not include the ski pack, and that is my finding. It is impossible, in my judgment, therefore, simply to say: Because in a loose sense the French ski school was a supplier that there is, as it were, a contractual chain of liability. The analysis and construction I put on clause 5 of the Fair Trading Agreement is that, in the context of all this, suppliers are those people who are making supplies in relation to the holiday which she had bought. And the holiday which she had bought did not include the ski pack.

I turn now to the regulations ... I can take this fairly shortly. If one looks at " *Interpretation Package* ", it has this definition:

" *'Package' means the prearranged accommodation of at least two of the following components when sold or offered for sale at an inclusive price and when the service covers a period of more than 24 hours: (a) transport, (b) accommodation (c) however ... not ancillary to transport or accommodation and accounting for a significant proportion of the package.* "

... So the short answer is that [the] argument that the ski pack is part of the package founders on a closer analysis of the *Consumer Protection Package, Travel Package Holiday and Package Tours Regulations 1992*. In short order, the argument contended for by learned counsel for the claimant does not pass muster when one reads to regulation 9 and when one looks at schedule 2. He tries to argue that the ski pack must be regarded as being part of the package.

... I would suggest that a proper reading of the whole regulations provides the answer as to what is regarded as being in the package, because it is an implied condition of the contract – and this is regulation 9.3 – that the other party to the contract complies with the provisions of paragraph 1 and that is to ensure that a contract contains at least the elements specified in regulation 2 of these regulations. It does not contain the requirements of paragraph 7; that is to say, other services which are included in the total price agreed for the package.

So the result is that the claimant has failed to succeed under the three lines of attack which have been adopted. ... it is not the law of this country that simply suffering very nasty injuries means that you have a claim against somebody for something.

Rochead v *Airtours Holidays Limited,* unreported, 18 June 2001, Central London County Court (HHJ Crawford Lindsay QC)

In this action the claimant seeks to recover agreed damages of £21,000 as a result of a skiing accident which occurred on 24th March 1997 when the claimant was skiing on a slope in Soldeu, Andorra. At the material time she had purchased a package holiday from the defendants who are tour operators. The claimant contends that the defendants are liable to pay her damages under the terms of the contract between them, under the provisions of the Package Travel, Package Holidays and Package Tours Regulations 1992 and in negligence.

The claimant I find to be an entirely frank and truthful witness. I accept the totality of what she said and in particular:-

(a)   that she was not asked her weight when she went into a shop called Ski Calbo where she was fitted with ski's and boots and bindings. She said she was positive that she was not asked her weight. While she was in the queue she realised that she did not know her weight in kilos. She was potentially embarrassed and told me that she had forgotten about her embarrassment when she made her witness statement in January 2001 and hence there was no reference to this in that statement. I accept this evidence.

(b)   that the boots she was provided with fitted her. They had three clips on the side that snapped shut and when she fell and injured herself, the boot was fastened.

(c)   that she was given no choice of ski equipment supplier and she assumed that Ski Calbo were a reputable firm and that the defendants would use a firm who " did things properly" .

(d)   that her skiing was reasonably competent and she was not in need of a refresher course.

(e)   that prior to her fall, she had skied on a blue run and on part of a blue and part of a red run and on the occasion of her fall, she was on a red run. She had fallen once before the fall which caused the injury and on that occasion her left ski had popped and the right did not.

(f)   in the coach travelling from Toulouse Airport, she bought her ski pass from one of the defendant's representatives and she was given a voucher to take to Ski Calbo. She paid for the ski pack in local currency.

(g)   on 24th March 1997 when she went to Ski Calbo to be issued with the equipment, she obtained a lift pass from one of the defendants representatives who was in the shop.

(h)   an employee of Ski-Calbo sized her up against skis which he gave her and she told him when he asked her about her experience that she was a novice/intermediate skier.

(i)   at the material time she weighed about 9 stone and was 5ft.2" and took size 4 shoes. When she fell the binding which fixed her ski boot to her left ski released. The binding which fixed her ski boot to her right ski did not do so.

The expert evidence comprised the written reports of both Mr Exell and Mr Foxon, their joint statement and both of them gave oral evidence. ... the experts state:-

> " ... *the court should be aware that the injuries sustained by the claimant is very uncommon. When a skier is supplied with the appropriate ski equipment (and that equipment is used in a responsible and appropriate manner), a spiral tibial fracture has one of the lowest probabilities of occurrence of any of the major categories of skiing injury.*"

In view of the factual and expert evidence in this case, I conclude that when [the Claimant] fell, the binding affixing the claimant's ski boot to her right ski did not release as a result of an act or acts of omission of an employee of Ski Calbo. The employee failed to ask the claimant her weight and either failed to obtain the appropriate binding settings and/or failed to adjust the binding or bindings to the setting 6.

Given the above finding, are the defendants liable to the claimant? I consider first the position under the *Package Travel, Package Holidays and Package Tours Regulations 1992.* [The Judge then sets out regulations 2 and 15 of the Regulations].

[Counsel for the defendant] submitted that the contract is the pre-arranged package contract bought from the tour operator, the defendants. There has to be a pre-arranged combination of two of the relevant components particularised in the definition of " package" sold or offered for sale at an inclusive price. In this case ... " the package" [was set out on the confirmation invoice]; five paying customers including the claimant purchased their holiday in the sum of £219.00 each, together with the flight supplement. The claimant purchased her ski-pack separately. This purchase was not included in the pre-arranged combination of the relevant components and it was not offered for sale at an inclusive price. The " package" did not include the ski-pack arrangements and therefore the regulations ... do not apply. The ski-pack was an available option: the price was fixed locally. Thus ... the brochure relating to Soldeu set out details of ski-pack prices, but stated " *the above prices are approximate, based on 95/96 rates and therefore should only be used as a guide*". ... under the heading " *What are extras?*" includes " *ski-packs as detailed on the resort pages.*" Under the general heading " *Ski-Packs*" it is stated: " *these are additional to the holiday price and only some may be pre-booked in the UK. Children and senior citizens should book in resort, as often there are special discounts available. " Ski-boot hire". Deposits are frequently required on hire equipment, these must be paid locally to the supplier. All equipment is of good mid-range standard, for those wishing to hire superior equipment, a supplement must be paid to the shop in the resort*".

Ski-Packs are tailor made to individual requirements and indeed not everyone who goes on a skiing holiday wishes to have the facility of a ski-pack.

In the light of the foregoing counsel submitted that the defendants were under no liability pursuant to the terms of the regulations.

[Counsel for the claimant] submitted that the contract was wider than the " package" . Ski hire was not part of the " package" but was part of the contract. There is a distinction in the drafting between regulations 15.1 and 15.2 and 15.3 and 15.4 and the regulations impose liability for the proper performance of the contract as a whole.

I am persuaded by [the defendant's] submissions. The Regulations apply to packages sold or offered for sale in the territory of the United Kingdom. The " package" involves a pre-arranged combination of two of the relevant components offering for sale at an inclusive price. The ski-pack did not form part of any pre-arranged combination of the relevant components and was not sold or offered for sale at an inclusive price. In my judgment the defendants are not liable to the claimant under the provisions of the Regulations.

Is there liability under the terms of the contract?

There is clearly an overlap between the submissions on this part of the case and the submissions under the provisions of the Regulations. [The defendant] submits that Ski Calbo was not a supplier of a service within the contract. There is no liability under Clause 5(b) of the Fair Trading Agreement if any failure is the fault of someone " *not connected with the provision of the services which make up the holiday which we have confirmed to you.*" " That holiday was confirmed [as set out in the confirmation invoice]. Suppliers are those who supply services contracted for under the confirmed contract.

[In my judgment] ... The failure here was " *the fault of someone else not connected with the provision of the services which make up the holiday which we have confirmed to you*". I further agree ... that Ski Calbo was not a supplier of [a] service within the package holiday contract because at the time the contract was made, no ski-pack had been purchased.

The alternative contract concluded on the coach cannot, in my judgment, be relied upon. It is not pleaded specifically and the defendants might well have wished to raise an issue as to the proper law of such an agreement. If there was such an agreement which was subject to English law, I do not consider that the regulations would apply to it. As to implied terms, I cannot see any way in which the claimant could establish a breach of any implied term on the particular facts of this case.

I turn now to consider the claim in negligence. ... such duty, if it exists, was one whereby the defendant was obliged to exercise reasonable care and skill in the provision of ski hire.

In response [the defendant] asserted that this was not a case where the claimant was entitled to an additional remedy in tort. Her contractual obligations were sufficient. She would in any event have a remedy in France or Spain and it is the case that she, living in Glasgow, is in any event bringing proceedings in a different jurisdiction.

I am not persuaded that this is a case where the claimant should be in a position to bring a claim in negligence in addition to her contractual claims. However, if the claimant is entitled to sue for negligence, then the duty of care owed is a narrow one as set out above. On the facts of this case I consider that there has been an isolated error by one employee of Ski Calbo. There is no evidence to suggest that there were numerous instances of bindings not being released. One has to put this incident into its context. Hundreds of people were being fitted with skis and the proper procedures seem to have been followed in relation to [others]. ... the defendants still work with Ski Calbo and that they have worked with them for a number of years. Likewise other foreign tour operators work with them and they have a large ski hire operation which they manage very well. [They are] a reputable shop owned by the Calbo family.

I am certainly not persuaded that there were regular errors appearing in binding adjustments. Unless there was a substantial number of complaints about bindings not releasing or some other evidence to suggest that Ski Calbo were unsuitable to provide ski packs, I do not consider that the defendants were in breach of any duty of care. There were no facts of which the defendants had or should have had to give rise to any such breach. For these reasons the claims in contract and tort as well as pursuant to the Regulations fail and the claim is dismissed.

Patrick v *Cosmosair Plc*, 5 March 2001, Manchester County Court (HHJ Lyon)

This case arises out of a very sad accident which occurred to the Claimant when she went on a holiday to a very interesting destination, the Gambia. The holiday was organised by the Defendant company Cosmosair. On the holiday, she met the representative of Cosmosair who introduced her to various excursions available to guests and a leaflet entitled " Cosmos Out and About" . Mrs Patrick had no reason to believe that anyone other than Cosmos was providing those excursions, at that time.

It seems from the oral evidence that it was probably the next day when Mr and Mrs Patrick decided which tours they wished to go on, and booked them. Their chosen tours included one to the nature reserve where the accident occurred. I am satisfied she was given a ticket headed " West Africa Tours" . I am also satisfied that the Defendants representative Ms Proctor warned them about the need to carry mosquito repellent and water, and gave to Mrs Patrick a description of the bus which would be taking her on the tour, and the uniform which would be worn by the employees. One knows that a number of buses are likely to pull up in front of the hotel and so one clearly needs the information in order to get on the right bus. It makes sense that Ms Proctor would say " *look out for the West Africa Tours bus*" – I accept that this meant nothing to Mrs Patrick who just wanted to deal with a respectable organisation.

They reached the park on the bus. They then walked 1 kilometre through the bush with the West Africa Tours guide from the car park to the clearing. As I understand it, they all stayed together as a group until they reached the clearing. They then split up as one might expect. On the evidence one does not know where the West Africa Tours representative went at this point.

Mrs Patrick was outside the monkey cage with about 15 or 20 of the group, when the keeper invited them in to take photographs while he fed the monkeys. One of the monkeys apparently stressed, leapt on Mrs Patrick and scratched her with its claws, infecting her with some nasty bacteria. This resulted in many operations and very unpleasant consequences; for a period Mrs Patrick feared she might lose part of her leg although in the end this became unnecessary. Still she is left with a nasty scar and it troubled her greatly.

Are the Defendants responsible for this injury? ... I am satisfied as a matter of fact that there was a real risk of entering the monkey enclosure. The risk foreseen might not be bacteria, but there was a risk nonetheless. It is not stretching Judicial notice too far to understand that there is a difference between looking at monkeys in the wild, where they have the opportunity to escape from the humans; and a group of people entering their cage at feeding time, which would make them feel threatened. In any event the risk is clear from the Defendant's own evidence – Dr Camara says that the practice was discouraged and this was a one off. It is clear that it was thought that some danger existed.

I am equally satisfied that a claim in negligence does not run in this case, because of the well known rule that the responsibility of Cosmos towards West Africa Tours would merely be to make a reasonable choice of sub contractor. There is no doubt that West Africa Tours were that, as all the Defendant's evidence, including the agreed statement of Patrick Southern, testifies.

So the claim must be brought in contract. As a matter of fact the relationship between Cosmos and West Africa Tours was one of agency as is shown by the documents. As a matter of law, Mrs Patrick was aware of the separate existence of West Africa Tours, if she read the ticket. Even if the Defendants were principals to the contract, my view is that their duty extended to transportation to the park and a valid entry ticket; in addition they should have on hand a tour guide. The guide however was not required to supervise every single person as they wondered around the park; but the guide was on hand in case anyone got into trouble – although the help; they were able to give on this occasion was not much.

For these reasons I cannot find in favour of the Claimant. Sometimes there are circumstances where an accident occurs, but no claim exists. There will therefore be judgment for the Defendant.

Norfolk v *My Travel Group Plc*, 21 August 2003, Plymouth County Court (HHJ Overend)

JUDGMENT

1. The preliminary issue in this case concerns the answer to the question as to whether or not the claimant's claim against the defendants is barred by Art.16 of the Athens Convention as applied by s.183 of the Merchant Shipping Act 1995. The preliminary issue proceeds upon the assumption that the facts set out in the particulars of claim as amended.

2. In a brief it is said that there was a contract entered into on 6th September 1999 between Mr. Norfolk, the claimant's husband, and the defendants, whereby the defendants agreed to organise and retail a package holiday to Mr. Norfolk and his wife. The package holiday comprised a sea cruise on the motor vessel Carousel starting at Palma. The package included flights to and from Bristol. The vessel sailed from Palma on 18th September 1999 and after no doubt enjoying a happy holiday until then, on 30th September 1999 unfortunately Mrs. Norfolk was injured in an accident on the vessel. She slipped on water on the floor of a lift and, as a result, suffered personal injuries. She claims in her claim form consequential losses including losses for pain, suffering and loss of amenity, and also including enjoyment of the rest of her holiday.

3. That claim form was issued on 25th September 2002 against the defendants under the Package Travel, Package Holidays and Package Tours Regulations 1992. In particular the claim was made under Regulation 15 ...

4. In addition to the facts in the particulars of claim certain admissions have also been made by and on behalf of the claimant. They include the following:

> " 1. That the contract was a contract of carriage within the meaning of Art.1.2 of the Athens Convention.

> " 2. That in relation to the contract the defendant was a carrier within the meaning of Art.1.1 of the Athens Convention.

> " 3. That the contract included carriage by sea within the meaning of the Athens Convention; and

> " 4. That The Carousel was a sea-going vessel."

5. There are other admissions. The combination of all those admissions enables this court to concentrate solely on the preliminary issue to which I have already referred. The original order of District Judge Meredith of 17th May 2003 had also ordered at a trial of two earlier preliminary issues:

> " (a) Whether the claimants alleged cause of action against the defendant arises out of a contract of carriage made by or on behalf of the defendant as a carrier, within the terms of Article 1 of the Convention...

> " 2. Whether, if so, the carriage which was the subject of the aforesaid contract was 'international carriage' within the meaning of that term as used in the Convention."

The answer to both those questions in the light of the admissions is yes.

6. The Athens Convention goes back to 1974 and has been part of English law from shortly after that date. Its current status is that it is applied under s.183 of the Merchant Shipping Act 1995 which provides, s.183(1):

> " *The provisions of the Convention relating to the Carriage of Passengers and their Luggage by Sea as set out in Part 1 of Schedule 6 (hereinafter in this section and in Part II of that Schedule referred to as 'The Convention') shall have the force of law in the United Kingdom.*"

The 1995 Shipping Act was a consolidating act.

7. The Convention itself contains a number of Articles of relevance to this preliminary issue. It includes Article 7, which limits liability for personal injury to an amount not exceeding 46,666 units of account per carriage. Article 8 which limits liability for loss of or damage to luggage to figures which include 833 units of account per passenger per carriage, and Article 10, which enables carrier and passenger to agree in writing and expressly to higher limits of liability than those I have referred to in Art.7 and 8.

8. For this preliminary issue, the most significant provisions of the Convention are Article 14, Basis for Claims:

> " *No action for damages for the death of or personal injury to a passenger, or for the loss of or damage to luggage shall be brought against a carrier or performing carrier otherwise than in accordance with this Convention.*"

and Article 16:

> " *Time-bar for actions.*

> " *1. Any action for damages arising out of the death of or personal injury to a passenger or for the loss of or damage to luggage shall be time-barred after a period of two years (my emphasis).*

> " *2. The limitation period shall be calculated as follows:*

> *(a) in the case of personal injury, from the date of disembarkation of the passenger;*"

9.   It is common ground between the parties that if the Athens Convention applies, then Mrs. Norfolk's claim is caught by the two year time bar in Article 16, having regard to the date when the claim form was issued.

10.   ... the defendant, says that the Athens Convention does apply. ... this is a claim for damages for personal injury to a passenger, however it is dressed up or labelled. She relies by parity of reasoning upon the House of Lords decision of *Sidhu v. British Airways* [1997] 2 W.L.R. p.26 which was concerned with the interaction of the Warsaw Convention and common law claims made by passengers in an aircraft. A similar situation arose in that case regarding the time bar limitations of the Warsaw Convention. Lord Hope in his speech concluded at p.46, paragraph E:

> " *I believe that the answer to the question raised in the present case is to be found in the objects and structure of the Convention. The language used and the subject matter with which it deals demonstrate that what was sought to be achieved was a uniform international code which could be applied by the courts of all the high contracting parties without reference to the rules of their own domestic law. The Convention does not purport to deal with all matters relating to contracts of international carriage by air, but in those area with which it deals and the liability of the carrier is one of them. The code is intended to be uniform and to be exclusive also of any resort to the rules of domestic law.*
>
> " *An answer to the question which leaves the claimant without a remedy is not at first sight attractive. It is tempting to give way to the argument that where here is a wrong there must be remedy. That indeed is the foundation upon which much of our own common law has been built up.* "

And he continued on p.47 at letter A:

> " *It was not designed to provide remedies against the carrier to enable all losses to be compensated. It was designed instead to define those situations in which compensation was to be available. So it set out the limits of liability and the conditions under which claims to establish that liability, if disputed, were to be made. A balance was struck in the interests of certainty and uniformity.* "

He continued further at letter C:

> " *The conclusion must be therefore that any remedy is excluded by the Convention as the set of uniform rules does not provide for it. The domestic courts are not free to provide a remedy according to their own law because to do this would be to undermine the convention. It would lead to the setting alongside the Convention of an entirely different set of rules which would distort the operation of the whole scheme.* "

11. ... the claimant, says that nothing could be clearer. One need only look at the regulations under which this claim is brought. ... this is a separate scheme devised for the regulation of package holidays enabling actions to be brought against retailers and organisers of package tours. ... times have moved on since sailing tickets were bought directly from the Cunard Line, to the world of the mass travel package for which the Regulations were designed. They are designed not only to be effective in this country, but also the whole of the European Union has to respond to the Directive. [The claimant] invites the court to say that the intention of the European Directive, and of the Regulations made thereunder, is to require transparency. That is to say, to insist that the exclusion provisions contained in international convention such as the Athens Convention should continue to apply but only if they are brought expressly to the notice of the consumer, whose protection is envisaged by the Regulations. He relies for that proposition upon regulation 15(3) of the Regulations which provides:

> " *In the case of damage arising from the non-performance or improper performance of the services involved in the package, the contract may*

provide for compensation to be limited in accordance with the international conventions which govern such services. "

... those words only make sense if they are construed to mean that the Athens Convention is only to apply if there has been an express reference to it in the contract.

Again, it is common ground between the parties that there is no such reference in the relevant contract.

12. [The Defendant's reply] is a blunt one. ... such a construction would, if adopted, drive a coach and horses through the Athens Convention, and she argues that if that interpretation is to be applied one would have expected clear words in the Regulation.

13. I agree with [the Defendant]. If the effect of s.183 of the Merchant Shipping Act 1995, and indeed the earlier statute which was codified therein, was to have been qualified, indeed effectively partially repealed so as to make the Convention applicable only in circumstances where there had been an express reference in the contract involving a carrier, rather than the Convention applying as a matter of law, then in my judgment the draughtsman would and should have said so in clear terms.

14. I go further and consider the words of regulation 15(3) and in particular the words: *" may provide for compensation to be limited in accordance with the international conventions"*. It does seem to me that that limitation can be interpreted as being a reference to the damage-capping provisions of Articles 7 and 8 rather than to the time-bar provision in Art.16. Accordingly, I hold that there is no conflict between the Merchant Shipping Act and the regulations on the issue of the time-bar. The Regulations do not contain any provisions relating to a specific time-bar and the Athens Convention applies without the need for any express reference.

15. There is a subsidiary point advanced ... to this effect, that this is not a claim for damages for personal injury but a statutory claim for damages for improper performance of the contract. In my judgment to accept such a submission would be to undermine the international scheme of the Athens Convention in the manner envisaged by Lord Hope and eschewed by him. The fact that the regulations ... flow from a directive, which emanated from the Council of Europe, in my judgment does not affect the standing of the international Convention. I gain support for that view from the further remarks of Lord Hope at p.37 of the report of the judgment in Sidhu. He was dealing with a submission that it would be inconsistent with the obligations of the United Kingdom under the European of Convention of Human Rights to accept the time-bar of Art.17 of the Warsaw Convention. He said at letter F:

> *" Your Lordships had no hesitation in rejecting that argument. The provisions of the European Convention have no bearing on the interpretation of international conventions such as the Warsaw Convention on carriage by air - and there are many other examples - which are concerned with commerce between countries and which seek, by a process of compromise, to achieve uniformity across international frontiers in the application of trade law.*

"*It must also be observed that, while some parties to the Warsaw Convention are parties to the European Convention of Human Rights, some, notably the United States of America - are not.*"

I would observe that there is a similar disparity between the signatories to the Athens Convention and the members of the Member States of the European Union. True it is that the aim of the international Convention is harmonisation as is the expressed aim of the council Directive. But be that as it may the reality remains that one group's harmony may be another group's distortion. The Court of Appeal in the decision of *Howe v. David Brown Tractors* [1991] 4 A.E.R. 30 (at p.36) asked the question: " What is the firm's action all about?" The answer to a similar question in this case is that this is a claim for damages for personal injury which, in my judgment, is caught by Arts.14 and 16 of the Convention.

Accordingly, for those reasons the answer to the remaining preliminary issue is, yes, this case is time barred.

Lee and Lee v *Airtours Holidays Ltd and Airtours Plc*, 26 April 2002, Central London County Court (HHJ Hallgarten QC)

JUDGMENT

1. This is in the nature of test case arising out of the fire and consequent sinking of the cruise liner 'Sun Vista' on 20.5.99. The Claimants were two of many holidaymakers on board at the time and they seek damages against the Defendants for personal injury (including psychiatric damage), loss of possessions (including valuables) and loss of their holiday (including disappointment consequent upon that loss).

2. The claim is brought under Reg. 15 of the Travel, Holiday and Package Tours Regulations 1992 (hereafter "the Regulations") ...

    There is no need to explore the distinction between the Defendants, and matters have proceeded on the basis that the Second Defendants (hereafter, save where the context otherwise requires, "the Defendants"), were indeed "the other party to the contract". The Defendants admit liability to the Claimants as consumers, i.e. t5hey admit that there was a failure to perform the contract made with the Claimants in April 1999 which included some five nights on board the 'Sun Vista' within a holiday intended to last for some three weeks or that there was improper performance of such contract.

3. What the Defendants say is that liability in relation to personal injury and loss of personal possessions is limited under Arts. 7 and 8 of the Athens Convention, incorporated into English law by s.183 of the Merchant Shipping Act 1995; and that, insofar as personal possessions comprised valuables, liability is excluded by reference to Art. 5 thereof.

4. Turning to consider the facts in somewhat greater detail, the only evidence was from the Claimants' side and that evidence was not challenged in respect of any of the issues which I was asked to decide. According to the Defendants' own documents, the First Defendants, carrying on business as Tradewinds, acted as agents for the Second Defendants, and the Second Claimant's evidence was that she came across the possibility of a holiday/cruise departing London 11.5.99 on the 'Sun Vista' through a teletext advert under the name of Tradewinds, giving the telephone number in Swansea of Travelfest Ltd., a concern which it is admitted were travel agents acting for the Second Defendants. In consequence, the Second Claimant spoke to someone at Travelfest Ltd, who confirmed that the holiday/cruise was still available, comprising carriage by air from London, Heathrow to Singapore, a five-night stay in Singapore, a five-night cruise on the 'Sun Vista', starting and ending at Singapore, a flight from Singapore to Penang, accommodation in Penang for some eight days, carriage by air from Penang to Kuala Lumpur, two days stay in Kuala Lumpur and finally a return flight from Kuala Lumpur to London, Heathrow. The Second Claimant stated then and there that she wished to book the holiday and did

so, using a Mastercard. There was no mention of any terms or conditions, but the Second Claimant was asked whether the Claimants wished to take out insurance, which the Second Claimant declined, stating that they had their own insurance.

5.   Shortly thereafter, by a letter dated 8.4.99, Travelfest Ltd provided booking details in relation to what was described as a 'Far East cruise and stay', stating also that 'a full confirmation invoice showing your flight times and itinerary will follow shortly'. The Claimants were asked to complete and return a "passenger declaration form", which was said to be required by 'Sun Vista', to ease embarkation on to the ship at Singapore. If such form was completed by the Claimants, it was not included in the evidence before me. As I understand it, Tradewinds only came on to the scene in respect of what was described as an 'Itinerary' dated 11.5.99, which document compendiously treated the 'Sun Vista' as a hotel, and generally gave a step-by-step account of each stage of the intended holiday. The document concluded with the statement:- "Vouchers – Please ensure all hotel vouchers are presented on arrival". On the same day, Tradewinds sent to Travelfest Ltd a document headed 'Confirmation of Invoice' which contained like details in respect to the Claimants' itinerary. The reverse of that document set out the Second Defendant's so-called 'Fair Trading Agreement' and the body of the document referred to a Brochure, but it was common ground that no copy of such Agreement or Brochure was at any time brought to the Claimants' attention.

6.   The Claimants left for Singapore on 11.5.99 and after a stay of some five days at the Concorde Hotel, boarded the 'Sun Vista' on 16.5.99. I deduce that they would at that point have surrendered the Tradewinds voucher, which gave rudimentary details of the booking and of their requirements. Although not referred to in the Claimants' witness statements, I deduce also that on boarding the vessel, the Claimants would have been provided with a brochure headed 'All you need to know before you cruise', issued by 'Sun Vista/Sun Cruises', giving an address in Singapore. Among other matters, it was stated as follows:-

> **"VALUABLES**
> Should fragile items, valuables and medications be carried on board, such items should be deposited in the safe available free of charge in every cabin...."

The Second Claimant's evidence was that at an early point she asked a member of the ship's staff whether valuables which the Claimants had with them, might be put into the ship's safe, which is what the Claimants had done on previous cruises, but she was told that they could not use such safe, it being represented that the one installed in their cabin was more than adequate. In consequence, the Claimants say that they did indeed use the cabin safe, their case being that, placed within it was silver wedding anniversary jewellery, cash, a Parker fountain pen and a Longines watch.

7.	The fire broke out on 20.5.99 and in due course the Captain gave the order to abandon ship, with passengers and crew taking to lifeboats. For present purposes it is not necessary to go into the circumstances of the vessel being abandoned or of conditions endured in the lifeboats, but suffice it to say that in due course the Claimants were rescued. At some point, the 'Sun Vista' sank, taking with her all the Claimants' belongings, save for the clothing which they were wearing and a video camera.

8.	Such being the background, I now turn to the issues in the case which broadly can be summarised as follows:

	(1)	Do the limitation of liability provisions of the Athens Convention apply to claims under the Regulations?

	(2)	If so, do they only apply to the extent that the Defendants can establish that they were 'carriers'?

	(3)	Even if prima facie the Convention applies, on the facts does Art 5 exclude any claim arising from loss of valuables?

9.	The case was presented by counsel dealing first with issue (2). For my part I prefer the above order as being more logical, but in any event it is clear that issues arising under heads (1) and (2) to some extent overlap.

(1)	**DO THE LIMITATION OF LIABILITY PROVGISIONS IN THE ATHENS CONVENTION APPLY TO CLAIMS UNDER THE REGULATIONS**

10.	The provisions contained in the Athens Convention were first adopted by the United Kingdom in consequence of s.14(1) of the Merchant Shipping Act, 1979, it being stated that they should 'have the force of law in the United Kingdom'. This was repeated in s.183(1) of the Merchant Shipping Act, 1995 which I was told was a consolidating Act (at any rate in the area with which I was concerned), and thus did not represent new law. Turning to the Convention, Art. 1 contains a number of definitions to which I may have to return and its application is by Art. 2 directed to 'International Carriage'. It is common ground that the present case indeed concerned international carriage. The liability provisions of the Convention read as follows:

"Article 3
Liability of the carrier
*1.	The carrier shall be liable for the damage suffered as a result of the death of or personal injury to a passenger and the loss of or damage to luggage if the incident which caused the damage so suffered occurred in the course of the carriage and was due to the fault or neglect of the carrier or of his servants or agents acting within the scope of their employment.*

2.   The burden of proving that the incident which caused the loss or damage occurred in the course of the carriage, and the extent of the loss or damage, shall lie with the claimant.

3.   Fault or neglect of the carrier or of his servants or agents acting within the scope of their employment shall be presumed, unless the contrary is proved, if the death of or personal injury to the passenger or the loss of or damage to cabin luggage arose from or in connexion with the shipwreck, collision, stranding, explosion or fire, or defect in the ship. In respect of loss of or damage to other luggage, such fault or neglect shall be presumed, unless the contrary is proved, irrespective of the nature of the incident which caused the loss or damage. In all other cases the burden of proving fault or neglect shall lie with the claimant.

Article 14

Basis for claims

No action for damages for the death of or personal injury to a passenger, or for the loss or damage to luggage, shall be brought against a carrier or performing carrier otherwise than in accordance with this Convention".

11.   As to limits of liability, these are contained in provisions reading as follows:

"Article 7

Limit of liability for personal injury

1.   The liability of the carrier for the death of or personal injury to a passenger shall in no case exceed 700,000 francs per carriage. Where in accordance with the law of the court seized of the case damages are awarded in the form of periodical income payments, the equivalent capital value of those payments shall not exceed the said limit.

....

Article 8

Limit of liability for loss of or damage to luggage

1.   The liability of the carrier for the loss of or damage to cabin luggage shall in no case exceed 12,500 francs per passenger, per carriage.

2.   The liability of the carrier for the loss of or damage to vehicles including all luggage carried in or on the vehicle shall in no case exceed 50,000 francs per vehicle, per carriage.

3.   The liability of the carrier for the loss of or damage to luggage other than that mentioned in paragraphs 1 and 2 of this Article shall in no case exceed 18,000 francs per passenger, per carriage.

4.   The carrier and the passenger may agree that the liability of the carrier shall be subject to a deductible not exceeding 1,750 francs in the case of damage to a vehicle and not exceeding 200 francs per passenger in the case of loss of or damage to other luggage3, such sum to be deducted from the loss or damage.

Article 10

Supplementary provisions on limits of Liability

1.   The carrier and the passenger may agree, expressly and in writing, to higher limits of liability than those prescribed in Articles 7 & 8.

Article 13

Loss of right to limit liability

1.   The carrier shall not be entitled to the benefit of the limits of liability prescribed in Articles 7 and 8 and paragraph 1 of Article 10, if it is proved that the damage resulted from an act or omission of the carrier done with the intent to cause such damage, or recklessly and with knowledge that such damage would probably result."

The Convention also contains provisions, inter alia, for passengers to give written notice in relation to damaged luggage (lArt. 15) and for a two-year time-bar (Art. 16).

12.   Turning now to look at the Regulations in somewhat greater detail, the preamble makes it plain that they were introduced pursuant to s.2(2) of the European Communities Act 1972 "in relation to measures relating to consumer protection as regards package travel, package holidays and package tours", prompted by Council Directive 90/314 EEC, referred to in Reg. 2 as 'the Directive'. Reg. 2(1) also indicates that lines are to be drawn between on the one hand the consumer and on the other hand the operator, i.e. the organiser or retailer – the organiser being the person who organises packages and sells or offers them for sale whether directly or through a retailer; and the retailer being the person who sells or offers for sale the package put together by the organiser. Reg. 2(1) also defines 'package' as follows:-

> *"Package means the pre-arranged combination of at least two of the following components when sold or offered for sale at an inclusive price and when the service covers a period of more than twenty-four hours or includes overnight accommodation:-*
>
> *(a)   transport;*
> *(b)   accommodation;*
> *(c)   other tourist services not ancillary to transport or accommodation and accounting for a significant proportion of the package...."*

13.   Taking an overview of the Regulations, Regs. 4 and 5 provide protection to consumers in relation to descriptive matter and the contents of brochures; and Reg. 6 sets out circumstances in which particulars in a brochure are to be binding on the operator. Regs. 7 and 8 impose on the operator the obligation in a timely way to provide certain appropriate information. Reg. 9 sets out certain minimum requirements as to the contents and form of the relevant contract, including the provision that 'all the terms of the contract are set out in writing or such other form as is comprehensible and accessible to the consumer'. Regs. 10-14 then provide the consumer with protection in relation to the transfer of bookings, price revision, significant alteration of essential terms and significant proportion of services not being provided. It is against this background that one comes to Reg. 15. I have already set out the material terms of Reg. 15(1) and (2) above. The limitation provisions are as follows:-

> *"(3)   In the case of damage arising from the non-performance or improper performance of the services involved in the package, the contract may provide for compensation to be limited in accordance with the international conventions which govern such services.*
>
> *(4)   In the case of damage other than personal injury resulting from the non-performance or improper performance of the services involved in the package, the contract may include a term limiting the amount of compensation which will be paid to the consumer, provided that the limitation is not unreasonable.*

14.   It is, of course, Reg. 15(3) which is relied upon by the Defendants. As I read that paragraph, it has the following characteristics:

(1)   It is permissive;

(2)   It cannot be imposed by the operator – it can only arise if it can be identified as an express term of the contract between the consumer and the operator;

(3)   It does not provide for the wholesale incorporation/adoption of relevant international conventions – it only allows for their application to the extent that they 'provide for compensation to be limited'.

15.   Reg. 15(3) also contains an ambiguity: it is made clear whether the reference to '*conventions which govern such services'* is only effective to the extent that the operator would be able to show that, but for the Regulations, he would *personally* be entitled to rely upon the limitation provisions of whichever convention was invoked.

16.   Putting the above ambiguity to one side, the Claimants' case is very simple: no contract was ever issued, let alone a contract which purported to refer to compensation being limited in accordance with any international convention, and thus the Defendants cannot rely on Arts. 7 or 8 of the Athens Convention.

17.   How did the Defendants seek to meet this apparently conclusive argument? [There were] two submissions:

(a)   that the Convention has the force of law and thus unless applies, save to the extent that it is expressly ousted by the Regulations;

(b)   that in any event, the Regulations should be read purposefully, in particular having regard to the terms of the Directive which prompted them.

I shall deal with these submissions in turn.

(a)   Convention having the force of law

18.   ... my attention [was drawn] to *The Lion* [1990] 2 Lloyd's Rep. 144 and in particular the passage in the judgment of Hobhouse J @ 153 reading as follows:

> "*All this Convention does is to provide a regime and lay down a code which is to apply to govern the rights and liabilities of carriers and passengers. It is that type of scheme. It is not one which is contractually dependent. So it is not a scheme which depends upon the incorporation of particular provisions into a contract. **It is a scheme which imposes its provisions as a matter of law upon the parties**". [Emphasis added]*

19.   ... also ... in respect of contracts of carriage to which the Convention applies, Art. 14, expressly provides that there will be no cause of action for death or personal injury to a passenger or for loss of or damage to luggage otherwise than pursuant to the Convention: the regime expressly excludes other bases of liability.

20. In my view [this] submission was misconceived, because it is quite plain in the present case that the Regulations represent an *alternative* regime which, in so far as it conflicts with UK domestic law, must pursuant to the European Communities Act, prevail. That the regimes are indeed different is well illustrated by the facts of the present case. Had liability been contested, it would have been for the Claimants to prove in the ordinary way that the fire was a consequence of 'improper performance' of the contract in accordance with Reg. 15(2). By contrast, under Art. 3(1) of the Convention, the relevant test is 'fault or neglect', and, even more to the point, by Art. 3(3) there is the presumption that, among other events, fire is caused by the carrier's fault or neglect, whereby the burden of proof is reversed. In my view, it makes no sense that there should be two essentially conflicting liability regimes. As I have already said, in so far as a conflict might arise, the Regulations must prevail. But what of the areas where one can see no necessary conflict? Could an operator, sued under Reg. 15, claim the protection of Arts. 5, 7 or 8 of the Convention? In my view the answer is that he could not: I consider that once the *liability* provisions of the Convention are over ridden by the Regulations, it is impossible to see upon what the limitation or indeed other ancillary provisions of the Convention could fasten and in my view, prima facie, they can have no application. As I see it, therefore, Reg. 15(3) was inserted for the purpose of giving to the operator the opportunity to incorporate one particular aspect of the Convention – that in relation to limitation of liability – which, absent Reg. 15(3), would be wholly inapplicable.

(b)   The effect of the Directive

21. In my view, [the] argument based upon the Directive really carries [the Defendant] no further. The basis of [the] submission was a paragraph in the preamble to the Directive reading as follows:

> *"Whereas in cases where the organizer and/or retailer is liable for failure to perform or improper performance of the services involved in the package, such liability should be limited in accordance with the international conventions governing such services, in particular the Warsaw Convention 1929 in International Carriage by Air, the Berne Convention of 1961 on Carriage by Rail, the Athens Convention of 1974 on Carriage by Sea and the Paris Convention of 1962 on the Liability of Hotel-keepers; whereas, moreover, with regard to damage other than personal injury, it should be possible for liability also to be limited under the package contract provided, however, that such limits are not unreasonable."*

22. The expression 'should be limited' of course has a mandatory air, but this is not carried through to the substantive part of the Directive, contained in Art. 5. Art 5.1/2 imposed on a Member State the duty to 'take necessary steps' to ensure that the operator was liable to the consumer for failure to perform or for improper performance, subject only to exclusions which were

in due course reflected in Reg. 15(2).   Art. 5.2 of the Directive then significantly continued as follows:

> *"In the matter of damages arising from the non-performing or improper performance of the services involved in the package, the Member States may allow compensation to be limited in accordance with the international conventions governing such services.*
>
> *In the matter of damage other than personal injury resulting from the non-performance or improper performance of the services involved in the package, the Member State may allow compensation to be limited under the contract.   Such limitation shall not be unreasonable."*

23.   The expression 'may allow' was not in my view intended merely to be declaratory of what might or might not be the position under the existing law of a particular Member State; I consider that it was intended to confer a power on each Member State, either to allow compensation to be limited in accordance with the Convention or not to do so.   So far as the United Kingdom was concerned, this power was exercised in the way set out in Reg. 15(3):   compensation was to be limited in accordance with International Convention if and in so far as the contract provided for that eventuality.   In the present case there was, of course, no written contract and no relevant contractual provision.

24.   Before moving on to the next issue, I would just mention the decision of the Court of Appeal in *Hone v Going Places Leisure Travel Ltd* [2001] EWCA Civ 947, which involved claims arising out of a package holiday in respect of which it was said that the relevant service – air carriage – was improperly performed.   As I read the judgment of the Court of Appeal, the Regulations were regarded as representing an autonomous regime, Longmore L.J. stating as follows:

> *"17. There is a clear contrast with the terms of the Warsaw Convention. In that Convention, Article 17 imposes a liability for death or personal injury without any requirement of improper performance. Article 18 does the same for loss or damage to baggage and cargo, and Article 19 the same for delay to passengers, baggage and cargo. There are then specific provisions for exclusion or diminution of liability and for limitation. The 1992 Regulations could have adopted a similar scheme but; by the use of the term "improper performance", it is patent that they have not done so. The fact that it is open to the travel agent (or other party to the contract) to incorporate the limitation provisions of any applicable international convention, if they wish to do so, cannot make any difference to this conclusion."*

25.   So far as I can see, no argument was addressed that the limitation of liability provisions in the Warsaw Convention applied, but in my view it is reasonably plain from the above passage that the Court of Appeal would have been of the same view as I am, namely that no part of the Warsaw Convention can have any impact upon a claim under the Regulations, save to the extent that the limitation provisions are expressly incorporated by contract.

(2)   WERE THE DEFENDANTS CARRIERS WITHIN THE MEANING OF THE ATHENS CONVENTION

26.   In light of my conclusion above, this no longer arises. If relevant, however, I consider that the question should be approached without any regard for the Regulations, and I begin by setting out certain of the definitions contained under Art. 1 of the Convention, reading as follows:

"Definitions

1.   (a)   "carrier" means a person by or on behalf of whom, a contract of carriage has been concluded, whether the carriage is actually performed by him or by a performing carrier;

(b)   "performing carrier" means a person other than the carrier, being the owner, charterer or operator of a ship, who actually performs the whole or part of the carriage;

2.   "contract of carriage" means a contract made by or on behalf of a carrier for the carriage by sea of a passenger or of a passenger and his luggage, as the case may be;

8.   "carriage" covers the following periods:

(a)   with regard to the passenger and his cabin luggage, the period during which the passenger and/or his cabin luggage are on board the ship or in the course of embarkation or disembarkation, and the period during which the passenger and his cabin luggage are transported by water from land to ship or vice versa, if the cost of such transport is included in the fare or if the vessel used for this purpose of auxiliary transport has been put at the disposal of the passenger by the carrier...."

I would also refer to Art. 4.1, reading as follows:

"Performing carrier

If the performance of the carriage or part thereof has been entrusted to a performing carrier, the carrier shall nevertheless

> *remain liable for the entire carriage according to the provisions of this Convention...."*

27.   ... can it be said that the Defendants' position was that of 'carrier'? [It was submitted that]:

> "The intention of the Athens Convention is to treat as the 'carrier' the person (usually a shipping line) who makes a **promise** by way of a 'contract of carriage' **to carry the passenger,** regardless of whether the carrier intends to perform the carriage or delegate the performance of its promise in respect of part or all of the carriage to the 'performing carrier' (usually another shipping line)."

28.   [The] submission [was] that the highest that the case could be put is that the Defendants promised 'absolutely to secure that' the Claimants were carried, and that on such analysis it was impossible to characterise the Defendants as carriers.

    ...

32.   In my view, none of the authorities really assist in determining the question before me, for the simple reason that I do not consider that the Convention is concerned with *status* at all: there is nothing which confines its application to concerns in the nature of shipping lines., Basically what emerge from the Convention are two categories:

(1)   the carrier – being the person by or on whose behalf a contract of carriage has been concluded; and

(2)   the performing carrier – being the person to whom such carriage is entrusted.

As I see it, the essential question is whether, as between the Claimants and the Defendants there was a contract of carriage by sea: if so then the Defendants assumed responsibilities as carriers, with the word carrier being used in a non-technical sense. On this issue the Convention affords no real guidance, although Art. 1.8 lends a little support to the Claimants' case in referring to consideration as "the fare" – language more consistent with the carriage aspect of a contract representing if not the sole then at any rate the dominant element. The matter is very largely one of impression, but for my part I see no difficulty in saying that the Defendants were carriers, in that the agreement with the Claimants included obligations pertaining to carriage by sea and to that extent, it represented a contract for the carriage by sea of the Claimants by the Defendants. Indeed, if Mr Reeve were right, it would, I believe, follow that even if the contract between the Claimants and the Defendants were exclusively for a cruise (with the vessel being provided by a different concern), Art. 1 of the Convention would not apply, and this is a conclusion from which I would recoil.

33.   I would mention that at the conclusion of … submissions, referring to *Hone v Going Places* above … the point [was made] that if an operator were to be treated as a carrier, he might be exposed to strict liability claims under the Warsaw Convention in respect to carriage by air. In my view, the answer to this may well lie in the wording of the Warsaw Convention itself, but for my part, I see nothing particularly startling in subjecting a tour operator to strict liability. Whether an operator might be regarded as a carrier would, however, substantially depend on a correct analysis of the Warsaw Convention which, so far as I can discern, contains no definition of "air carrier" and also has certain provisions – e.g. in relation to the issue of a ticket – which may involve a different approach being taken to the one which in my view is appropriate to a consideration of the provisions of the Athens Convention.

34.   In all the circumstances, had the Athens Convention been applicable, I would have concluded that the Defendants were indeed carriers thereunder.

35.   (3)   **EXCLUSION OF THE VALUABLES CLAIM?**

36.   Art. 5 of the Convention reads as follows:

> ***"Valuables***
> *"The carrier shall not be liable for the loss of or damage to monies, negotiable securities, gold, silverware, jewellery, ornaments, works of art, or other valuables, except where such valuables had been deposited with the carrier for the agreed purpose of safe-keeping, in which case the carrier shall be liable up to the limit provided for in paragraph 3 of Article 8 unless a higher limit is agreed upon in accordance with paragraph 1 of Article 10."*

37.   For the reasons set out under Head (1) above, in my view, Art. 5 of the Convention has in fact no application …

38.   But supposing that I am wrong, and the Convention is applicable, can the Defendants in fact rely on Art. 5?
      …
      It may well be that had the valuables been deposited with the carrier at some central point, rather than left in the cabin, such would have made no difference – the items would, in the circumstances that occurred, have been lost in any event. But I cannot see how that overcomes the impediment represented by the express language of Art. 5: unless initially there is a deposit for safe-keeping, liability is excluded.

39.   [There was] an alternative argument in respect of which I gave permission to amend, namely that the Claimants were vested with a separate cause of action based on the circumstance that one of the services which ought reasonably to have been provided was the facility whereby valuables might be deposited with the carrier for safe-keeping. On this basis, the Claimants' claim was not so much for the loss of the valuables as for being deprived of

the right to make a claim for such loss. In my view, the Claimants did make out this separate cause of action. Indeed, having regard to the very terms of the Convention itself, it is plainly incumbent upon a carrier to provide appropriate facilities for safe-keeping and on the evidence, either such were not available or the Claimants' tender of valuables was wrongfully rejected. In either event, in my view a breach was established and the measure of damages is the amount which the Claimants would otherwise have recovered, on the assumption that the Convention applied, up to the limit as set out under Art. 8.3.

CONCLUSION

40.   For the reasons set out ... above, my conclusion is that liability in respect of the claims is not limited or excluded by reference to the Athens Convention.

Higham v *Stena Sealink Ltd*, 16 February 1996, CA (Civ)
(Hirst and Pill LLJ)

JUDGMENT

LORD JUSTICE HIRST:

Introduction

This case raises an important point in international maritime law in relation to the time limits for actions for damages arising out of the death of or personal injuries to a passenger, or for the loss of or damage to luggage. On 16th August 1991 the plaintiff, while a passenger on the defendant's ferry the M.V. Stena Cambria sailing between Holyhead and Dunlaoghrie in the Republic of Ireland, suffered injury when she slipped on some broken glass on the deck and fell. She disembarked later the same day. Over two years later, on 2nd September 1993, she issued proceedings in the Liverpool County Court claiming damages for negligence and/or breach of statutory duty on the part of the defendants.

The Convention Relating to the Carriage of Passengers and their Luggage By Sea (the Athens Convention 1974) has the force of law in the United Kingdom pursuant to section 14 and Schedule 3 of the Merchant Shipping Act 1979 (the MSA), which was the statute in force at the material time, now replaced by section 183 and Schedule 6 of the Merchant Shipping Act 1995. Article 16 of the Convention lays down the following provisions as to time-bars:-

> "(1) Any action for damages arising out of the death of or personal injury to a passenger or for the loss of or damage to luggage shall be time-barred after a period of two years.
> (2) The limitation periods should be calculated as follows:-
> (a) in the case of personal injury, from the date of disembarkation of the passenger;
> (b) In the case of death occurring during carriage, from the date when the passenger should have disembarked, and in the case of personal injury occurring during carriage and resulting in the death of the passenger after disembarkation, from the date of death, provided that this period shall not exceed 3 years from the date of disembarkation;
> (c) In the case of loss or damage to luggage, from the date of disembarkation or from the date when disembarkation should have taken place, whichever is the later.
> (3) The law of the Court seized of the case shall govern the grounds of suspension and interruption of limitation periods, but in no case shall an action under this convention be brought after the expiration of a period of 3 years from the date of disembarkation of the passenger or from the date when disembarkation should have taken place whichever is the later.
> (4) Notwithstanding paragraphs (1) (2) and (3) of this article, the period of limitation may be extended by a declaration of the carrier or by agreement

of the parties after the cause of action has arisen. This declaration or agreement shall be in writing".

On 18th January 1994 the defendants applied to the court for an order striking out the plaintiff's claim on the basis that the proceedings were issued outside the time limit laid down in Article 16 above.

This application came before Deputy District Judge Wright on 14th April 1984, who dismissed it on the footing that, on the proper construction of Article 16, section 33 of the Limitation Act 1980 applied to this action for personal injury, and she then proceeded in the exercise of her discretion to disapply the time-bar.

The defendant appealed to Her Honour Judge Bernstein, who on 17th June 1994 allowed the appeal and struck out the action; it is against this decision that the plaintiff presently appeals. The basis of the judge's decision, in a nutshell, was that the words suspension and interruption as contained in Article 16(3) were inapplicable to section 33, so that the 2 year time-bar was effective.

The Limitation Act 1980. (The 1980 Act).

Part I, headed " Ordinary Time Limits for Different Classes of Action" provides in Section 1, under the heading " Time limits under Part I subject to extension or exclusion under Part II" as follows:-

> *"(1) This Part of this Act gives the ordinary time limits for bringing actions of the various classes mentioned in the following provisions of this Part.*
> *(2) The ordinary time limits given in this Part of this Act are subject to extension or exclusion in accordance with the provisions of Part II of this Act."*

Sections 11, 11A, and 12 in Part I lay down time limits for actions in respect of personal injuries, product liability, and fatal accidents respectively. Part II is headed "Extension or Exclusion of Ordinary Time Limits".

Sections 28 and 28A deal with extension in cases of disability.

Sections 29 to 31 inclusive deal with extension in cases of acknowledgement or part payment. Section 32 deals with postponement in the case of fraud, concealment or mistake.

Section 33, which is headed " Discretionary exclusion of time limit for actions in respect of personal injuries or death" provides so far as relevant as follows:-

> *"(1) If it appears to the court that it would be equitable to allow an action to proceed having regard to the degree to which*
> *(a) the provisons of Section 11 or 11A or 12 of this Act prejudice the plaintiff or any person whom he represents; and*
> *(b) any decision of the court under this sub-section would prejudice the defendant or any person whom he represents; the court may direct that*

those provisions shall not apply to the action, or shall not apply to any specified cause of action to which the action relates."

Section 39, under the heading "Saving for other limitation enactments" provides:-

"This Act shall not apply to any action or arbitration for which a period of limitation is prescribed by or under any other enactment (whether passed before or after the passing of this Act) or to any action or arbitration to which the Crown is a party and for which, if it were between subjects, a period of limitation would be prescribed by or under any such other enactment".

The Athens Convention. (" The Convention")

The Convention governs actions by passengers against vessels on which they are being carried at the time of the incident giving rise to the claim. The countries which are presently parties to the Convention, numbering about 30, have a wide variety of limitation laws.

Recently the Comite Maritime International commissioned Professor Francesco Berlingieri, the leading maritime lawyer who was formerly Professor of Maritime Law at the University of Genoa, and who is Honorary President of the CMI, to compile a book on comparative international maritime time-bars, including that in the Convention. He submitted a questionnaire to all relevant countries, and the result is contained in Time Bar Actions published in 1993 by Lloyds of London.

This illustrates in great detail the very wide variety of different codes of limitation throughout the world; in the particular case of provisions which might potentially fall within the scope of Article 16(3), Professor Berlingieri's research shows that some countries (e.g. Belgium) make no such provision, and that, of those who do, the regimes differ widely from country to country. It is common ground between the parties in the present case that, on the proper construction of Article 16(3), the *lex fori* of the court seized of the case govern the grounds (if any) of suspension or interruption of limitation periods, subject of course to the 3 year long-stop.

The Issues.

The questions at issue are as follows:-

(1) Does section 39 exclude altogether the application of the 1980 Act to the Convention?
(2) If the answer to (1) is in the negative:-
      (a) Does section 33 fall within the scope of Article 16(3) as being a stipulation which governs the grounds of suspension and interruption of limitation periods? and
      (b) If so, does section 33 on its proper construction apply to the Convention?

To succeed on this appeal, the appellant must not only successfully rebut the respondent's argument on section 39, but also obtain affirmative answers to both questions 2(a) and 2(b).

Section 39.

[The appellant's] submission is a very simple one, namely that, since the Convention, as enshrined in the MSA, prescribes a period of limitation, the 1980 Act as a whole, and in particular Part II in its entirety, does not apply.

In my judgment, section 39 on its proper construction cannot be interpreted as excluding from the ambit of the 1980 Act this stipulation in the MSA which by its very terms incorporates the 1980 Act to the extent provided in Article 16(3).
I would theefore reject [the] submissions on Section 39...

It follows that the whole of Part II of the 1980 Act is potentially applicable to the MSA, but we are presently concerned only with section 33, and there is no need in this judgment to determine either way whether or not any of the other sections in Part II would qualify under Article 16(3); I would only say that although sections 28 to 32, (and in particular section 32 which provides for the postponement of the limitation period in the case of fraud, concealment or mistake) might well appear at first sight to be eligible candidates, the fact that in each case the section refers to periods of limitation " prescribed by this Act" , or words to that effect may disqualify them; but it would be not appropriate to decide that point until it arises specifically in relation to one of these other sections.

Section 33.

Section 33 ... empowers the court to exclude altogether a period which has already run its course, and so cannot in my judgment possibly be treated as a ground of suspension or interruption eligible under Article 16(3).

However, even if it were so eligible, I would be unable to construe section 33(1), which expressly refers to "the provisions of section 11 or 11A or 12 of the Act" as embracing the Convention.

Unauthenticated Decisions

Gow v *TUI UK Ltd (t/a Crystal Holidays)*, 27 April 2006, Watford County Court (Deputy District Judge Perusko)

C booked a package holiday with D through a travel agent, B, over the telephone, paying to B the holiday price before completion of the call. As per D's standard terms and conditions, C was allocated a room in the annexe of the hotel as B did not charge a supplement. C was unaware the hotel had an annexe and B did not inform at the time of the call that the booking was subject to D's standard terms and conditions. B's invoice received by C prior to travel stated that it was so subject. C sued D for breach of contract.

Held, dismissing the claim: (i) whilst B were at all material times agents for D, the contract was not formed during the telephone call, notwithstanding that B had accepted C's offer without stating that acceptance was subject to D's standard terms and conditions – standard practice in the industry was for the contract between the tour operator and holiday-maker not to be concluded when the travel agent communicates the tour operator's provisional acceptance of the booking; (ii) accordingly, B's invoice was a contractual document; (iii) the reference made therein to D's standard terms and conditions was sufficient to incorporate them into the contract, as C had accepted that he knew where they could be found, namely in D's brochure or on its website.

Costelloe v Thomson Tour Operations Ltd Current Law Cases: 00/4046

C alleged that he had been injured as a result of the negligence of a ski lift operator while on a package skiing holiday in Italy. He had bought his ski lift pass from the same travel agent through which he had also bought the package holiday. The tour operator, T, maintained that the pass did not form any part of the package and that there was no commercial link between itself and the lift operator. T's brochure stated that there were 29 ski lifts at the resort and that passes could be bought there but did not state that such purchases would be organised by T. C brought unchallenged evidence that, having paid the travel agent for the pass, he was told to hand a photograph of himself to T's representative at the resort. After he did so, the representative procured the pass for him. The brochure stated that T accepted liability for personal injuries sustained while C was using the services it had arranged. C contended that (1) there was an implied term in the contract between himself and T that the ski lifts would be operated with due skill and care, and that failure to exercise the appropriate level of care would result in T's liability, and (2) by reason of having obtained the pass, T's representative had "arranged" the services of the ski lift operator within the meaning of the brochure.

Held, giving judgment for T, that (1) the pass was not part of the package and had not been sold by T, and (2) T had not arranged for the purchase of the pass, it had been "arranged" and supplied by the travel agent.

J v *First Choice Holidays and Flights Limited,* 27 November 2001, Blackpool County Court (DJ Bryce)

J, a 15 year boy and his friend, S, a sixteen year old boy, were taken on a package holiday to Tenerife by J's parents. J had, for several years, suffered from a form of bone cancer and had been fitted with a prosthetic femur and hip joint. At the start of the holiday J, S and J's parents enquired about suitable excursions for young adults. They spoke to the local representative of FC: the tour operator. The parents explained J's medical history and informed FC's representative of the boys' ages. The parents were aware that the consumption of alcohol was an invariable feature of the young adult excursion package. The boys signed up for 4 excursions. The first 3 excursions passed without incident; the boys left one excursion early by taxi because they ran out of money. The fourth excursion was a Caribbean night at a local nightspot. The guests made their own way to the excursion. They would also have to make their own way home. There was free alcohol. Soft drinks were available as an alternative, although the boys might not have been aware of this. J did not drink any significant quantity of alcohol. S did indulge in the free alcohol and felt ill. Therefore, the boys left the excursion early. They could not find FC's representative to tell her that they were leaving early. The boys caught a taxi back to the resort. Another taxi followed them and the driver of that taxi quarrelled with the driver of the taxi in which they were riding. When they arrived back at the resort the driver of the other taxi attacked the boys using his belt as a weapon. In the course of the assault J was knocked to the ground and dislocated his hip. He was taken to hospital by ambulance. The reason for the assault was a mystery; the evidence of J was that nothing had been done to provoke it. FC's representative made one visit to the family in hospital, save for this visit the family arranged their own (delayed) flights home and visited the local police on their own. J brought an action for breach of contract. He acted in person, with the assistance of his parents, at trial complaining that there had been a lack of supervision at the excursion. He complained that if S had not become drunk then the boys would not have left the excursion early and would not have travelled home by taxi. J also complained that FC had not provided assistance in resort after the assault.

Held, dismissing J's claim, that (1) it was ill advised for the parents to permit the boys to participate in an excursion in which alcohol was consumed, but FC was not in breach of its contractual duty to exercise reasonable care and skill in failing to ensure that the two boys stayed to the end of the excursion – a requirement of this kind was not reasonably practicable; (2) the boys would, if they had stayed to the end of the excursion, have been returning to the resort by their own means in any event; (3) FC accepted no liability for the actions of the unconnected third party taxi driver and no liability could be attached to FC in this context in law; (4) permitting S to drink did not cause the assault – his drunkenness played no part in the injury that was suffered by J; (5) the assault by the taxi driver was not reasonably foreseeable by FC; (6) FC could and should have done more to assist the family after the assault; (7) the family had, however, liaised with the police and their insurers and obtained all of the services that they required; (8) accordingly, any breach of contract by FC in failing to provide assistance after the assault did not sound in damages.

This was an excursion booked and paid for in resort and, therefore, was not part of the Package holiday within the meaning of regulation 2(1) of the Package Travel etc. Regulations 1992.

Derbyshire v *First Choice Holidays and Flights Limited,* 5 October 2004, Central London County Court (HHJ Karsten QC)

The Claimant, C, booked a package holiday to Canada with the Defendant tour operator, FC, for the period 29 March 2000 until 8 April 2000. The price paid for the package holiday included the following elements: accommodation; return flights from London Gatwick to Calgary; transfer from airport to Hotel; the services of a local representative. C could have pre-booked and paid in advance for his skiing equipment and lessons through FC. C neither pre-booked nor paid in advance for the hire of ski equipment or ski lessons (the combination of these two elements was referred to as a "*ski pack*"). C arrived at Calgary airport on 29 March 2000. He was met by the transfer coach and FC's local representative. On arrival at the Hotel C and his partner hired ski equipment and booked skiing lessons which were provided by Altitude Sports: an independent local business. C made a payment to FC's local representative for the hire of the ski equipment and the lessons and the representative issued a "*Ski Pack Ticket*" with Altitude Sports written at the top which C presented to Altitude Sports for the provision of the equipment and the lessons. The ticket also featured FC's logo. The evidence was that FC selected Altitude Sports to supply ski equipment to all of its guests. C attended the Altitude Sports shop on 29 March 2000. He was provided with ski boots and skis which he wore on 30 March 2000 for his first lesson and first day's skiing without incident. The accident happened on 31 March 2000 (the second day of skiing). C was attempting a snowplough turn to his right. As he pressed down on his left ski, his ski stopped suddenly while his body continued to rotate in a clockwise direction and he fell to the ground. His right ski detached from his foot, but his left ski was still attached. The reason for this was that the assistant in the Altitude Sports shop had (as the Judge found at trial) negligently supplied the wrong sized boot for C's left ski and bindings. C sustained a cruciate ligament injury to his left knee as he fell. C brought an action against FC for the negligence of the Altitude Sports employee. He relied on causes of action in contract pursuant to the Package Travel etc. Regulations 1992 and FC's booking conditions. He also argued, in the alternative, that he had a separate contract, parallel to the main package contract, for the fitting and hire of his ski equipment which he had entered into in Canada with FC through FC's local representative. Further and alternatively, C argued that FC had negligently selected an unsafe supplier of ski equipment for its guests.

Held, dismissing the claim, (1) the purchase of the ski pack was not regulated in accordance with the Package Travel etc. Regulations 1992 because it was neither pre-arranged nor inclusively priced and was sold separately outside the United Kingdom and, therefore, was not part of the "*package*" as defined in reg 2(1) to which the 1992 Regulations applied by virtue of reg 3(1); (2) on a true construction of the contract made for the fitting and provision of skiing equipment C's contract was with Altitude Sports and FC's local representative had simply acted as their agent (FC's local representative had disclosed the existence and identity of Altitude Sports and FC's promotional literature for ski packs made it clear that FC only "*recommended*" suppliers of ski packs, rather than supplying the same itself); (3) FC's status as agent was not affected by the fact that FC's local representative had taken the money for the ski pack; (4) there was no evidence that FC had been negligent in failing to select an appropriate local supplier for the fitting and hiring out of ski equipment and, therefore, no liability arose on this basis (the accident was the result of an isolated lapse).

Allison Rochead v Airtours Holidays Limited [2001] CLCC (*per* HHJ Crawford Lindsay QC), *Gallagher v Airtours Holidays Limited* [2001] CLY Preston CC (*per* HHJ Appleton) and, *Wong Mee Wan v Kwan Kin Travel* [1998] 1 WLR 38 (PC) considered.

> **Comment:** This case is important not because the Court declined to accept the argument that the ski pack formed part of the regulated package; there is already ample first instance authority on this point (*Rochead v Airtours Holidays Limited* [2001] CLCC (*per* HHJ Crawford Lindsay QC) and *Gallagher v Airtours Holidays Limited* [2001] CLY Preston CC (*per* HHJ Appleton) are the clearest examples). Instead, *Derbyshire* is significant because it is the first case in which the parallel contract issue has been fully ventilated (see, discussion in "*Excursions: Tour Operators and the negligence of local suppliers*" (2002) *International Travel Law* Journal). While each case in this difficult area will turn on its own facts, *Derbyshire* provides some comfort for tour operators. If a tour operator alerts consumers to the existence and identity of the third party supplier before contracting and if it is signalled to the consumer that the tour operator will not itself be supplying the service contracted for then it should be possible for the tour operator to escape liability on the parallel contract.

Thompson v Airtours Holidays Ltd (No.2) Current Law Cases: 02/Mar.

T and his wife sought to recover damages from a tour operator, A. T booked a one week holiday in Portugal which was selected from A's "Winter Sun" brochure. The brochure listed a number of facilities available at the hotel and classed the hotel as "four star". T made a request for a quiet room at the time of booking. Upon arrival, T was allocated a room which overlooked a very busy dual carriageway. Noise was constant throughout the day, increased at night and was exacerbated by the arrival of young guests who played loud music until late at night. A number of the advertised facilities were closed, namely the outdoor swimming pool, snack bar, gym, sauna, tennis and squash courts and the hotel bar did not open until 4.30 pm. T was a keen swimmer. T's room had no heating as advertised and was damp and cold. T's wife had to sleep with her clothes on. T complained at the hotel reception but was told that he could not move from the room allocated. A relied on a term in the brochure which stated that, outside peak season, it was common for facilities and services to be less widely available, both in the accommodation and the resort generally, and declined to accept liability in those circumstances. It also stated "We will try to meet any special requests that you tell us about before you leave but we cannot guarantee anything. If we cannot meet your special request, we will not pay any compensation."

Held, giving judgment for T, that although the exclusion clauses were very clear, A could not rely on them to avoid liability. The hotel was advertised as a holiday in the winter sun. The fact that a number of facilities were not available at all was very different to some being "less widely available". Further, it was misleading to take a booking and accept the request to allocate T a quiet room and then do nothing to fulfil the request. The court took account of the fact that some facilities were available and that T had access to the restaurant and bar. T and his wife were each awarded GBP 300 for the misleading nature of the brochure and GBP 300 and GBP 250 respectively for loss of enjoyment.

Currie v Magic Travel Group (Holidays) Ltd Current Law Cases: 01/4278

C, a couple, booked a two week holiday in Spain at a cost of GBP 894 each. The hotel was rated as "platinum" in M's brochure and was described as being of a high standard and quality. At the time of booking, C specifically requested a quiet room, although they were aware that M would only endeavour to fulfil the request. In fact, their room was above the kitchen and was adjacent to the restaurant. The noise carried on until 12.30 am and started again at 6.00 am. After the first night, C requested to be moved, but that was not possible because M did not have the use of any other rooms at the hotel. They were offered a room in another hotel over 10 km away, but were told they would have to pay additional costs. C decided to pay to fly home immediately. Relying on the Package Travel, Package Holidays and Package Tours Regulations 1992, C sought to recover the entire cost of the holiday together with damages for loss of enjoyment of the holiday.

Held, giving judgment for the claimants, that the room could not be described as "quiet" however subjective that test was. M had made no endeavour to fulfil the special request and, indeed, it appeared that it was impossible for M to fulfil the request at that hotel. M had not discharged its obligations under the Regulations and C had been entitled to act as they did. They were entitled to a refund of the total cost of the holiday, the cost of the flight home and GBP 225 each for the loss of enjoyment.

Marsh v Thomson Tour Operators Limited Current Law Cases: 00/4044

M booked a package holiday with T at the Savoy Hotel, Madeira for himself and his wife. The brochure contained a guarantee that if a customer found that T had failed to fulfil the promises in its brochure, T would spend 24 hours trying to put the problem right, and if it could not do so to the customer's satisfaction, it would fly the customer home and refund the cost of the holiday. The hotel was advertised in the brochure as having a "magnificent lido complex", two salt water pools and a private jetty. Those facilities were closed for refurbishment when M arrived at the hotel. M was offered a transfer to a nearby hotel of similar standard, but refused it in favour of being flown home. T eventually agreed to fly M home, but declared that it was not doing so under the terms of the guarantee and that the holiday cost would not be refunded. M claimed a full refund under the terms of the guarantee. T argued that it had done all that it reasonably could to rectify the problem, that it was unreasonable for M to fly home when he had been offered a satisfactory alternative, and that in doing so he had failed to mitigate his loss.

Held, giving judgment for M, that the guarantee did not specify that a customer's dissatisfaction had to be "reasonable", and such a term could not be implied. The guarantee was included by T as a sales gimmick, to provide something extra to set it apart from the competition. If the operation of the guarantee was limited to situations where it was reasonable for a customer to request to be flown home, it would be worth little.

***Djengiz* v *Thomson Holidays Ltd* Current Law Cases: 00/4038**

D brought an action for damages against a tour operator, T, on his return from a package holiday in the Dominican Republic. The holiday consisted of 14 days at an all inclusive resort complex. D contended that the holiday brochure promised that a programme of activities would form part of the package. On the final day of his holiday, D, who had undergone a bilateral hip replacement some years earlier, took part in a beach volleyball game organised by the resort complex staff. The game formed part of a programme of events advertised daily. The volleyball pitch was located on a beach adjacent to the resort complex, but was actually owned by the local authority. As D jumped for the ball, he fell on his side. The area on which he fell had a concrete base and only a fine covering of sand. D passed out, suffered extreme pain and personal injuries. D argued that a warning ought to have been given by the hotel, or displayed at the volleyball pitch, to alert holidaymakers to the concrete base of the pitch. T argued that, while it had, by its standard booking conditions, contractually accepted liability for personal injury caused by the negligence of its suppliers, such acceptance of liability only extended to personal injury suffered while D was using the services that T had arranged for him. D had been injured while playing volleyball at a location that was off the resort complex and was not owned or run by the resort complex. In addition, the volleyball game was not one of the activities which D had booked and paid for in advance. It was not mentioned expressly in the brochure and thus did not form part of the holiday contract for the purposes of the Package Travel, Package Holidays and Package Tours Regulations 1992 Reg.15(2). In the alternative, T argued that, in the absence of evidence from D as to safety standards for volleyball pitches in the Dominican Republic, D could not establish a breach of duty on T's part, *Wilson v Best Travel Ltd* [1993] 1 All E.R. 353 cited.

Held, giving judgment for D, that (1) the volleyball game was organised by the entertainments staff; (2) while the beach was not part of the resort, the volleyball game organised to take place there was a service arranged by the resort; (3) the volleyball game was impliedly part of the entertainment promised in the brochure; (4) in the circumstances, the volleyball game was a service arranged by T, or its supplier, and T had accepted liability for the injury that D suffered in the course of the game; (5) the failure to warn D of the hazard constituted by the concrete base of the pitch constituted negligence, and (6) Wilson could be distinguished on the ground that D was encouraged to take part in the volleyball game and that a warning would have deterred him from taking part.

Excursions and Ski Packs Revisited
Matthew Chapman [2005] ITLJ 7

Introduction

This article revisits, in the light of recent first instance decisions, the question of tour operator liability in respect of the provision of excursions and other services sold in-resort by local representatives. It is a common feature of package holidays that the local representative employed by the tour operator markets, sells and collects money for a variety of local excursions. The venue for this activity is, typically, the welcome meeting hosted by the local representative at the start of the holiday.

Equally typically, the tour operator does not itself provide the excursion on the day. This is, instead, undertaken by a local entity (often, but by no means invariably, a company registered locally). If something goes (negligently) wrong during the course of the excursion then the UK holidaymaker (left injured or dissatisfied) would generally prefer the convenient option of suing the UK registered tour operator, rather than taking the risk and bearing the cost of suing the local company which provided the excursion. As a result of recent first instance cases like *Allison Rochead v Airtours Holidays Limited* [2001] CLCC (HHJ Crawford Lindsay QC) and *Gallagher v Airtours Holidays Limited* [2001] CLY Preston CC (HHJ Appleton) it is now tolerably clear that the Package Travel etc. Regulations 1992 will not assist. If the excursion is booked and paid for in resort, rather than in advance, then it will not satisfy the conditions of pre-arrangement and inclusive pricing in order to form part of the regulated package (on which, see regulations 2(1) and 3(1) of the Package Travel etc. Regulations 1992). If the Package Travel Regulations 1992 do not apply then, of course, neither does regulation 15 and the consumer cannot take advantage of the extended vicarious liability which it imposes on tour operators for the defaults of their local suppliers.

Most tour operators are careful in their brochures and booking conditions to demarcate the boundaries of what does and does not form part of the (inclusively priced) package holiday contract. The significance of this is that tour operators (most of those who subscribe to the ABTA Code of Conduct) include in their booking conditions an acceptance of liability for injury, loss and expense which results from the negligence of their suppliers. However, the same tour operators generally make it clear (although there are some exceptions) that this contractual acceptance of liability extends only to negligence by suppliers in the performance of holiday services arranged before departure from the UK (that is, such services as are confirmed on the Holiday Confirmation Invoice). This is generally thought sufficient to defeat the argument that, under the Booking Conditions, tour operators bear a vicarious liability for negligence by the local excursion company (on which, see again, Rochead).

Accordingly, in the typical case the consumer will be left with just one line of attack: the parallel contract. Namely, that he entered into a contract – running parallel to the main package holiday contract – with the tour operator through the tour operator's local representative. The consumer's argument in these circumstances has to be that it was a contractual term that the tour operator would exercise reasonable care and skill in the performance of the excursion contract (as per section 13 of the Supply of Goods and Services Act 1982), even 'though, in reality, it was a local company that provided the excursion on the day.

In *Rochead* the Claimant attempted to run this argument, but this was raised so late in the trial process (during closing submissions and without pleading the new cause of action) that the trial Judge declined to hear argument on it.

There is authority for the proposition that such an argument might be available to a consumer as a common law (contractual) alternative to the causes of action provided by the Package Travel etc. Regulations 1992 (see, *Wong Mee Wan v Kwan Kin Travel* [1998] 1 WLR 38 (PC)). It is, however, only very recently that this issue has been fully argued and tested in Court.

Derbyshire v First Choice Holidays & Flights Limited [2004] CLCC (HHJ Karsten QC)

The facts

In this case, the Claimant booked a package holiday to Canada with the Defendant tour operator for the period 29 March 2000 until 8 April 2000. The price paid for the package holiday included the following elements: accommodation; return flights from London Gatwick to Calgary; transfer from airport to Hotel; the services of a local representative. It was a classic package. This was a skiing holiday and the Claimant could have prebooked and paid in advance for his skiing equipment and lessons through the Defendant (the combination of these two elements was referred to as a 'ski pack'), but he chose not to do so. The Claimant arrived at Calgary airport on 29 March 2000. He was met by the transfer coach and the Defendant's local representative. On arrival at the Hotel the Claimant and his partner hired ski equipment and booked skiing lessons which were provided by an independent local ski shop business. The Claimant made a payment to the Defendant's local representative for the hire of the ski equipment and the lessons and the representative issued a 'Ski Pack Ticket' with the name of the local ski shop written at the top. The Claimant presented the ticket to the local ski shop for the provision of the equipment and the lessons.

The ticket also featured the Defendant tour operator's logo. The evidence was that the Defendant selected the local ski shop to supply ski equipment to all of its guests (or, at least, as many as wished to take up this option, rather than make their own arrangements). The Claimant attended the ski shop on 29 March 2000. He was provided with ski boots and skis which he wore on 30 March 2000 for his first lesson and first day's skiing without incident. The accident happened on 31 March 2000 (the second day of skiing). The Claimant was attempting a snowplough turn to his right. As he pressed down on his left ski, his left ski stopped suddenly while his body continued to rotate in a clockwise direction and he fell to the ground. His right ski detached from his foot, but his left ski was still attached. The reason for this was that the assistant in the shop had (as the Judge found at trial) negligently supplied the wrong sized boot for the Claimant's left ski and bindings. The Claimant sustained a classic skiing injury: a cruciate ligament injury to his left knee. He brought an action against the tour operator for the negligence of the ski shop's employee. He relied on causes of action in contract pursuant to the Package Travel etc. Regulations 1992 and the Defendant's booking conditions. Unsurprisingly, these arguments failed for the reasons sketched above; the trial Judge referred, in the course of judgment, to *Rochead.*

The Claimant also argued, in the alternative, that he had a parallel contract for the fitting and hire of his ski equipment which he had entered into in Canada with the Defendant through the Defendant's local representative. Alternatively, the Claimant argued that the Defendant had negligently selected an unsafe supplier of ski equipment for its guests.

The claim was dismissed.

Parallel contract

The Claimant's argument at trial was summarised by the Judge in the following terms:

> a. the Defendant's holiday brochure indicated that the Defendant's local, representatives would advise on the provision of ski packs;
>
> b. there was a contract between the Defendant and the local shop which appointed the latter as the exclusive supplier of ski packs to the Defendant's clients;
>
> c. the ticket supplied to the Claimant by the Defendant's local representative contained the logo of the Defendant;
>
> d. the Defendant's local representative took the payment;
>
> e. these matters, taken together, meant that the Defendant was in law (and pursuant to *Wong Mee Wan*) undertaking to provide the ski pack services itself.

This argument was rejected by the trial Judge for the following reasons:

> a. the existence and identity of the local ski shop had been disclosed at an early stage (in fact on the transfer coach to the Hotel) and on the ski pack ticket;
>
> b. the ski packs were described on promotional material supplied to the Claimant as 'recommended' services (in other words, the Claimant received only a recommendation and had a choice about where to hire his ski equipment);
>
> c. *Wong Mee Wan* was distinguishable because it dealt with what was an overall package of services, rather than a parallel contract for the provision of a discrete service;
>
> d. it would be an unreasonable extension of a tour operator's potential liability (at least at common law) for the tour operator to be liable for negligence in the provision of services simply by virtue of the fact that its employees collected the money (the Judge was, for example, concerned at the prospect of tour operators being held liable when things went wrong with the ski lift during a skiing holiday in circumstances where its local

representative had simply collected from guests the money for the lift passes).

The Judge accepted the argument for the Defendant that the principals to the parallel contract were the Claimant and the local ski shop and that the Defendant had acted simply as agent.

Accordingly, the parallel contract argument failed.

Negligent selection

This left the Claimant only with the argument that the Defendant had selected an unsafe or inappropriate local shop to recommend to its guests for the hire of their skiing equipment.

Claimant's evidence on this was weak. There was no evidence that the negligence found by the Judge in the fitting and supply of skis, boots and bindings was anything other than an isolated incident. The Defendant had adduced evidence that the shop was well-run and that a check of the shop had been made by the local representatives when the shop had first been approached. The claim therefore failed on this basis as well.

The Judge went on to make some brief observations about the law (Canadian or English) that would have applied to the parallel excursion contract between Claimant and Defendant in the event that it had existed. However, in the light of his dismissal of the claim these observations were wholly obiter.

Derbyshire is significant because it appears to be the first case in which the parallel contract issue has been fully ventilated. While each case in this difficult area will turn on its own facts, Derbyshire provides some comfort for tour operators. If a tour operator clearly alerts consumers to the existence and identity of the third party supplier before contracting and if it is signalled to the consumer that the tour operator will not itself be supplying the service contracted for locally then it should be possible for the tour operator to escape liability on the parallel contract; an agency argument will likely defeat the claim. Much will, of course, turn on what is said by the local representatives and what is written both in the main package holiday brochure and in any promotional material handed to consumers in resort.

It is a question of getting the wording right.

Gadd v *Lotus International Limited* (t/a Supertravel) *(Manchester County Court, 24th August 2000)* [2000] ITLJ 201

The liability of travel agents is one of the great mysteries of travel law. Are they agents or independent contractors? If they are agents whose agent are they, the client's or the tour operator's, or perhaps they are the agent of both? Are they liable in contract or tort? This case, fortunately for the protagonists, manages to avoid those difficult issues but is nevertheless worth reporting simply because it adds to the thin line of existing authority on travel agency liability.

Judge Bloom QC: This is an appeal from a judgment of District Judge Shannon dated 3rd May 2000 whereby he adjudicated that the defendants were liable to the claimants in the tort of negligence in the sum of £2,298 plus interest.

The facts are as found by the District Judge and are not in dispute and indeed are unchallengeable.

The claimants have a young child. They were interested in a holiday abroad. On the 18th March 1997 they rang the defendants, who are booking agents, a limited company who trade as Supertravel. In connection with this transaction, they were booking agents for a company called Sunworld.

The communication was by telephone, and there were a series of calls between 7pm and 9pm, which is outside normal office hours for the defendants, but they did hold themselves out as available to accept telephone bookings at that time.

The facts as found by the District Judge were: the employees were Tony Reilly and Tim Denby.

The claimants were offered a holiday in the Dominican Republic. They were anxious to know whether they should obtain vaccinations against diseases or illnesses, prior to travelling. They were informed correctly that it was not a legal requirement for travelling to the Dominican Republic. This information was available to the employees. The information was correct, so that if the claimants were to travel, there would be no impediment to their entry.

They were still anxious to know whether vaccinations were advisable in that without them they would be at risk of disease or illness. That information was not then available to Tony Reilly or Tim Denby. It was somewhere within the defendant's computer system but only available to employees during normal office hours, not between 7pm and 9pm in the evening.

However, the information would be readily available at the commencement of business the next morning via the defendants themselves, or elsewhere, for example the School of Tropical Medicine, or other holiday providers.

Tim Denby read out to the claimants some information from a Thomson Brochure.

The claimants were informed that the information was not available to Tim Denby or Tony Reilly. They could not say whether vaccinations were recommended. So the claimants were aware there was a distinct possibility that they were recommended, but Tim Denby and Tony Reilly did not know.

The claimants were also informed that the booking might not be available the next day, but this information was not used to put any pressure on the claimants to book.

It seems to me that the claimants took a commercial risk. They were aware that if they cancelled, Sunworld would retain the whole price.

The claimants decided to go ahead in the hope that vaccinations were not recommended.

The next day they found out that vaccinations were recommended, by enquiry from the School of Tropical Medicine. Alternative holidays were offered to them but they chose not to take them, and no criticism can be made of them for that.

The District Judge found that the conduct of Tim Denby and Tony Reilly was beyond criticism.

But he found the defendants were in negligent breach of duty, adopting clauses 7a and 7c from the Particulars of Claim, in that the defendants via their employee Tim informed the claimants that no vaccinations were required whereas they were in fact recommended; and that in all the circumstances the defendants failed to provide the claimants with the proper advice before they entered into the contract notwithstanding that they knew that the claimants had no knowledge of the Dominican Republic and were relying upon the defendants knowledge and expertise.

It is difficult to see how the District Judge arrived at this conclusion. As has been submitted to me, paragraph 7a is just a statement of the facts, but not a complete statement because Mr. Denby went on to say that he did not know the answer.

As to paragraph 7c, the District Judge finding must depend on what was the extent and scope of the duty to advise. The case of *Hedley Byrne v Heller* [1963] 2 All ER 575 has been referred to, and in particular the speech of Lord Reid at page 583 letters C and D in which he said:

> "A reasonable man knowing that he was being trusted, or that his skill and judgment were being relied on, would, I think, have three courses open to him. He could keep silent or decline to give the information or advice sought; or he could give an answer with a clear qualification that he accepted no responsibility for it or that it was given without that reflection or enquiry which a careful answer would require; or he could simply answer without any such qualification. If he chooses to adopt the last course then he must, I think, be held to have accepted some responsibility for his answer being given carefully, to have accepted a relationship with the enquirer which requires him to exercise such care as the circumstances require".

In my view, Lord Reid is expressing the view that there is no liability for a statement if there is a clear disclaimer of it; but if a person chooses not to give advice, then he would not be liable for economic loss.

The claimants seek to distinguish this by saying that the information was in the Lotus computer, but their employees did not have access to it at the time and therefore the defendants were in negligent breach of duty of care to prevent financial loss in failing positively to make the information available.

In my view this would be a considerable extension of the duty of care to prevent economic loss - it would be a duty to prevent a person from being put into a situation where that person might decide to take a risk, the consequences of which he is fully aware.

I know of no authority in support of that contention.

The case of *James McNaughten Paper Group Ltd v Hicks Anderson & Co* [1991] 2 QB 113 (see Clerk and Lindsell on Tort paragraph 770) shows the duty on a claimant to take their own independent advice in these circumstances.

This case is even stronger from the defendants point of view. Their employees said the advice was not available and the claimants in knowledge of the risk decided to take a chance rather than wait until the next day.

In my judgment there was no duty of care to prevent a person of full capacity and mature judgment taking a risk the consequences of which he was fully aware.

There is no duty to protect a person from financial losses resulting from the consequences of their own ill-judged decision.

The defendants were not negligent towards the claimants and the appeal will be allowed.

The claimants are to return the monies paid by the defendants under the judgment and to pay the defendants costs in the sum of £800 within 14 days.

SECTION 2

CAUSATION

Section 2

CAUSATION

Cases in this Section

Sheila Mawdsley v *Cosmosair Plc* [2002] EWCA Civ 587 (18 April 2001)

1. LORD JUSTICE JONATHAN PARKER: This is an appeal by Cosmosair Plc ("Cosmos"), the defendant in the action, against an order made by His Honour Judge Singer in the Manchester County Court on 26 September 2001, whereby he awarded Mrs Sheila Mawdsley, the claimant in the action, damages in the sum of £17,500 in respect of personal injuries which she suffered on 29 September 1997 as a result of a fall at the Marmaris Palace Hotel in Turkey whilst on a package holiday supplied by Cosmos. Permission to appeal was granted by Hale LJ on the papers on 27 November 2001.

2. It is common ground that the fall occurred when Mrs Mawdsley and her husband were descending a flight of stairs leading to the restaurant in the hotel. They were carrying their bay baby daughter, Charlotte, in a pushchair between them. In the process Mrs Mawdsley lost her footing, slipped and fell. The only issue was as to liability. The quantum of any damages to be awarded in respect of the injuries which Mrs Mawdsley suffered in the fall was agreed at £17,500. Although Mrs Mawdsley also claimed general damages for inconvenience, distress and discomfort, by the time of the trial this additional claim had been compromised so the judge was only concerned with the issue as to whether Cosmos is liable for damages in respect of the injuries suffered by Mrs Mawdsley in her fall.

3. By her Particulars of Claim, Mrs Mawdsley alleges that in the brochure advertising the hotel, in reliance on which she and her husband booked the holiday, Cosmos represented that the hotel restaurant could be accessed by a lift when in fact it could not, and that the hotel was suitable for parents with young children when in truth it was not so suitable.

4. Mrs Mawdsley claims damages against Cosmos in respect of these alleged misrepresentations on three different basis.

> (1) She pleads that Cosmos breached its duty under Regulation 4 of the Package Travel Regulations 1992 ("the Regulations"), in that its brochure contained "misleading information", and that under that Regulation Cosmos is liable for any loss suffered in consequence of that breach of duty.

> (2) In the alternative, she claims damages for negligent misrepresentation.

> (3) In the further alternative, she claims damages for breach of contract on the footing that the representations were a term of the contract with Cosmos for the purchase of the holiday; that she relied on the misrepresentations; and that, in consequence, she suffered the injuries which resulted from her fall.

5. By its Defence, Cosmos denies that the information contained in its brochure was misleading or that the representations in it were false. It goes on to plead that there was nothing unusual, difficult or dangerous about the flight of stairs down which Mrs Mawdsley was descending when she suffered her fall. Cosmos further denies that it was a term of the contract that it would be possible to have access to the restaurant without using any steps. It further denies that if there was a breach of contract, that breach was causative of the accident. It is further pleaded that it was not in the reasonable contemplation of Cosmos that personal injury would result from the

provision of what is described in the pleading as "an ordinary staircase". The Defence goes on to deny that Mrs Mawdsley and her husband were obliged to carry a buggy and a pram up and down the relevant staircase. It put Mrs Mawdsley to proof of the injuries in respect of which she claims damages.

6. Mr and Mrs Mawdsley have two children, Jack and Charlotte. At the time of the holiday Jack was aged about 3½ and Charlotte about six months. The brochure issued by Cosmos on which, as the judge found, Mr and Mrs Mawdsley relied when booking the holiday, shows photographs of the hotel and pool area. The photograph of the hotel shows it as a modern concrete type structure facing the sea with rising ground to the rear. To the rear of the hotel, viewing it from the sea, is the main building. To the front of the main building at a lower level is a substantial terrace. The terrace extends underneath the main building and also outward towards the sea beyond the line of the front wall of the main building. Immediately below that terrace is another terrace which in turn gives access via a single flight of steps to the pool area. The photograph shows two substantial flights of steps leading from the upper terrace to the lower terrace.

7. The written part of the brochure draws attention to various features of the hotel and of the holiday which is offered. Under the heading "Facilities" appear the words, "Lifts (in main building)". The brochure also lists a number of facilities which are available for children and to price reductions for children.

8. The holiday booked by Mr and Mrs Mawdsley included full board, which entailed their visiting the hotel restaurant at least twice a day. The restaurant for those enjoying full board is situated on the upper terrace, which is on level 1. Level 1 is one floor down from the ground floor of the main building where the hotel reception is situated. The pool area is at level 2, one floor below level 1. There is a lift in the main building between the reception and the pool area (level 2), but it does not stop at level 1 which is a mezzanine floor.

9. Direct access to the restaurant from the reception area is provided by four flights of steps, 39 steps in all. This route is described in the judge's judgment as route 2. There is an alternative route from the reception area to the restaurant via a ramp and some steps outside the main building. This route, which involves negotiating 14 steps, is referred to in the judgment as route 1. Direct access to the restaurant from the pool area is provided by two flights of steps, 24 steps in all. This route is referred to in the judgment as route 3.

10. Mr and Mrs Mawdsley and their two children were accommodated in a maisonette or bungalow in the grounds of the hotel separate from the main building. On the fifth day of the holiday, Mrs Mawdsley suffered the fall which forms the basis of her claim. The judge described what happened on page 10B-E of his judgment:

> "On the day in question the Claimant on day five was going down the first of the 11 steps of the 39 steps that they had to negotiate from the reception to the restaurant. She was holding the handle of the pushchair, which was facing downstairs. Her husband, having his back to the pushchair, was holding the foot area, a position in which wives and husbands can regularly be seen to take in carrying a pushchair downstairs. That is something which, whilst I cannot claim I can take judicial notice of, is accepted by all the

parties as a fairly usual way of going down the stairs, and it is not suggested that they were adopting anything that was a negligent way of carrying the pushchair down the stairs. She says in her statement that she lost her footing and slipped, and I find that that is what happened."

11. The judge turned, first, to the holiday brochure. He began by rejecting the argument, put forward on behalf of Cosmos, that it was obvious from the description in the brochure of the various activities which were available, and from the photograph of the hotel itself, that there were bound to be a number of steps to be negotiated. As to that argument, the judge said at page 3D:

> *"I take the view that there is absolutely no reason why an hotel, overlooked as the description said by the scenery described and as depicted in the photographs and having the facilities that were described, should not itself have been on fairly level ground."*

12. The judge went on to find that Mrs Mawdsley relied on, among other things, the words "Lifts (in main building)" as a representation that the hotel was suitable for young children.

As to that, the judge said at page 4E-F:

> *"I see no reason to throw any doubt on the Claimant's assertion that that made her feel that since there were lifts in the main building, she and her husband would have no difficulty in transporting their children round the hotel either in or out of the pushchair or buggy that they took with them. One could reasonably suppose that the lift would provide access to the pool and to every other floor."*

13. Later in his judgment, at page 5B, the judge said:

> *"...if you say there are lifts in the main building, it clearly implies that that will provide access to everything."*

14. The judge recounted what happened when the Mawdsley family arrived at the hotel and discovered there was no access to the restaurant by lift. He said at page 5F-G:

> *"Accordingly, they found that there were two ways that they could get to the restaurant. The ways that in fact have been described have been described as routes 1, 2 and 3. There was a route 4, which was from the bungalow to the reception, which does not appear to be relevant at that stage."*

15. He then described route 2 (the direct route from the reception area to the restaurant), and route 3 (the route from the pool area to the restaurant) as being the route which the Mawdsleys took. He described route 1 (the alternative route from the reception area to the restaurant), but concluded, rejecting the evidence of the Cosmos' representative, Mr Goodwin, to the contrary, that Mr and Mrs Mawdsley were not told about route 1. The judge further found that, not only were they not told about it, but there was no reason why they should have discovered it. The judge said at page 6H-7C:

> *"On the evidence, I am satisfied that there is no way that the Claimant could have reasonably discovered this round about way to the restaurant, and accordingly I find that it was not a route which she ought to have taken. It is accepted by the Claimant, I believe, through her counsel, that had she known of that route, that would have been one which would not have put her to the risk and danger which the Claimant claims she was put to by virtue of the other two routes."*

16. In relation to that last reference to an acceptance by Mrs Mawdsley through her counsel that route 1 would have posed a lesser risk, the position as I understand it, is that in the course of her cross-examination Mrs Mawdsley made a comment to that effect, which the judge has recorded, but that aspect of her evidence was not explored in re-examination.

17. The judge went on to find that when Mr and Mrs Mawdsley complained to Mr Goodwin about the stairs to the restaurant he said:

> "In that case you can leave the buggy and the pushchair at the top."

18. The judge commented, "This they could not do". He went on to conclude that it was reasonable for them to take Jack, Jack's buggy and Charlotte in her pushchair at the same time. At page 8D he said:

> *"I also find it entirely reasonable, and it has not been challenged that the Claimant and her husband should take baby Charlotte in what is described as the pushchair."*

19. The judge returned to the allegation of misrepresentations in the brochure. He concluded that the brochure represented that the hotel was suitable for young children. There is nothing controversial in this conclusion. Cosmos asserts that the brochure does so contain that representation. But the judge went on at page 9A-B:

> *"In my judgment, it was unsuitable for children, because for an hotel to provide the only available accesses to the restaurant which holiday makers had to use together with their children, via 24 or 39 steps, is not providing a hotel which is suitable."*

20. The judge elaborated on this conclusion at page 9D of the judgment:

> *"It was misleading to say that there was a lift in the main building because the lift only gave access to all the floors bar the restaurant."*

21. The judge went on to hold that, in making this misrepresentation, Cosmos was in breach of the Regulations, in breach of contract and liable in the tort of negligence subject to establishing damage. He then turned to the issue of causation of damage. That is the issue whether the injuries which Mrs Mawdsley suffered in her fall were caused by the misrepresentations he had found.

22. After referring to a number of authorities which had been cited to him, including *Kemp v Intasun Holidays*, an unreported decision of the Court of Appeal dated 20 May 1987; *Quinn v Birch Brothers (Builders)* [1966] 2 QB 370 CA; and *Manning v Hope*, an unreported decision of the Court of Appeal dated 16 December 1999, the

judge expressed his conclusion on the causation issue in following passage in his judgment at page 17E-18F:

> "*This is a situation in which I find as a fact that the claimant and her husband were required by the failure of the Defendants to supply lift access two or three times a day to negotiate stairs, carrying a pushchair in the way that they have described, which was a tricky situation. I will come back to that later on - the issue of foreseeability. But, in my judgment, the description of Mr Kilvington that she loses her footing because she was put in the position of going up and down steps with the pushchair and cannot watch her feet and the way she is descending is a fair and accurate way of explaining the matter.*
>
> *If you are having to concentrate in part on carrying the pushchair, your six month old baby being in it, you cannot be paying as much attention as is reasonably necessary to where your feet are going on the stairs*".

He also characterises it in this way.

> "*The Claimant was put in an unsuitable position by the misleading information and suffered injury by the lack of suitability of the premises, the lack of suitability being requiring her to carry a baby in a pushchair down 39 or up 24 steps to get to and from the restaurant. He said that is why the injury was suffered.*
>
> "*Whilst we do not know precisely how she came to lose her footing, in fact it is reasonable to suppose in my judgment, that she did so because she was unable to pay sufficient attention to how she was descending the stairs because of the task that she and her husband had to perform so many times a day on so many occasions. There is, in my judgment, a clear causal connection between the misrepresentation which directly put them in that difficult situation and the injury that was suffered. Therefore, the Claimant does satisfy the issue of causation in relation to each of the three grounds upon which the matter is argued.*"

23. The judge then went on to the consider the issue of foreseeability. He concluded at page 19B that it was "not unlikely" that Mrs Mawdsley would lose her footing as she did. At 19D of his judgment he said:

> "*In my judgment any reasonable person considering the circumstances would say that, whilst not dangerous, it is a hazardous thing to require somebody to do two or three times a day in the way the claimant was required to do.*"

24. ... Cosmos submits, addressing the claim in contract, that there was no basis upon which the judge could conclude that the description of "Lifts (in main building)" could amount to an implied term of the contract between Mrs Mawdsley and Cosmos that the restaurant could be accessed by lift, and that his conclusion that that description implied that the lift would provide access to "everything" (ie all the facilities in the main building) is unsustainable. [It is submitted] that there is no representation that the lift would stop at all levels in the main building, including the mezzanine level on which the restaurant is situated. [It is said] that there was indeed a

lift in the main building and that that particular facility was provided as stated in the brochure.

25. ... the brochure says nothing about where in the hotel complex the relevant restaurant is situated, and that there was no reason to suppose that it was necessarily situated in the main building. As to the alleged misrepresentation that the hotel was suitable for parents with young children, [it is submitted] that, although the judge found that Mr and Mrs Mawdsley were not told about route 1 ... route 1 was undeniably available to hotel guests and it cannot be said that the hotel was unsuitable for young children [and] that it is unrealistic to conclude that a hotel with steps leading to and from guest facilities is unsuitable for young children. [Cosmos points out] that a parent carrying a child may trip on a single step [and] therefore that the fact that the restaurant could only be accessed by negotiating flights of steps, did not and could not be said to render the hotel in its entirety unsuitable for young children.

...

27. As to the case pleaded under the Regulations, [Cosmos] submits, correctly in my judgment, that this claim adds nothing to the two other heads of claim pleaded by Mrs Mawdsley.

28. As to causation, which Cosmos put this at the forefront of [the] oral submissions, [it is submitted] that Mrs Mawdsley's injuries were caused by the fact she lost her footing, no doubt because she had her hands full with Charlotte in her pushchair. ... this could have happened anywhere in the hotel complex, and the fact that it happened on the stairs leading to the restaurant is purely coincidental and does not provide the necessary causal link between the representation and the injury. ... there is no finding, nor has it been alleged, that the stairs in question were in themselves inherently unsafe, that the surface material was compromised in any way, or that the stairs were not properly maintained. Nor was it alleged that, as a result of what she read in the brochure, Mrs Mawdsley expected the hotel complex to be entirely free of steps or other difficulties for guests and children.

29. [Cosmos] submits that the precise reason why Mrs Mawdsley lost her footing is a matter in respect of which no finding is, or could on the evidence be, made. ... Mrs Mawdsley had a number of choices as to the manner in which she descended the stairs and that, in making the choice which she did, she effectively broke the chain of causation with the consequence that the liability for the injuries cannot be laid at the door of Cosmos because of the misrepresentations contained in the brochure.

30. ... an appropriate test is to ask whether, but for Cosmos' conduct, Mrs Mawdsley would have avoided an accident of this character in some other situation on some other different family holiday. ... the answer to that must in all probability be "No".

31. ... however reasonable Mrs Mawdsley's conduct it was, nevertheless, one of a range of reasonable choices which she could make. ... therefore, that the fact that the accident occurred on the stairs leading to the restaurant is neither here nor there and does not provide sufficient causal link.

32. Cosmos relies on *Quinn v Birch Bros (Builders)* [1966] 2 QB 370, to which I shall return.

33. Accordingly, even if otherwise actionable, [Cosmos] submits that the statement in the brochure "Lifts (in main building)" did not cause Mrs Mawdsley to suffer injuries for which she seeks damages.

...

35. [The Claimant] submits that the judge was right to conclude that the description "Lifts (in main building)" was a representation that, in effect, all levels in the main building, including the mezzanine level, could be accessed by lift. As to the allegation that the admitted representation that the hotel was suitable for parents with young children was a false representation in that the hotel was not so suitable by reason of the absence of a lift giving access to the restaurant, [the Claimant] relies on the finding of the judge and the passages from the judgment to which I have referred. [It is submitted] that the particular defect which renders the hotel not suitable for young children is the very defect highlighted by the misrepresentation arising, as he contends, out of the description "Lifts (in main building)".

36. As to causation ... the misrepresentation not only provided the opportunity for Mrs Mawdsley to suffer the injuries she suffered when she fell, but that it was the effective or dominant cause in that the misrepresentation itself exposed her to the risk of injury because it exposed her to a hazardous situation. There was ... a direct link between the misrepresentation that the restaurant could be accessed by lift and the presence of Mrs and Mrs Mawdsley and their children on the stairs leading to the restaurant.

...

38. [It is submitted] that the flights of stairs created a particular risk for guests with pushchairs in the same way as they would they would create a risk for the disabled, elderly or infirm. ... Cosmos' misrepresentations and breaches of contractual duty exposed Mrs Mawdsley to the very risk of the kind of accident which, in the event, she suffered.

39. ... the necessity for the Mawdsley family to traverse flights of stairs two or three times a day in accessing and leaving the restaurant only served to increase the particular risk to parents with young children. He says that in every case it is a matter of degree and that in the instant case the level of risk resulting from the misrepresentations rendered the misrepresentations actionable.

40. In the first place I agree with the judge that the description "Lifts (in main building)" in the brochure does represent that all levels in the main building can be accessed directly by lift. That, as it seems to me, is how a potential customer would naturally read and understand that description. The fact that the brochure describes the hotel us a "Holiday Village" standing in landscaped gardens and lists a large number of facilities seems to me to be immaterial for present purposes. The representation is expressly limited to the mainbuilding. Nor does the fact that the brochure makes no specific mention of the restaurant assist in this connection. Absent any such specific mention, a reader of the brochure would, it seems to me, naturally assume that the restaurant was situated somewhere in the main building and consequently accessible directly by lift.

41. Accordingly, I would conclude that description "Lifts (in main building)" is a misrepresentation. On the other hand, I am unable to agree with the judge's further conclusion that the fact that there is no direct access to the restaurant by lift rendered the hotel unsuitable for parents with young children. I agree with [Cosmos] that it is unrealistic to conclude that the mere fact that access to the hotel restaurant involves negotiating stairs renders the hotel unsuitable for young children; the more so when one looks at the nature of the hotel complex as shown in the photographs in the brochure. It is plain from the photographs that, given the differing levels as described earlier, enjoyment of at least some of the hotel's facilities must be likely to involve negotiating a flight of steps.

42. I proceed, therefore, on the basis that the operative breach of contract/misrepresentation is that which is constituted by, or embodied in, the description in the brochure "Lifts (in main building)"; that is the representation that, in effect, all levels in the main building, including the restaurant, could be accessed by lift. In my view that was "misleading information" for the purposes of Regulation 4 of the Regulations, with the result that Cosmos is liable under that Regulation for all consequent damage. Since Regulation 6 of the Regulations provides that particulars in the brochure are implied warranties in the contract, it follows that Cosmos was also in breach of contract in that respect. Moreover, in the context of negligent misrepresentation, the judge's finding that Mrs Mawdsley relied on the misrepresentation seems to me to be unassailable in this court.

43. I turn, then, to the issue of causation. I turn first to Quinn v Birch Brothers (Builders) ... In that case the claimant was a plasterer carrying out work under a subcontract. The defendants, the main contractors, in beach of contract failed to supply him with a step-ladder despite his request for one. In order to complete his work in the absence of a step-ladder, the claimant chose to prop a folded trestle against the wall and use it as a ladder. The foot of the trestle was not made firm and it slipped causing the claimant to fall and suffer injuries. The claimant claimed damages against the defendants in respect of those injuries.

44. At first instance Paull J held that, although the defendants were in breach of contract, that breach did not cause the accident since the claimant's negligent failure to make the trestle secure broke the chain of causation. It was, he held, a new intervening act. The Court of Appeal upheld his decision. In the course of his judgment Sellers LJ said at page 389D:

> "*The breach of contract was not a cause of the subsequent events which brought the plaintiff's accident.*"

45. At page 390A-B Sellers LJ said:

> "*....this cannot be said to be an accident which was caused by the defendant's breach of contract. No doubt that circumstance was the occasion which brought about this conduct of the plaintiff but it in no way caused it. It was in no way something flowing probably and naturally from the breach of contract.*"

46. Dankwerts LJ, agreeing, said at page 391G:

"The failure of the defendants to provide the equipment required may have been the occasion of the accident but it was not the cause of the accident."

47. Salmon LJ, also agreeing, said at 395A:

"The breach of contract merely gave the plaintiff the opportunity to injure himself and was the occasion of the injury. There is always a temptation to fall into the fallacy of post hoc ergo properter hoc; and that is no less a fallacy even if what happens afterwards could have been foreseen before it occurs."

48. [Cosmos] submits that, although there is an additional element in Quinn in that the course of conduct chosen by the plaintiff was negligent, that is not a factor which distinguishes Quinn from the instant case. In the instant case, as he has submitted, Mrs Mawdsley was faced with a number of choices as to the course which she should take in reaching the restaurant.

49. In relation to causation of damage, [Cosmos] submits that Quinn is on all fours with the instant case in that all that the misrepresentation in the instant case has done is to provide Mrs Mawdsley with an opportunity to suffer the very accident which she suffered.

50. I cannot accept that submission. In my judgment, Quinn is distinguishable from the instant case in that there was not in the instant case, whereas there was in Quinn, a new intervening act breaking the chain of causation. The sole causes of the claimant's accident in Quinn, as I read that decision, were his choice of using a trestle in place of a ladder when he could have waited for a ladder to be supplied, and his own negligent failure to secure the trestle properly. In that case it was truly said that the defendant's breach of contract provided no more than the opportunity for the claimant to do what he did. In the instant case there is, in my judgment, a sufficient causal link between the misrepresentation that the restaurant could be accessed by lift and the accident which occurred on the stairs. As [was] submitted, the misrepresentations served to expose Mrs Mawdsley to the risk of suffering the very type of accident which in the event she suffered. It is not just that "but for" the representation Mrs Mawdsley would not have been in the hotel at all; the misrepresentation related directly to the means of access to the restaurant. Nor, as I have already pointed out, is there any finding of negligence on the part of Mrs Mawdsley. The judge expressly found that it was reasonable for her to descend the stairs in the way she did.

51. In my judgment, therefore, on the facts of this case, the judge was right to find as he did at page 18E of the judgment that:

"There is, in my judgment, a clear causal connection between the misrepresentation which directly put them in that difficult situation and the injury that was suffered."

52. Since no separate issue arises on foreseeability, it follows that, for the reasons I have given, I would dismiss the appeal.

Purcell v Thomson Holidays Ltd, unreported, 15 October 2003, York County Court (HHJ Barry)

1. Very sadly when the claimant in this case was meant to be enjoying herself on her holiday in August 1999, the holiday was spoilt on the 9th August when she went to have a shower. While she was in the shower, in circumstances which I do not think she has explained particularly well, and she has in evidence relied upon the concussion she suffered as a result of the accident as supporting her contention that she cannot remember very well what happened, she fell. She hit her head, was knocked out it seems for a time and suffered a series of unfortunate injuries, particularly soft tissue injuries, which have lasted quite a long time and would redound in substantial damages if she establishes liability.

2. She says that is the fault of Thomson's who are vicariously liable for the fault of the hotel administration (the combination of course of the hotel administration and the representatives' efforts on behalf of Thomson's) at the site on which she was on holiday.

3. It is accepted that under the Package Travel Regulations 1992, particularly Section 15, Thomson's are, by regulation, made responsible for what their suppliers in the hotel do as far as their customers are concerned. So that is one potential legal problem that is out of the way. If the hotel failed her essentially then Thomson's failed her and it would be proper to make an award against them.

4. What are their duties here? Their duties are, of course, to provide for this holiday, including the accommodation and the amenities such as the bathroom attached to her room, with reasonable care and skill and that obviously has her safety in mind, and although I do not find necessarily that there was a specific implied term of the agreement that the bathroom would be reasonably safe, it seems to me a facet of the general duty of care owed by Thomson's to their customers, and that if it is shown that they have failed in that reasonable skill and care, in providing a safe bathroom then they are liable and therefore if the hotel failed to provide such a reasonably safe bathroom then Thomson's have fallen below the appropriate standard.

5. What do I know about the bathroom? I take the view that the oral descriptions of it given by the witnesses I have heard to date are, to some degree, a reaction to the accident itself. They say that the bath was particularly narrow. They complain that the bath and shower were one unit, rather than two separate units, so people had to stand in the bath in order to have a shower and they say because it was narrow and the sides curved up, it was not possible to stand safely on the floor of the bath in order to have a shower and that led to the accident that Mrs Purcell suffered.

6. I have some relatively objective data about the bathroom from the evidence of Samantha Hicks. It is right to say that one has to be careful about this sort of hearsay evidence adduced for convenience because the witness is abroad and therefore has not been susceptible to cross-examination, about the safety of the bath. She has not been here to be asked did she have to put

her feet against the curve of the bath. It may be that she is a smaller woman than Mrs Purcell was at the time. Her husband, rather ungallantly, volunteered the information she was rather bigger when the accident took place than she is now. But it may well be that she is considerably smaller than Mrs Perkins, who gave evidence about the nature of the bath, because that lady said she is a foot size 7. Samantha Hicks apparently is foot size 5 and therefore one imagines a smaller woman.

7. What she has done is provide photographs which show me what the bathroom is like and there is nothing in the photographs which make it look anything out of the ordinary. There are photographs particularly of her own feet in the bath, where she is standing with her small size 5 feet, alongside each other with a gap between them. She is not standing to attention with her heels together, like a soldier on sentry duty, and both her feet appear to me on the base of this bath to be flat on the ground, on the base of the bath without having to be cocked at an angle against the curving walls of the bath. She says, and quite frankly I cannot see how any cross-examination could have established anything different, that she did this standing where she would have a shower in the bath.

8. It seems perfectly possible therefore for a lady to stand with her feet flat on the base of the bath and have a shower. Perhaps it would be awkward, perhaps it would not be convenient, and I accept Mrs Perkins evidence, when she gave me one or two demonstrations of her posture, that it was too cramped for a robustly built lady like her to swing round to wash conveniently under her arms in an upright posture, and she demonstrated that she would have to crouch a little in order effectively to do it. That is an inconvenience but it does not seem to me to suggest that the bath is in any way dangerous.

9. One has to accept, and I think I can take judicial notice of the fact that when one goes away to stay in hotels, one is apt to find bathroom accommodation which is more cramped than one would have at home. It is almost unheard of for a bathroom in a hotel, unless it is a very expensive one which you are paying very high fees for, to have a bath of the same size as one's domestic one back home and certainly there is nothing irregular about having a bath and shower unit combined. That is very common, particularly in hotels. It is pretty common in domestic use. It all depends on how much space you have got available, I suppose.

10. So there is nothing to criticise about the provision of the baths, either from the fact that the unit is combined, a combined bath and shower nor, I find on the evidence of the photographs and what I have been told about it, the width of the bath at its base.

11. I have evidence, again it is susceptible to criticism because it is hearsay evidence adduced under the statute because the witnesses are abroad, of the provision of the baths by the suppliers of the particular bath. I see no reason to imagine that the manager of the hotel or the informant from the bath company, who wrote letters about the matter enclosing the specifications of the bath, would dare to mislead the Court about the provenance of this

bath. I accept, therefore, that it is built according to European standards which are numbered and cited in the documents which would be the same standards which would apply in this country and I do not have to rely upon Miss Allen's late evidence about a particular hotel in this country and the particular width of the bases there, to see if it complies with British standards.

12. It is, of course, for the claimant to establish that it was the fault of Thomson's or the hotel, that she suffered this accident and insofar as it is based upon criticisms of the structure of the bath, the design of the bath and the shower, I find that she has failed to establish that that is in any way out of the ordinary or likely to have caused an accident.

13. Now, getting in and out of baths and walking about in baths is always susceptible to slipping. One of the problems about bathing is that one uses water, water gets onto relatively smooth surfaces, although the evidence about this particular bath is that it is a non-slip surface. Well, one can take that with a pinch of salt perhaps as one is always susceptible to slipping in baths and to the extent that the witnesses say this has never happened to them before, I just have to find that they are very lucky. Slipping is a constant danger in bathrooms and adults have to be aware of it and so conduct themselves that they look after their own interests properly.

14. Up to the 9th August from the 31st July, the Purcells did not notice anything particularly wrong with this bath. The narrowness one would have thought would be more of a nuisance to those sitting in the bath to wash than someone standing in it. But the bath was perfectly acceptable to Mrs Purcell in her ordinary use of it as a tub up to the 9th August and Mr Perkins makes no complaints about it at all.

15. So far as the Perkins are concerned, they did seem to find more difficulties that they complained about. Mrs Perkins, of course, thought the whole holiday was a disgrace and this was a particularly bad hotel. The rooms were dreadful, the staff were dreadful, the assistance of the representatives were meagre and she looked at this whole hotel through what are the opposite of rose coloured glasses, through tinted glasses of a gloomy nature, and it seems to me that her evidence is, to some degree, informed by the shock of finding that her friend had had an accident in these circumstances.

16. She may well have asked for a bathmat if she had known they existed because she has two children, one with particularly long hair she wanted to wash, and she might have been concerned about children slipping in the bath because, of course, of the known propensity of children to lark about when they are having baths. She may have done, I do not know. I have no reason to suppose that if this accident had not happened the Purcells would have ever thought anything in the nature of a bathmat was necessary. I do not believe they would have asked for one if they had known one was in existence and I have no reason to believe that the provision of a bathmat would have prevented the particular accident that befell Mrs Purcell.

17.   From time to time people lose their footing in baths. Mr Perkins did once or twice, once before the accident of Mrs Purcell, once afterwards. It did not cause him any real difficulty. It is something that happens to us all and if we want bathmats we could ask for them, of course. Nobody thought of doing that. It does not seem to me to matter that no notice was given to them that bathmats were available if they wanted them.

18.   These welcome meetings by tour representatives at holiday places are, of course, something that we can all go to when we go on holiday and hear what advice is to be tendered, if one can put up with the waste of time and deduction of it from one's holiday when one goes. But what the representatives often do is to warn English people of the sort of problems that exist in Mediterranean countries which do not exist over here to put them on enquiry about problems. They warn people, do they not, about the larger measures of alcohol that are served in the Mediterranean than in England. They warn people about the marble floors and the marble surrounds to swimming pools, so that when people get out they do not slip on the wet pools. That sort of thing is done but they do not have to because adult people are expected to know when things are dangerous and one thing we all know is that we can get in and out of the bath only with care. We can move about in the bath and stand in it only with care because in the wet environment of a bathroom there is always a danger of slipping.

19.   Of course, of one is old, suffering a disability, has weight problems or poor balance or perhaps suffers a certain amount of confusion, it would be wise to draw that to the attention of those looking after you at the hotel to make sure that special provisions are made, such as the provision of one of these rather unpleasant sticky rubber mats to put in the bottom of the bath. To make life, if somewhat uncomfortable, that degree safer, but for ordinary robust healthy adults it seems to me that that is an unnecessarily nannying standard which the law does not require of those who provide the facilities here.

20.   I do not think that the claimant and her witness are lying witnesses. I am inclined to believe that what they say is entirely what they believe. However, it seems to me that a lot of their evidence and their opinions, is a construct arising from the shock and distress of the accident happening itself and had it not happened it would not have occurred to them that any of these matters were required.

21.   I accept the evidence, again I know adverse comment can be made of it, that somebody who works for this hotel group is bound to have an interest in supporting it and also that it is easy enough to say without fear of cross-examination that people in Greece do not bother about bathmats for whatever reasons of their own. However, I believe it is true that Miss Allen's evidence was quite clear that there is a small supply of bathmats just for the sort of people I have canvassed who might need to ask for them for special reasons, but there was no general tradition of supplying them in Greece and I do not believe there is a general tradition of supplying them in England or indeed in any other country. Well, O do not know what goes on, of course, in Switzerland or some states of the United States of America but these

things are, as the defence submit, sometimes provided, sometimes not, and it is certainly not an indication of negligence neither to provide them nor to warn people before they have a bath that they might slip and tell them of the availability of bathmats if necessary.

22. The experience of those running the hotel appears to me to be made very clear by Miss Allen's evidence that there would only be about a dozen, certainly less than 50, bathmats available and if there was a run on them, some of the customers would have to be denied.

23. It seems to me that no question of contributory negligence arises here. What appears to me is that the claimant has not established what caused the accident at all and has given me no reason to suppose that it is either the design of the particular bath in question or the failure to provide or to give notice of the availability of bathmats, which has caused this accident. It is something of a mystery, one of those unfortunate mysteries that an affect us all at sometime or other. It is an accident in which no negligence is involved and so I will give judgment for the defendant in this case entirely.

24. If it helps, in case this matter has to be considered elsewhere, I would have accepted Mr Gore's submissions to some degree about the impact of the permanent continuing slight disabilities that Mrs Purcell has and would make her damages in the region of £4,600.00 generally, with an extra £200.00 for the loss of enjoyment of the holiday, £4,800.00 in all there. So far as the special damages are concerned, the sum is admitted, I accept her evidence about paying £400.00 to the decorator. It is not as certain evidence as it might have been had invoices been available but I accept her as a witness of truth on that matter and would allow her the £400.00 that she claims. So far as her husband's contribution to the household chores are concerned, I am inclined to say that it is not a case that falls within the *Mills -v- BR Engineering Limited* rules and would make any award very reluctantly. It seems to me that just a small addition to her general damages for inconvenience and the impact of that upon domestic life of say £500.00 would be appropriate and since it is claimed as part of the special damages, I think the whole special damages come to £942.00.

25. So there is general damages of £4,800.00 and special damages of £942.00 but they are not awarded in this case because I do not believe that the claimant, as she is bound to do, has established, on the balance of probability, that any negligence on the part of the hotel or the tour operator caused her very unfortunate and distressing injuries.

Clough v *First Choice Holidays and Flights*, 26 January 2005, David Foskett QC (Deputy Judge QBD)

Introduction

1.   On 13 November 1999 the Claimant, then aged 26, sustained a very serious injury to his cervical spine rendering him tetraplegic. In common parlance, he broke his neck. The consequences for him have been devastating: he is now wheelchair-bound, has only very limited use of one hand, has no bladder or bowel control and is totally dependent on others for virtually all his daily needs.

2.   He sustained the injury in what, for shorthand purposes, can be described as a "swimming pool accident" at a holiday complex in Lanzarote. He had been drinking during the few hours prior to the accident and was approximately 2½ times the legal limit for driving purposes. On any view, he was under the influence of alcohol at the material time.

3.   Referring, as I understand it, to statistics for the UK alone, Lord Hoffmann in *Tomlinson v Congleton Borough Council* [2004] 1 AC 46 (at paragraph 39) said that every year about "25 to 35 [people] break their necks diving". He returned to this statistic later in his speech (at paragraph 49) when referring to the evidence of an expert (Dr Penny) given in that case in March 2001:

> "Each year, as I have mentioned, there are about 25 to 35 fracture-dislocations of the neck. Almost all those affected are males and their average age is consistently around 25 years. In spite of greatly increased safety measures, particularly in swimming pools, the numbers (when Dr Penny gave evidence) had remained the same for a decade:
>
> > "This is probably because of the sudden, unpredictable nature of these dangerous dives, undertaken mostly by boisterous young men ... hence the common description the 'macho male diving syndrome'." "

4.   There was no alcohol involved in Mr Tomlinson's case and the statistics to which Lord Hoffmann referred do not indicate the extent to which alcohol may have contributed to the circumstances in which the serious injuries reflected in those statistics were sustained. However, one only has to read cases such as *Ratcliff v McConnell* [1999] 1 WLR 670, *Donoghue v Folkestone Properties Ltd* [2003] QB 1008 and *Balram Singh v Libra Holidays* [2003] EWHK 276 (Holland J) to see the influence that alcohol may bring to bear on accidents of this kind. Indeed all commonsense supports the proposition that swimming, diving and all other activities in the vicinity of water when significantly affected by alcohol are fraught with potential danger.

5.   In this case it is the Defendant's case that the Claimant, under the influence of drink, deliberately dived from a substantial height above its surface into what he knew (or certainly ought to have appreciated) was a children's pool containing only relatively shallow water. The Defendants say that, tragic

though it was, the accident was the Claimant's own responsibility. Although Mr Ritchie's closing submissions for the Claimant kept open the possibility of some finding in his favour even if he did execute a deliberate dive into the pool, the reality is that if he did so then he could not establish any liability against the Defendants whatever failings there might have been about "no diving" signage around the pool.

6. However, there is a crucial (and surprisingly difficult) issue about whether the Claimant did indeed execute a deliberate dive as suggested by the Defendants. If I resolve that issue against the Defendants, the question of how the Claimant came to fall into the relevant pool arises and, consequent upon that finding, whether, and if so to what extent, the Defendants are responsible legally for the consequences.

7. Before turning to the first crucial issue of fact, I must set out some of the general background a little more fully.

...

30. I do not doubt the honesty of the evidence given by the witnesses to whom I referred ... above. However, each was undeniably (and wholly understandably) sympathetic to the Claimant's cause and there is always in that situation an unconscious desire to put forward material in a way that supports the cause. Mr Saggerson made the point (which was, I think, accepted by most, if not all, the witnesses) that there is always a risk of slipping around a swimming pool. That, I am sure, is the common experience of everyone who uses a swimming pool, whether at home or abroad. In those circumstances, I find it difficult to draw much from accounts of incidents of slipping such as those to which these witnesses referred. There is other evidence that those using the complex did not experience slipping accidents routinely and Mr Saggerson has submitted that the complex does not have what he called "an accident profile". Mr Ritchie, however, invited me not to attach to much significance to that submission because no accident book has been disclosed.

31. Mrs Sleigh said that she had no reason to believe that the pool edges were slippery. She said that there is an element of slipperiness in the situation where water and suntan oils mix. The only comment she had made about the pool surrounds was as I have already recorded in paragraph 26 above. Having re-read her report for the purposes of composing this judgment, I am inclined to think that she was addressing principally concerns relating to the signage, depth markings, the need to keep children from falling into adult pools and so on, and rather less on matters such as non-slip paint. She may well have assumed that the paint was non-slip and, as she said herself, there was nothing very technical about the inspection that she undertook. She did not, of course, walk on the Fountain pool wall as did Mr Morgan.

32. Mr Morgan has concluded (correctly, in my judgment) that no kind of proprietary brand of non-slip water-proof paint was used at the complex at that time. He drew attention to certain brands obtainable in the UK. Mr Saggerson submitted that there was no basis for saying that a Spanish

proprietary brand would have made a difference or that it would have guaranteed a non-slip surface. As to that submission, I would make this observation: the Spanish Regulations from which I quoted partially in paragraph 18 above do place significant emphasis on provisions designed to avoid slipping. In addition to the need for "anti-slippery and water-proof material" to which I have already referred, there is a requirement that the floor of a pool should have "a wrinkled surface to avoid people slipping". Against that background it is difficult to believe that there are not effective proprietary brands of non-slip paint available for use around the (doubtless many) swimming pools in Spain.

33.   Endeavouring, then, to pull together the various pieces of evidence in this regard, my conclusions, on the balance of probabilities, can be stated shortly as follows:-

    (a)   the horizontal surface of the Fountain pool wall was not coated in a proprietary brand of non-slip paint;

    (b)   the paint with which it was coated was less effective than a proprietary brand of non-slip paint in minimising the risk of slipping;

    (c)   the horizontal surface of the wall was such that someone walking upon it with wet feet would be exposed to an increased risk of slipping compared with a surface coated with a proprietary brand of non-slip paint.

34.   These conclusions do not, of course, necessarily establish that the Claimant slipped or that, if he did, his fall into the paddling pool would have been prevented had a proprietary brand of non-slip paint been used. I will return to this issue later should it become material.

...

65.   Doing the best I can on what, on any view, is a difficult evidential basis, I am not satisfied that it has been established that the Claimant deliberately dived into the childrens' pool.

66.   It seems to me, therefore, that what probably happened was that the Claimant got out of the adult pool on the side of the Fountain pool furthest away from where Mr Plazier was sitting, spoke briefly to Mr Hannigan and let him and his daughter pass. Not long after this he climbed up on to the Fountain pool wall, either with a view to looking into the area where the (then non-operational) fountain was or, perhaps more likely, simply taking a short cut to where he had left his clothes, when he slipped and in the process toppled over and fell essentially head-first into the children's pool. It is possible that he stopped or slowed down to look at the view out to sea back in the direction of the reception area, as Mr Lloyd thought that he did, but it was in this general process (possibly with various ideas in his mind of what he was there for, but undoubtedly under the influence of drink) that the Claimant lost his footing and fell in the manner I have described.

...

69. For all those reasons, particularly as a slip from the surface of the wall in the absence of any barrier to prevent a fall could cause injury, it was, in my judgment, incumbent on the owners of the complex to use good-quality non-slip paint for the surface. That they did not do so was a breach of the local regulation and represented "a failure to exercise reasonable care and skill" in the provision of facilities at the complex.

70. For reasons I will give later (see paragraph 78), I have some reservations about whether the Claimant is someone who can claim the benefit of these regulations in the sense of being someone for the protection of whose well-being they were designed. However, assuming for present purposes that they were, does this breach have causative potency in this case?

71. Mr Ritchies' Closing Submissions contained the proposition that the lack of non-slip paint must have made a "material contribution" to the Claimant's fall if I found that there was indeed a fall rather than a dive. After I had intimated my likely findings on the central issues to him and to Mr Saggerson, they each provided me with additional written arguments on various matters for which I express my appreciation. Mr Ritchie developed the argument concerning "material contribution" further in those submissions. I should say that this was against the background of my indication that my likely conclusion was that, whilst the Claimant's slip occurred on a surface with an increased risk of slipping compared with the surface that ought to have been provided, it had not been established that this made any difference to his fall.

72. Mr Ritchie reminded me of the definition of what constitutes a "material" contribution as set out in *Bonnington Castings -v- Wardlaw* [1956] AC 613 (*per* Lord Reid at p.621) and to the way in which the issue of causation was dealt with in the well-known case of *McGhee -v- NCB* [1973] 1 WLR 1, a case where what Mr McGhee's employers did (or failed to do) materially increased the risk of his contracting dermatitis. Mr Ritchie argues that if I find (i) that the risk of slipping was materially increased by virtue of the surface of the wall and (ii) that the Claimant slipped, I should conclude that the surface made a "material contribution" to the injury sustained as a result of that slip. He also drew my attention to the cases of *Lee -v- Nursery* [1945] 1 AER 387 and *Cook -v- Kirkby* [1952] 2 AER 402, cases where there were breaches of statutory duty owed to workmen in which the inference of causation was drawn by the court when the particular workmen suffered the kind of injury that the relevant safety regulations had been designed to prevent.

73. Notwithstanding these forceful submissions, I am not persuaded that the provisional view I had formed about the issue of causation was wrong. I will endeavour to explain why in paragraphs 74 – 78 below.

74. On the issue of causation, in my view, the Claimant has to prove, on the balance of probabilities, that but for the absence of proper non-slip paint he would not have slipped as I have found that he did. The other way of putting it, as Mr Ritchie submitted, is that he must prove, on the balance of probabilities, that the absence of proper non-slip paint caused or materially

contributed to his slip and his subsequent fall. However, in my judgment, if the slip is as likely to have occurred irrespective of the absence of a proprietary brand of non-slip paint as it would have had such paint been provided, or the evidence does not permit of a conclusion on the balance of probabilities, then the necessary evidential hurdle has not been surmounted and the "but for" test has not been passed.

75. If, as Mr Ritchie has effectively submitted, the law applicable to a case such as this was that a breach of duty that increased the risk of a claimant sustaining injury in a particular way is to be taken to have caused or materially contributed to an injury sustained by the claimant within the area of that risk, then, subject to the duty being owed to him, the Claimant would certainly have the makings of a case on that issue. He slipped where the surface carried an increased risk of doing so compared with the risk on the surface that ought to have been provided. However, that approach to causation is, as the law now stands, limited to certain specific situations and, notwithstanding Mr Ritchie's very well-argued written submissions, I do not consider that it applies to this one: see generally *Fairchild v Glenhaven Funeral Services Ltd and others* [2003] 1 AC 32. But there does seem to me to be a more fundamental difficulty in applying such an approach to this case in any event.

76. I can illustrate the difficulty of applying the "material contribution" approach to a case such as this in the following way. I have held that the risk of slipping on the surface of the wall was greater than it should have been. Since an increased risk is "material" if the increase is "more than minimal", it would follow that the increased risk here was "material". However, I have no way of concluding what the true magnitude of that increased risk was in this case. If the evidence had established that people were habitually slipping on its surface, I might have been able to conclude that the increased risk was so significant that it must have contributed materially to the Claimant's slip and that, but for that material contribution, he would not have slipped at all. However, the evidence does not establish that: people did walk on it safely as I have observed in paragraphs 30 and 78. Indeed so did the Claimant for some part of his journey. Whilst the role that percentages can play in this context is debatable, even, say, a 10-15% increased risk would be "material" within the definition of that word mentioned above. But even if I was satisfied that an increased risk of that order existed here, I would find it impossible to conclude that but for it the Claimant's slip would not have occurred. I am, however, unable on the evidence to say what magnitude of increased risk arose here. Some objective assessment of the "slipperiness" of one surface as against the other might have helped, but since the inevitable conclusion would have been that no surface is likely to have been risk free so far as slipping is concerned, it may be that such evidence would not have led me much further in the inquiry. However, I can only express my conclusion, as I have, in a very general way by making the comparison between what was provided (which was not the best quality non-slip paint, but which must have had *some* effect otherwise people would have been slipping all the time) and what was not (the best

quality non-slip paint, but which could not of itself guarantee that no-one would ever slip).

77.   In his oral submissions at the close of the case Mr Ritchie recognised, I think, that there is a gap to be bridged for the necessary causal link to be established in this case. He invited me to adopt an approach similar to that adopted by Judge Brunning in the case of *Burns v Airtours plc and another*, 18 February 2000. I was provided with a transcript of the judgment in that case. It is clear that Judge Brunning had been referred to the well-known case of *Rhesa Shipping Co. S.A. v Edmunds* [1985] 1 WLR 948 in which the House of Lords reflected on how a judge should approach a fact-finding exercise when various improbable scenarios arise for consideration. However, the issue in *Burns* was simply whether the infant claimant is likely to have slipped on the top step or bar of a ladder leading to a pool-slide, that top step not being made, as it should have been, of a non-slip surface. It was argued by those alleged to have been responsible for the accident that the claimant might have tripped, slipped or lost his foothold in various ways and that it could not be said, on the balance of probabilities, that he slipped on the relevant top step. However, given that there was no suggestion that the claimant was using the slide in an irresponsible way or that there was any medical reason for how he might have lost his grip and fallen, Judge Brunning held that the clear inference was that he fell as of result of something untoward. There being no other explanation than the slippery bar on to which he must have put his foot, the inference drawn was that it was putting his foot on that bar which caused him to slip.

78.   It does seem to me that the circumstances of that case are different from those in this case. In that case, when all unlikely explanations had been discarded, there was only one likely explanation left. In this case, whilst I have found it likely that the Claimant did slip, and did indeed do so on a surface where there was an increased risk of doing so compared with the risk if the surface had been of the correct quality, it does not, in my view, follow as a matter of necessary inference that his slip was caused or materially contributed to by that surface. He had circumnavigated a fair part of the surface of the wall without apparently slipping before he reached the point at which the slip occurred. Others must have done so safely before. Mr Morgan, doubtless walking with circumspection, was able to walk safely on the wall some 18 months later when, by reasonable inference on the assumption that the wall had not been resurfaced in the meantime, the surface was likely to have been even more slippery than it was at the time of the Claimant's accident. And there is the inevitable consideration that no surface can be made completely non-slip when water and suntan oil mix no matter how good the quality of the non-slip paint. There must have been a good measure of water and suntan oil on and around many parts of this complex. Taking all those considerations into account, it seems to me that the highest I could put it in the Claimant's favour is that it was as likely that he would have slipped on this surface had it been of the correct quality from the non-slip point of view as it was that he slipped because of its inferior quality. If, of course, it had been established that there was (as in *Burns*) one

particularly slippery area where, on the balance of probabilities, the slip occurred, the conclusion as to causation can follow so much more readily.

79.   I would add that whilst the matter of alcohol consumption in the context of an accident such as this is probably to be viewed as a factor principally going to the issue of contributory negligence, it is impossible to avoid the reflection that the provision of non-slip paint in an area such as this is really intended for those who are behaving responsibly and are taking reasonable care for their own safety. Whilst I have already concluded that he was not behaving in a reckless fashion when on the surface of the wall, it is difficult to resist the inference that the Claimant would probably not have gone onto the wall and thus have slipped but for his own alcohol intake, or at least that but for that intake he would probably have recovered from such a slip. I have resolved this issue against the Claimant on the grounds of causation, but I am bound to say that had I not decided that issue in that way I would have been inclined to say that someone such as him would not be within the group of persons for whom the existence of the duty to provide non-slip paint is imposed.

80.   The next issue is the question of whether some railings or other form of barrier should have been provided on the outer perimeter of the Fountain pool wall to prevent someone from falling (or indeed diving) over that side into the shallow children's pool. Railings would undoubtedly have prevented the Claimant's fall and some other form of barrier would, on the balance of probabilities, have done so.

81.   In his report Mr Morgan said that he believed "that a physical barrier should have been provided along the edge of the wall surrounding the ornamental fountain to prevent the possibility of either diving or slipping from this elevated position." He amplified this in his oral evidence when he said that such a barrier would operate to prevent people, particularly children, falling into the pool on either side of the central fountain area. By reference to a photograph of a barrier provided between an adult and a children's pool at another hotel that he saw during his stay, Mr Morgan was suggesting what may be described as a fairly substantial metal fence with a number of horizontal bars between uprights. The height would appear to have been about one metre. The precise dimensions do not really matter for present purposes: what was required, in Mr Morgan's view, was a suitable barrier that would have prevented the possibility of a fall.

82.   I will revert to Mr Morgan's view shortly, but it is worth drawing attention to what Mrs Sleigh had said about the Reception pool in her report to which I have referred previously. In paragraph 12 I described it as follows: "It comprised a clover leaf-shaped adult pool and a kidney-shaped children's pool, each separated from the other by a circular island upon which a bar was situated." At the time of Mrs Sleigh's inspection she expressed concern about what she described as the "edge protection" around the edge of the circular island, her concern being that people, including children in particular, might fall off the central island into the surrounding water. She expressed her concern in this way:

"The current edge protection comprising uprights and ropes to the front and rear of the bar is inadequate, particularly in view of bar activities.

I would advise that a more robust, visible barrier is installed to extend along the exposed raised edges between bar and pools. This should be flush with the edge of the raised area to prevent formation of an outside ledge from which to dive, and I would recommend that it is extended beyond the exposed edge where practicable .... You may wish to consider various other forms of edge protection, possibly utilising planters or urns to perform this function. The barrier used should not cause additional safety problems."

She illustrated the kind of barrier that she had in mind on some photographs in her report. The height of the barrier she illustrated appears to be about the same height as the barrier suggested by Mr Morgan, although her diagrammatic representation of the barrier was in the form of a fence with more vertical struts than the kind of fence described by Mr Morgan. Those differences are, apart from one reason, immaterial: either kind of fence would prevent someone who slipped falling into whatever water there was beyond. As I understood her, Mrs Sleigh was of the view that vertical rails or struts were better because it made it more difficult for people to climb on them, something that has to be borne in mind when a barrier in this kind of situation is contemplated.

83. Mrs Sleigh did not make a similar recommendation in relation to the Fountain pool wall when she saw it. Her concern about the Reception pool was largely centred on the sale of alcoholic drinks in the central area and what she described as the "pinch point" caused by people walking backwards and forwards across that area. A great deal of her concern related to the possibility of children falling into the deeper pool when their parents may not have been watching. The specific concerns of alcohol and a pinch point would not have arisen in connection with the Fountain pool. Furthermore, the arrangement at the Fountain pool had changed between her visit and when the Claimant's accident occurred. Both side paddling pools (as they later became) were, at the time of Mrs Sleigh's visit, filled ("piled up", she told me) with decorative rocks of various sizes. She would not have contemplated that people would ordinarily have gone into those pools when she visited, but was concerned that if they did "the rocks in the decorative rock pool features could be slippery and present a risk of falling." She advised warning people not to try to paddle in these pools. As I have indicated, certainly by the time of the Claimant's accident, any such rocks had been removed from those side pools and the pools had become paddling pools proper. At all events, for whatever reason, I am inclined to think that Mrs Sleigh had not identified the Fountain pool wall as an area where people, including children, could get to easily. I think that had she done so,

she would probably have made a similar recommendation to that which she made in relation to the Reception pool, albeit for slightly different reasons.

84.   She did draw attention to possible disadvantages of a barrier, particularly the consideration that people will sometimes pull themselves up upon such a barrier. Mr Morgan accepted that it is necessary to weigh advantages and disadvantages when considering the provision of such a barrier, but, bearing in mind the kind of injury that could be sustained in a fall from the wall, the greater good would be done by providing such a barrier.

85.   This seemed a logical and sensible view and I accept it. My only *caveat* (which I think Mr Morgan would accept) is that a barrier of the sort that he and Mrs Sleigh described would only be put in place in this situation to reduce so far as practicable the risk of injury to children. That injury could be the kind of bodily injury sustained in a fall into the children's pool or the risk of drowning by falling into the adult's pool on the other side. The barrier would not be put there to protect adults who ought to know how to look after themselves and not put themselves in danger.

86.   On balance, therefore, I find that it fell below acceptable standards for a barrier not to be provided around the edge of the Fountain pool wall as suggested by Mr Morgan, the actual design being closer to that recommended by Mrs Sleigh in relation to the Reception pool. As I have said, any such barrier would have been there for the protection of children.

87.   The next issue, upon which I felt I should seek the further specific assistance of Counsel after intimating to them my provisional findings since the issue had not been canvassed in argument, is the question of whether the Claimant could rely upon this breach of duty towards children to say that liability to him had been established. I repeat my appreciation for their subsequent written submissions. I hope they will forgive me for expressing my conclusion quite shortly.

88.   They are, as I understand it, agreed that the Claimant cannot make a claim in tort for damages based upon a breach of a tortious duty which is owed not to him but only to children. Adapting Mr Saggerson's formulation for this purpose, a generalised "breach of duty" or a breach of duty owed to someone else is not a proper foundation for a claim by a specific claimant who falls outside the class of person to whom a duty is owed. Unless the existence of a duty can be established an action in negligence must fail. He drew attention to *Bottomley v Bannister* [1932] 1 KB 458, where Greer LJ said, at 476:

> "It is a commonplace of the law of negligence that before you can establish liability for negligence you must first show that the law recognizes some duty towards the person who puts forward the claim. The plaintiffs in this action alleged that the defendants were guilty of a negligent breach of duty towards the deceased in that they failed to attach to the Halliday boiler a flue to carry off the poisonous fumes through the wall into the open air. When the defendants installed the boiler they had not then and might never

have had any relations with the deceased. English law does not recognize a duty in the air, so to speak; that is, a duty to undertake that no one shall suffer from one's carelessness."

Instances of this general approach can be found in many cases and I will not extend this judgment by reference to them.

89.   Mr Ritchie did, however, submit that the obligation to fence, as I have found it to have existed, was also a contractual obligation because of the operation of Regulation 6 of the Package Travel, Package Holidays and Package Tours Regulations 1992 which had the effect of converting into implied warranties particulars given in the Defendant's brochure. He argues that the statements I recorded in paragraphs 18 and 19 above have thus been converted into warranties and that the Claimant is entitled to the benefit of these warranties since they are warranties incorporated into any contract with the Defendant irrespective of whether the party going on holiday includes children or not.

90.   I cannot accept this argument. Whilst it may well be that making safety a "high priority" is to be regarded as a contractual obligation, it is not, even as expressed, an obligation to provide complete safety, certainly for an adult who, at the material time, is to be expected to be looking after him or herself properly. If a child had fallen as I have found that the Claimant fell, I would have found liability established. I might well have found liability established if an adult, not under the influence of alcohol, had gone on to the wall to protect a child from the risk of falling, but had fallen him or herself. But I do not think that those considerations advance the Claimant's case here. Those conclusions would have been reached as much as part of the tortious liability as a contractual liability and I do not see anything in this particular brochure that extends the scope of the overall duty of care to this Claimant in a way that entitles him to the benefit of the obligation to fence the Fountain pool wall.

91.   At the end of the day, the Claimant decided to go on to the Fountain pool wall for whatever reason, quite significantly affected by drink, and he has to take the risks of doing so on his own shoulders. It is, of course, a terrible tragedy that he slipped and fell, but I do not think he did so because of some failing either on the part of the owners of the complex or on the part of the Defendants as such.

Conclusion

92.   For all those reasons, I regret to say that I cannot find that any liability is established in favour of the Claimant. I do reach this conclusion with regret, because it is very sad to see a young man such as the Claimant disabled in the way that he is leaving the court without even modest compensation which would, of course, make a difference to his life. Unlike some, however, he is fortunate to have had in place some insurance policies that have yielded funds to enable him to acquire and adapt accommodation suitable for his needs. I am sure that he has received realistic advice prior to this case and will understand that, even had I felt able to make some finding of

liability in his favour, it would have been in very modest proportions, certainly no more than 25%. He may take some comfort from the fact that, having reviewed the evidence as thoroughly as I can, I have rejected the suggestion that he deliberately dived from a substantial height into a children's paddling pool, an allegation with which he has doubtless found it difficult to live.

Clough v First Choice Holidays and Flights Ltd [2006] EWCA Civ 15 (25 January 2006)

President of the Queen's Bench Division:

1.   This is an appeal by Michael James Clough against the decision of Mr David Foskett QC sitting as a deputy High Court judge in London dated 27th January 2005 dismissing his claim for damages against First Choice Holidays and Flights Ltd.

2.   The claim followed a catastrophic accident on 13th November 1999 when the appellant, a young man then 26 years old, slipped from a wall and broke his neck in a swimming pool accident at a holiday complex in Lanzarote.

3.   The general background to the accident is summarised in Mr Foskett's careful judgment. Much of the analysis of the background, the description of the layout of the complex, and the circumstances of the accident is taken directly from it.

4.   The appellant, his then girlfriend, Zoe Laws, and their friends Ricky Lloyd and Viv Mallett, booked a holiday with the defendants for 14 days at the Las Lomas Apartments in Lanzarote. The booking was made through Eclipse, a division of the defendants, a company in business as tour operators supplying package holidays. The essential information provided by Eclipse to the claimant asserted that the safety and wellbeing of customers was a matter of high priority. It was a contractual term that responsibility was accepted for "any death, bodily injury or illness caused to you as a result of the proven negligent acts and/or omissions of our employees and agents and our suppliers and subcontractors and their servants and/or agents while acting within the scope of or in the course of their employment".

5.   The Las Lomas complex was comprised essentially of apartments of varying sizes, built around various swimming pools provided for the use of clients. The complex attracted families and couples from different European countries, including the United Kingdom. It was a typical "package holiday" destination for relatively young couples or couples with young families.

6.   The holiday began on 4 November 1999. After their arrival the appellant and his friends stayed in apartments that did not overlook either the reception pool (otherwise described as pool 1) or the fountain pool (otherwise as pool 2), the pool where the claimant's accident occurred. The apartment in which the appellant was accommodated meant that he had walked past the fountain pool on many occasions before the accident happened, and indeed had used it as well. He also knew that at the easternmost pool of the fountain pool there was a shallow circular paddling pool. It was in this part of the fountain pool that the appellant's accident occurred.

7.   In general the pools were closed after 7pm. Nevertheless from time to time residents at the complex would use the pools after they were formally closed for "after hours" swimming.

The fountain pool

8.   This pool derived its name from the fountain arrangement at its centre. It was laid out so that there was an adult pool, shaped as two adjoining circles in a "figure of eight" fashion with trees planted at the point where the two circles narrowed to form a neck. The pool was 1.1 metres deep at the shallowest end

increasing in depth to 2 metres at the point where the pool was nearest to the fountain. The fountain was raised above the level of the water in the middle of a circular area surrounded by a wall. There were two half-moon shaped paddling pools to the north and south, and to the east of the fountain there was a shallow paddling pool. The judge appended an illustrative photograph (photograph A) to his judgment, ensuring that the identity of those shown in the photograph are blurred. I shall do the same.

9.   The overall diameter of the circular area in which the fountain was located was 17 feet. The horizontal surface of the surrounding wall was 32" wide. The distance from the top of the wall to the bottom of the paddling pool was 64". No physical barrier, adequate to prevent a fall, was provided. The depth of the water in the paddling pool was 18", too shallow to produce any possible "cushioning effect".

10.   The horizontal surface of the surrounding wall was painted white with standard paint to which marble dust was added as the paint was applied. The paint itself was not "non-slip". The marble dust was susceptible to acid, and in time would dissolve through the effect of water from the swimming pool. It was conceded by the respondents at a late stage in the litigation that, notwithstanding repeated earlier claims to the contrary, the paint used on the surface was not "designed to be non-slip", and eventually accepted that the use of such paint constituted a breach of Spanish regulations which governed the structure and surrounds of swimming pools. In particular the walls around such pools, and the pavements around the edges, should have been made of or covered with "anti-slippery and waterproof material".

11.   In his submissions, Mr Frank Burton QC on behalf of the appellant drew attention to some of the written and oral evidence from the appellant and his friends, and an expert called on the appellant's behalf, which he was anxious that we should consider. It is however unnecessary to repeat it. The judge made specific findings of fact. He concluded:

> (a) the horizontal surface of the fountain pool wall was not coated in a proprietary brand of non-slip paint.

> (b) The paint with which it was coated was less effective in minimising the risk of slipping than a proprietary brand of non-slip paint: effective brands for use around swimming pools were available in Spain.

> (c) The horizontal surface of the wall was such that someone walking upon it with wet feet would be exposed to an increased risk of slipping compared with a surface coated with a proprietary brand of non-slip paint.

> (d) The wall was an attractive feature of the complex, regularly used by holiday makers, and indeed "a dive allurement".

> (e) The failure to use non-slip paint constituted a negligent breach of duty by the respondents for the purposes of the contractual arrangements between them and the appellant, and a breach of contract. It was "incumbent" on the owners of Las Lomas to have used good quality non-slip paint. Their failure to do so constituted a breach of the local regulations, and a failure to exercise reasonable skill and care in the provision of facilities at the complex, and the respondents were responsible in law for this negligence.

(f) A physical barrier should have been provided around the wall, for the protection, not of adults, but children.

12.   These findings speak for themselves, and are not to be criticised merely because the judge did not identify the precise nature of the increased risk of slipping consequent on the failure to use non-slip paint.

The accident

13.   In the course of his evidence, the appellant accepted that he was familiar with the fountain pool, and the nature of the surface underfoot, and that he had not previously slipped. During the afternoon of 13 November, the appellant and Mr Lloyd spent some hours drinking together while they watched a football match between England and Scotland on television. On his own account the appellant drank up to six pints of lager. His friend drank a little more. By about 6pm they were in high spirits. In evidence, Mr Lloyd accepted that he would have been a bit intoxicated, and that his judgment would not have been 100%. He and the appellant were in a state of high spirits, and they decided to take a dip in each of the pools of the complex. With hindsight, he thought it was probably not the best of ideas.

14.   After a swim in the first pool, the two of them moved to the fountain pool. The appellant got on to the horizontal wall adjoining the pool and, while walking along in an anti-clockwise direction in his bare wet feet, fell into the paddling pool. The judge rejected the respondents' case that he had deliberately dived into it. He also concluded that the appellant was indeed in high spirits and under the influence of alcohol, approximately two-and-a-half times over the legal limit for lawful driving. Nevertheless, he was not incapable of realising the general nature of what he was doing.

15.   The judge explained the appellant's fall in the following words. "If he did not dive, the natural inference is that he lost his balance in some way and fell into the pool. This could have been because he simply stood too near the edge of the wall, and, given his intoxicated state, merely toppled over, or it could be because he slipped from some point on the horizontal surface of the wall and fell following a slip." The judge then examined the various possibilities in the light of the evidence. On balance, he drew the inference that the appellant slipped and fell in a "toppling movement" into the pool, where, unsurprisingly, he struck his head on the surface at the bottom. Having reached that conclusion, he noted that just before his fall the appellant's feet would have been wet, and that he would have been less steady on his feet than he would have been if completely sober.

16.   Paragraph 66 of the judgment reads:

"... what probably happened was that the claimant got out of the other pool on the side of the fountain pool furthest away from where Mr Plazier was sitting, spoke briefly to Mr Hannigan and let him and his daughter pass. Not long after this he climbed up onto the fountain pool wall, either with a view to looking into the area where the (then non-operational) fountain was, or perhaps more likely, simply taking a short cut to where he had left his clothes, when he slipped and in the process toppled over and fell essentially head first into the children's pool. It is possible that he stopped or slowed down to look at the view out to sea back in the direction of the

reception area, as Mr Lloyd thought that he did, but it was in this general
process (possibly with various ideas in his mind of what he was there for,
but undoubtedly under the influence of drink) that the claimant lost his
footing and fell in the manner I have described."

At the conclusion of his judgment, the judge summarised his findings in paragraph
91. This reads:

> "At the end of the day, the claimant decided to go to the fountain pool wall,
> for whatever reason, quite significantly affected by drink, and he has to take
> the risks of doing so on his own shoulders."

17.   On the judge's findings, the appellant slipped on a surface which should
have been but was not painted with non-slip paint. His feet were wet, and he had
consumed a great deal of alcohol, but by walking where he did and being where he
was when he slipped, he was not doing anything abnormal or prohibited by the rules
of the complex. He did not dive into the shallow pool, nor miss his footing because
he was walking too close to the edge, nor topple from it in a drunken stupor.

Causation

18.   The claim failed on causation: hence this appeal. In summary, the judge
concluded that the negligence and breach of duty established against the respondents
lacked "causative potency".

19.   The judge highlighted a number, but not all, of the features of the evidence
relevant to this conclusion. Other users of the fountain pool, and in particular the
wall from which the appellant slipped, had used it safely on previous occasions: so
had the appellant himself on the day of his fall for part of his journey on foot. Mr
Burton suggested that this did not directly address the evidence of "slipperiness"
advanced by honest, but partial, witnesses called on behalf of the appellant, and
perhaps overemphasised the very short distance covered by the appellant on the wall
itself immediately before he slipped. The judge commented that Mr Morgan, an
expert called on behalf of the appellant, was able to walk safely on the wall when
examining it some eighteen months after the accident, when the surface would have
become even more slippery than it had been at the time of the accident. Mr Burton
suggested that that did not perhaps fully convey Mr Morgan's concern about the
degree of stiction, the effect of which was that even when he was walking on the
surface feeling relatively secure, if once his foot overcame the static friction beneath
it, it would slip. Mr Morgan believed that the risk of slipping was appreciable, and
that the wall surface was not safe. No engineering or other expert evidence was
advanced on behalf of the respondents directly to contradict Mr Morgan.

20.   The judge thought that it was virtually "inevitable" that, given the mixture
of water and suntan oil, even the best quality of non-slip paint would not have been
sufficient to make the surface of the wall completely non-slip. He was not prepared to
conclude that there was any individual "particularly slippery area" from which the
appellant fell. The judge reflected further on the issue of the alcohol consumed by the
appellant. Notwithstanding his conclusion that the appellant was "not behaving in a
reckless fashion" when he was on the surface of the wall, the judge found it difficult
to resist the inference that if the appellant had not taken alcohol, he would probably
not have gone on to the wall, but even if he had done so, and slipped, he would

probably have been able to avoid the consequent fall. Reading the judgment as a whole, he was plainly troubled by the consumption of alcohol and the final comments in his judgment need no repetition.

21.   At the conclusion of his judgment the judge considered a distinct possible basis of liability arising from the absence of a physical barrier to protect against a fall. This was not in issue before us. He noted that if a child had fallen in the way that the appellant fell, liability would have been established, and he "might well" have found liability if the appellant had gone on to the wall to protect a child from the risk of falling and, unburdened by alcohol, had slipped while doing so.

22.   Mr Edward Faulks QC suggested that the judge found that the appellant was outside the class to whom the duty to provide non-slip paint was owed. It was limited to children. I doubt whether the judge reached that conclusion, but if he had, I should have disagreed with him. The risk of slipping on the wall surface and swimming pool surround was shared by all the holiday makers at the complex, adults as well as children. If the judge had concluded that the duty was owed to children, but not adults, he would have said so in terms. Rather, he approached the case as if the obligation to provide non-slip paint was intended to benefit "holiday makers", including children, unless the adult holiday makers had somehow put themselves outside the protective duty of care. The judge's hesitation about whether the duty extended to the appellant personally on the day of the accident was based on his concern about his consumption of alcohol, and it was this that led the judge to reflect that the appellant was not taking appropriate care for his own safety.

23.   Mr Burton suggested a contrary criticism: an over-concentration in the judgment on alcohol consumption which is not without some justification. As it seems to me, this was indeed a holiday complex, used by holidaymakers. People on holiday relax, drink, and play about, sometimes with their children, sometimes with other adults. They are relaxed and less inhibited than they are in the normal daily grind. As they indulge themselves, an appropriate and reasonable degree of protection should be provided for them. In my view, their safety, even when inebriated, is one of the purposes of the regulations which required the provision of "anti-slip" material on the walls and edges of swimming pools. This claim may fail on causation, but not through the absence of a duty owed to the appellant.

24.   In written and oral submissions both sides subjected the reasoning which led the judge to his conclusion, and the conclusion itself, to a close analysis. For the respondents, Mr Faulks contended that the judge applied the correct test in law, and having done so, without expressly referring to all the evidence which supported his conclusion, decided as a matter of fact that the appellant had failed to establish causation. This court was not entitled to interfere. Mr Burton, for the appellant, suggested that the judge had overlooked, and certainly had not referred to all, the material relevant to this issue, but he had in any event misdirected himself in law.

25.   To do justice to Mr Burton's sustained argument I must refer to the judge's analysis of the legal issue. At paragraphs 74-76 of his judgment he said:

> "74. On the issue of causation ... the claimant has to prove, on the balance of probabilities, that but for the absence of proper non-slip paint he would not have slipped as I have found that he did. The other way of putting it ...

is that he must prove, on the balance of probabilities that the absence of proper non-slip paint caused or materially contributed to his slip and his subsequent fall. However, in my judgment, if a slip is as likely to have occurred irrespective of the absence of a proprietary brand of non-slip paint as it would have had such paint been provided, or the evidence does not permit of a conclusion on the balance of probabilities, then the necessary evidential hurdle has not been surmounted and the "but for" test has not been passed.

75. If, ... the law applicable to a case such as this was that a breach of duty that increased the risk of a claimant sustaining injury in a particular way is to be taken to have caused or materially contributed to an injury sustained by the claimant within the area of that increased risk, then, subject to the duty being owed to him, the claimant would certainly have the makings of a case on that issue. He slipped where the surface carried an increased risk of doing so compared with the risk on the surface that ought to have been provided. However, that approach to causation is, as the law now stands, limited to certain specific situations and notwithstanding ... very well argued written submissions, I do not consider that it applies to this one: see generally *Fairchild v Glenhaven Funeral Services Ltd* & ors [20003] 1 AC 32. But there does seem to me to be a more fundamental difficulty in applying such an approach to this case in any event.

76. I can illustrate the difficulty of applying the "material contribution" approach to a case such as this in the following way. I have held that the risk of slipping on the surface of the wall was greater than it should have been. Since an increased risk is "material" if the increase is "more than minimal", it would follow that the increased risk here was "material". However I have no way of concluding what the true magnitude of that increased risk was in this case. If the evidence had established that people were habitually slipping on its surface, I might have been able to conclude that the increased risk was so significant that it must have contributed materially to the claimant's slip and that, but for that material contribution, he would not have slipped at all. However the evidence does not establish that: people did walk on it safely as I have observed ... indeed so did the claimant for some part of his journey. While the role that percentages can play in this context is debatable, even, say, a 10-15% increased risk would be "material" within the definition of that word mentioned above. But even if I were satisfied that an increased risk of that order existed here, I would find it impossible to conclude that but for it the claimant's slip would not have occurred. I am, however, unable on the evidence to say what magnitude of increased risk arose here. Some objective assessment of the "slipperiness" of one surface as against the other might have helped, but since the inevitable conclusion would have been that no surface around the swimming pool is likely to have been risk free so far as slipping is concerned, it may be that such evidence would not have led me much further in the enquiry. However, I can only express my conclusion, as I have, in a very general way by making the comparison between what was provided (which was not the best quality non-slip paint, but which must have had some effect otherwise people would have been slipping all the time) and what was not (the best quality non-slip paint, which could not of itself guarantee that no-one would ever slip)."

26.   Mr Burton submitted that these passages from the judgment demonstrate the flaws in the judge's approach to the issue of causation. He misapplied the "but

for" principle, and failed to appreciate the true ambit of the concept of material contribution to damage, indeed, according to Mr Burton, he confused it with what Mr Burton suggested was the distinct concept, material contribution to the risk of damage. It was, according to the argument, not necessary for the appellant to demonstrate that the safety feature provided by the non-slip paint would have prevented or avoided his accident. If the use of non-slip paint was likely to have made a difference, its omission should be treated as having made a material contribution to the accident. That was sufficient to establish liability. The appellant was not required to establish that the slip was caused by the absence of non-slip paint rather than his own careless movements, or lack of balance, or the degree of his inebriation.

27.   Mr Burton developed his submission by identifying two categories of case in which what he described as the "doctrine" of material contribution might apply to establish causation in negligence or for breach of statutory duty. The first was material contribution to damage, which applied where more than one cause of the harm complained of was present, and the tortious cause, on the balance of probabilities, either made or was capable of making a material contribution to that harm. He relied on *Bonnington Castings v Wardlaw* [1956] AC 613 and *Wilsher v Essex Health Authority* [1998] AC 1074 as examples of and providing support for this principle. Material contribution to risk arose, exceptionally, where as a matter of policy, the court allowed causation to be proved (perhaps more accurately, found that causation was proved) even though due to the limits of current knowledge the evidence did not permit a factual inference that the increase in risk materially contributed to the damage. He identified *McGhee v National Coal Board* [1973] 1 WLR 1, *Fitzgerald v Lane* [1987] 3 WLR 249 and *Fairchild v Glenhaven Funeral Services Ltd* [2003] 1 AC 32 as examples of and sustaining this doctrine in an exceptional case.

28.   Mr Burton accepted that the precise ambit of the two categories had yet to be fully analysed, but he suggested that there was no reason in principle why cases in the first category should not apply to all accidents in which there were competing causes, some of which were tortious, and some of which were not. This therefore could apply where there were multiple or single parties, multiple or single agents, provided the court could be satisfied that the negligence complained of made a material contribution to the damage, or where it was legitimate to draw an inference to that effect. Whenever cases in either category arose, the claimant was not required to show that "but for" the negligence he would not have sustained the harm. All that was required of him was to show that the negligence made a contribution which was more than minimal.

29.   These were very wide-ranging submissions. Perhaps it would be as well at the outset to notice that Mr Burton was not inclined to identify any distinction between the claim for negligence or breach of duty or breach by the respondent of the contract with the appellant. In effect, any claim for breach of contract is subsumed in the claim that the claimant's catastrophic injuries resulted from negligence for which the respondents were responsible. The only significant issue in this appeal was causation.

30.   As a matter of first principle, the appellant is entitled to recover damages for personal injuries caused by the respondents' negligence: no more, no less. Lord

Bingham of Cornhill encapsulated this principle in his dissenting speech in *Chester v Afshar* [2005] 1 AC 134. At 142, where he observed:

> "It is trite law that damage is the gist of the action in the tort of negligence. ... A claimant is entitled to be compensated for the damage which the negligence of another has caused to him or her. A defendant is bound to compensate the claimant for the damage which his or her negligence has caused the claimant. But the corollaries are also true: a claimant is not entitled to be compensated, and a defendant is not bound to compensate the claimant, for damage not caused by the negligence complained of."

Trite law needs no reinforcement by an anxious parade of supporting authority. Nevertheless, given the judge's express reference to the "but for" test, perhaps reference to the broad approach to this issue identified by Lord Nicholls of Birkenhead in Fairchild will be forgiven. He said:

> "In the normal way, in order to recover damages for negligence, a plaintiff must prove that but for the defendant's wrongful conduct he would not have sustained the harm or loss in question. He must establish at least this degree of causal connection between his damage and the defendant's conduct before the defendant will be held responsible for the damage. Exceptionally this is not so. ..."

In effect, Mr Burton submitted that this is such an exceptional case to which, again in Lord Nicholl's words later in his speech, "a lesser degree of causal connection" sufficed.

31.   I should record at the outset that, after considering Mr Burton's submissions, I have concluded that what I have described as the first principle of causation remains the applicable starting and the finishing point in this case. Nevertheless in deference to his argument, I must consider his analysis of the authorities.

32.   This began with *Bonnington Castings Ltd v Wardlaw*. An employee claimed that he had contracted pneumoconiosis as a result of inhaling silica dust in the course of his employment. The dust came from two sources, and there was a breach of duty in relation to only one of them. The critical question was whether the dust inhaled from that source materially contributed to the disease. In a passage echoed in the judgment presently under consideration, Lord Reid observed:

> "What is a material contribution must be a question of degree. A contribution which comes within the exception de minimis non curat is not material, but I think that any contribution which does not fall within that exception must be material. I do not see how there can be something too large to come within the de minimis principle yet too small to be material."

Mr Burton drew particular attention to the observation of Lord Rodger of Earlsferry in *Fairchild*, commenting on *Bonnington*, that it was "enough that the defendant's wrongful act materially contributed to the claimant's injury" and that accordingly "the law is not applying the causa sine qua non or "but for" test of causation".

33.   In *McGhee v National Coal Board* the House of Lords was concerned with another problem of fault exposure to unacceptable conditions at work over a lengthy

period. In consequence Mr McGhee developed dermatitis. His case was that the provision of a shower would have reduced but not eliminated the risk of dermatitis, which might have developed in any event. Lord Reid commented:

> "From a broad and practical viewpoint I can see no substantial difference between saying that what the defendant did materially increased the risk of injury to the pursuer and in saying that what the defendant did made a material contribution to his injury."

34.   Lord Simon regarded it as unreal to draw a sharp distinction between the breach of duty and causation. Lord Salmon, too, suggested that the distinction between materially increasing the risk of contracting the disease and having materially contributed to causing the disease was "far too unreal to be recognised by the common law". In short, not altogether helpfully to Mr Burton's present submissions, together with Lord Simon and Lord Reid, in the context then receiving attention, he examined and rejected the purported distinction.

35.   Mr Burton drew attention to the text in Munkman on Employer's Liability (13th edition, 2001) summarising the test in the context of the liability of employers for accidents at work. The proposition he relies on is summarised in this passage:

> "The courts are prepared to infer that increased exposure to risk has contributed to, and hence caused, the accident. Examples provided to sustain this proposition include *Lee v Nursery* [1945] 1 All ER 387; *Cork v Kirby* [1952] 2 All ER 402; *McClymont v Glascow* [1971] SLT 45."

36.   Mr Burton referred specifically to the first two decisions. In my view, however, both decisions must now be approached with considerable caution. *Bonnington* made plain that the normal burden of proof was not to be shifted. Referring to this line of authority, Lord Reid agreed that a court should not be "astute to find against any party", but should apply the ordinary standards. Lord Tucker emphasised that the question whether the plaintiff had proved that the injury complained of had been caused by breach of duty depended on the particular facts and the proper inferences to be drawn from them. The same principle was described by Lord Keith of Avonholme as "elementary". To the extent that in *McGhee*, Lord Wilberforce suggested a different approach to the burden of proof, his views did not find favour when they were considered later in the House of Lords in *Wilsher* and *Fairchild*.

37.   If further emphasis were needed, it is perhaps to be found in the rejection by the House of Lords, again in *Wilsher* and *Fairchild*, of the principle, as Mustill LJ endeavoured to identify it in the Court of Appeal in Wilsher v Essex Area Health Authority [1987] QB 730. He suggested:

> "If it is an established fact that conduct of a particular kind creates a risk that injury will be caused to another or increases an existing risk that injury will ensue; and if the two parties stand in such a relationship that one party owes a duty not to conduct himself in that way; and if the other party does suffer injury of the kind to which the risk related; then the first party is taken to have caused the injury by his breach of duty, even though the existence and extent of the contribution made by the breach cannot be ascertained."

38.   Sir Nicholas Browne-Wilkinson VC disagreed. *Wilsher* was "wholly different" from *McGhee*. The context was clinical negligence. There were a number of possible causes for the development of retrolental fibroplasias, which resulted in the blindness of a premature baby. The defendant failed to take reasonable precautions to reduce excess oxygen. That was one possible cause of the plaintiff's condition, constituting a breach of duty by the defendant which could have caused it. However, although the breach increased the risk that this plaintiff's unhappy condition might develop, liability was not established. As the Vice Chancellor explained, in *McGhee* brick dust was the only explanation for the onset of dermatitis, and the failure "to take a precaution against brick dust causing dermatitis was followed by dermatitis caused by brick dust ... I can see the common sense, if not the logic, of holding that in the absence of any other evidence, the failure to take the precaution caused or contributed to the dermatitis." On the other hand, "a failure to take preventative measures against one out of five possible causes is no evidence as to which of those five caused the injury". In the House of the Lords, the reasoning of the Vice Chancellor was adopted, and that of Mustill LJ rejected. In *Fairchild*, that rejection was endorsed. Lord Bingham supported the reasoning of the Vice Chancellor. Lord Hoffman rejected the broad principle identified by Mustill LJ. Lord Rodger of Earlsferry stated in terms that this approach would result "in obvious injustice to the defendants."

39.   In the House of Lords in *Wilsher v Essex Area Health Authority* the only opinion was given by Lord Bridge of Harwich, with whom the other members of the House agreed. Lord Bridge commented that the decision in *McGhee* did not support any attempt "to extract from it some esoteric principle which in some way modifies, as a matter of law, the nature of the burden of proof of causation" after a breach of duty had been established. This particular observation is no longer treated as authoritative (see per Lord Bingham of Cornhill in Fairchild at paragraph 22; per Lord Nicholls at paragraph 45; per Lord Hoffmann at paragraph 70; per Lord Rodger of Earlsferry at paragraph 150), but its rejection does not advance Mr Burton's argument. The correctness of the decision in *McGhee* – that the claim for damages failed, notwithstanding that the defendant health authority's breach of duty increased the risk of injury to the plaintiff – was not doubted.

40.   *Fitzgerald v Lane* was an action for personal injuries by a plaintiff who was struck by two vehicles. The first threw him onto its bonnet, from whence he was propelled into the road, where another car struck him. Four possible causes of his tetraplegia were established. For present purposes it is sufficient only to notice that this Court was plainly influenced by the decision of the majority of the Court of Appeal in the then recently decided *Wilsher*, and in particular the principle identified by Mustill LJ, now deprived of authority. As Nourse LJ put it:

> "... The majority have now shown us that the decision in the McGhee case established a principle whose application is wide enough to bridge the evidential gap in this case as comprehensively as it did in the other two. The decision of the majority now binds this Court ... a benevolent principle smiles on these factual uncertainties and melts them all away."

It is unnecessary to comment on the correctness, or otherwise, of the eventual decision in *Fitzgerald,* but sufficient for present purposes to highlight that the apparent benevolence of the principle has not enabled its further extension beyond the limitations laid down by the House of Lords in *Wilsher,* and in *Fairchild.*

41.   The litigation in *Fairchild* arose from the development of industrial disease, mesothelioma, following fault exposure to asbestos fibres at work. The disease may be caused by a single fibre, a few fibres, or many fibres, and once malignancy has developed, the condition is not exacerbated by further exposure. The problem for the plaintiffs was that they had worked for a number of different employers at different sites where they had been negligently exposed to asbestos fibres. The Court of Appeal concluded that causation was not established. Although fault exposure to a fibre or fibres occurred at their places of employment, the plaintiffs could not establish that the fibres which caused the onset of mesothelioma resulted from any particular breach of duty by any particular employee. The court was therefore unable to close the "evidential gap". The House of Lords addressed the problem whether, in the special circumstances, the conventional approach to causation was appropriate, and concluded that the interests of justice required that the normal rules of causation should be relaxed and modified. It was not necessary for the claimant to establish that the disease from which he suffered would not have occurred "but for" an individual defendant's breach of duty. "The ordinary approach to proof of causation" was varied (per Lord Bingham). It was one of those cases where "a lesser degree of causal connection" sufficed (per Lord Nicholls). When medical science could not yet establish which particular moment of fault exposure caused the claimant's condition, it was open to the House of Lords "to formulate a different causal requirement in this class of case" (per Lord Hoffmann). The circumstances in which it may be appropriate to modify or extend the conventional approach to causation were identified by Lord Bingham, Lord Hoffmann and Lord Rodger, but in ways which were not identical. Although Fairchild undoubtedly represents a development in the conventional principles relating to causation, the reasoning does not undermine but rather reinforces what Lord Bingham himself was later to identify in Chester, in the passage quoted in paragraph 30, as "trite law", at any rate in cases of personal injury consequent on an individual, specific occasion of negligence for which (discounting situations like vicarious liability) a single party was responsible.

42.   I must return to *Chester,* to observe that the conclusion of the majority, favouring a narrow development of causation principles to enable the court to uphold the right of a patient to be properly informed by her doctor of the possible risks of agreeing to a surgical procedure, did not dilute the essential principle. (See per Lord Steyn at paragraph 23; per Lord Hope at paragraph 85; per Lord Walker at paragraph 101, applying *Fairchild.*) What happened, in essence, is that the approach to causation was modified to emphasise a wider principle. This was a policy decision with no application to cases like this.

43.   The authorities to which Mr Burton drew attention establish that the "but for" test, applied in its full rigour, should no longer be treated as a single, invariable test applicable to causation issues, in whatever circumstances they may arise. The question in the present appeal is whether *Fairchild,* and the series of decisions developing the law of which it represented the culmination (subject of course to subsequent developments) have any application here. In my judgment, in agreement with the judge, they do not. On any view, it would be absurd to describe this unfortunate accident as exceptional. Accidents like this happen all too frequently, and

even though negligence by an identified tortfeasor is established, the question still remains whether the negligence caused the claimant's injuries. A successful claim for damages for personal injuries consequent on negligence or breach of duty requires the court to be satisfied that the injuries were indeed consequent on the defendant's negligence. Even if it may have some application in different situations, the distinction sought to be drawn by Mr Burton between material contribution to damage and material contribution to the risk of damage has no application to cases where the claimant's injuries arose from a single incident. In this Court any modification of the principles relating to causation in the context of claims for damages for personal injury must be approached with the greatest caution. Certainly, however the law of causation may develop, save in the House of Lords, it cannot develop in a way which revives or is dependent on the approach adopted by Mustill LJ in *Wilsher*, and subsequently twice rejected in the House of Lords. That route is closed. In reality, for the purposes of cases like this, trite law is unchanged.

44.   The breadth of Mr Burton's submission may have distracted attention from a single but potent consideration. In the context of causation, the two words "but for" are shorthand. They encapsulate a principle understood by lawyers, but applied literally, or as if the two words embody the entire principle, the words can mislead. They may convey the impression that the claimant's claim for damages for personal injuries must fail unless he can prove that the defendant's negligence was the only, or the single, or even, chronologically the last cause of his injuries. The authorities demonstrate that such an impression would be incorrect. The claimant is required to establish a causal link between the negligence of the defendant and his injuries, or, in short, that his injuries were indeed consequent on the negligence. Although, on its own it is not enough for him to show that the defendant created an increased risk of injury, the necessary causal link would be established if, as a matter of inference from the evidence, the defendant's negligence made a material contribution to the claimant's injuries. As Lord Rodger explained and demonstrated in *Fairchild*, there was "nothing new" in Lord Reid's comment in *Bonnington* that what was required was for the plaintiff to make it appear at least "that, on a balance of probabilities, a breach of duty caused, or materially contributed to, his injury". Lord Rodger observed that there was ample authority for the proposition in English and Scots law, both before and after Lord Reid had, in effect, treated it as so elementary that it required no support from authority.

45.   This, as it seems to me, was precisely reflected in the approach taken by the judge. In paragraph 74, he referred to the "but for" principle, but accepted, alternatively, that it would be sufficient for the claimant to prove "on the balance of probabilities, that the absence of proper non-slip paint caused or materially contributed to his slip and subsequent fall". In short, the judge correctly identified the appropriate principle, and rightly rejected the suggestion made to him that *Fairchild* had any application to the present case. Thereafter he examined what he described as a fundamental difficulty arising from the argument that the appellant's claim should succeed because he had established that the surface of the wall carried an increased risk of a slip when compared with the risk of slipping if the wall had been painted with non-slip paint. However as he had already correctly directed himself in law, for the reasons I have endeavoured to explain, it was not strictly necessary for him to have decided this issue.

46.   The single question, therefore, is whether any proper basis for interfering with the judge's factual findings on causation has been shown. This has not been an easy decision, and I shall not disguise that as I have reflected on it, my view of the case has varied. This hesitation has been reinforced by my concern about the possible impact of the judge's erroneous failure to recognise that the application of non-slip paint was intended to protect the inebriated as well as the sober.

47.   Mr Faulks's submissions on the facts had the attraction of simplicity. The judge remained unpersuaded that the claimant's slip was caused, or materially contributed to, by the absence of non-slip paint on the surface of the wall. Non-slip paint would have made the surface less slippery, but not non-slippery, nor removed altogether the risk of a slip by someone walking on the top of the wall with wet feet. So the risk of a slip was inevitable, and the fact that the claimant slipped did not of itself demonstrate that the slip resulted from the absence of non-slip paint. There was therefore no sufficient evidence to establish a causal link between the negligent absence of non-slip paint and the appellant's subsequent fall. He reminded us of the need to respect the factual conclusion reached by the judge, a consideration of particular force here, where the judgment under consideration has examined the issues with great care.

48.   This is persuasive reasoning. The practical reality of the case is that the judge was not satisfied on the balance of probabilities that the appellant's accident would have been avoided if non-slip paint had been used on the surface of the wall. In short, the risk represented by the absence of non-slip paint was just that, an increased risk which in his judgment, as a matter of fact, did not cause or materially contribute to the appellant's accident. These are findings with which this Court should not interfere.

49.   For these reasons, this appeal must be dismissed.

Healy v Cosmosair Plc & Others 28 July 2005 QBD Eady J. (EWHC 1657)

International Travel Law Journal [Bathing in the Waters of Truth] 2005 ITLJ 167. (Saggerson)

Introduction

In June 2002 Mr. Healy (a family man in his mid-thirties) went on holiday to the Colina Da Lapa apartments in Carvoeiro in Portugal. At about 8pm on 11 June after a day out in the town with his children (part of which was spent watching Ireland play World Cup football) he returned to the apartments where he was persuaded to join his son Jack in the pool. As he went to jump in (he alleged) he lost his footing and fell, twisting in the air as he did so, and landing at about 90 degrees with his head hitting the bottom of the pool. He broke his neck as a result.

Issues

The basis of the Claimant's claim against the tour operator was pursuant to the express terms of the package holiday contract and regulation 15 of the Package Travel (Etc.) Regulations 1992. It was alleged that:

(a) The pool terrace tiles caused Mr. Healy to slip;

(b) The tiles were deficient and not of a reasonable (non-slip) standard;

(c) The tiles did not comply with Portuguese regulations that required a 2 metre non-slip ring around the edge of the pool (there being only 410mm of non-slip material);

(d) These failing constituted a breach of contract and an improper performance of the obligations under the holiday contract that had caused the accident entitling Mr. Healy to damages.

The Defendant raised a number of issues:

(i)   On the facts it was alleged with the help of a number of eye witnesses that the Claimant had deliberately dived into the (shallow) pool;

(ii) The Claimant's judgment was impaired by alcohol;

(iii) In any event the terrace tiles on which the slip was alleged *did* comply with Portuguese non-slip regulations for 3 reasons. First because they were sold and supplied under the description of non-slip. Secondly, because they were indeed non-slip when dry and thirdly the Portuguese architect and local authority regulator had certified the complex as compliant with local regulations at the time the recently built resort had been completed.

(iv) The Claimant could not prove he had slipped on a deficient tile.

Just in case, however, the Defendant joined in the management of apartments as Part 20 Defendants on the basis of a written indemnity clause which provided so far as is material as follows:

> "The Hotelier shall indemnify and keep indemnified Cosmos against all losses, liabilities, claims or expenses for or in respect of injury ... which may arise form any cause whatsoever arising out of or in connection with the supply of services to Cosmos (excluding the negligence or default of Cosmos ... but including the failure of the Hotelier to comply with [local] laws. Degrees and regulations ...".

The Facts

Save that he was sure that he would not have dived into the pool, Mr. Healy did not know what caused him to lose his footing. Endless evidence was forthcoming from various eye witnesses. Those in the pool (all relatives of Mr. Healy) describing an accidental loss of control, and those standing by (all independent) describing a dive – but importantly all describing a sort of shallow or racing dive of the sort one might expect to form an entry into shallow water.

There was also evidence from the Defendant's local representative to the effect that one member of the family had more or less admitted to seeing the whole thing in the immediate aftermath of the incident and that it *was* a dive. The judge thought this evidence unconvincing.

The clincher for the Claimant on this vital issue of fact was probably the medical evidence which described the nature of his neck fracture and concluded that the type of injury sustained was only consistent with a (more or less) 90 degree impact with the floor of the pool – head first in other words. This flatly contradicted the independent eye witnesses various descriptions of a shallow or racing dive.

Accordingly, the judge was able to conclude on the balance of probabilities that the entry into the pool came about other than by means of a voluntary dive and that the probabilities pointed to an "uncontrolled fall".

Slippery Tiles?

So far so good from the Claimant's point of view, but was this uncontrolled fall triggered by a slip on tiles that were wet, slippery and failed to comply with Portuguese non-slip requirements?

There was a volume of anecdotal evidence from various family and independent sources (including the Defendant's own local representative) to the effect that the terrace tiles surrounding the pool were slippery when wet and a number of previous slipping incidents were revealed. The expert health and safety evidence was agreed that when wet the tiles were as slippery as smooth glazed tiles even though they were to some extent "textured". Again, one senses from the judgment that the expert evidence was more compelling than the anecdotal evidence which was repeatedly described as being "impressionistic". When dry, the non-slip effect was as good as the 410mm dedicated non-slip surface that was there (which the Claimant alleged should have been 2 metres wide to accord with Portuguese standards).

Breach of Portuguese Regulations

For the second time in recent history (see also *Singh v Libra Holidays* 2003 EWHC 276 QB; 2003 *ITLJ* 123) a Defendant attempted to excuse what was plain failure to comply with specific local regulations on the local regulators or enforcers. The judge said, no doubt risking a statement of the obvious:

> "*I came to the decision, as a matter of construction, that the local stipulation for a two-metre (non-slip) strip is not met by the provision of a strip of 410mm.*"

> "*...I should have been inclined to hold that the Defendant was to that extent liable for improper performance.*"

The Defendant's contention that the court could not go behind the certificates provided by the architect and the local authorities (each by implication accepting that the textured terrace tiles constituted non-slip tiles for the purpose of measuring the 2 metre strip) was rejected – not least of all because the stipulation that there should be a non-slip "strip" (as indeed there was if only of 410mm) was inapt to describe the whole of the pool terrace covered by the terrace tiles.

Causation

For the second time in the space of 12 months (see *Clough v First Choice Holidays and Flights Limited* 28 January 2005), despite the judge's findings of fact indicating that the Claimant and his witnesses were "bathed in the waters of truth" (although the actual expression has been appropriated from another judgment) the Claimant's case fell apart on causation.

The Claimant had two hurdles to surmount on causation. First, that his uncontrolled fall was caused by a slip, and secondly, that he slipped on a *wet* terrace tile. The judge reminded himself by quoting from *Clough* that people *do* slip from time to time whether or not the surface is non-slip or wet. He was also concerned about expert biomechanical evidence suggesting that a fall (from the general area where the Claimant recalled being) straight into the pool without touching the ground was not a physical possibility, whilst accepting that the Claimant's understandably "patchy" recollection of events meant it was possible he had touched the ground on his way into the pool but simply did not recollect so doing.

Of even more concern was the fact that originally (and for some time as the proceedings progressed) the Claimant's contention had been that the terrace tiles were wet because they were in an area shaded by the pool bar and would not have dried in the period since most guests had finished using the pool at the end of the afternoon. At trial, the Claimant's attention had re-focused on the suggestion that the tiles were wet because his son had hopped out of the pool to get a soft drink from the bar dripping water on the tiles in the process.

The "shaded area" theory was not supported by the health and safety experts who concluded in broad terms that the area would not have been shaded for long enough for this to be an issue. The problem with the evidence about the son was that it was a very late addition to the factual matrix (the evidence was served only a few months before the trial) with the almost inevitable consequences that the judge was hesitant about its reliability.

In the event, the trial judge did not decide even on the balance of probabilities *what* had triggered the Claimant's "uncontrolled fall" and he concluded that the Claimant had failed to prove (the burden being on him) that he had been on a wet terrace tile at the time the uncontrolled fall was triggered.

Not Proven

> *"It is of course* possible *that the Claimant slipped on a wet tile less than 2 metres from the edge of the pool; it is also* possible *that the area had become wet by reason of Jack getting out of the pool. Nevertheless in these circumstances it is difficult conscientiously to draw the conclusion that the Claimant has proved on the balance of probabilities that he actually slipped on a wet area of tiling within the relevant margin."*

The outcome on the main action was a resounding "not proven" and in this the result shares some startling similarities with that of *Clough.*

SECTION 3

CONSTRUCTION OF THE PACKAGE TRAVEL, PACKAGE HOLIDAYS & PACKAGE TOURS REGULATIONS 1992

Section 3

CONSTRUCTION OF THE PACKAGE TRAVEL, PACKAGE HOLIDAYS AND PACKAGE TOURS REGULATIONS 1992

Cases in this Section

6. Keppel-Palmer v *Exsus Travel and Royal Westmoreland Villas*   **Page 218**

To qualify as "transport" within regulation 2 of the Package Travel [Etc.] Regulations 1992 the transport had to be more than *de minimis* when looked at in the context of the holiday arrangements (inlcuding the price) as a whole and should not be merely ancillary to another package component such as accommodation. Agency: liability of retailers.

7. Josephs v *Sunworld Ltd (t/a Sunworld Holidays)*   **Page 222**

Multiple, cumulative breaches of regulations 4, 5, 12, 13 and 15 of the Package Travel (Etc) Regulations 1992 in respect of pre-contractual promotional material and the supply of contractual services.

8. Minhas v *Imperial Travel Ltd*   **Page 223**

Liability of retailers under Package Travel [Etc.] Regulations 4 and 5. Villa holiday not up to standard. Travel agent was a "retailer" and because it had accepted the money for the holiday it was "the other party to the contract" under regulation 15. [Query whether rightly decided without a determination of the capacity in which the money was accepted.]

9. Lambert v *Travelsphere Limited*   **Page 224**

"Sars" virus. Regulations 12 and 13 of the Package Travel [Etc.] Regulations 1992. A tour operator is only constrained to alter significantly an essential term of the holiday contract to trigger a consumer's right to regulation 13 remedies when there is no "flicker of hope" that each part of the original contract can be honoured.

10. Clark and Others v *Travelsphere Limited*   **Page 227**

"Constrained" in regulation 12 means "forced". Foreign and Commonwealth Office advice.

11. Westerman v *Travel Promotions Ltd*   **Page 231**

Application of Package Travel [Etc.] Regulation 14(2) and (3) –"suitable alternative arrangements"; compensation where appropriate.

12. Martin v *Travel Promotions Ltd*   **Page 232**

Package Travel [Etc.] Regulations 1992 regulations 14(2) and (3). Delay to an internal flight resulting in missed international connection was a failure to provide a significant proportion of package services contracted for. Claimants entitled to small amount of damages but not the cost of alternative first class international flights.

3.1 Definition of Package Components

Pre-arranged combination – Inclusive price – Regulation 2

R (The Association of British Travel Agents Ltd) ("ABTA") v The Civil Aviation Authority ("CAA") and The Secretary of State for Trade and Industry [2006] EWHC 13 (Admin) (16 January 2006)

GOLDRING J.

The issue

1.   The claimant is the Association of British Travel Agents ("ABTA"). It is the leading trade association for travel agents and tour operators. The defendant is the Civil Aviation Authority ("CAA"). The Secretary of State as Interested Party has not appeared or made representations. One of the CAA's functions is "the licensing of the provision of accommodation in aircraft." At issue in this application for judicial review are the circumstances in which a travel agent is obliged to have an Air Travel Organiser's Licence ("ATOL"). At the heart of the dispute between ABTA and the CAA is the definition of "package" for the purposes of the Civil Aviation (Air Travel Organisers' Licensing) Regulations 1995 as amended in 2003 ("the ATOL Regulations"). ABTA challenges the CAA's view in that regard contained in its Guidance of 4 March 2005 under the rubric "Sale of Air Package Arrangements: Advice on the need to provide consumer protection" ("the Guidance"). It sets out how the CAA intends to interpret and enforce (including by possible criminal sanction) the applicable regulations.

2.   The CAA also takes the point that judicial review is not in any event an appropriate remedy in the case.

The statutory background

The Civil Aviation Act 1982

3.   The CAA was constituted by the Civil Aviation Act 1971. The provisions relating to it were consolidated in the Civil Aviation Act 1982 ("the Act"). It is section 3(b) of the Act, as amended, which provides that a function of the CAA is "the licensing of the provision of accommodation in aircraft."

4.   Section 71 of the Act provides that,

"(1) Provision may be made by regulations made by the Secretary of State for securing that a person does not...

(a) make available, as a principal or an agent, accommodation for the carriage of persons...on flights...or

(b) hold himself out as a person who, either as a principal or an agent or without disclosing his capacity, may make such accommodation available, unless he...holds and complies with the terms of a licence issued in pursuance of the regulations..."

5.   As Lord Justice Gibson said when giving the judgment of the Court of Appeal in R (on the application of Jet Services Ltd.) v Civil Aviation Authority [2001] 2 All ER (Comm) 759 at page 771,

> "The need for such licensing was perceived following a number of financial failures by tour operators providing package holidays...which left holiday makers stranded abroad or with no flight to take them on the holiday for which they had paid."

6.   The ATOL is such a licence.

...

43.   As it seems to me, what the CAA is effectively saying to Government is this. First, there is an inexorable trend towards buying separate travel facilities. Second, what is in substance the sale of separate facilities may appear to the consumer to be a package when it is not. Third, the sale of such "quasi-packages" is outside the protection of the Directive, the PTR and the ATOL Regulations. They only protect the consumer if the substance of the transaction is a real package. In other words, the definition of package in the Regulations only encompasses packages "narrowly defined." It does not encompass "quasi-packages". For in such a situation there is in substance "no contractual package." The consumer may think he is protected when he is not. Fourth, the only way this lacuna in the law can be filled is by legislation.

44.   The submission appears to accept (and it seems to me to be the case) that whether the transaction takes place on the internet or at the travel agent cannot affect its substance.

Guidance Note 26

45.   The Guidance Note was issued in March 2005: in other words, a little over 12 months after the Advice to Government.

46.   In paragraph 1 what is said to be the "Background" is set out.

> "1.1 This Guidance Note deals with the financial protection of holidaymakers. It has been produced to help travel organisers and agents understand the definition of an air package set out in the relevant...Directive...the [PTR] and the...[ATOL Regulations]...it also takes account of decisions of the European Court...It is a response to market developments such as split contracts and is designed to help travel organisers and travel agents decide what parts of their businesses need ATOL protection."

47.   In fact, the Guidance Note affects not only holidaymakers. It deals with the sale or offer for sale of any sort of travel package.

> "1.2 This Guidance...explains the types of air package business which a travel company is required to protect under an...ATOL. The Note should be read in conjunction with the Regulations. The purpose of this Guidance...is to explain the background to the Regulations and to offer an interpretation of certain provisions. Only the courts can give a determinative view on the law...

1.4 The...Regulations were amended on 1 October 2003 with the intention that the practice of splitting an air package contract by way of separately documenting the flight, accommodation and other services, was brought within the scope of the ATOL Regulations. As part of the amendment, the ATOL Regulations incorporated a description of a package identical to that contained in the PTR...

1.5...[which] mirrors the definition...in the [Directive]."

...

50.   Under the heading "package," the Guidance states at paragraph 2.3,

"The definition is at paragraph 1.5. One reasonable test is to consider what the consumer thinks he is getting when he approached the agent or travel organiser; artificial arrangements to sell components at separate times and with separate billing would not mean that a package had not been sold."

51.   Under the heading "pre-arranged," the Guidance states at paragraph 2.4,

"Where a combination of facilities is advertised in any form, including in a brochure, on Teletext or on a website, this will be taken as evidence of a pre-arrangement. Additionally, if a combination of travel facilities is offered from which a consumer is able to choose their (sic) holiday arrangements, then these will also be taken as evidence of prearrangement; it does not mean that it is necessary to have made reservations or taken allocations in advance."

52.   Under the heading "inclusive price," the Guidance states at paragraph 2.5,

"This term refers to the price of the package. It does not matter if the cost of a package is made up of separate sums relating to the value of each element (travel, accommodation, other ancillary tourist services). In these circumstances, the whole arrangement can still be sold at an inclusive price."

53.   Paragraph 2.6 states that,

"...it should also be noted that whether a combination of travel facilities does or does not amount to a package for the purposes of the Regulations will depend on the facts of each individual case; the mere fact that the word "package" is not used by the consumer is not decisive."

...

55.   Paragraph 3.3 states that,

"The introduction of new sales channels, and particularly web based sales, has enabled travel companies to source individual items rather than simply retail another company's travel arrangements to their customers. In addition, the sale of individual holiday items over the internet and the rapid expansion of no-frills airlines has led consumers to expect that their travel arrangements can be "dynamically packaged" or "tailor made" to suit their own requirements. Consequently, travel companies are able to construct packages from individual components and arrangements are quite different from the scenario at 3.2."

56.   Paragraph 3.4 states that,

"As travel agents' sales of combinations of arrangements, including air transport, potentially become packages, there are circumstances in which travel agents will need an ATOL to provide the public with financial protection for this activity. The following sections describe the ways in which the sale by an agent of combinations of travel arrangements, including air transport, may become sales of a package with a consequent requirement of an ATOL; this guidance is based upon the regulatory requirements..."

57.   Paragraph 3.5 states that,

"In the ultimate analysis the question of whether an ATOL is required for any individual transaction will depend upon the particular facts of that transaction. The examples given in sections 4 and 5...are just that- examples. "

...

58.   Paragraph 4 deals with those situations where an ATOL is required.

"...4.2 If travel facilities are advertised by an agent in a brochure, a shop window display, on Teletext, in a newspaper advertisement or on a website, and it is clear that these can be combined to form a package, or the agent offers to provide individual package quotations based on an advertised range of options, then such packages require ATOL cover..."

"4.3 If an agent offers a consumer a choice of travel facilities, including a flight, the resulting sale will be a package requiring the agent to hold an ATOL...."

"4.4 If a consumer requests a flight and accommodation and/or other tourist services to a particular resort or destination and asks an agent for details of suitable arrangements and the agent provides information on a combination of services, rather than a package from an ATOL holder, then this is a package under the [Regulations]..."

"4.5 In some instances a consumer may have been offered an ATOL protected package, but asks the agent whether there is a cheaper alternative; if the agent decides to offer an alternative that he has selected himself, rather than a package from another ATOL holder, then the agent will need his own ATOL."

4.6 Following the 2003 ATOL...amendment, if an agent puts together a package utilising a scheduled flight, provided to the consumer on a "ticket provider" basis, (ie the consumer paid for the flight and received a valid ticket for travel [from the agent] immediately in return,) then the package will require to be covered by an ATOL."

4.7 If an agent advertises that he can provide tailor-made holiday arrangements or he can provide dynamic packages, then he will need an ATOL to cover the majority of such sales..."

4.8 If an agent has taken commitments or contracts with a supplier for any item offered as part of an air package, then the package will require an ATOL."

59.   Paragraph 5 sets out examples of where an ATOL is not needed.

"5.2 A consumer may approach an agent to buy a number of services which the customer specifies with no influence from the agent...this is not defined as a package...as there is no prearrangement by the agent and the agent cannot be held responsible for a service over whose choice the agent had no influence. All services must...be separately documented. If one or more elements are not available and the agent recommends alternatives/changes, this may become a package."

"5.4 A consumer buys a flight from an agent (which may be ATOL protected) and at a later date returns to buy accommodation. The sale of the two services at different times does not unless they are linked by documentation, create a package. However such transactions must genuinely take place at different times and cannot be a device to avoid providing package protection."

60.   In the "Summary" in paragraph 6 it states,

"6.1 Travel firms which sell air package arrangements which they have constructed themselves will in the majority of cases need to hold an ATOL to protect those sales. From the agent's perspective this means that if they have selected specific travel components, or they have offered for sale travel facilities including a flight, then the resultant sale will usually be a package. From the customer's perspective, if he approaches an agent and explains that he wants to buy a flight and accommodation and/or other services, or merely that he wants to buy a holiday, then it is likely that the arrangements will have been sold or offered for sale to him as a package."

61.   Paragraph 6.3 deals with consequences to the travel agent who fails to comply.

"The CAA undertakes monitoring of travel firms to ensure compliance with the ATOL Regulations. With the issue of this new guidance the CAA will be carrying out increased monitoring of travel agents, and firms should be aware that it is the CAA's policy to prosecute in cases where firms have been made aware of the compliance requirement but have failed to obtain a licence..."

62.   This is clearly stating that the Guidance now sets out the basis upon which the CAA will monitor and prosecute travel agents, among others.

The CAA's current advice to consumers

63.   On its website (and in a leaflet) the CAA seeks to explain what a package is. Under the heading "How can I tell if a holiday is a package," it states,

> "The best guide is that if you pay one firm, in a single transaction, for a range of holiday items...it's a package. It can be offered in a brochure or on a website, and will normally be sold at a single inclusive price. Some points to look out for are:
>
> - If you ask a travel agent to meet your specific requirements...it won't normally be a package.
>
> - ...some tour operators offer brochures (or websites) from which you can create a "tailor made" holiday by choosing your flights and hotel from limited lists, and what you buy from these operators will usually be a package.
>
> - Many websites...will offer you the ability to put together a package by choosing a flight from the airline, and then choosing the other items you want. But you may find that the firm providing the hotel or car hire is quite separate from the airline, and that you pay for the two items separately. If so, it won't be a package."

64.   Mr. Haddon-Cave submits this guidance is correct. It effectively defines a package more narrowly than does the Guidance. It reflects a correct understanding of the ATOL Regulations.

.....

79.   In my view, this is a case appropriate for judicial review. I say so for several reasons.

80.   The CAA is a statutory body. It is the regulatory and prosecution authority for the travel industry. Although the Guidance is said to be only that and subject to the decision of the court, it is elsewhere described as formal and is plainly intended to be a basis of regulating and possibly prosecuting travel agents. It says as much in paragraph 6. It would not be appropriate for a public body to regulate and possibly prosecute on the basis of guidance which is manifestly wrong in law. It is in the public interest, if that be the case, that such erroneous guidance be withdrawn.

81.   The Guidance has the clearest effect on travel agents. Most will obtain ATOLs on its basis. Doing so will incur substantial cost. That is not hypothetical. If the Guidance is not in accordance with the law, that cost will be unnecessarily incurred. Although Mr. Griffiths submits the travel agent may take his own advice and act accordingly, given the possible sanctions, it would be a brave travel agent who did so. In the final analysis he would leave himself open to the possibility of up to two years' imprisonment. It is not in the public interest for travel agents effectively to be pressurised into obtaining ATOLs if the law manifestly does not require them to.

82.   The claimant's case is that on a proper understanding of the ATOL Regulations parts of the Guidance cannot on any factual basis be right. They reflect a misunderstanding of the law. It is not in my view necessary in such circumstances for

the claimant to agree some facts upon which the court could rule. There is no question of the court considering hypothetical factual situations.

... It is eminently a matter for the court to decide what the ordinary and natural meaning of a statutory provision is. In most cases it will do so with a specific factual background. However, if the words in dispute are incapable of having the meaning ascribed to them the court can say so. That is not hypothetical.

... it seems to me apparent that in the Guidance the CAA has taken a different and wider view of the effect of the ATOL Regulations than it has often, although not invariably, taken previously. The CAA's apparent inconsistency as to the legal definition of a package does not of itself help me in construing the ATOL Regulations. However, it may suggest that the CAA is not as confident in the legal effect of the Regulations is as is now submitted. It could lend force to a suggestion by ABTA that the CAA is by the Guidance seeking to legislate by the back door. For if the effect of the Guidance is effectively to force travel agents to take ATOLs because they do not wish to take the risk of not doing so, the lacuna apparently previously accepted by the CAA would for practical purposes be closed. That reinforces my view that if the Guidance is manifestly wrong, the court should say so.

...

The argument on the merits

90.   Mr. Haddon-Cave submits the following is the appropriate approach when construing the ATOL Regulations.

91.   First, the words should be given their ordinary and natural meaning in their context, having regard to their obvious legislative purpose of providing protection to passengers who have paid for flight accommodation: see Jet Services (above).

92.   Second, Mr. Haddon-Cave submits that what amounts to a package for the purposes of the ATOL Regulations is a question of substance, not form. If the reality is that what the travel agent sells the consumer is a package, then the form in which it is sold is irrelevant. He submits that the invariable legal effect of the sale of a package by the travel agent will be a single contract between the consumer and the travel agent. Mr. Griffiths agrees that what is important is the substance of the transaction. He agrees that such things as the billing arrangements are irrelevant to that substance. He submits however that the contractual arrangements "should not be allowed to result in the non-application" of the regulatory regime.

93.   Third, Mr. Haddon-Cave submits that the meaning of package for the purposes of the ATOL Regulations should be the same under the PTR Regulations. Again, I do not understand that to be in dispute.

94.   Fourth, for there to be a package, the three requirements under the ATOL Regulations must be satisfied. It must be "pre-arranged." There must be a "combination." It must be "sold or offered for sale at an inclusive price." I do not understand Mr. Griffiths to disagree.

95.   Fifth, Mr. Haddon-Cave submits that the mischief at which the 2003 amendments were directed was the public being misled by "contract splitting:" in other words, directed against the travel agent who sold what was in reality a package

and pretended that he was selling separate or unconnected components of a journey. There is an issue about this.

96.   Sixth, Mr. Haddon-Cave submits that given this is a penal Regulation, if there is any doubt or ambiguity as to its meaning, it should be resolved in favour of the travel agent. I agree. That of course does not necessarily mean, as Mr. Griffiths emphasises, it must be interpreted in a narrow way. If his submissions as to the width of the meaning of ATOL Regulations are unambiguously right, then that wide interpretation must be applied.

A sale or offer for sale "at an inclusive price"

97.   This is at the heart of Mr. Haddon-Cave's submissions. His submission comes to this. An inclusive price is a single, comprehensive or overall price. It is more than a total or aggregate price. "Inclusive" connotes something extra. It is analogous to the distinction between the sale in the supermarket of "three for the price of two," as opposed to the bill produced at the checkout. The bill is simply an arithmetical total of different and separate purchases. An "inclusive price" imports an element of things tied or linked together in a financial sense. If it is a package, one element cannot be removed. The buyer has the choice of taking or leaving it. A sale at an inclusive price does not mean, submits Mr. Haddon-Cave, that the individual components cannot be identified, or made up in different ways; for example, with different choices of hotels or flights or whatever.

98.   If, submits Mr. Haddon-Cave, an inclusive price is no more than a total price, there would be no purpose in the reference to "inclusive." It would be enough for it to be an "inclusive price" if the travel agent presented the consumer with a bill containing several different and separate elements. As he rhetorically puts it, what on the CAA's case would not be inclusive?

99.   Subsection (i), submits Mr. Haddon-Cave, means that if the reality is that the sale is of a package, the travel agent cannot escape that reality merely by submitting different accounts for different components.

100.   Mr. Griffiths disagrees. He submits that the concept of an "inclusive price" focuses on whether the different components are sold or offered for sale together, on a composite basis. That is emphasised by subsection (i). It is enough that the travel agent should be asking the consumer to pay a price which may reflect several completely separate or discrete components of a holiday, provided they were bought or offered for sale together. It is irrelevant that each component may be provided by a different supplier without any connection with another supplier or that one component has no relationship, whether financial or in any other way, with another component. The total amount due represents an inclusive price (whether on a single bill or different bills representing the different component parts). The price is "inclusive" if it is no more than the arithmetical total of different and discrete components provided by any number of suppliers through the agency of the travel agent. In such a case the travel agent will be selling or offering to sell a package holiday. In other words, the price may be inclusive and what is sold a package irrespective of the number of different contractual relationships there may be.

101.   Mr. Haddon-Cave further submits that if the substance of the sale is of a package at an "inclusive price," there will only be one contract between the consumer and the travel agent. If what is sold amounts to the sale of several separate components with different legal characteristics: for example, the sale of a flight on behalf of one principal: the sale of a hotel room on behalf of a different one and so on, then what is sold will not be a package. In short, Mr. Haddon-Cave submits that giving the words "inclusive price" their ordinary and natural meaning will result in there being a single contract between the travel agent who sells the package and the consumer who buys it. A single contract is a characteristic of the sale of any package. An arrangement involving several contracts between the consumer and different parties cannot amount to a package. The ATOL Regulations go no further than preventing the travel agent falsely separating the components of what in truth is a single contract.

....

107.   In support of his (further) submission that the English law of agency is not excluded by the PTR and the ATOL Regulations, Mr. Haddon-Cave relies upon the decision of Mr. Justice Douglas Brown in Hone v Going Places Leisure Travel MA993390.

...

109.   Mr. Justice Douglas Brown held that

> "[Regulation 15] taken with...Regulation 2, does not...make a retailer liable for the performance of the contract unless...[the] agent is acting for an undisclosed principal in which case the claimant can sue either principal or agent...[or] the retailer, either on his own or jointly with another operator provides the package."

110.   He found that the first was the case on the facts. The defendant only disclosed he was acting for a principal after the contract was made. In the Court of Appeal (reported at [2001] EWCA Civ 947), Lord Justice Longmore, with whose judgment Lord Justice Henry and Mr. Justice Carnworth (as he then was) agreed, said that by Regulation 15, the other party to the contract was responsible for the proper performance of the contract, whoever actually performed the service.

...

112.   Mr. Griffiths disagrees. He relies on both the Directive and the PTR as showing that there can be a "package" where different components are provided by two or more different principals.

...

116.   In short, the language used in both the Directive and the PTR envisage that there may be more than one contract in a "package." The English law of agency does not apply. Construing a "package" to embrace a combination of elements supplied by two or more principals is perfectly natural. There may be a "package" when there is more than one contract involving the travel agent and the consumer. The word "inclusive" must be construed in that light.

"Pre-arranged"

117.   Mr. Haddon-Cave submits that the word "arranged" in its ordinary and natural meaning means something that is put together. "Pre-arranged" means something that is put together by the travel agent before the consumer sees it. The ordinary and natural meaning of "pre-arranged" having regard to the wording in subsection (ii) means, first, that the combination can be put together at any time up to the sale; second, that the consumer can wholly dictate the component parts of the package.

118.   It follows, submits Mr. Haddon-Cave, that advice or information from the travel agent is not necessarily needed for something to be "pre-arranged."

119.   In support of that submission Mr. Haddon-Cave relies on the decision of the European Court of Justice in *Club-Tour, Viagens e Turismo SA v Garrido* [2002] ECR 1-4051. In that case, among other things, the European Court held that Article 2(1) of the Directive,

> "...must be interpreted so as to include holidays organised in accordance with the consumer's specifications...[it may be] put together at the time the contract is concluded between the travel agent and the consumer..." See paragraphs 19 and 20.

...

A sale or offer for sale at an inclusive price

153.   As it seems to me a number of things follow from the definition of "package" within the ATOL Regulations.

154.   First, the definition contemplates that a travel agent may sell or offer to sell to the consumer the component parts (transport, accommodation and other tourist services) outside a package. In other words, the fact a travel agent may sell or offer to sell these component parts at the same time does not automatically mean that what he is selling or offering to sell is a package.

155.   Second, to amount to a package what is sold or offered for sale must accord with the definition in the ATOL Regulations: crucially, the component parts must be sold or offered for sale at a price which is "inclusive." The sale or offer for sale of the component parts at a price which is not "inclusive" means that what is sold is not a package.

156.   Third, the words "inclusive price" should be given their ordinary and natural meaning. The ordinary and natural meaning of the word "inclusive" connotes more than a mere arithmetical total of the component parts of a price. If the substance of a transaction is the sale by the travel agent of separate and discrete components of (for example) a holiday, with no one part being connected with or dependent upon any other part (other than that they are sold together), to call the resulting price "inclusive" is in my view to stretch the ordinary and natural meaning of that word. It is in reality no more an "inclusive price" than is the total price of goods at the check out of a supermarket. For the sale of a package at an inclusive price the relationship between the component parts of that package must be such as to mean that the consumer is buying and paying for them as a whole: that the sale or

offer for sale of one component part is in some way connected with or dependent on the sale or offer for sale of the others.

157.   Fourth, while not determinative of the meaning, that would accord with what most members of the public would understand when considering the words "inclusive price" in conjunction with the word "package."

158.   Fifth, again, giving the words their ordinary and natural meaning, subsection (i) says no more than this: the "submission of separate accounts for different components shall not cause the arrangements to be other than a package" if the substance of the arrangement is a package: in other words, if, among other things, it is a sale or offer for sale at an "inclusive price."

159.   Sixth, the interpretation above does not involve inserting words. It is a question of interpreting the words which are there.

160.   Seventh, the use of the words "inclusive price" in the context of the Directive and/or the PTR does not in my view mean a broader interpretation should be given to the words: that a meaning different from the ordinary and natural one should be applied.

161.   Eighth, the PTR do not exclude the application of the English law of contract. There is continual reference to "the" contract and "the other party to the contract:" see paragraphs 2, 6(3), 7(1), 8(1) and 9(1). In my view, whether the agreement links the consumer to the organiser or retailer or both depends upon the application of the English law of contract, in particular the law of agency. So too do decisions as to whether the organiser or retailer or both are parties to the contract or whether under Regulation 15, the organiser or retailer or both are liable under it. If by application of the English law of contract the retailer is liable under the contract between him and the consumer, he cannot escape his liability by blaming the lack of proper performance of the obligations under it on someone else. For, additionally, he is responsible for the proper performance by others who may supply services under the contract. Equally under Regulation 16 the retailer must provide sufficient evidence of security. In short, that there may be such an additional obligation upon the retailer does not mean that the normal English law of contract has no relevance. It means that in the case of the sale of a package, the retailer cannot escape liability by pointing to someone else's failure: that he must provide sufficient bonding to give that obligation value.

162.   Furthermore the ATOL Regulations in terms refer to and rely on the English law of contract. Paragraph 3(1)(c) speaks of a person acting as "an agent on behalf of an disclosed and identified principal." Paragraph 3(1A)(a) speaks of a person acting "in the capacity of an agent." The reference in that paragraph to a "single contract" is a reference to the English law of contract. There are further references to people acting as agents or to the capacity in which a person acts: see paragraphs 3(2)(a), 3(2)(b), 4(2)(a).

163.   Although the PTR provide for an extension of liability in the limited and specific ways set out within them, they do not, as it seems to me, mean that a wider definition of "inclusive price" than that understood to be the ordinary and natural one, should be applied.

164.   Although in the Preamble to the Directive and elsewhere the obligations said to arise as a result of it are expressed in broad terms, the Directive relies in its definition of "package" upon the concept of an "inclusive price." For the reasons I have expressed when considering the PTR and the ATOL Regulations it does not seem to me that the Directive results in the broad definition of a package as advocated by the CAA.

165.   Ninth, it does seem to me that a single contract between the travel agent and the consumer will be the usual characteristic of the sale or offer for sale of a package at an inclusive price. However, it is not necessary for present purposes to go as far as deciding that in every sale or offer for sale by a travel agent at an inclusive price there will invariably be a single contract. What is crucial is that the price is inclusive in the way I have defined that concept.

166.   I have of course considered the authorities mentioned earlier in the judgment. However, in the final analysis, they do not seem to me decisive of the issue I have to decide. The issue resolves itself into one of the application of the ordinary and natural meaning of the words used.

167.   ... Applying its ordinary and natural meaning in its context means, first, that the combination can be put together at any time up to the sale. Second, that the consumer can wholly dictate the component parts of the package. Advice or information from the travel agent is not necessarily needed for something to be "pre-arranged."

The Guidance

168.   In the light of my interpretation of the ATOL Regulations, I turn now to the individual paragraphs of the Guidance.

Paragraph 2.5

169.   By omitting any mention of the proper interpretation of an "inclusive price" this paragraph is in my view inadequate and misleading. It does matter if the cost is made up of separate sums. If I am right, it is only if the total of those separate sums amount to an inclusive price as I have defined it that what is sold can be a package.

Paragraph 5.2

170.   First, there can be a pre-arrangement for the purposes of the ATOL Regulations whether or not the consumer specifies those arrangements and whether or not they are modified by the travel agent. The Regulations say so. That is consistent with *Garrido* (see above). It is wrong to state that the travel agent cannot be held responsible for a service over whose choice he had no influence. Second, whether or not the arrangement may be a package depends not upon the features set out in the paragraph, but crucially upon whether what the travel agent sells or offers to sell is at an "inclusive price." Third, whether or not it is sold at an inclusive price depends upon those features to which I have already referred.

171.   In short, therefore, it does seem to me that the paragraph wrongly sets out the law. To some extent, that error benefits ABTA. However, it is wrong to say without more that if "one or more elements are not available and the agent recommends alternatives/changes, this may become a package."

Paragraph 4.3

172.   The paragraph appears to state that there will inevitably and without more be a package for the purposes of the ATOL Regulations when the travel agent offers the consumer a choice of travel arrangements (provided a flight is included). That does not seem to me to be right. It is not enough to bring the arrangements within the ATOL Regulations for the travel agent without more to offer a whole range of different and discrete possible travel arrangements on behalf of different providers. Such a sale will not necessarily be at an inclusive price as properly understood.

Paragraph 4.8

173.   It seems to me that while what the consumer thinks he is getting may be a relevant consideration, it cannot be a test. Indeed, as the CAA's Advice to Government makes clear, the problem is that the consumer may well be misled into believing that what may appear to be a package is not for the purposes of the ATOL Regulations.

...

Paragraph 4.2

177.   If this amounts to saying that the advertisement of any individual travel facilities which can be combined inevitably amounts to a package for the purposes of the Regulations, that seems to me wrong. Whether it amounts to a package depends upon the features to which I have already referred, particularly that of an inclusive price.

Paragraph 4.4

178.   This seems to me too wide. The provision by a travel agent of information on a combination of services does not without more amount to a package. It requires an offer to sell them (or the sale of them) at an inclusive price. In other words, whether it amounts to a package depends upon whether the nature of what is offered or any agreement which is reached between the agent and the consumer. The agent may sell the consumer a package as defined by the Regulations. He does not necessarily.

...

Conclusion

184.   It follows that I have concluded that the Guidance is wrong to the degree which requires it be quashed. The remedy now sought by ABTA is limited to such an order. In the light of what I have said, that is the order I make.

The Association of British Travel Agents Ltd v Civil Aviation Authority [2006] EWCA Civ 1356 (18 October 2006)

Chadwick LJ

1.   This is an appeal from an order made on 16 January 2006 by Mr Justice Goldring in the Administrative Court in proceedings for judicial review brought on the application of The Association of British Travel Agents Limited ("ABTA"). By his order the judge declared that a guidance note issued by the Civil Aviation Authority ("the CAA") – Guidance Note 26: "Sale of Air Package Arrangements: Advice on the need to provide consumer protection" – was unlawful. The judge went on to quash the guidance note.

2.   Guidance Note 26 ("the Guidance Note") was issued by the CAA on 4 March 2005 in order "to help travel organisers and agents understand the definition of an air package set out in the European Council Directive (PTD), the Package Travel Regulations (PTR) and the Civil Aviation (ATOL) (Amendment) Regulations ('The Regulations')" and "to help travel organisers and travel agents decide what parts of their business need ATOL protection" – paragraph 1.1 of the Guidance Note. It is said to be a response "to market developments such as split contracts" – (ibid).

3.   Paragraph 1.2 of the Guidance Note is in these terms:

> "This Guidance Note explains the types of air package business which a travel company is required to protect under an Air Travel Organiser's Licence (ATOL). The Note should be read in conjunction with the Regulations. The purpose of this Guidance Note is to explain the background to the Regulations and to offer an interpretation of certain provisions. Only the courts can give a determinative view on the law."

The objective is admirable. The criticism advanced by ABTA – a leading trade association of travel organisers and travel agents – is that the interpretation of the regulations set out in some parts of the Guidance Note is misleading and wrong.

4.   The force of that criticism (if made out) is compounded by the warning in paragraph 6.3 of the Guidance Note:

> "The CAA undertakes monitoring of travel firms to ensure compliance with the ATOL Regulations. With the issue of this new guidance the CAA will be carrying out increased monitoring of travel agents, and firms should be aware that it is the CAA's policy to prosecute in cases where firms have been made aware of the compliance requirement but have failed to obtain a licence. The maximum penalty on summary conviction is a fine of £5,000 and on conviction on indictment to fine or imprisonment for a term not exceeding two years or both."

The clear message to travel organisers and travel agents is that the CAA will adopt the views which it has set out in the Guidance Note – and, in particular, its view as to the circumstances in which accommodation in aircraft is made available as a component of a package - in deciding whether to prosecute for infringement of the ATOL Regulations. It is of little comfort to travel organisers and travel agents who may disagree with those views to learn – as is obviously the case – that "Only the courts can give a determinative view on the law." If the CAA's views are wrong, a travel agent should not be required to choose between accepting those views and testing the point as defendant to a prosecution.

5.   It was in those circumstances that the judge rejected the submission, advanced on behalf of the CAA, that the Guidance Note was not susceptible to challenge in proceedings for judicial review. He rejected that submission for the reasons which he set out at paragraphs [80] to [88] of his judgment [2006] EWHC 13 (Admin). The submission was not pursued, as such, in the appellant's notice or in the skeleton argument filed on behalf of the CAA; although it was said that the judge should not have embarked on the exercise which he did in what was described as "a factual vacuum". It is, I think, enough to observe at this stage that, if the judge was correct in his view that the Guidance Note contains an interpretation of the requirements in the ATOL Regulations which was wrong or misleading, then it is clearly in the public interest that the Guidance Note be amended or withdrawn.

...

15.   It is important to keep in mind that a "package", for the purposes of the Directive and the Package Travel Regulations, may or may not include flight accommodation. Whether the package includes flight accommodation or not, the person who takes or agrees to take the package will be the "consumer" for those purposes; the person who organises the package and sells or offers it for sale (whether directly or though a retailer) will be the "organiser"; and the person who sells or offers for sale the package put together by the organiser will be the "retailer". The "contract" will be the agreement linking the consumer to the organiser or to the retailer (or to both) as the case may be; and "the other party to the contract" will be the party to the contract other than the consumer – that is to say, the other party to the contract will be the organiser or the retailer (or both) as the case may be. For convenience I will refer to the other party to the contract as "the counter-party". Whether the package includes flight accommodation or not the counter-party will be liable for the proper performance of the obligations under the contract (regulation 15(1) of the Package Travel Regulations) and the counter-party will be obliged to provide sufficient evidence of financial security (regulation 16(1) of those Regulations). But, if the package is one in respect of which the counter-party is required to hold an ATOL, the obligation imposed by regulation 16(1) of the Package Travel Regulations does not require the counter-party to ensure that arrangements described in regulations 17, 18, 19, 20 or 21 of the Package Travel Regulations are in force. In such a case, the obligation is, in effect, met through the CAA's requirements for the grant of an ATOL.

16.   The ATOL Regulations – in relation to the provision of flight accommodation which constitutes a component of a package - must be read in conjunction with the provisions of the Directive and the Package Travel Regulations. The effect of the ATOL Regulations – in the case where flight accommodation is a component of a package – is to restrict the persons who can be "the other party to the contract" for the purposes of the Package Travel Regulations. The counter-party, in such a case, must be the holder of an ATOL ("a licence holder") or the operator of the relevant aircraft. Further, it is only where all the components of the package are

made available under a single contract between the customer (or consumer) and a licence holder, that flight accommodation can be made available by a person acting in the capacity of an agent; and then only if that person is acting in the capacity of an agent for a licence holder – regulation 3(1A) (a) of the ATOL Regulations. Flight accommodation which constitutes a component of a package cannot be made available by a person acting in the capacity of a ticket provider – regulation 3(1A)(b). It will follow that, where flight accommodation is a component of a package, the person who will be liable (under regulation 15(1) of the Package Travel Regulations) for the proper performance of the obligations under the contract will be a licence holder or (perhaps) the operator of the relevant aircraft; and the financial security of that person (if a licence holder) will be ensured by the fact that he is the holder of an ATOL.

17.   It is against that regulatory background that the concept of "package" – as a pre-arranged combination of at least two of the prescribed components "when sold or offered for sale at an inclusive price" – falls to be addressed.

"Package"

18.   The enquiry, in any given case within the scope of the Guidance Note, is whether the flight accommodation which is made available "constitutes a component of a package". If it does, then the restrictions to which I have just referred – imposed by regulation 3(1A) of the ATOL Regulations – apply. If it does not, then the position remains as it was before the introduction of that regulation in 2003.

19.   There can be no doubt that flight accommodation is capable of being a component of a package – it falls squarely within sub-paragraph (a) of the definition (transport). Nor can there be any doubt that flight accommodation will not be a component of a package unless it is sold or offered for sale with some other service which falls within one or other of sub-paragraphs (b) and (c) of the definition (accommodation and other, non-ancillary, services). And the two (or more) components together must cover a period of more that twenty-four hours or include overnight accommodation. But there are the further requirements that the components of the package must be sold or offered for sale as a "pre-arranged combination" and "at an inclusive price".

20.   The requirement that the components of the package must be sold or offered for sale as a "pre-arranged combination" is met not only where the components are put together by the organiser without input from the customer (typically, the brochure holiday) but also where the components are put together by the organiser in accordance with the specifications of the individual customer (or consumer) or group of customers (typically, the 'customised' holiday) – *Club-Tour, Viagrens e Turismo SA v Alberto Carlos Lobo Gonçalves Garrido* (Case C-400/00) [2002] ECR I-4051. And the requirement is satisfied not only in cases where the components have been put together and offered for sale by the organiser in advance of any contact with the individual customer but also in cases "where the combination of tourist services is the result of the wishes expressed by the customer up to the moment when the parties reach an agreement and conclude the contract" – ibid, paragraph [19]. It can be seen, of course, that the principle is expressly stated, as proviso (ii), in the definition of "package" in both the Package Travel Regulations and the ATOL Regulations (as

amended in 2003). That proviso did not appear in the Directive, which was the text which the Court of Justice was required to consider in the *Garrido* case.

21.   The question, then, is what (if anything) does the requirement that the components be sold or offered for sale "at an inclusive price" add to the requirement that the components be sold or offered for sale as a pre-arranged combination. It is the answer to that question which lies at the heart of the dispute between ABTA and the CAA. The CAA's view, expressed at paragraph 2.5 of the Guidance Note, is that:

"This term refers to the price of the package. It does not matter if the cost of a package is made up of separate sums relating to the value of each element (travel, accommodation, other non-ancillary tourist services). In these circumstances, the whole arrangement can still be sold at an inclusive price."

ABTA's submission, in the Administrative Court, was that that was to equate or confuse an inclusive price with a total or aggregate price. As it was put in the written skeleton argument deployed in that court:

"The natural and ordinary meaning of 'inclusive price' is a single, comprehensive price which includes all of the travel components being sold.

. . .

An 'inclusive price' is different from simply adding up the various prices of the different services to arrive at a total price."

22.   The judge addressed that question at paragraphs [153] to [166] of his judgment.

...

23.   The CAA does not challenge the judge's conclusion that: "For the sale of a package at an inclusive price the relationship between the component parts of that package must be such as to mean that the consumer is buying and paying for them as a whole"... It is said that it did not dispute that proposition in the Administrative Court: "nor is it inconsistent with the Guidance". It submits that the proposition "is an echo of the CAA's argument that the concept of 'inclusive price' taken in conjunction with that of 'pre-arranged combination' focuses on whether the different components are sold or offered for sale together, on a composite basis".

24.   At first sight, therefore, there is now little, if anything, between the parties on this question. The requirement that the components be sold or offered for sale "at an inclusive price" must be read in conjunction with the requirement that the components be sold or offered for sale as a pre-arranged combination. The price is the price of the combination.

25.   In many cases – indeed, I suspect, in the majority of cases – the price of the combination will not be the aggregate of the prices for which the components within the combination would have been sold or offered for sale if each component had been sold or offered for sale as a separate service outside the combination. That may be because some of the components (for example, the services of the organiser's local representative) would not be available as a separate service outside the combination. Or it may be because some of the components can be provided more cheaply if

provided in conjunction with other components - the hotel may provide a courtesy airport transfer service. Or it may be that, in order to sell the package, the organiser will price attractively: the organiser will offer the package of services at a price which is below the aggregate of the prices which would be charged if the components had been sold separately. In those cases there is unlikely to be difficulty in reaching the conclusion, on the facts, that the components (including flight accommodation) are being sold as a pre-arranged combination and at an inclusive price. The same could be said of cases – which, I suspect, are likely to be rare indeed – in which the price of the combination exceeds the aggregate of the prices for which the components would have been sold or offered for sale separately.

26.   The more difficult cases are those in which the price for the whole is equal to the aggregate of the prices for which the components would have been sold or offered for sale separately. The principle is, perhaps, easier to state than to apply in practice. If the components are offered for sale as a pre-arranged combination – albeit that the components are not combined (and, perhaps, not all identified) until "the moment when the parties reach an agreement and conclude the contract" (to adopt the language of the Court of Justice in the *Garrido* case) – then the price for the combination will be "an inclusive price" notwithstanding that it may have been calculated, arithmetically, by aggregating the prices of the components: that is to say, notwithstanding that the price for the combination is the aggregate of the prices for which each component would have been sold or offered for sale if it had been sold or offered for sale as a separate service outside the combination. The factual question to be resolved – on a case by case basis – is whether the services are being sold or offered for sale as components of a combination; or whether they are being sold or offered for sale separately, but at the same time.

27.   The point may be illustrated by examples. Suppose a customer, in London, who wishes to spend a week at a named hotel in, say, Rome. He asks his travel agent what the trip will cost him. The agent ascertains that the cost of the return flight will be £X, the cost of accommodation will be £Y and the cost of the airport transfers will be £Z. Without disclosing the individual cost of each service, the agent offers the customer flights, accommodation and transfers at a price of £(X+Y+Z). The customer accepts without further inquiry. In that case there would be little doubt – as it seems to me – that the services were sold as a pre-arranged combination and at an inclusive price.

28.   Now suppose that the agent has informed the customer that the cost of flights will be £X, the cost of accommodation will be £Y and the cost of transfers will be £Z; and has explained to the customer that he can purchase any one or more of those services, as he chooses, without any need to purchase the others. He has explained, in effect, that the customer can choose to purchase the other services elsewhere; or to make other arrangements. In that case – as it seems to me – there would be little doubt that the services are not offered for sale as a pre-arranged combination and at an inclusive price.

29.   What, then, if the customer chooses, and contracts for, one of those services. It is plain that that service would not be sold as a pre-arranged combination: it is not sold in combination with any other service. And it is plain that that position would not alter, if having paid for one of those services, the customer subsequently decides to take, and contracts for, another of the services. Nor would the position alter if,

after paying for the second service, the customer later decides to take, and contracts for, the third service. And it would make no difference if, having entered into three separate contracts and received three separate invoices, the customer were to pay the three invoices with a single cheque. The position would be the same. There would have been no sale of a pre-arranged combination of components at a single inclusive price. Rather, there would have been three separate sales of independent services, the aggregate of the prices payable for the three separate services being satisfied by a single payment.

30.   Nothing in the preceding paragraph is inconsistent with proviso (i) to the definition of "package" in the Package Travel Regulations or the ATOL Regulations ("the submission of separate accounts for different components shall not cause the arrangements to be other than a package") or with the proviso to the definition in the Directive ("The separate billing of various components of the same package shall not absolve the organiser or retailer from the obligations under this Directive"). As the judge explained at paragraph [158] of his judgment, if the arrangements would otherwise be a "package" – because the services are sold or offered for sale as components of a pre-arranged combination and at an inclusive price – the substance of the arrangements is not altered by invoicing the components separately. But, if the arrangements would not otherwise be a "package" – because the services are, in fact, sold or offered for sale separately – separate billing merely reflects the substance of the arrangements. The most that could be said is that composite billing might be evidence (in the particular case) that the services had been sold as a package.

31.   Returning to the second of the examples which I have set out, difficult questions of fact are likely to arise if the customer chooses and contracts for two or more of the services on the same occasion. The principle is not in doubt. If the services are sold or offered for sale as components of a combination, there is a package: if they are sold or offered for sale separately but at the same time, there is no package. The question whether they are sold as components of a combination - or separately but at the same time - is a question of fact. That question may not be easy to resolve in the particular case.

ABTA's challenge to the views expressed in the Guidance Note

...

34.   The judge identified "the four principal errors" on which ABTA relied at paragraphs [121] to [130] of his judgment. He addressed those alleged errors at paragraphs [169] to [173] of his judgment; and held that each had been made out.

35.   The first of the "principal errors" is in paragraph 2.5 of the Guidance Note. The paragraph appears under the heading "Inclusive price"... The issue between the parties is whether, in stating that "it does not matter" if the cost of a package is made up of separate sums relating to the value of each element, the paragraph is to be taken to mean that where services are sold at the same time in circumstances where the total price is the aggregate of the individual prices there will necessarily be a package for the purposes of the ATOL Regulations; or is to be taken to mean only that there may be. ABTA submits that the paragraph has the former meaning; and that, understood in that sense, the paragraph is misleading. The CAA submits that the paragraph means only that there may be (but not necessarily will be) a package if the total cost

is the aggregate of the individual prices; and that that is a correct view of the regulations.

36.   The judge held (at paragraph [169]) that:

> "By omitting any mention of the proper interpretation of an 'inclusive price' this paragraph is in my view inadequate and misleading. It does matter if the cost is made up of separate sums. If I am right, it is only if the total of those separate sums amount to an inclusive price as I have defined it that what is sold can be a package."

There is force in the judge's observation that paragraph 2.5 of the Guidance Note is inadequate; in that the paragraph gives no insight into what is meant by the phrase "sold or offered for sale at an inclusive price". Taken alone, the two sentences of which complaint is made – "It does not matter if the cost of a package is made up of separate sums relating to the value of each element . . ." and "In these circumstances, the whole arrangement can still be sold at an inclusive price" – are not inaccurate. The vice, as it seems to me, is that – in the absence of any explanation as to what is meant by the phrase "sold or offered for sale at an inclusive price" – the uninformed reader might be led to think that "inclusive price" was synonymous with "total price" – so that where services are sold at the same time in circumstances where the total price is the aggregate of the individual prices there will necessarily be a package for the purposes of the ATOL Regulations. If a reader might be led to that conclusion, the paragraph is potentially misleading.

37.   In the Administrative Court ABTA criticised paragraph 5.2 of the Guidance Note. The paragraph is in these terms:

> "A customer approaches an agent to buy a number of services which the customer specifies with no influence from the agent (i.e. a specific hotel and airline/flight number); this is not defined as a package by the DTI as there is no prearrangement by the agent and the agent cannot be held responsible for a service over whose choice the agent had no influence. All services must however be separately documented. If one or more elements are not available and the agent recommends alternatives/changes, this may become a package."

The judge accepted ABTA's criticism that the statement that a combination of services, sold at the same time and in circumstances in which the agent had no input into the customer's choice, cannot be pre-arranged is inconsistent with the decision in the Garrido case and is contradicted by proviso (ii) to the definition of "package" in both the Package Travel Regulations and the ATOL Regulations. The judge was correct to take the view (at paragraph [171] of his judgment) that "the paragraph wrongly sets out the law". He might have said the same of the final sentence in paragraph 3.2: ". . . such arrangements are not seen as creating a package because the travel agent would not have played a role in influencing the arrangements." [

38.   ABTA did not need to pursue its criticism of paragraph 5.2 in this Court. The point was conceded by the CAA. The criticism remains well-founded.

39.   The third of the "principal errors" addressed by the judge is in paragraph 4.3 of the Guidance Note:

> "If an agent offers a customer a choice of travel facilities, including a flight, the resulting sale will be a package requiring the agent to hold an ATOL. However this will not be the case where the travel facilities all form part of a package sold by the travel agent on behalf of a single ATOL holder."

The second sentence is unobjectionable. It reflects the saving provision in regulation 3(1A)(a) of the ATOL Regulations. But the judge accepted ABTA's submission that the first sentence was misleading. An offer of a choice of travel facilities will not necessarily lead to the conclusion that the resulting sale will be a package. The judge said this, at paragraph [172] of his judgment:

> "It is not enough to bring the arrangements within the ATOL Regulations for the travel agent without more to offer a whole range of different and discrete possible travel arrangements on behalf of different providers. Such a sale will not necessarily be at an inclusive price as properly understood. "

40.   I agree with that view. The question, in the particular case, is whether the services are sold or offered for sale as components in a pre-arranged combination; or whether they are being sold or offered for sale separately, but at the same time. It is only in the former case that the price – the price of the combination – is properly to be regarded as an "inclusive price" for the purposes of the ATOL Regulations.

41.   The fourth of the "principal errors" was said to be in paragraph 4.8 of the Guidance Note:

> "If an agent has taken commitments or contracts with a supplier for any item offered as part of an air package, then the package will require an ATOL."

The judge took the criticism of that paragraph to be "without more this cannot be right" – paragraph [130] of his judgment. In addressing that criticism, the judge observed, at paragraph [173]:

> "It seems to me that while what the consumer thinks he is getting may be a relevant consideration, it cannot be a test. Indeed, as the CAA's Advice to Government makes clear, the problem is that the consumer may well be misled into believing that what may appear to be a package is not for the purposes of the ATOL Regulations."

42.   For my part, I do not find it easy to see what it was that the judge had in mind in making that observation in the context of paragraph 4.8. It may be (as the CAA suggests at paragraph 60 of its skeleton argument on this appeal) that paragraph [173] of the judgment was directed at paragraph 2.3 of the Guidance Note, and not at paragraph 4.8. But, if so, the criticism of paragraph 4.8 which the judge identified at paragraph [130] is not addressed at all. [I note that the CAA does not address it in its skeleton argument on this appeal].

43.   ABTA's criticism of paragraph 4.8 - as it appears from sections D, G and H(5) of the skeleton argument which was before the Administrative Court - was that the paragraph suggests that, whenever an agent has taken commitments from, or

made contracts with, a supplier for travel services which are sold or offered for sale to a customer at the same time as other travel services, the transaction will be treated as the sale or offer for sale of a package. ABTA made the point (correctly) that the fact that an agent has taken commitments from, or made contracts with, a supplier for any item sold or offered for sale (with other travel services) to a customer does not necessarily lead to the conclusion that the services which are the subject of those commitments or contracts are sold as a package for the purposes of the ATOL Regulations.

44.   If the paragraph were to be read as ABTA suggests, the criticism would be well-founded. But, as it seems to me, that would be to give the paragraph a meaning and effect which it does not have. Its meaning is controlled, I think, by the words "any item offered as part of an air package". The premise underlying the paragraph is that the service in respect of which the agent has taken commitments from, or made contracts with, a supplier is offered for sale as part of an air package. Given that premise the conclusion is correct: "then the package will require ATOL cover". Properly understood, the paragraph does not suggest that whenever the agent has taken commitments from, or made contracts with, a supplier for a service which the agent then sells or offers for sale to a customer at the same time as other travel services the transaction will be treated, necessarily, as the sale or offer for sale of a package.

45.   There are other statements in the Guidance Note which are said to contain or reflect errors of law. Paragraph 2.3 – under the heading "Package" - is in these terms:

> "The definition is at paragraph 1.5. One reasonable test is to consider what the consumer thinks he is getting when he approached the agent or travel organiser; artificial arrangements to sell components at separate times and with separate billing would not mean that a package had not been sold."

The second limb of the sentence is unobjectionable: it reflects the proviso to the definition of "package" in the Directive (proviso (i) to the definition in the regulations). The first limb is open to the criticism that the test is not subjective. But the fact that the customer thinks he is buying two or more separate services at the same time rather than a combination of services at an inclusive price – (or vice versa) - may be a powerful evidential pointer to the true nature of the transaction.

46.   As I have already indicated, the reason which is relied upon in support of the final sentence of paragraph 3.2 - "such arrangements are not seen as creating a package because the travel agent would not have played a role in influencing the arrangements." - is open to the same criticism as that made of paragraph 5.2. ABTA did not pursue the point in this Court. It does, however, criticise the final sentence of paragraph 3.3:

> "Consequently travel companies are able to construct packages from individual components and these arrangements are quite different from the scenario at 3.2."

This is a variant on the same point. In a case where the price paid by the customer is the aggregate of the prices for which the services would be sold or offered for sale (if sold or offered for sale separately) the agent's input is irrelevant; save, perhaps, as an evidential pointer to the true nature of the transaction.

47. ABTA criticises much of the guidance given by way of example in section 4 of the Guidance Note. In addition to the "principal errors" which it identifies in paragraphs 4.3 and 4.8, ABTA takes issue with all or part of the following paragraphs:

> (1) Paragraph 4.2:
>
> > "If travel facilities are advertised by an agent in a brochure, a shop window display, on Teletext, in a newspaper advertisement or on a website, and it is clear that these can be combined to form a package, or the agent offers to provide individual package quotations based on an advertised range of options, then such packages require ATOL cover. However if these facilities were offered or sold by the agent on behalf of a single ATOL holding tour operator, then the agent would not need its own ATOL."

The first sentence seems to me unobjectionable. It describes circumstances in which travel facilities are offered for sale as components of a pre-arranged combination. It is immaterial that the components within the combination will not become known until the customer makes his choice: see the decision in the Garrido case and proviso (ii) to the definition of package in the regulations. It is self evident from the context that an "individual package quotation" will be an inclusive price. The second sentence is plainly correct: see the saving provision in regulation 3(1A)(a) of the ATOL Regulations.

(2) Paragraph 4.4:

> > "If a consumer requests a flight and accommodation and/or other tourist services to a particular resort or destination and asks an agent for details of suitable arrangements and the agent provides information on a combination of services, rather than a package from an ATOL holder, then this is a package under the PTR and the agent will need to hold an ATOL"

The provision of information would not, of itself, contravene regulation 3(1A) of the ATOL Regulations; nor would the provision of information, of itself, be a component "sold or offered for sale" within the definition of "package" in the Package Travel Regulations. But, of course, it would not be difficult to infer from the provision of travel information by an agent that the agent was offering to sell the services to which that information related. An agent who offered to sell travel services in combination at an inclusive price (otherwise than under a single contract between the holder of an ATOL and the customer) would, if the services included flight accommodation, need to hold an ATOL. In my view the judge was correct to say of paragraph 4.4 of the Guidance Note:

> > "This seems to me too wide. The provision by a travel agent of information on a combination of services does not without more amount to a package. It requires an offer to sell them (or the sale of them) at an inclusive price. In other words, whether it amounts to a package depends upon whether the nature of what is offered or any agreement which is reached between the agent and the consumer. The agent may sell the consumer a package as

defined by the Regulations. He does not necessarily." [paragraph [178] of the judgment]

(3) Paragraph 4.5:

> "In some instances a customer may have been offered an ATOL protected package, but asks the agent whether there is a cheaper alternative; if the agent decides to offer an alternative that he has selected himself, rather than a package from another ATOL holder, then the agent will need his own ATOL."

It seems to me that the reader of that paragraph would understand that the customer (having been offered a package) was seeking an alternative, but cheaper, package; and that what the agent was prepared to offer was indeed a package. On that basis the paragraph does not misstate the law: the agent does need his own ATOL. The position would be different if, on a proper analysis of the facts in a particular case, the agent was offering to sell (as an alternative to the package) a number of separate services, each at its own price. But that is not, I think, the factual situation to which paragraph 4.5 is addressed.

(4) Paragraph 4.6:

> "Following the 2003 ATOL Regulations amendment, if an agent puts together a package utilising a scheduled flight, provided to the consumer on a 'ticket provider' basis, (i.e the customer paid for the flight and received a valid ticket for travel immediately in return) then the package will require to be covered by an ATOL."

That, as it seems to me, is a correct statement of the law – see regulation 3(1A)(b) of the ATOL Regulations: "A person shall not make available flight accommodation which constitutes a component of a package in the capacity of a ticket provider". The premise which underlies paragraph 4.6 is that the scheduled flight is a component of a pre-arranged package. The paragraph does not purport to describe the circumstances in which that premise will, or will not, be established.

(5) Paragraph 4.7:

> "If an agent advertises that he can provide tailor-made holiday arrangements or he can provide dynamic packages, then he will need an ATOL to cover the majority of such sales. However if all facilities were offered and sold by the agent on behalf of a single ATOL holder, an ATOL would not be required."

The first sentence is a correct statement of the law in so far as it relates to "dynamic packages" – provided, of course, that the package includes flight accommodation. On the other hand, "tailor-made holiday arrangements" are not necessarily within the definition of "package"; although some (indeed, perhaps, the majority) will be. That issue will turn on the facts of the particular case: is the advertisement to be seen as an offer to sell a pre-arranged combination of travel services (including flight accommodation) or as an offer to sell a number of separate services, each at its own price. If the latter, the agent will not need to hold an ATOL. The second sentence is plainly correct – see the saving provision in regulation 3(1A)(a) of the ATOL Regulations.

48.   As I have said, section 5 of the Guidance Note contains examples of cases in which the CAA takes the view that an ATOL is not required. I have already addressed the criticism of paragraph 5.2 which was made in the Administrative Court. As I have said, it was not necessary for ABTA to pursue that criticism in this Court, I am satisfied that it was well-founded. Criticism is made, also, of words in paragraph 5.4. The paragraph is in these terms:

> "A customer buys a flight from an agent (which may be ATOL protected) and at a later date returns to buy accommodation. The sale of the two services at different times does not, unless they are linked by documentation, create a package. However, such transactions must genuinely take place at different times and cannot be a device to avoid providing package protection."

If it were not for the words "unless they are linked by documentation" the paragraph would be unobjectionable. But it is said, correctly in my view, that the fact that two sales at different times may be recorded in common documentation – for example, on a common invoice or on a monthly statement of account – does not necessarily lead to the conclusion that the services are sold or offered for sale as a package. The question, in each case, is whether, at the time of the first sale, the combination of the service then sold with the service to be sold by the second sale was pre-arranged. Common documentation might point to the conclusion that there was a pre-arranged combination; but it will not always do so. The second sentence of paragraph 5.2 is plainly correct. The need for ATOL protection cannot be avoided by presenting what is, in substance, a single transaction as if it were two separate transactions.

49.   Paragraph 6.1 contains the following general observation, by way of summary:

> "Travel firms which sell air package arrangements which they have constructed themselves will in the majority of cases need to hold an ATOL to protect those sales. From the agent's perspective this means that if they have selected specific travel components, or they have offered for sale travel facilities including a flight, then the resultant sale will usually be a package. From the customer's perspective, if he approaches an agent and explains that he wants to buy a flight and accommodation and/or other services, or merely wants to buy a holiday, then it is likely that the arrangements will have been sold or offered for sale to him as a package."

Taken as a general observation, that paragraph is unobjectionable. The first sentence is plainly correct. The premise which underlies that sentence is that the arrangements are sold as an air package. The second sentence is also correct. The fact that the agent has selected the travel components is likely to point to the conclusion that the components are offered for sale as a pre-arranged combination. The position may be less clear where the agent has "offered for sale travel facilities including a flight". As I have explained, an offer to sell two or more separate travel services at the same time does not necessarily lead to the conclusion that the services are being sold or offered for sale as components in a pre-arranged combination and at an inclusive price; but, on the facts of the particular case, it may do so. I do not think that ABTA is in a position to challenge the CAA's view that an offer made in the circumstances described in the second sentence will usually lead to that conclusion. Similar points can be made in relation to the third sentence. If the customer approaches an agent "to buy a holiday", it is likely that what will be sold or offered for sale will be a pre-arranged combination of services at an inclusive price: that is to say, "a package". If the customer wants to buy "a flight and accommodation and/or other services", then (as I have explained) it will not necessarily follow that the services sold or offered for sale will be sold or offered as a package: but they may be. Again, I do not think that ABTA is able to challenge the CAA's view that a sale or offer for sale made in the circumstances described in the third sentence of paragraph 6.1 is likely to be a sale or offer of a package. Properly understood, the paragraph does not suggest that the circumstances described in the second and third sentences will always lead to the conclusion that the services are sold or offered for sale as a package.

...

The CAA's proposal is aimed essentially at sales that the customer would perceive as packages, which fall generally into two categories. One is where the separate items have clearly been packaged before being offered for sale; the second category is that of 'tailor made' holidays where an operator offers a limited selection of flights and accommodation from which the customer is intended to make his choice to form a package. In many cases the clearest evidence that a package falls into one of these two categories may be the existence of advertising (in any medium) or a brochure, and where this is the case enforcement action can be both effective and cost-effective.

...

Conclusion

63.   I am satisfied that the Guidance Note is misleading, or potentially misleading to the uninformed reader, in the following respects:

(1) In the absence of any explanation as to what is meant by the phrase "sold or offered for sale at an inclusive price", the uninformed reader might be led by the two sentences in paragraph 2.5 of which complaint is made to think that "inclusive price" was synonymous with "total price" – so that where services are sold at the same time in circumstances where the total price is the aggregate of the individual prices there will, necessarily, be a package for the purposes of the ATOL Regulations. As I have sought to explain, that is not the effect of the Regulations.

(2) The statements in paragraphs 3.2 and 5.2 to the effect that arrangements are not seen as creating a package where the travel agent has taken no part in influencing the customer's choice are misleading. In the light of the decision of the Court of Justice in the *Garrido* case and proviso (ii) to the definition of "package" in both the Package Travel Regulations and the ATOL Regulations, it is irrelevant whether or not the agent has influenced the customer's choice.

(3) The statement in the first sentence of paragraph 4.3 that, if an agent offers a customer a choice of travel facilities including a flight the resulting sale will be a package, is over-simplistic and misleading. It is only where the services are sold or offered for sale as components in a pre-arranged combination that there will be a "package" for the purposes of the ATOL Regulations. Where flight accommodation is made available as one of a number of services sold or offered for sale separately

(albeit at the same time) the agent is not to be treated as a person within regulation 3(1A) of those Regulations.

(4) The statement in paragraph 4.4 is not accurate. The provision of information does not, of itself, bring the agent within regulation 3(1A) of the ATOL Regulations. What is required is that flight accommodation is made available as a component of a package. The provision of information may, but will not necessarily, lead to the conclusion that the flight accommodation is offered for sale as one of a number of components in a pre-arranged combination.

(5) The statement in paragraph 4.7 that "he will need an ATOL to cover the majority of such sales" is unhelpful. "Tailor-made holiday arrangements" are not necessarily within the definition of "package" for the purposes of the ATOL Regulations; although some will be. The statement does not enable the uninformed reader to identify the circumstances in which an ATOL will, or will not, be required.

(6) The words "unless they are linked by documentation", which qualify the first sentence in paragraph 5.4, are misleading in that they suggest that common documentation will, necessarily, lead to the conclusion that the sales which are the subject of that documentation are components in a pre-arranged combination. That is not a necessary conclusion.

64.   In my view the cumulative effect of the statements to which I have referred is that the Guidance Note is likely to give the uninformed reader a misleading impression as to the circumstances in which regulation 3(1A) of the ATOL Regulations requires that the agent be a licence holder. It is clear, from the circumstances which gave rise to the issue of the Guidance Note, that the CAA appreciated that the definition of "package" in the Directive and the Package Travel Regulations gave rise to difficulties of interpretation and that the introduction of that concept into the ATOL Regulations by the amendments made in 2003 was, at best, a compromise which did not really meet the need for consumer protection in the changed market conditions which the CAA had identified. In my view it is not satisfactory that the uninformed reader of the Guidance Note might be led to think that regulation 3(1A) has a wider reach than, on a proper interpretation, it can be given.

65.   The judge quashed the Guidance Note. But the Guidance Note contains nothing which affects existing or future rights: there is no need for an order that it be quashed. It is, I think, accepted that an order directing that the Guidance Note be withdrawn would be the appropriate relief in the circumstances that it has been found to be misleading. Subject to any further representations which the parties may wish to make on that point, that is the order which I would make. Save to that extent necessary to make that substitution, I would dismiss the appeal.

Lady Justice Arden:

66.   I agree.

The President of the Family Division:

67.   I also agree.

Does the Package Travel Directive apply to promotional holidays where consumers do not pay the full price, or any price attributable to some package components?

Walter Rechberger, Renate Greindl, Hermann Hofmeister and Others v *Republik Österreich* ECJ C-140/97; [1999] ECR I-3499

Opinion of Mr Advocate General Saggio delivered on 25 June 1998.

1 The present case affords this Court a further opportunity to interpret Council Directive 90/314/EEC of 13 June 1990 on package travel, package holidays and package tours (hereinafter 'the Directive'). (1) In this matter, the Court is asked first of all to clarify whether travel offered at a reduced price to the subscribers of a newspaper falls within the scope of the Directive, particularly where the payment demanded from those travelling is referable to just one part of the package ...

2 As this Court has already made clear, (2) the purpose of the Directive is, as stated in its Article 1, to approximate the laws, regulations and administrative provisions of the Member States relating to packages sold or offered for sale in the territory of the Community...

6 The Directive was transposed into Austrian law by a series of legislative provisions...

7 The plaintiffs before the national court are all subscribers to an Austrian daily newspaper, the Neue Kronenzeitung. In November 1994, the company publishing the newspaper decided to offer subscribers, as a reward for their loyalty, a holiday under an arrangement with the travel agency Arena-Club-Reisen. It consisted of four or seven day stays in foreign tourist resorts, including flight with on-board refreshments, airport-hotel-airport transfers, overnight accommodation with breakfast, in a double or single room (the latter on payment of a supplement) and a tour in the company of a German-speaking tour guide.

8 Under the terms of the offer, subscribers were only asked to pay the Austrian airport tax of ÖS 40 per person and the Greek airport tax of ÖS 280 per person. Subscribers travelling alone were required to pay a single room supplement of ÖS 500 per night. Persons accompanying subscribers, on the other hand, were required to pay the full price as set out in a brochure annexed to the offer. Accordingly, the publisher distributed vouchers to subscribers which they could use to book a trip, choosing from a variety of dates. The subscriber would then receive a booking confirmation from the company organising the travel, to which a deposit of 10% of the sum due from him was to be paid within ten days of the confirmation, the balance being payable no later than ten days before departure.

9 The plaintiffs before the national court booked their trips between 19 November 1994 and 12 April 1995. Some intended to travel alone, others with one of more companions. The holidays were to take place 10 April and 23 July 1995, according to the booking.

10 The offer was far more successful than the organisers had anticipated. Whilst the travel agency had planned a flight capacity of 30,000, bookings were made by no

fewer than 52,260 subscribers with a further 33,041 people travelling as companions. The organiser consequently encountered serious operational difficulties as no more places were available on board flights, and these difficulties led in turn to financial problems. On 4 July 1995, insolvency proceedings were instituted upon application by the company Arena-Club-Reisen itself. As a result of the organiser's insolvency, two of the plaintiffs were unable to take their holidays, while the other four had already had their holidays cancelled due to the lack of available places. All the plaintiffs, however, had paid the whole cost of the trip.

11 It appears from the order for reference that, in the absence of statutory requirements, no guarantee was provided in respect of the payments made by the three plaintiffs who had booked their trips during 1994. Two of them consequently sought to assert their rights as creditors in the insolvency proceedings relating to the organiser, but to no avail. The guarantee referred to in the November 1994 Order operated, however, in favour of the other three plaintiffs who, after 1 January 1995, booked trips to be made after 1 May 1995. For these customers, a bank guarantee in excess of ÖS 4 000 000 had been provided, yet this still covered only 25.38% of the travel costs paid in advance by the plaintiffs.

12 In the cases pending before the national court, all the plaintiffs have accordingly asked that the Austrian State be held liable for having failed to fulfil its obligation under the Treaty promptly and faithfully to implement the Directive. They therefore asked for the State to be ordered to pay damages corresponding to the amounts paid over and unrecovered following the insolvency of the company which organised the travel.

13 The Landesgericht (Regional Court) Linz decided to refer to this Court the following questions [amongst others] for a preliminary ruling:

(1) Does the protection afforded by [the] Council Directive 90/314/EEC of 13 June 1990 on package travel, package holidays and package tours ("the Directive") extend to travel for which the principal contracting party must, on the basis of the contract, only pay

(a) the airport security tax (departure tax) and a single room supplement, if he travels alone,

or

(b) the airport security tax (departure tax), if he travels with one or more accompanying persons paying the full price,

and nothing in respect of the flight and accommodation in a multiple occupancy room?

(2) Does such travel fall within the Directive's scope of application even when it is offered by the largest circulation daily newspaper in a Member State as a free gift exclusive to subscribers as part of an anti-competitive advertising campaign?

14 With the first two questions, the Austrian court is essentially asking this Court to clarify whether the Directive covers the trips booked by the plaintiffs in the proceedings before it. Doubt arises, according to the order for reference, from the fact that, in this case, the trips were offered as a 'free gift' to the subscribers of a daily

newspaper, with the result that the principal contracting party was not required to pay any sum which could, under normal market conditions, be considered proper consideration for the travel offered.

15 I would begin by saying that the conditions laid down by the Directive to establish whether given tourist services fall within its scope are, I find, satisfied for each of the plaintiffs in the main proceedings. There is no doubt that these were package services within the meaning of Article 2(1) of the Directive, in that the trips in question included flights, accommodation and other tourist services not ancillary to the first two, including the tour in the company of a German-speaking tour guide.

16 It is less obvious, however, whether the conditions laid down by the first part of that provision and by Article 1 of the Directive are met. The Austrian Government disputes that, in the present case, package services sold or offered for sale at an inclusive price in the territory of the Community are in point. In its view, the holidays booked by the plaintiffs in the main proceedings were given away, not sold, to the subscribers to the daily newspaper. In support of its argument the Austrian Government maintains that both the context and the wording of the Directive show that for there to be a `package' there must be a close relationship between the services offered by the organiser or retailer of the holiday and the consideration demanded of the consumer. This means that the consumer must be asked to pay a price which corresponds to the value of the service as a whole and which is calculated by reference to that service, even if the payment does not necessarily cover all of the costs.

17 I do not find the interpretation advanced by the Austrian Government convincing for a number of reasons. It should be observed at the outset that interpretation of the Directive must always be informed by the general principle that, in cases of doubt, its provisions must be interpreted as far as possible in favour of the party to whom protection is intended to be given, in this case the consumer of tourist services. This conclusion is reached on the basis of a systematic analysis of both the text of the Directive and its objectives and also in the light of its preamble...

18 That said, it must then be pointed out that the text of the Directive contains nothing to imply that tourist services do not fall within its scope where the price paid by the consumer does not correspond to the economic value of the services offered in return, or where the monetary consideration demanded from the consumer is imputed to one part of the 'package' only...

19 There can, on the other hand, be no doubt that the tourist services offered by the newspaper were sold in the context of a relationship which was clearly contractual in nature or that the price demanded as payment was an inclusive price paid in advance by the consumers. This is the case as regards both the subscribers who intended travelling alone (who were asked to pay only the single room charge and the airport taxes) and those who made bookings for themselves and their companions (who had to pay only the airport taxes). Admittedly, the fact that these consumers were required to make only a reduced payment will in turn limit the damage or loss sustained in the event of the organisers insolvency and, consequently, any liability on the part of the State in the event of its having failed to implement the Directive properly or at all, but I do not think it is correct to infer from this that the services in question should be excluded altogether from the scope of the Directive. I also think

that, with regard to those subscribers who intended to take up the offer along with their companions, the fact that it was the subscriber who was asked to pay the full price, which was then formally attributed to the companions, is not without significance. (8) Those travelling as companions could not have taken part in the trips offered by the newspaper without the intervention of a subscriber, and from this it can ultimately be said, in accordance with the opinion expressed by the United Kingdom Government, that in cases of this sort the `package' must be considered as a unit: the price paid by the subscriber, whether it is attributed to the subscriber himself or to his companion(s), acts as consideration for the participation of both in the holiday offered for sale by the organiser. From this perspective, it is indisputable that what are concerned are tourist services which fall within the scope of the Directive.

20 I should add that, for all the plaintiffs, the fact that the payment was attributed to just one or two of the services offered (either the flight alone, or the flight and the overnight accommodation), does not alter the terms of the question. If it did, the organiser of package travel would, as the United Kingdom Government has observed, be able to prevent the rules for the protection of consumers from applying simply by attributing the payment of the price to a single part of the package.

23 As to the second question, I do not think it necessary to say very much. The fact that the tourist services in question were offered in the context of a misleading promotional campaign, which was expressly held by the Austrian Courts to infringe competition law, does not alter the terms of the question. Indeed, the recognition of the misleading nature of the offer, presented by the newspaper as `free' whilst in fact it was not, serves at most to confirm that the tourist service in question was in fact offered for sale for valuable consideration and so could not fail to fall within the scope of the Directive.

24 Nor do I think any greater merit can be attached to the other objection raised by the Austrian Government to the effect that the travel offered in the case in point does not fall within the scope of the Directive because the offer was only addressed to a well defined group of persons (the subscribers to the newspaper). The scope of the Directive is clearly not limited to tourist services which are offered to a potentially unlimited number of consumers, it being sufficient that they are sold or offered for sale within the territory of the Community at an inclusive price, and that they include at least two of the components listed in Article 2(1).

25 For the reasons stated, I find that the tourist services in point in the main proceedings fall within the scope of the Directive.

55 On the basis of all the foregoing considerations, I therefore propose that the Court give the following answers to the questions put to it by the Landesgericht Linz:

(1) The protection referred to in Article 7 of Council Directive 90/314/EEC of 13 June 1990 on package travel, package holidays and package tours extends to travel for which the principal contracting party must pay

(a) the airport security tax (departure tax) and a single room supplement, if he travels alone, or

(b) only the airport security tax (departure tax), if he travels with one or more accompanying persons paying the full price.

(2) Such travel falls within the scope of the Directive even when it is offered by large-circulation daily newspapers of a Member State exclusively to their subscribers as part of a misleading advertising campaign.

Judgment

...

11 The plaintiffs in the main action are subscribers to the daily newspaper Neue Kronenzeitung. In November 1994 they received a letter from the publisher informing them that, to thank subscribers for their loyalty, the newspaper had arranged for the travel organiser Arena-Club-Reisen to offer them by way of gift (save for airport taxes) a four or seven day trip to one of four European destinations.

12 The offer included, in particular, the following services: flight with on-board refreshments, three or six nights' accommodation in a double room with breakfast in a four-star hotel, and guided tours. Persons travelling with subscribers were required to pay the price set out in a brochure. If a subscriber decided to travel alone, he was required to pay a single-room supplement of ATS 500.

13 Subscribers who accepted the offer received a confirmation of their booking from the travel organiser and were required to pay the organiser a deposit of 10% of the relevant charges, the balance being payable no later than ten days before the scheduled departure date.

14 The offer proved to be far more successful than the travel organiser had anticipated, and this caused the organiser logistical and financial difficulties which led it to apply, on 4 July 1995, for bankruptcy proceedings to be initiated against it. The advertising campaign organised by Neue Kronenzeitung was subsequently held by the Austrian Supreme Court to be incompatible with national competition law.

15 The plaintiffs in the main action booked their trips between 19 November 1994 and 12 April 1995. Some of them were to travel alone, others in the company of one, two or three persons. They all paid the whole of the travel costs in advance. However, the trips, which were to take place between 10 April and 23 July 1995 according to the individual bookings, were cancelled for a number of reasons.

16 For three of the plaintiffs in the main action who made bookings in 1994 no guarantee was provided since the Regulation only applied to package travel booked after 1 January 1995. Two of the three registered their claims as creditors in the organising company's insolvency, but although they were admitted as creditors they failed to obtain any settlement from the available assets in the estate. The payments of another three of the plaintiffs who booked their trips after 1 January 1995 and were to leave after 1 May 1995 were in principle covered by a guarantee issued in accordance with the Regulation. However, the bank guarantee of ATS 4 000 000 issued by the travel organiser was insufficient to reimburse the travel costs they had paid, the final level of cover being only 25.38% of the amount paid.

17 The plaintiffs brought an action against the Republic of Austria before the Landesgericht Linz, before which they claimed that Austria was liable for its failure to transpose Article 7 of the Directive in good time and in full, in order to recover the full amount they had paid over, in so far as they had not yet been reimbursed. The Republic of Austria disputed its liability, arguing inter alia that the subscribers who

had made bookings to travel alone did not fall within the scope of the Directive, that, given the date on which the Regulation entered into force and given the other measures adopted with a view to transposing the Directive, there had been no serious breach of Community law, and that there was no causal link in this case in that, quite aside from any liability on the part of the State, there were circumstances of fact, not ordinarily foreseeable, which had decisively contributed to the damage caused to the travellers.

...

The first and second questions

24 By its first and second questions, which it is appropriate to consider together, the national court is essentially asking whether Article 7 applies to trips which are offered by a daily newspaper as a gift exclusively to its subscribers as part of an advertising campaign that contravenes national competition law and for which the principal contractor, if he travels alone, pays only airport taxes and a single-room supplement or, if he is accompanied by one or more persons paying the full rate, airport taxes only.

25 The plaintiffs in the main action, the French and United Kingdom Governments and the Commission all submit that that question must be answered in the affirmative.

26 The Austrian Government, on the other hand, argues that there can be said to be a package only where the consumer is required to pay, as consideration for all the services stipulated in the contract, a price which corresponds to the value, and is calculated on the basis, of all those services. If the person travelling is only required to pay a single-room supplement instead of a global price for a trip which is essentially offered free of charge (apart from minor ancillary costs) then it is not a package within the meaning of the Directive. Moreover, the scope of the Directive does not extend to trips which are neither sold nor offered for sale on the market to an unlimited number of potential customers but are instead offered as a gift only to a predetermined class of persons.

27 It must be borne in mind first of all that the purpose of Article 7 is to protect consumers against the risks arising from the insolvency of the organiser of the package travel. Those risks, inherent in the contract concluded between the purchaser and the organiser, stem from the payment in advance of the price of the package and from the spread of responsibilities between the travel organiser and the various providers of the services which, in combination, make up the package. Consequently, the result prescribed by Article 7 of the Directive entails the grant to the traveller of rights guaranteeing the refund of money that he has paid over and his repatriation in the event of the organiser's insolvency.

28 In the present case, is should first be observed that the plaintiffs in the main action found themselves exposed to precisely those risks against which Article 7 was intended to provide protection. First, when the plaintiffs paid over money before their departure, they were exposed to the risk of losing that money; secondly, they were exposed to the risk of being stranded at their destination should the organiser become insolvent during their trip and the carrier refuse, because of that insolvency, to provide the service required for the return journey.

29 It must also be borne in mind that, according to Article 2(1) of the Directive, all that is needed to constitute a package is the pre-arranged combination of at least two of the three components mentioned in that paragraph, when sold or offered for sale at an inclusive price.

30 Taking into account the objective of Article 7, and having regard to that definition of 'package', it must be held that Article 7 applies even if the consideration the purchaser is required to pay does not correspond to the total value of the package or relates only to a single component of it.

31 Next, it must be observed that there is no basis in the text of the Directive for limiting its scope to packages offered to a potentially unlimited number of consumers and that it would be contrary to the purpose of the Directive to do so. In order for the Directive to apply, it is sufficient if the package is sold or offered for sale within the territory of the Community at an inclusive price and includes at least two of the components mentioned in Article 2(1) of the Directive.

32 Lastly, it must be noted that the fact that the advertising campaign consisting in the offer of free trips by the daily newspaper Neue Kronenzeitung was found to be incompatible with national competition law cannot prevent those trips from constituting package travel within the meaning of the Directive.

33 In those circumstances, the answer to the first and second questions must be that Article 7 of the Directive applies to trips which are offered by a daily newspaper as a gift exclusively to its subscribers as part of an advertising campaign that contravenes national competition law and for which the principal contractor, if he travels alone, pays airport taxes and a single-room supplement or, if he is accompanied by one or more persons paying the full rate, airport taxes only.

...

3.2 Pre-Arranged Combination

What constitutes a pre-arranged combination of package components? Does pre-arranged apply to circumstances where the components have been put together at the request of the consumer?

Club-Tour, Viagens e Turismo SA v *Alberto Calos Lobo Goncalves Garrido and Another* ECJ C-400/00; [2002] ECR I-4051

30 April 2002

1. By a decision of 31 October 2000, received at the Court on 3 November 2000, the Tribunal Judicial da Comarco do Porto referred to the Court for a preliminary ruling under Article 234 EC on two questions on the interpretation of Article 2(1) of Council Directive 90/314/EEC of 13 June 1990 on package travel, package holidays and package tours (OJ 1990 L 158 p. 59; the 'Directive).

2. Those questions arose in the course of a dispute between the travel agency Club-Tour, Viagens et Tourismo SA ('Club-Tour) and Mr Lobo Goncalves Garrido concerning payment of the price of a holiday.

Legal background

3. The purpose of the Directive is to harmonise the laws, regulations and administrative provisions of the Members States concerning package travel, package holidays and package tours sold or offered for sale within the Community.

4. Article 2(1) of the Directive provides:

'For the purposes of this Directive:

1. package means the pre-arranged combination of not fewer than two of the following when sold or offered for sale at an inclusive price and when the service covers a period of more than twenty-four hours or includes overnight accommodation:

(a) transport;

(b) accommodation;

(c) other tourist services not ancillary to transport or accommodation and accounting for a significant proportion of the package.

The separate billing of various components of the same package shall not absolve the organiser or retailer from the obligations under this Directive."

5. Point (j) of the Annex to the Directive states:

'Elements to be included in the contract if relevant to the particular package:

...

(j) special requirements which the consumer has communicated to the organiser or retailer when making the booking, and which both have accepted."

The dispute in the main proceedings and the questions referred

6. Mr Lobo Goncalves Garrido purchased from Club-Tour, for PTE 1 692 928, a holiday consisting of air tickets and accommodation for two weeks, full board, in the holiday village of Gregolimano (Greece).

7. For that purpose, Club-Tour bought a holiday from the travel agency Club Med Viagens Ld.[2] ('Club Med'). It was thus Club Med which undertook to make the necessary reservations at the holiday village of Gregolimano for accommodation, meals and transfers, organised and published the holiday programme, and fixed the overall price.

8. On their arrival at the holiday village, Mr Lobo Goncalves Garrido and his family noticed that it was infested by thousands of wasps, which prevented them - throughout their stay - from fully enjoying their holiday. Moreover, the immediate request by Mr Lobo Goncalves Garrido for the transfer of himself and his family to another village could not be dealt with by Club-Tour, as the Club Med which it contacted stated that it was not in a position to arrange appropriate alternative accommodation.

9. For that reason, on his return home, Mr Lobo Goncalves Garrido refused to pay the price of the holiday agreed with Club-Tour. The latter thereupon sought an order from the Tribunal Judicial da Comarca do Porto that Mr Lobo Goncalves Garrido pay the price of the holiday. Before that court, Club-Tour denied that the Directive applied to the present proceedings, arguing that the holiday sold was outside its scope.

10. Taking the view that the Directive aims to protect consumers of holiday services by making tour operators and travel agents liable for loss caused to consumers as a result of the improper execution of a contract, and that national law must be interpreted and applied in accordance with the Directive, the Tribunal Judicial da Comarca do Porto referred the following questions to the Court for a preliminary ruling:

"(1) Does a package organised by the agency, at the request and on the initiative of the consumer or a strictly defined group of consumers in accordance with their wishes, including transport and accommodation through a tourism undertaking, at an inclusive price, for a period of more than twenty-four hours or including overnight accommodation, fall within the scope of the concept of package travel as defined in Article 2(1)?

(2) May the expression pre-arranged which appears in the directive be interpreted as referring to the moment when the contract is entered into between the agency and the customer?"

The first question

11. By the first question, the court of reference essentially asks whether the word 'package' used in Article 2(1) of the Directive must be interpreted as including holidays organised by a travel agency at the request of and according to the specifications of a consumer or a defined group of consumers.

12. In line with the submissions of the governments and of the Commission to this Court, the answer to that question must be in the affirmative.

13. The Directive, which is designed amongst other things to protect consumers who buy 'package' holidays, gives a definition of that term in Article 2(1) whereby it is enough, for a service to qualify as a 'package', if, first, the combination of tourist services sold by a travel agency at an inclusive price includes two of the three services referred to in that paragraph (namely transport, accommodation and other tourist services not ancillary to transport or accommodation and accounting for a significant proportion of the package), and, second, that service covers a period of more than 24 hours or includes overnight accommodation.

14. There is nothing in that definition to suggest that holidays organised at the request and in accordance with the specifications of a consumer or a defined group of consumers cannot be considered as 'package' holidays within the meaning of the Directive.

15. That definition is reinforced by point (j) of the Annex to the Directive, which provides that, among the elements to be included in a contract covered by the Directive are 'special requirements' which the consumer has communicated to the organiser or retailer when making the booking, and which both have accepted.

16. In those circumstances, the answer to the first question is that the term 'package' used in Article 2(1) of the Directive must be interpreted as including holidays organised by a travel agency at the request of and according to the specifications of a consumer or a defined group of consumers.

The second question

17. By its second question, the referring court essentially asks whether the term 'pre-arranged combination' used in Article 2(1) of the Directive must be interpreted as including combinations of tourist services which are put together at the time when the contract is concluded between the travel agency and the consumer.

18. Given the answer suggested by them to the first question, the governments which have submitted observations to the Court and the Commission propose an affirmative answer to the second question.

19. As it has been held in paragraph 16 of this judgment that the term 'package' in Article 2(1) of the Directive must be interpreted so as to include holidays organised in accordance with the consumer's specifications, the term 'pre-arranged combination which constitutes one of the elements of the definition of 'package', necessarily covers cases where the combination of tourist services is the result of the wishes expressed by the consumer up to the moment when the parties reach an agreement and conclude the contract.

20. The answer to the second question must therefore be that the term 'pre-arranged combination' used in Article 2(1) of the Directive must be interpreted so as to include combinations of tourist services put together at the time when the contract is concluded between the travel agency and the consumer.

On those grounds, THE COURT (Third Chamber), in answer to the questions referred to it by the Tribunal Judicial da Comarca do Porto by decision of 31 October 2000, hereby rules:

1. The term 'package' used in Council Directive 90/314/EEC of 13 June 1990 on package travel, package holidays and package tours, must be interpreted so as to include holidays organised by travel agents, at the request of and in accordance with the specifications of a consumer or limited group of consumers.

2. The term 'pre-organised' combination used in Article 2(1) of Directive 90/314 must be interpreted so as to include combinations of tourist services put together at the time when the contract is concluded between the travel agency and the consumer.

3.3 Accommodation

Is student exchange accommodation qualifying accommodation within the meaning of the Package Travel Directive?

AFS Intercultural Programs Finland ry ECJ C-237/97; [1999] ECR I-825

11 February 1999

Judgment

1. By order of 23 June 1997, received at the Court on 27 June 1997, the Korkein hallinto-oikeus (Supreme Administrative Court) referred to the Court for a preliminary ruling under Article 177 of the EC Treaty two questions on the interpretation of Council Directive 90/314/EEC of 13 June 1990 on package travel, package holidays and package tours (OJ 1990 L 158, p. 59, hereinafter 'the Directive').

2. Those questions arose in the context of administrative proceedings brought by AFS Intercultural Programs Finland ry ('AFS Finland'), a non-profit-making association operating in Finland which coordinates student exchanges at international level, with regard to whether the Directive, and in particular Article 7 thereof, applies to activities such as those engaged in by AFS Finland.

3. The first recital of the preamble to the Directive provides that one of the main objectives of the Community is to complete the internal market, of which the tourist sector is an essential part; the fifth recital provides that the Council welcomed the Commission's initiative in drawing attention to the importance of tourism and took note of the Commission's initial guidelines for a Community policy on tourism; and the seventh recital provides that tourism plays an increasingly important role in the economies of the Member States and that the package system is a fundamental part of tourism.

4. According to Article 1, the purpose of the Directive is to approximate the laws, regulations and administrative provisions of the Member States relating to packages sold or offered for sale in the territory of the Community.

5. Article 2 is worded as follows:

'For the purposes of this Directive:

1. "package" means the pre-arranged combination of not fewer than two of the following when sold or offered for sale at an inclusive price and when the service covers a period of more than twenty-four hours or includes overnight accommodation:

(a) transport;

(b) accommodation;

(c) other tourist services not ancillary to transport or accommodation and accounting for a significant proportion of the package.

The separate billing of various components of the same package shall not absolve the organiser or retailer from the obligations under this Directive;

2. "organiser" means the person who, other than occasionally, organises packages and sells or offers them for sale, whether directly or through a retailer;

...'

6.   Articles 3 to 6 contain provisions relating to the protection of the consumer against certain risks inherent in package travel, namely misleading information in the descriptive matter concerning a package, the method of payment of the price of the package and blurring of the responsibility to be apportioned as between the organiser and/or the retailer of the package and the various suppliers of services whose combined services constitute said package.

7.   Article 4(3) of the Directive provides that the consumer may transfer his booking, where he is prevented from proceeding with the package, after having first given the organiser or the retailer reasonable notice of his intention before departure, to a person who satisfies all the conditions applicable to the package.

8.   Article 7 of the Directive provides that 'the organiser and/or retailer party to the contract shall provide sufficient evidence of security for the refund of money paid over and for the repatriation of the consumer in the event of insolvency'.

9.   The Directive was implemented in Finland by two laws: the valmismatkaliikelaki (Law on package travel firms) No 1080/1994 and the valmismatkalaki (Law on package travel) No 1079/1994.

10.   Under Law No 1080/1994, persons engaged in the business of organised travel must be registered in the register kept by the Kuluttajavirasto ('Consumer Protection Office'). Paragraph 8 of that Law requires travel organisers to provide a security approved by the Consumer Protection Office to protect the rights to which the traveller is entitled under Law No 1080/1994, in the event of insolvency.

11.   According to its statutes, AFS Finland's object is to promote international cooperation and exchanges between various cultures. To that end, like its sister organisations in other countries, it organises exchange programmes for students aged between 16 and 18 years of age. AFS Finland relies for its activity on the support of various donors and foundations as well as on the work of volunteers. It receives aid from the Finnish State in order to finance its activity.

12.   AFS Finland sends students abroad twice a year, usually for a period of 6 to 11 months. The students attend school in the host country and lodge with families which put them up free of charge. AFS Finland selects the students

and places them in families on the basis of interviews. Next, the association arranges the students' transport to the host country by scheduled flights and, as a rule, the host family collects the student at the arrival point. Before departure, the students and their parents follow preparatory courses on conditions abroad.

13.   10% of the cost of the journey is paid when the student is admitted to the exchange programme, that is to say normally about 10 months before departure. The balance is then paid before the beginning of the visit, in three instalments. On departure, the student receives a pre-paid return air ticket. Part of AFS Finland's fees goes to a reserve fund which ensures, in particular, the students' transport home where the return ticket issued to them cannot be used.

14.   On 25 August 1995 the Consumer Protection Office informed AFS Finland that it considered the student exchange activities of that association to be comparable with the exercise of package travel business. The Consumer Protection Office set a time-limit of one month for AFS Finland to register in the register of package travel businesses warning it that, should it fail to do so, it could prohibit it from pursuing its activities. Since AFS Finland did not comply with the request to register, the Consumer Protection Office, by decision of 14 October 1996, ordered it to suspend its business.

15.   AFS Finland applied to the Korkein hallinto-oikeus for an order annulling the decision, claiming that it was not a package travel organiser within the meaning of the directive.

16.   In those circumstances, the national court decided to stay proceedings pending a preliminary ruling by the Court of Justice on the following two questions:

"(1) Does a student exchange of approximately six months' or one year's duration, the purpose of which, so far as the student is concerned, is not a holiday or tourism but to attend an educational establishment in a foreign country and familiarise himself with the people and culture of that country by staying free of charge with a local family as a family member fall, wholly or in part, within the scope of Council Directive 90/314/EEC of 13 June 1990 on package travel, package holidays and package tours? Are certain characteristics which indicate the non-commercial nature of the organiser of the exchanges, such as the facts that participants in the exchange programme are only required to pay part of the costs of the programme, that the exchanges are devised by way of collaboration between non-profit-making associations in various countries, and that they rely largely upon voluntary work and are financed with public funds set aside for cultural activities, relevant to the question whether the student exchanges fall within the Directive's scope?

(2) In the event that the student exchanges do fall with the general scope of the Directive, the Court is then asked to answer the following questions concerning the detailed interpretation of Article 2:

(a) Is a long-term stay, free of charge, with a family, where the guest is treated almost like a child of the family, to be considered accommodation within the meaning of Article 2(1)(b)?

(b) Are the training of the students and their parents, the selection of the host families and educational establishments in the host country and the preparation of documentation relating to the host country to be considered other tourist services within the meaning of Article 2(1)(c)?"

17.   By the first part of its first question, the national court is asking essentially whether the Directive applies to journeys:

- consisting of student exchanges of six months' or one year's duration;

- the purpose of which is attendance by students at an educational establishment in a host country in order to familiarise themselves with the people and culture of that country; and

- during which the students are accommodated free of charge with a local family as a family member.

18.   AFS Finland submits that applying the Directive, in particular Article 7 thereof, to its activity would cause it to incur excessive costs for providing a security and these would give rise to an increase in costs to each student, which would have a detrimental effect on student exchanges at both international and national level. It observes that the purpose of such exchanges is to promote education in an international spirit as well as international peace and understanding. In order to attain that objective, AFS Finland must convey young people to host countries and find them host families, but that package is not organised with touristic purposes in mind and the journey cannot be considered to be a significant proportion of the experience to be gained from the student exchange.

19.   AFS Finland further submits that the specific need to protect the consumer, for which the Directive is intended to provide, has been brought about by the stiffening of competition in the tourist industry. However, non-profit-making organisations do not operate in a similar competitive context and their operation does not present characteristics which could undermine consumer protection. AFS Finland takes the view that travel in the context of a student exchange programme is therefore excluded from the scope of the Directive.

20.   The Finnish Government submits that the Directive cannot be interpreted as meaning that only holiday travellers benefit from the protection introduced by the Directive. Nor does the Directive mean that journeys must be organised or offered for sale in the context of a business. Only an activity pursued occasionally is excluded from its scope. Moreover, no special condition as to the type, level or duration of accommodation was provided for in the Directive. According to the definition given, packages are to be sold or offered for sale at an inclusive price. The fact that, in the case in the main proceedings, accommodation is of a certain duration and free of charge is of no relevance to the application of the Directive. The essential

element is whether the organisation of accommodation is included in the package. Travel in the context of student exchanges includes therefore the organisation of transport and accommodation simultaneously, so that it is not appropriate to interpret the concept as 'other tourist services'.

21.   The United Kingdom Government submits that it is plain from the purpose and general scheme of the Directive that it applies to the tourist sector and that it does not cover educational activities of the kind engaged in by AFS Finland. The fact that Article 2(1)(c) of the Directive refers to 'other tourist services' means that, in order for the package to fall within the scope of the Directive, the other two elements must also be offered within the context of the provisions of tourist services.

22.   According to the Commission, the Directive is applicable irrespective of the purpose of the journey, even if, for example, the consumer is travelling to his destination for educational purposes. Moreover, student exchanges do not fall outside the scope of the Directive merely because their organisers are not engaged in a commercial activity. Furthermore, the Directive is applicable even where the consumer does not himself pay the full cost of the journey.

23.   The Commission claims in addition that the fact that admission to exchange programmes is subject to an assessment of the student's personality and of his ability to adapt to the place where the programme is held and to the family which hopes to host him indicates that it is not a package within the meaning of the Directive. Thus, participation in student exchanges is not based on objective factors and Article 4(3) of the Directive, under which the consumer is entitled, where he is prevented from proceeding with the package, to transfer his reservation to a person who satisfies all the conditions applicable to the package, does not apply. Next, the Commission submits that the student exchanges organised by AFS Finland are not a package within the meaning of the Directive on the ground that a long-term stay free of charge with a family where the student is treated as a member thereof cannot be considered to be accommodation within the meaning of the Directive. Finally the Commission states that the tourist services which they comprise are not a significant proportion of the packages.

24.   First of all, it should be borne in mind that, according to Article 2(1) of the Directive, a package is comprised of the pre-arranged combination of not fewer than two of the following three elements: 'transport', 'accommodation' and 'other tourist services not ancillary to transport or accommodation and accounting for a significant proportion of the package' when the service covers a period of more than 24 hours or includes overnight accommodation.

25.   Since AFS Finland organises student travel to the host country on scheduled flights, the journey in question contains the transport element required by Article 2(1) of the Directive.

26.   So far as concerns the interpretation of 'accommodation', it should be observed that, even if, traditionally, it is hotels, hostels or similar

establishments which provide such a service for consideration, the fact that the stay is at such an establishment providing such service for consideration does not constitute an essential element of the definition of accommodation for the purposes of the Directive.

27.   It should further be pointed out that, even if the accommodation included in package travel is normally of relatively short duration, that cannot be regarded as a defining element of the term 'accommodation' within the meaning of the Directive. As the Finnish Government points out, under Article 2(1) of the Directive, any travel exceeding 24 hours falls within the definition of packages, since no 'maximum' duration has been provided for.

28.   None the less, it does not necessarily follow from the foregoing that the period spent by a student with a host family where he is treated as a member of that family and as if he were another child should be described as accommodation within the meaning of the Directive. Even though the type of accommodation, the fact that it is free of charge and the duration thereof are not, as such and taken in isolation, defining elements of the concept of accommodation for the purposes of the Directive, their combined effect is such that 'hosting' which possesses all those characteristics cannot be described as accommodation within the meaning of the Directive.

29.   It must therefore be concluded that student exchanges such as those at issue in the main proceedings do not contain the element of accommodation required by Article 2(1) of the Directive. It is therefore necessary to come to a conclusion on the question whether such exchanges comprise 'other tourist services not ancillary to transport or accommodation and accounting for a significant proportion of the package'.

30.   In this connection, it should first be observed that selection of a school by the organiser of the package cannot in itself be regarded as a tourist service within the meaning of Article 2(1)(c) of the Directive. The specific purpose of such a service, offered to the students taking part in international student exchanges, is the education of the participants.

31.   Next, the service constituted by the selection of a family to host a student during his stay is in any event an ancillary service within the meaning of Article 2(1)(c) of the Directive and is therefore not covered by the concept of other tourist services.

32.   Finally, even supposing that preparation of the documentation necessary for a stay in another country and the courses which the students follow with their parents before departure in order to prepare for life abroad could be considered to be covered by the concept of other tourist services, they do not fulfil one of the criteria specified in Article 2(1)(c) of the Directive, namely that of accounting for a significant proportion of the package.

33.   In those circumstances, it must be held that student exchanges such as those in issue in the present case do not contain the necessary elements to be regarded as package travel within the meaning of the Directive.

34.   The answer to the first part of the first question must therefore be that the Directive does not apply to travel:

- comprising student exchanges of about six months' or a year's duration;

- the purpose of which is attendance by the student at an educational establishment in the host country in order to familiarise himself with its people and culture; and

- during which the student stays with a host family as if he were a member thereof free of charge.

35.   In view of the foregoing, there is no need to reply to the other questions put by the national court.

3.4 Transport and Regulation 4

Keppel-Palmer v Exsus Travel & Royal Westmoreland Villas [2003] All ER Digest 183 (June)

Gage J.

01   This is a claim by the Claimant for damages arising out of a holiday over the Millennium period 1999/2000 in Barbados. The holiday was between 12 December 1999 and 13 January 2000 and took place at Villa Frangipani, the Royal Westmoreland Club in Barbados. There are two Defendants; they are Exus Travel Limited, the First Defendant, which arranged the holiday, and Royal Westmoreland Villas Limited, the Second Defendant, which is the company which built the villa and the owner of the resort. The villa itself was owned by a private individual or individuals. Following the issue of the claim solely against the First Defendant, the First Defendant served a Part 20 notice on the Second Defendant; the Second Defendant was joined as a Defendant by the Claimant.

02   The Claimant paid the sum of US$142,425 for the holiday. At the then current exchange rates that is equivalent to £88,025. It is the Claimant's case that the holiday was to be a truly luxurious holiday for herself, her husband, her two grown-up children, her sister and her brother. Not all members of the family were scheduled to be present all the time. The Claimant's case is that the accommodation at Villa Frangipani did not measure up to the requisite standard and was a sad disappointment to her and her family. She claims damages under two heads; first, she claims a sum representing the diminution in value of the holiday; secondly, she claims a sum for loss of enjoyment of the holiday.

03   A number of issues arise. They are as follows. (1) Which of the two entities, the First or Second Defendant, was the contracting party? (2) Do the Package Travel, Package Holidays and Package Tours Regulations 1992 Statutory Instrument 1992 No 3288 apply? (3) What are the terms of the contract? (4) Were there breaches of the terms of the contract and/or the regulations? (5) If there are breaches, what is the proper sum to be awarded in damages?

. . . .

09   The first issue with which I shall deal is which of the two Defendants was the contracting party?

. . . . . . As between the two Defendants, there is no dispute; the Second Defendant concedes it was the contracting party, and the First Defendant its agent. The documents show that the brochures were all headed 'The Royal Westmoreland, Barbados'. Faxes sent by Mr Roth were headed 'Royal Westmoreland'. The invoice, on the other hand, was sent on the First Defendant's (or rather its predecessor in title) headed notepaper. The name and address at the bottom stated that the First Defendant was the general sales agent for the Second Defendant. The Claimant said that at all times she dealt with Mr Roth, believing him to be involved with the First Defendant.

11   It is submitted on behalf of the Claimant that because she dealt exclusively with Mr Roth at his London office, and the invoice was made out by the First Defendant, I should find that the contract was between the Claimant and the First Defendant. The fact that the invoice showed the First Defendant as being the general sales agent of the Second Defendant did not alter the position. Sales agent, it is submitted, is to be distinguished from a letting agent.

12   I cannot accept these submissions. I see no reason to reject the assertion made on behalf of the First and Second Defendant that the Second Defendant was the principal and that the First Defendant was its agent. All the documents point to this being so. That being the case, the only way that the First Defendant would be contractually liable to the Claimant is if it was acting for the Second Defendant but the Second Defendant was an undisclosed principal. In my view, this cannot be said to be the case. At all times the Claimant knew the Second Defendant ran the resort. In 1997, before she and her husband acquired the property at Sandy Lane, they had been shown round the resort by employees of the Second Defendant. In June 1999, she had dealt directly with the Second Defendant when leasing for five days a villa at the resort. In the circumstances, in my judgment, the contract was clearly made by the First Defendant as agent of the Second Defendant. The fact that the invoice e was made out in the First Defendant's name does not alter this conclusion.

13   The next issue is the application of the Package Travel, Package Holidays and Package Tours Regulations 1992 which hereafter I shall refer to as 'the Regulations.' There is no dispute that if the Regulations apply, the First Defendant is a 'retailer' and the Second Defendant 'an organiser' as defined by Regulation 2. The question whether the Regulations apply depends upon the proper meaning of 'package' as defined by Regulation 2 and as applied to the facts of this case. Mr. Chapman submits that the contract in this case was a package as defined by Regulation 2. That Regulation reads, in its material part, as follows:

> "Package means the prearranged combination of at least two of the following components when sold or offered for sale at an inclusive price and when the sale covers a period of more than 24 hours or includes overnight accommodation (a) transport, (b) accommodation, (c) other tourist services not ancillary to transport or accommodation, and accounting for a significant proportion of the p[package."

At first sight it would seem curious to describe the contract in this case as a package holiday. The Claimant and her husband flew by Concorde at their own expense to Barbados and the rent for the villa for 33 days was US$142,425, as I have already indicated. The basis of the submission is that the Second Defendant provided other tourist services; in this instance said to be a housekeeper and private cook and certain facilities in local hotels and within the resort.

14   The Defendant submit first, that in this case the provision of transport to and from the airport does not qualify as one of the component parts of a package holiday. Secondly, that the facilities provided were ancillary to the accommodation. Thirdly, he submits that neither the transport nor the facilities were prearranged.

15   In my judgment, there is force in all of these submissions. First, I have great difficulty in accepting that the provision of transport to and from the airport, a

journey of some 45 minutes' duration, can in the context of this case qualify as transport under the definition in Regulation 2. I accept that there is no quantitative definition of transport, but in my view in each case it must be a question of fact and degree as to what constitutes transport under the Regulation. Here, in my judgment, what was provided was so minimal that it can be disregarded. In any event, on the facts of this case, on a balance of probabilities, I find that it was not prearranged. True it is that in her second witness statement the Claimant described Mr Roth as stating that the price included a limousine service from the airport. I accept that this may have been said, and I accept that the Claimant and her husband were transported by one of the Second Defendant's vehicles from the airport to the villa. However, as the documents show, a fax dated 09 December 1999 from the Second Defendant to the Claimant's secretary or employee shows that at the Claimant's request the Second Defendant agreed to arrange for a car hired by the Claimant for the holiday to be sent to the airport to pick up herself and her husband. There would seem to have been no need for this if it had always been agreed that the Second Defendant would send a limousine to carry out that task as part of the contract. There is nothing in any of the pre-contract documents or faxes which refer to this item of transport. On the assumption it was mentioned by Mr Roth, I find it was mentioned in passing, not as part of the prearranged contractual package.

16   I also accept the submission that the facilities provided were, in this case, ancillary to the accommodation.

17   In view of these conclusions, it is strictly unnecessary for me to rule on the submissions on the issue which concerns Regulation 4. Regulation 4 reads, in the material part:

> "(1)   No organiser or retailer shall supply to a consumer any descriptive matter concerning a package, the price of a package or any other conditions applying to the contract which contains any misleading information."

18   [The] submission is that the words 'supply to a consumer any descriptive matter' do not comprehend supply by the First Defendant (the retailer) of a brochure produced by the Second Defendant.... further that the words 'descriptive matter' import something of substance, such as written material, and do not include oral descriptions.

19   I reject this submission on the meaning of supply in this Regulation. In my view, given its ordinary meaning, it must include supply of a brochure itself obtained from the organiser. The fact that the source of the brochure was the Second Defendant, the organiser, does not, in my judgment, enable the retailer, the First Defendant, to avoid liability as a supplier under the Regulations. As far as the submission that descriptive matter does not include oral descriptions, I am aware that a District Judge has held that it is wide enough to include oral descriptions, but since it is unnecessary in this case for me to decide this issue I decline to do so.

. . . .

42   I turn therefore to the final issue, which is the issue of damages. It is agreed that damages are to be assessed in this case under two heads, although both may be combined in one sum. The two heads are diminution in value of the holiday, and loss of enjoyment or disappointment. The Claimant claims under the first head a sum

representing half the cost of the holiday and under the second head a sum of £500 per day, making a total under this head of £16,500. Mr Saggerson reminds me that I should not leave out of account the undoubted benefits provided by the Second Defendant. The Claimant and her party did get premises according to the advertised specifications; it did have magnificent views; it was over the Millennium period; and a number of additional features such as a golf course, private beaches, the sanctuary's central facilities and a gym with a large pool were provided. Both counsel accept that I have to assess both elements of damages on a pragmatic or broad basis.

43   In my opinion, the Claimant is entitled to a sum representing diminution in value of the holiday. In assessing this sum, I take into account that this was on any view a very expensive holiday. As such, the Claimant and her party were entitled to expect very high standards. As I have found, what she was provided with fell below these high standards. Doing the best I can, and taking into account what was provided, the location and the time of the year, I assess damages under this head in the sum of £22,000. As will be obvious, I calculate this on the basis of a deduction of some 25% from the contract price.

44   In my opinion, she is also entitled to a sum representing loss of enjoyment. In this respect, I take into account that this was designed to be a very luxurious holiday, coming after her and her family's, difficult year. This is, however, not the case of a family unused to holidays. To be able to afford the cost of such a holiday indicates a degree of financial resources from which I infer that the Claimant and her family are used to some of the more expensive things in life, including regular holidays. For that reason, in my judgment, the sum for loss of enjoyment must be modest; I assess it in the sum of £3,000.

45   Accordingly, I give judgment for the Claimant against the Second Defendant in the sum of £25,000.

3.5 Regulations 4 and 5: Liability of Retailers

Josephs v *Sunworld Ltd (t/a Sunworld Holidays)* [1998] CLY 3734

J booked a family holiday in the Algarve for his wife and two children aged five and eight years to stay at the Vale do Lobo Villas. The holiday was booked six months before departure at a cost of GBP 2,933.60. On arrival, they were allocated a villa in another resort, Vale De Garro, which was a 15 minute drive from the resort they had booked. The accommodation was terraced, it was in close proximity to a main highway and had confined grounds. It had a small swimming pool which J claimed was overfilled with chemicals. Further allegations comprised a failure to provide barbecue utensils, the television remote control did not work, the sun loungers were broken, balcony doors did not lock, the bed linen was not changed for the duration of the holiday and the fridge and kettle did not work. Further, a new hotel was being constructed at the rear of the property. J had expected exclusive accommodation of a high standard in the resort of Vale Do Lobo which would according to the brochure "stand in its own (usually enclosed) grounds with mature gardens and lawns and many will be on small exclusive estates". In addition, a car hired by J broke down, but S failed to provide any assistance. J brought an action against S, the tour operator for breach of contract.

Held, granting judgment to J, that S was in breach of contract and of the Package Travel, Package Holidays and Package Tours Regulations 1992. In particular, S was in breach of the 1992 Regulations Reg.4 because the descriptive matter in the brochure was misleading. It was in breach of Reg.12 because there had been a significant alteration to central terms due to the change of resort, Vale De Garro did not fall within the Vale Do Lobo area and therefore was a separate resort. J had not been offered the alternative of continuing with the holiday and claiming compensation or returning home therefore S was in breach of Reg.13. A significant proportion of the services were not provided and the aspects of the villa were not as indicated, therefore there had been a breach of Reg.14 in relation to the standard of accommodation. Under Reg.15(1) the tour operator was strictly liable for any problems with the holiday. Further S was in breach of Reg.15(7) due to its failure to assist J following the breakdown of the hire car even though the car had not been hired through S. Under Reg.15(7) the tour operator must provide every assistance even if the loss suffered was due to another party. Damages of GBP 1,500 were awarded in respect of diminution in value of the holiday together with GBP 500 general damages for distress and inconvenience.

Minhas v Imperial Travel Ltd CLY 03/o2/02

M brought an action against I under the Package Travel, Package Holidays and Package Tours Regulations 1992 Reg.4 and Reg.5, for loss and damage arising from a 14 day holiday in Cyprus which M and her boyfriend had booked with I, who had acted as agent for the tour operator, S. I had described the accommodation as being open plan and suitable for three people; therefore M had to pay an under occupancy fee. It was also stated that the hotel had a roof top swimming pool. M discovered that the room was very small and would not accommodate three people. The swimming pool was located approximately 400 yards down a busy main road on the roof of the hotel reception building; the toilet in the apartment did not flush adequately; the sink taps leaked continuously, the hotel reception toilets smelt of urine and were littered with toilet paper, and on their first day, M discovered vomit on the stairwell. Neither I nor S offered alternative accommodation. Therefore M made her own arrangements on the first day of her holiday, incurring additional accommodation and mobile phone charges, and taxi fares in moving luggage to the new hotel and back again. In total M suffered four days of inconvenience and distress. I did not raise issue with the allegations concerning misdescription and substandard accommodation, but contended that as agent they were not responsible for the misdescription nor the facilities provided and it was S who was responsible.

Held, granting judgment in favour of M, that a travel agent was defined as a "retailer" in the Regulations and therefore is bound not to provide misleading matter. Further, as I had received payment directly from M, I was the "other party to the contract" as described in Reg.15. M was entitled to bring a claim on behalf of herself and her boyfriend in her name only, *Jackson v Horizon Holidays Ltd* [1975] 1 W.L.R. 1468 (»»digest) followed. I was liable to pay damages for the alternative accommodation expenses of GBP 418, travel and telephone expenses of GBP 25 and inconvenience and distress assessed at GBP 300 for both M and her boyfriend in total. As I had not availed themselves of the Regulations they were ordered to pay the costs unreasonably incurred by M in pursuing the matter to the hearing, because the matter had been capable of settlement prior to the instant hearing.

3.6 Regulations 12, 13 and 14

Lambert v *Travelsphere Limited,* 1 September 2004, Peterborough County Court (HHJ Darroch)

Regulations 12 and 13

This is an appeal from the decision of the District Judge, District Judge Elliott, given on the 23rd June 2004, when he awarded damages to the Claimants, Mr and Mrs Lambert, that being the balance of the money they had paid for a proposed holiday to China and Hong Kong.

...

I turn to look at some of the uncontested facts.

The first one is that on the 10th January 2003 the Claimants booked the holiday which, as I say, was to China with an add-on to Hong Kong.

On the 2nd April 2003 a document ... came out. That was some guidance and health advice from the Department of Health. What we refer to as SARS had broken out in various places – Hong Kong and parts of China and Singapore. It was an unpleasant infection. Sadly a number of people died. It was very uncertain, at least at that stage, how long it would last; how far it would spread. It arose very quickly. I think I am right in saying that it disappeared rather quickly.

...

On the 8th April a letter was sent by the Defendants, the travel company.

... It seems to me to say very clearly that the travel company is considering the position. There is concern. "We will re-arrange your itinerary to omit Hong Kong if it is necessary to do so", pointing out that normal booking conditions apply. I do not find that really a misleading letter. I point out that the Defendants did not indeed have to circulate anything at that stage.

......

After referring to the letter of the 8th April the District Judge said this:

> "I think that that is certainly a major change. It significantly alters an essential term of the contract, and that is that the trip to Hong Kong would or might be cancelled".

The Claimants put it in this way. They say that the District Judge was stating, and rightly stating, that that letter itself imported a variation into the contract. There was a change between certainty and uncertainty, and it was an alteration of a significant term. That being so, they say that the regulations, which I will have to look at in a moment – Regulation 12 of the Package Travel Holiday Regulations – is brought into play.

The Defendants see it differently. They say that there is a finding of fact there by the District Judge that the trip to Hong Kong would or might be cancelled, and that that is very different from saying that the regulation is engaged.

...

Do I agree with the District Judge as to his finding?

It seems to me that there is a finding of fact, as the Defendants say, that the trip to Hong Kong might be cancelled...

Dealing with the legal argument, I am bound to say that I cannot see that writing a letter, which I think was meant to be helpful, which seems to have been understood by the Claimants, in itself altered the terms of the contract. One has to remember that there would have been quite a degree of uncertainty in the minds of anyone thinking of going to China or to Hong Kong at that time that SARS was around and about. I do not think that that letter itself altered the terms of the contract at all.

. . . .

I therefore reject the first argument that there was an alteration in the contract by virtue of the letter.

. . . .

[On 18 April 2003] the Claimants write to the Defendants and say:

> "Thank you for your courtesy during our telephone conversations in which we discussed our reasons for *considering* [my emphasis] cancellation".

It goes on:

> "Thank you also for taking our telephone cancellation of the above holiday....We look forward to receiving the appropriate refund, including the commission".

It goes on to say that they are reserving their position as to the 60% balance. There is some further correspondence about that balance.

I find it quite impossible to read that letter as anything other than a cancellation, especially when I see it in the context of the telephone conversation. The Claimants had made a difficult and deliberate decision that they did not want to bring this virus back. They were aware of the consequences that they might only get 40%. They wrote a letter which the Defendants were entitled to take as confirming the cancellation. The Defendants are in the travel business which tries, and I can take notice of this, to provide holidays at affordable prices. ~They can only do that if they know how many people are going to go on a particular trip, what commitments they have got to meet and what income they are having coming in. They are entitled to read that letter as being a fairly clear, indeed totally clear, cancellation. *I am not able to accept that writing a further paragraph saying, "We reserve our position" in any way makes it some sort of conditional cancellation. I have no doubt that the Claimants did cancel the holiday.

...

We now come to what I consider to be the heart of the case. I am now looking at paragraph 12 of the Regulations.

"In every contract there are implied terms to the effect that where the organiser is constrained...."

....

"...before the departure to alter significantly an essential term of the contract, he will notify the consumer...and then the consumer is entitled in broad terms to a substitute holiday or a refund".

A number of points arise. What is meant by "constrained" and what is meant by "an essential term of the contract"?

In the course of argument the Claimants' representative has said that taking Hong Kong out was a significant term. I am bound to say that I agree with that. If Hong Kong were to be removed, that would be an essential term........

What then is meant by "the organiser is constrained"? That is a strong word. It really seems to me to mean that he had absolutely no other choice. He was forced into doing what he did.

....

The interpretation I put upon it, as a matter of law, is this. You may not shut your eyes to the absolutely obvious, but you may also keep open the contract until the last moment. Whilst there is some flicker of hope that you may be able to carry it out, you are not constrained. You are exercising a choice.

I find as a fact that, on the documentation, it is not possible to say that at the stage before the cancellation, which I find to have been made via telephone before that date, it was absolutely inevitable and unavoidable. One may well conclude that some operators reading the documents would have made the decision earlier, but this is not, in my view, what is meant by "constrained". They were exercising a judgment, in my view, in trying to keep the holiday open. They were, I have no doubt, mindful of the fact that if they pulled out too early they might face a claim. It is correctly described as a "tightrope" upon which they walk. .... I am quite unable to say that when they made that decision they were not exercising choice. Just as the Claimants exercised the decision to pull out, so at that point the Defendants were exercising the option to try to keep the holiday alive.

In my view, therefore, there was nothing to engage Rule 12. The organiser was not constrained to alter the contract. The organiser was constrained to do so before departure, but that is not relevant in this case. He was not so constrained before the contract was terminated.

Unauthenticated Decisions

Clark and others v Travelsphere Limited, 22nd October 2004, Leeds County Court (HHJ Hickinbottom)

Regulations 12 and 13

In the summer of 2003, the world found itself in the grip of a devastating epidemic. The SARS (Severe Acute Respiratory Syndrome) virus infected over 4,000 people worldwide, with cases reported as far afield as Canada, South Africa and Malaysia. In Hong Kong the outbreak was particularly severe, with 1755 people infected and 299 killed between February and March. Hundreds of thousands of residents donned surgical masks and up to 10,000 people were quarantined in an attempt to contain the virus.

Against this background, the Claimants, two couples, had booked package holidays with the Defendant tour operator to travel to China and Hong Kong between the 12th and 27th April 2003. The holidays were to consist of an 11-day tour of China and a 3-day add-on trip to Hong Kong and Guangdong province. Both couples paid the full cost of the holiday in advance.

Acting in response to the extensive media coverage of the SARS outbreak, and mindful of advice issued by the World Heath Organisation and the Foreign Office (FCO), the Claimants expressed concerns to the Defendant about the Hong-Kong section of the tour and asked to discuss the possibility of alternative arrangements, including returning home after the 11 day tour of China with a full refund of the 'add-on'. The Defendant's reply, which in evidence was said to be based upon information obtained from local contacts in Hong Kong and the Far East, was that the situation was being monitored constantly (on an 'hourly' basis according to the Defendant's representative at trial) and that the Defendant was still hopeful that it would improve in time for the tour to take place. The Claimants were therefore told that the holiday would go ahead, subject to the proviso that if FCO guidance on Hong Kong remained the same at the end of the 11-day tour of China, holidaymakers would be flown home.

On the 12th April, the Claimants did not turn up at the Airport and the tour party left without them. In the event, the holiday was in fact curtailed after the 11-day tour of China and the Hong Kong add-on did not go ahead. Those holidaymakers who went on the trip were refunded the cost of the add-on. An email was sent by the Claimants to the Defendant on the day of departure in which they explained that they were not going on the trip because of fear of the outbreak. The Defendant went ahead with all its non HK tours until 23 April 2003 when the FCO included Beijing in its avoidance advice.

The Holiday Contract between the parties provided, in summary, that if the Consumer cancelled the holiday less than 72 hours prior to departure they would not be entitled to a refund, but that if it was 'necessary' for the tour operator to make a major change to the itinerary, compensation would be offered.

The Claimants' case, in which the full cost of the holiday was claimed, was pleaded on two bases:-

1)   Breach of a duty of care in 'indicating that [the Claimants] should travel to an unsafe country'; and

2)   Breach of contractual obligations in 'failing to be in a position to confirm that each element of the trip would be [undertaken] safely'.

Although not specifically pleaded, it was also accepted by both parties that the holiday contract was a package holiday and therefore subject to the provisions of the Package Travel etc. Regulations 1992 ('the 1992 Regulations').

The Defendant's case.

At trial, it was argued on behalf of the Defendant that looking at events not with hindsight, but from the standpoint of the tour operator in April 2003, the Claimant's case was unsustainable.

First, it was argued, it could not be said that the Defendant had indicated that the Claimants should travel to an unsafe country. On the contrary, they had expressly stated that as long as FCO guidance advised against travel to Hong Kong, then that part of the tour would not go ahead.

Secondly, the Defendant was not under a contractual obligation to confirm that every element of the tour would be carried out when they were dealing with what was, in essence, a 'moving target'. FCO advice was fluid: it could move from one extreme to another in a matter of hours and the Defendant's responsibility was simply to monitor this advice and alert customers to the risk of possible alterations to the holiday.

The Defendant also argued that Regulation 12 of the 1992 Regulations did not apply. Regulation 12 provides that where an organiser is 'constrained before departure to alter significantly an essential term of the contract ... he will notify the consumer as quickly as possible in order for him to take appropriate decisions and to withdraw from the contract without penalty'. The Defendant conceded at trial that the Hong Kong add-on was a 'significant' part of the tour and that if it had decided prior to departure that that element was not going ahead at all, then this would have entitled the Claimants to a refund of the price paid.

However, on the facts, it was the Defendant's case that, as at the 12th April (the date of departure) it was not 'constrained' within the meaning of the Regulations because the Hong Kong part of tour was still some 12 days away and FCO advice could change at any moment. Reliance was placed upon an earlier decision of HHJ Darroch in *Lambert v Travelsphere*, Peterborough County Court, 1st September 2004, in which it was stated that an organiser is not constrained as long as there is a 'flicker of hope' that the holiday may still be carried out.

The Defendant drew the judge's attention to Regulation 15, which provides an exception to the liability of the tour operator for improper performance of the contract for reasons beyond either party's control: a 'force majeure' clause.

Moreover, Regulation 14, it was argued, provided consumers with substantial protection against changes made after departure, so that this was not a case in which the Claimants would have been left without a remedy if they had chosen to go on the holiday.

It was also emphasized that although this was a consumer dispute, it could not be viewed in isolation. If the Defendant had cancelled the trip prior to departure, the Claimants in this case would have been satisfied but the other holidaymakers who had chosen to go on the tour of China would have been up in arms. Put simply: you cannot please everybody all of the time and by not turning up at the airport, the Claimants had attempted to short circuit the regulatory framework and shut out the force majeure clause in Regulation 15.

The Claimant's case.

The Claimants' arguments were pinned upon what it argued was the completely unambiguous nature of FCO guidance at the time: that travel to Hong Kong should be avoided. It was suggested to the Defendant's representative in cross-examination that the only reason for going ahead with the tour in the face of this advice was to maintain its commercial advantage. In effect the Defendant knowingly manipulated the contract terms and Regulations and deliberately refused to make a significant alteration even though one was required.

The date at 'constraint' should be measured, it was argued, should be the 'last reasonable moment before departure'. In this case, that would mean that, as at the 11th April, the day before departure, if the FCO guidance had not changed then the Defendant was constrained to alter a significant element of the tour and the Claimants were entitled to act as they did.

The Judgment

The judge found as follows:

1)   Both parties were honest and respectable.

2)   The Defendant was a reputable company with agents and contacts operating in the Far East.

3)   The Defendant's belief, on the basis of information being provided to it from Hong Kong, that it may still be able to provide the add-on, was an honest and reasonable one.

4)   The situation with SARS at the time was in a state of flux and FCO guidance could change at any moment, with immediate effect. The Defendant was monitoring this situation on an hourly basis.

5)   It was not therefore possible to say, on the 12th April, that the trip to Hong Kong would not go ahead.

6)   The Defendant never had any intention to take the Claimants to Hong Kong unless the FCO guidance changed. The Claimants were aware of this.

7)   The reasons given by Mrs Clarke in her evidence at trial – that not knowing in advance whether the Hong Kong trip would go ahead made such matters as collecting the dogs from the kennel and booking a taxi from the airport very difficult – were exaggerated and unrealistic.

8)   The Claimants had accepted before the 12th April that they would have been prepared to go for the 11-day trip to China even if the Hong Kong element didn't go ahead.

The judge concluded that this was a case which could be decided simply by looking at the terms of the Holiday Contract itself. The Defendant, he said, never suggested that the Claimants should travel to an unsafe country, and there was no contractual term obliging it to confirm that each part of the trip would be undertaken safely. The Defendant could not be expected to 'predict the future'.

This was a case, he said, in which the issue was a common one: which of two innocent parties to a contract should bear the financial burden of events beyond the control of either of them? The Claimants, by cancelling the contract first, and within 72 hours of departure, engaged clause 4 of the Holiday Contract and were not entitled to any compensation. The fact that if the Defendant had cancelled first the Claimants would have been entitled to compensation should not, and did not, alter the situation.

What of the Regulations? The judge preferred to focus on the Holiday Contract itself, which he found it was accepted by both parties mirrored the Regulations. However, for the sake of clarity, he decided simply that 'constrained' in Regulation 12 meant 'forced', and that the Defendant was not 'forced' at the material time to cancel the tour. It was as simple as that.

Westerman v Travel Promotions Ltd

Regulation 14

W brought an action for damages against a tour operator, T, after he and his wife returned from a package holiday in Switzerland, Italy and the Mediterranean. The holiday consisted of a sightseeing programme with transport between locations to be provided by rail, bus and boat. The cost of the holiday was GBP 795 per person. The holiday brochure promised that part of the travel arrangements on days 3 and 10 of the holiday would be on a "unique" 1939 built train, "the Red Arrow". W's evidence was that himself and his wife were rail enthusiasts and would not have booked the holiday but for the attraction of the Red Arrow and the rail travel thereon. Days before the tour commenced W was informed by letter that the Red Arrow had been withdrawn from service. T provided an alternative itinerary which provided instead for first class travel on Swiss Rail and for a significantly longer period to be spent travelling by train than would have been provided on the Red Arrow as originally scheduled. T also made provision for a flight in place of a stretch of the journey that was scheduled to be covered by bus and the Red Arrow. W and his wife embarked on the holiday and upon their return, sought compensation for the failure to provide the Red Arrow train journeys. T provided a GBP 50 per person refund and argued that, given only three hours in total would have been spent on the Red Arrow and that more than adequate alternative arrangements had been made, that satisfied their liability to compensate W under the Package Travel, Package Holidays and Package Tours Regulations 1992 Reg.13 and Reg.14. T relied upon Reg.14(2) in support of its refusal to make any further payment to W.

Held, giving judgment for the claimants, that (1) the primary reason why W and his wife had booked the package holiday was the Red Arrow element of the package; (2) the changes to the Red Arrow element of the package, which also formed a major part of T's brochure advertising for the holiday, constituted a significant alteration to the itinerary and/or a failure to provide a significant proportion of the package holiday services; (3) while T had made alternative arrangements and had paid GBP 50 per person in compensation, that did not amount to adequate compensation in accordance with T's duty under Reg.14(2) of the 1992 Regulations, and (4) in the circumstances, W and his wife would be awarded GBP 100 each for the diminution of the value of their holiday and a further GBP 100 each for their distress and disappointment.

Martin v Travel Promotions Ltd (t/a Voyages Jules Verne) [1999] CLY 3821

Regulation 14

M1 and his wife, M2, brought an action for damages against a tour operator, T, after their return from a package holiday in India which cost GBP 795 per person. M1 and M2 were scheduled to fly to the UK from Bombay on April 17. They lived in Menorca and had pre booked a flight from London to Menorca on April 18. On April 16 an internal flight was to carry M1 and M2 from Delhi to Bombay to connect with the UK bound flight. The internal flight was delayed arriving at Bombay, but the evidence was that, even if it had arrived on schedule, there would not have been time to check in for the UK flight, which departed without them. M1 issued an ultimatum to T's local agents that, unless it was confirmed that he and his wife had seats on an alternative flight on April 18, he would purchase two first class tickets that he had reserved. On April 17, T was able to confirm places on board a UK flight scheduled to depart on April 18, by which time M1 had made arrangements for himself and his wife to return first class to the UK on the same flight. That flight arrived in the UK in time for the connection with the Menorca flight. M1 alleged that T's failure to ensure that the internal flight connected with the international flight put T in breach of an implied contractual term that T would use all proper skill to make arrangements to return M1 and M2 on April 17 and in time for them to catch the Menorca flight. M1 and M2 claimed the cost of two first class air fares, together with the cost of some telephone calls and a taxi fare.

Held, that (1) the Package Travel, Package Holidays and Package Tour Regulations 1992 Reg.14(2) and Reg.14(3) applied to the package holiday contract; (2) the implied term alleged by M1 and M2 was an unnecessary addition to the contract; (3) T's failure to ensure that M1 and M2 returned to the UK on April 17 constituted a failure to provide a significant proportion of the services contracted for within the meaning of Reg.14, and (4) T was under an obligation to make equivalent alternative arrangements at no extra cost to M1 and M2 and to compensate them for the difference between what was contracted for and what was provided. M1 and M2 were entitled to GBP 250 each in general damages for their loss of enjoyment occasioned by the delay and special damages in respect of telephone calls. However, they were not entitled to the cost of the first class air fares on the basis that that loss was not caused by any breach of T's contractual obligations. It resulted from hasty and disproportionate action by M1 and M2.

Holidays, Excursions, Trips, Tours, Promotions Packages? A Voyage Around Regulation 2(1) of the Package Travel Regulations 1992
Matthew Chapman [2004] ITLJ 129

The Judges of the European Court of Justice have been just as adept as their English counterparts in approaching the interpretation of the clear provisions of Article 2(1) of the 1990 Council Directive (translated into English law by the 1992 Regulations) in a creative manner which pays comparatively little attention to what Article 2(1) actually says.

Pre-arranged

The questions arising out of this part of the definition contained in Regulation 2(1) focussed on:

> (a) exactly when the combination of qualifying components had to be pre-arranged in order to satisfy Regulation 2(1) – e.g. at time of offer/invitation to treat; before contracting; before departure from UK;

> (b) the identity of the person responsible for the pre-arrangement; and,

> (c) the potential liability of travel agents.

Some answers have now been provided by the European Court of Justice in *Club-tour Viagens E Turismo SA v Alberto Carlos Lobo Goncalves Garrido* (Case No C-400/00) (ECJ). We now know, as a result of this case, that:

> (a) bespoke or (what the Advocate-General referred to as) *customised* packages are within Article 2(1) of the Directive (and these are defined as, *tourism services which are organised at the request and on the initiative of the consumers or a strictly defined group of consumers in accordance with their wishes and therefore not fixed in advance unilaterally by the travel agencies*);

> (b) it follows that there is no need for any proposal to be made to the consumer by the other party to the contract and changes made to any proposal by the consumer will not prevent the holiday arranged as a result of such changes from being a *package* (A problem of construction which does not arise in a UK context because of the provision contained in sub-para 2(1)(ii) of the 1992 Regulations referring to *the request of the consumer* which does not appear in the present text of the 1990 Directive);

> (c) it also follows, that, the term *pre-arranged combination ... necessarily covers cases where the combination of tourist services is the result of the wishes expressed by the consumer up to the moment when the parties reach an agreement and conclude the agreement.*

It should be noted that the Advocate-General in *Club-Tour* regarded the insertion of the word *pre-arranged* in Article 2(1) to be *superfluous* in the light of his conclusion that the Directive embraced customised holidays (at para 26 of his Opinion (a view also taken by the Commission in its representations), although this was not a view taken – at least not expressly – by the Court)).

In his Opinion for the Court Advocate-General Tizzano also expressed the view that, *the fact that the payment due from the consumer corresponds to only one of the components of the service does not preclude the application of the directive* (at para 16). This assertion appears superfluous to the reasoning which underlies the decision of the Court and is not found in the judgment. It refers, instead, to an earlier decision of the Court of Justice in *Walter Rechberger & Ors v Austrian Republic* [1999] ECR I- 3499 (ECJ). In this case the Claimants were subscribers to an Austrian daily newspaper which – as a reward for their loyalty – offered them a holiday under an arrangement with a travel agency.

The holiday consisted of all the traditional elements of a package: return flights, airport transfers, accommodation and a tour guide.

Subscribers were required to pay only the airport tax, provided that they travelled with someone who was not a subscriber and paid full price.

Subscribers travelling alone were required to pay a single room supplement (on a price per night basis) in addition to the airport tax. The offer was vastly more popular than the organisers had anticipated and the travel agency became the subject of insolvency proceedings. The Claimants were rewarded for their loyalty with the loss of the monies that they had paid out and did not get their *free* holidays.

On a reference to the European Court raising the question whether the holidays constituted a *package* the Court gave short shrift to the argument that the *free gift* status of the offer – so that the consumer was not required to pay any sum constituting proper consideration for the services to be provided – had any impact on the application of the Directive. It was *sufficient* for the application of the Directive that there be a *prearranged combination of at least two of the three components mentioned in ...* [Article 2(1)] *when sold or offered for sale at an inclusive price.*

It did not matter that the sale price did not correspond to the total market value of the package or that it related only to a single component of it, although one assumes that there would still – in some realistic sense – need to be a *sale* or an *offer for sale* in order to satisfy the definition contained in Article 2(1) and Regulation 2(1) and that, therefore, an entirely gratuitous gift or promotion would not be within their ambit.

It is interesting to note that, in both *Rechberger* and *Club-Tour*, the European Court of Justice made implicit reference to the clarity of the text of Article 2(1) and the need to construe the relevant Article in:

(a) a manner consistent with the principle that in cases of doubt such doubt should be resolved in favour of the class of persons intended to be protected by the Directive; and,

(b) that interpretation should not stray beyond the clearly expressed text of the Directive.

It is somewhat ironic that, in the next case to be considered, the Court of Justice might be said to have broken both of these golden rules in order to arrive at a pragmatic solution which bears more resemblance to a common law approach than that adopted in *Rechberger* and *Club-Tour*.

Accommodation and the purpose of the tour

AFS Intercultural Programs Finland ry [1999] ECR I-825 (ECJ) concerned student exchanges.

The Association was a non-profit making body established under Finnish law. Its admirable object was to promote cultural understanding and harmony between nations by sending adolescent Finns overseas. The length of stay varied between 6 and 11 months. The Association arranged transport in the form of scheduled flights. The participants were accommodated, free of charge, by host families and, during their stay, they attended local schools and took part in a range of cultural and other events. The only charge to the participants was a contribution of around 10% of the total cost which was due around 10 months before departure (payable in 3 instalments). On departure the participant received a pre-paid return air fare.

The Association received a request from the Finnish authorities to file an entry in a register of travel organisers which was established in the Finnish ordinance that gave effect to the 1990 EU Directive. The Association did not comply with the request to register and, accordingly, the Finnish authorities ordered the suspension of its business as a travel organiser and also levied a hefty contingent fine. The Association applied to the Finnish Administrative Court to quash the decision to suspend its activities and the Court made a reference to the European Court where the primary question was this:

Does a student exchange of approximately six months' or one year's duration, the purpose of which, so far as the student is concerned, is not a holiday or tourism but to attend an educational establishment in a foreign country and familiarise himself with the people and culture of that country by staying free of charge with a local family as a family member fall, wholly or in part, within the scope of ... [the 1990 Directive on Package Travel]?

Advocate-General Saggio was in no doubt that the Directive was engaged and that the cultural tours were packages:

> (a) the purpose of the tour was not a matter that required consideration under Article 2(1) of the Directive – the Court was not required by the Directive to embark upon the esoteric exercise of defining the *concept of tourism*;

> (b) the substantive scope of the Directive could be defined only by reference to the clear terms of Article 2(1) and if the criteria contained therein were satisfied then the Directive should apply;

> (c) there was no need for any commercial element to be applied to the Article 2(1) definition and the (earlier) *Rechberger* decision made it clear that the price paid for the package did not need to bear any resemblance to the total market value of the tour;

> (d) the duration of the stay and the *gratis* nature of the accommodation provided did not prevent the tour from constituting a package.

Among other representations made to the Court the UK government argued that educational tours – embarked upon without a clear *touristic* purpose – would not be caught by the Article 2(1) definition.

In the course of its judgment the Court acknowledged that:

(a) the transport element of Article 2(1) was satisfied by the provision of flights;

(b) the accommodation element of Article 2(1) was as capable of embracing a stay in a private home as more traditional stays in an hotel or hostel; and,

(c) no maximum duration of stay was stipulated in the Directive.

However, the Court went on to say this:

Nonetheless, it does not follow from the foregoing that the period spent by a student with a host family where he is treated as a member of that family and as if he were another child should be described as accommodation within the meaning of the Directive.

Even though the type of accommodation, the fact that it is free of charge and the duration thereof are not, as such and taken in isolation, defining elements of the concept of accommodation for the purposes of the Directive, their combined effect is such that 'hosting' which possesses all those characteristics cannot be described as accommodation within the meaning of the Directive.

This decision is open to the criticism that, having apparently directed itself that *hosting* was capable of being accommodation within the meaning of Article 2(1), the Court concluded – without detailed explanation – that the Directive was not engaged.

One might identify the result of *AFS Intercultural Programs* as flowing from the conclusion that *hosting* fell into some special category of tour to which the Directive did not apply. However, that does not provide any explanation why that is so.

In fact, it seems likely that the Court was adopting a pragmatic solution to the problem which confronted it. The reason that the UK government made representations, as did the Commission and other member states that the Directive did not apply, is because the likely effect of a decision applying the Directive to educational and cultural visits would be to subject schools and voluntary organisations (Scouts, Guides, Rotary Clubs and the like) to the full regulatory regime of the Directive. No doubt it was feared that doing so would inhibit the organisers of such trips from continuing to organise such trips.

Equally, the Court seems – at least implicitly – to have given credence to the representations of the UK Government that the Directive was intended – in the words of the Preamble – to introduce a *Community Policy on tourism* and not to regulate educational and cultural programs organised by people of goodwill (although this was probably because the Court concluded that the hosting, which did not comprise accommodation, was equally not the provision of *other **tourist** services not ancillary to transport or accommodation.*)

The decision appears, as I have argued, to represent a pragmatic solution which departs from the strict wording of Article 2(1) to achieve what the Court considered to be the just result. The Court came close to saying that the tours organised by the Finnish Association just did not look or feel like packages.

Transport and a quantitative threshold

A consumer rents a luxury villa over the Millennium New Year period on the island of Barbados. She flies to Barbados by Concorde which she organises herself and pays for separately from the price she pays for the accommodation.

Included within the cost of the villa rental which is sold to the consumer by the villa owner is the provision of a complimentary limousine service which collects the consumer at the airport and spirits her across the island to her luxury villa (a 45 minute journey one way). The luxury villa is a considerable disappointment and the consumer wants to bring a claim under the Package Travel etc. Regulations 1992. Can she do so?

One might think the answer to this is a simple yes:

> (a) the price paid for the villa included the prearranged, complimentary limousine service;
>
> (b) there is no quantitative element to the transport component of Regulation 2(1) – it does not require that the transport account for *a significant proportion of the package;*
>
> (c) the complimentary nature of the limousine service has no bearing – the fact that its hidden cost is wrapped up in the overall cost of the holiday should be immaterial (see, *Rechberger*);
>
> (d) the limousine transfer was the provision of what any layman would recognise as *transport.*

Last year the English High Court held that this was not a package in *Keppel-Palmer v Exsus Travel Limited and Royal Westmoreland Villas Limited* [2003] All ER (D) 183 (Jun) (QBD).

It should be noted that the observations made by Gage J in this connection were strictly *obiter* because he found as a fact that the Claimant in *Keppel-Palmer* had probably not been provided with a free limousine and had probably used a private hire car to get from airport to villa. However, he went on to say that, even if the limousine had been pre-arranged and provided on arrival, the holiday did not constitute a package. This was for two reasons:

> (a) the limousine service was *de minimis* and should not account for the transport element of Regulation 2(1) where:
>
> > • the holiday itself was of vast expense;
> >
> > • the return air flights (arranged separately by the consumer) also cost a large sum of money;
> >
> > • the holiday was for one month's duration whereas the transfer journey lasted only 45 minutes one way; and, in addition,
>
> (b) the limousine service was not separately invoiced or identified on any invoice – it was a gratuitous add-on and was not, therefore, sold or offered for sale within the meaning of Regulation 2(1) (cf. *Rechberger*).

This decision effectively adds to the definition of *transport* an additional requirement: namely, that the transport not be *de minimis*. It appears that what is and is not *de minimis* is – in that familiar common law phrase –a fact-specific matter and falls to be assessed on a case by case basis. The Judge appears to have found compelling the Defendant's submission that the holiday in *Keppel- Palmer* did not *look, feel or taste* like a package (see, A Saggerson, *One Man's Mansion is Another Woman's Monstrosity* [2003] 4 ITLJ 185, 186).

Conclusion

We have come a long way in the decade or so since the 1992 Regulations came into effect in the UK.

We now know that:

> (a) the purpose of a tour is irrelevant to its status as a *package*, unless, perhaps, it is clearly for *nontouristic* purposes;

> (b) that there is a minimum threshold of 24 hours or an overnight stay for a trip, tour or holiday in order for the same to constitute a *package*, but no maximum cut-off point – but that accommodation which is provided free of charge, in a private home and for a lengthy period of time (*hosting*) may not be *accommodation* within the meaning of Regulation 2(1);

> (c) there is no need for the transport component to account *for a significant proportion of the package* unless it is *de minimis* in which case it will not be taken into account;

> (d) we all know what *transport* and *accommodation* are, but we should not be confident that the Courts will agree with us.

As a result of the attentions of the ECJ and the English Courts the 1992 Regulations have accreted layers of interpretation and uncertainty which take the meaning of *package* beyond what might be suggested by a straightforward construction of Regulation 2(1). This means lots of lucrative fun for lawyers, but a great deal of uncertainty about what that ostensibly simple thing, a package holiday, actually is.

SECTION 4

STRICT AND FAULT LIABILITY

STRICT AND FAULT LIABILITY

Cases in this Section

6. *Thompson* v *Thomson Holidays Ltd*   **Page 262**

Removing the cause of an accident after the event is not evidence of any breach of contractual duty by the "occupier" of a hotel or a tour operator.

7. *James* v *Travelsphere Ltd*   **Page 263**

Tour operator not under any duty to warn tourists of obvious potential hazards at public recreational facilities (an elephant sanctuary). Allegation that the staff at such a facility were "suppliers" within the meaning of regulation 15 of the Package Travel [Etc.] Regulations 1992 abandoned.

8. *Langton* v *TUI (UK) Ltd*   **Page 264**

No responsibility for or duty to warn of power cuts at hotel.

9. *Grahame* v *JMC Holidays Ltd*   **Page 265**

Where significant delays had occurred in the provision of return holiday flights the tour operator was not liable for improper performance where the delays were caused by unusual in-flight technical problems – see also statutory defences.

10. *McRae* v *Thomson Holidays Ltd*   **Page 266**

A tour operator was not liable in a case where a consumer fell from a broken plastic chair in circumstances where there was no discernible pre-existing fault with the chair. No operational negligence against the hotel and so no liability on the tour operator.

11. *Martin* v *Thomson Tour Operations Ltd*   **Page 267**

It was incumbent on the Claimant to produce some evidence as what cryptosporidium was, how it could be contracted and what its incubation period was if he expected to succeed in a claim for gastric illness (cryptosporidiosis).

12. *Charlson* v *Warner*   **Page 268**

On a skiing holiday where the weather conditions were so adverse that skiing was not possible and the resort had to be evacuated, a tour operator was not liable for any failure to perform the holiday contract. See also statutory defences.

Hone v *Going Places Leisure Travel Ltd*, unreported, 16 November 2000, QBD, Manchester District Registry (Douglas Brown J)

The complainant, Mr Gerard Hone, claims damages for statutory compensation in respect of injuries allegedly caused by the Defendants failure to perform or the improper performance of, a contract for which the Defendant is liable to the Complainant by virtue of the provisions of Regulation 15 of the Package Travel, Package Holidays and Package Tours Regulations 1992. This claim gives rise to a number of disputed issues of law and fact. I am only concerned with the trial of the issue of liability.

The Defendant is a very well known Travel Agent with many high street shops and also invites business through advertisements on the ITV Teletext service. This branch of the Defendant's enterprise is called 'Late Escapes' and specialises in late or last minute holiday bookings. It is now agreed that the Defendant acts as a retail agent for tour operators but there was an issue as to whether the Defendant had made it known to, or clear, to the Claimant or his brother who actually made the holiday booking, that they were acting as retail agents for a tour operator. On 22 September 1996 the Claimant saw a holiday advertised on a Teletext message for 14 nights at a hotel at Gumbet in Turkey on a date convenient for him and at an acceptable price. Mr Iredale, the Sales and Operations Manager for Late Escapes, thought it unlikely that the advertisements would identify a resort and would have been more likely to name a country or general area as shown in the sample Teletext messages put in evidence. I accept the Claimant's evidence that the area and the identity of the location was important to him and the probability is he saw that on the screen. The following day his brother, Mr Duncan Hone, booked the holiday by telephone. Mr Hone himself looked at the Teletext message and then telephoned the number shown. He did not remember the details save that the holiday was through Going Places. He knew that his brother, then a serving police officer, was particularly anxious about booking through a reputable and well known concern. A telephone sales representative now known only as Gillian, dealt with Mr Hone. He asked if the holiday advertised was still available and it was. He gave the Visa number of the joint card held by himself and his wife and booked for four persons, that is, himself and his wife, his brother and his then fiancée. He is certain, and although pressed on this in cross examination, remained certain that there was no mention of Suntours or Sunways during the conversation. Gillian told him that a confirmation of the booking would be sent by post and the tickets were to be collected at the airport. There is no challenge on behalf of the Defendant that Suntours or Sunways had not been mentioned before the holiday was booked and paid for. It is a little surprising that Mr Iredale confirmed the contents of his witness statement namely, that the fact the holiday is provided by a tour operator, in this case Suntours, would not be made known to the customer until after the deal had been concluded and the credit card payment made. Although the precise Teletext message which the Claimant and his brother would have seen was not in evidence, specimens showing details of the resorts and prices at page 80 and 81 in the Core bundle are agreed to be representative of the screen text that would have been seen by them. There is a page which contains no details of holidays but which is a general advert for Going Places although they are not mentioned by name. There, in large letters 'GO DIRECT AND SAVE ££££££s' and at the bottom it says in small print "we act as retail agents for ATOL holders".

ATOL stands for Air Transport Operators Licence. Neither the Claimant nor his brother has any recollection of seeing that and indeed if they had, there is nothing to connect that advertisement with Going Places. All the sample pages contain the words "Retail Agt ATOL Hldr". The case put forward by the Defendant before me was that their advertisements make it clear that they were acting as agents for tour operators who were the holders of the appropriate licence. The sample pages in evidence show nothing of the kind. Mr Saggerson, counsel for the Defendant, conceded that it was open to the sensible construction that Going Places were retail agents who, themselves, held an Air Transport Operators Licence. That in my view is the only construction and true meaning of those words whatever they were intended to convey. Neither the Claimant or his brother however, remembers seeing those words. Their interest was in the location, date and price of the holiday and in dealing with a well known reputable firm such as Going Places. When the holiday documents arrived, the voucher to be exchanged for the tickets was headed in large print "Going Places Direct" and" Late Escapes" and in the top left hand corner in the representatives handwriting against the printed word operator, "Suntours" was written and the collection point for the air tickets was Suntours desk. Both the Claimant and his brother, particularly the brother who had these documents all the time with him, did not notice the reference to Suntours and have no recollection of which desk the air tickets were obtained from. Mr Duncan Hone said that he recollected a number of desks as they walked into the airport, which appeared to have a variety of agents. He handed over the letter and the tickets were located straight away. It was at this point for the first time that the name Suntours or Sunways was mentioned. He and his brother were cross examined carefully about this ... and as far as they were concerned they were dealing with Going Places or Late Escapes.

The party of four travelled to Turkey and the holiday passed uneventfully. The events giving rise to this claim arose on the return flight. The circumstances which are derived from paragraph 4 of the Particulars of Claim and the witness statements and oral evidence of the Claimant, his brother and the Claimant's wife, Mrs Hone. The return flight was on 19 October in an aircraft operated by Sunways, a Turkish airline operating apparently in partnership with a Swedish charter airline company. A short time into the flight from Adnan Menderes airport to Manchester, the aircraft was diverted to Istanbul following a bomb threat. The passengers were told to prepare for an emergency landing and as the aircraft was descending, instructions changed and the passengers were instructed to prepare for a crash landing. The Claimant, his brother and their ladies were sitting about eight seats back from the front on the starboard side. They had been told to leave by the door on that side but when they reached the front of the aircraft the port door had been opened by the only stewardess stationed at the front of the aircraft and she was struggling to open the door on the starboard side, pushing and kicking. The Claimant then left by the port side door from which ran a chute down to the tarmac. Before he began his descent he noticed a woman getting off at the bottom who he recognised as a woman he had met on holiday. He described her as huge, weighing approximately 25 stones. As he came down the chute he realised that the woman was struggling to get off and was in fact stuck at the bottom. He managed to open his legs wide enough to avoid striking her directly in the back but collided with her. Mrs Hone was right behind him and her feet struck him in the spine causing an acute pain which winded him. He managed to get to his feet and climbed over the woman over the side of the chute and then managed to get her to her feet and free of the chute and in so doing hurt his back again. The Statement of Case makes a number of allegations of failed or improper performance which in summary involved allegations of insufficient trained personnel were present at the top and bottom of the emergency escape chute and that instructions for the safe descent of the chute were not given. There was no evidence as to the type or size of aircraft involved. There was no evidence as to the number of airline staff onboard, no evidence as to any instructions given to the airline staff as to the evacuation of passengers and no evidence, expert or otherwise, to indicate whether the number of staff was adequate or inadequate, and in particular there was no evidence as to whether a stewardess or steward should have left the plane first to look after passengers at the bottom of the chute. The aircraft was deliberately made to land at a considerable distance from the terminal buildings. It crash landed about half a mile away. It was some minutes before any airport staff arrived at the scene.

The Claimant's case is that:

1. The contract was made by Mr Duncan Hone on behalf of the other members of the party and the Defendant as the provider of the holiday and tour operator. The Teletext pages made no reference to the fact that the holiday was with Suntours and instead emphasised the direct nature of the arrangement which was said to result in a money saving holiday, that the deals were not available in shops and that the retail agent i.e. the Defendant held an Air Transport Operator's Licence. The documentation stressed that the Defendant was a direct provider of the holiday. For example, the confirmation documents made it clear that Late Escapes was "the one-stop direct holiday shop". Although the Claimant and his brother did not notice the reference to Suntours it was too late for the Defendant to attempt to draw Suntours as operators to their attention when the contract had been made and the booking paid for before there was any mention of any other operator than Going Places.

2. Both Suntours and Sunways had now ceased trading and were insolvent but this was irrelevant because the wording of the 1992 regulations permits a claim to be made against a retailer in the circumstances of this case.

The interpretation section of the regulations is found in Regulation 2(1). Four definitions only need be referred to:

"*Contract*" means the agreement linking the consumer to the organiser or to the retailer, or to both, as the case may be."

"*The other party to the contract*" means the party, other than the consumer, to the contract, that is, the organiser or the retailer or both, as the case may be.

"*Organiser*" is the person who, otherwise and occasionally, organises packages and sells or offers them for sale whether directly or through a retailer.

"*Retailer*" is the person who sells or offers for sale the package put together by the organiser.

[It was] submitted that the object of the regulations was to give effect to the Directive of the Council of the European Communities on package travel, package holidays and package tours of 13 June 1990. The regulations follow closely the wording of the directive and implement for an incorporation into English law provisions which extend the liability of those in the travel trade, making, in this case, a retailer liable where he would not be liable under common law principles of the law of contract. It was the purpose of the directive and then of the regulations to put an end to escape routes which had up until then been used in the travel trade to avoid liability.

Because on the facts of this case, although in reality the Defendant did not provide the package and was not the operator, the Defendant held itself out as the operator and the contract here linked the consumer to the organiser and to the Defendant as retailer. [It was] accepted that a wider construction of the regulations putting liability on retailers who had made it clear they acted as agents for operators, was probably not permissible. This was because such a construction would represent such a substantial extension of liability for travel agents that much plainer words would be required to bring such liability about. For the purposes of [this] case [it was] contended on the perhaps unusual facts of this case the retailer was liable as the other party to the contract.

3. If the Defendant was "the other party to the contract" by regulation 15 there was absolute liability for the failure to perform the contract or the improper performance of the contract, in this case by the carrier Sunways. If, contrary to submission, fault had to be established then it was plainly proved here. It was obvious, [it was] submitted, that permitting the Claimant to descend the chute without any supervision and without any member of the airline staff stationed at the bottom of the chute there had either been a failure to perform the contract or an improper performance of the contract. It was so obvious that no evidence was needed of good airline practice and how it may have been breached by the Sunways personnel.

The Defendant's Case [was as follows]

[It was] accepted that the word "link" was a difficult word to give meaning to. It certainly could not be construed as to mean that the retailer should be generally liable under the regulations for the way in which a tour operator or its carrier provided the package holiday. ... a number of reasons [were advanced] of which I need only mention two. Firstly, there are statutory schemes compensating those who fall victim to insolvent airlines and tour operators e.g. the Air Travel Trust and the ATOL scheme itself run by the Civil Aviation Authority, and these are not applicable to retailers, unless the retailers are themselves actually providing the package holidays. Secondly, a travel agent does not have direct control over the services delivered as part of the package holiday. It has no control over, and cannot influence, standards of service or facilities provided during the holiday. Regulation 15 (1) does reserve rights of indemnity, but a travel agent would not be able to take advantage of those rights. There are circumstances, contemplated in the regulations where, for example, a travel agent enters into a contract itself with a consumer where e.g. there is a tailor made holiday put together by the retailer from a variety of sources and the retailer is a principal or Co-principal. In those circumstances the regulations plainly should apply. The construction of "link" put forward was this: before the regulations members of a family or other friends travelling in the party might be met with a plea that they were not in any contractual relationship with the retailer or organiser or both because the contract had been made with somebody else. The use of the word "link" makes it impossible for this defence to be maintained.

[It was submitted] that the breaches envisaged by Regulation 15 for which compensation could be obtained were of two kinds. The first which was probably an example of absolute liability was "*the failure to perform a contract*". An example he gave of this was an unconditional stipulation that the holiday would be at Hotel A whereas in fact it was provided in Hotel B. However, "*improper performance of the contract*" did import some degree of fault on the part of the supplier, in this case the airline carrier. ... there was no fault proved here and no breach made out. ... this being an emergency evacuation where the standards to be expected in respect of supervision could not be those of any conventional disembarkation. The reason for the emergency evacuation was that there was thought to be a bomb on the aircraft and therefore evacuation had to take place almost irrespective of incidental orthopaedic injuries. It was quite unrealistic to expect evacuating passengers to wait until the chute was empty before beginning their descent. The Claimant accepted that in his evidence. There was a complete lack of evidence that the staffing levels onboard were in any way inappropriate, and certainly nothing to support the bold allegation that the airline onboard staff should have been provided in sufficient numbers for one of them to be stationed at the bottom of each chute. If it be the case that the airport authorities should have provided someone to assist at the bottom of the chute, that could not be the responsibility of the Defendant as it was not the responsibility or fault of the supplier.

In any event, even if there was a breach on the part of the airline or its staff in the terms of inadequate supervision or advice the Defendant was entitled to avail itself of the statutory defence in Regulation 15(2)(c)(ii) that the failure was due to "*an event which the other party to the contract or the supplier of the services, even with all due care, could not foresee or forestall*". ... the circumstances of this evacuation were highly unusual. It was not suggested that the airline were in any way responsible for the crash landing, nor was it their responsibility that an immensely large lady got herself stuck at the bottom of the chute.

In the light of the view I have formed on the facts of this case it is only necessary to deal quite shortly with the submissions as to the meaning and effect of regulation 15. This regulation, taken with the interpretation provisions in regulation 2, does not in my view make a retailer liable for the performance of the contract unless:

1. The agent is acting for an undisclosed principal in which case the Claimant can sue either principal or agent at his option. See *Bowstead & Reynolds on Agency 16th Edition* Paragraph 9-012 at 559:

> "*Where the principal is undisclosed at the time of contracting the contract is made with the agent and he is personally liable and entitled on it*"

2. The retailer, either on his own or jointly with another operator, provides the package. On the evidence as I find it here the first situation obtained. At no stage until after the contract was made did the Defendant disclose that it was acting for a principal. This situation was brought about by the unusual business practice of the Defendant in firstly making no reference to acting for a principal in the only advertising material which the customer would see, the Teletext screen, and secondly instructing its sales staff to mention the existence and identity of the tour operator only when the contract had been made. In those circumstances the description "the other party to the contract", exactly fits the Defendant here. Any other construction

of the regulation would constitute any retailer a virtual insurer and the supply of services by the tour operator, the hotel and the carrier. Such a dramatic extension of the liability of travel agents is not in the contemplation either of the Directive or of the regulations.

As to the circumstances of the Claimant's unfortunate injury, there is no suggestion here that there was a failure to perform a contract. What is alleged is the improper performance of contract. [At the time the regulations were introduce] in both the House of Commons and the House of Lords, government ministers used the same language: "*Regulation 15 is important and makes the organiser, or possibly in certain circumstances the retailer, strictly liable for performance of the contract*". If that was the object of the regulations in their draughtsmanship, the object has not been achieved. Much clearer words would be required to impose strict liability in all circumstances on organisers and retailers. The case is pleaded as if it was a case of negligence with particulars being provided of "failed or improper performance"...

In my view on such facts as the Claimant has been able to prove, the Claimant has wholly failed to establish that his accident was anyone's fault. Before criticising employees of an airline in respect of failures arising in an emergency crash I would need to know much more than I am told in the evidence in this case. The court would need to know approximately the size of the aircraft, and particularly the number of escape doors and chutes that there were. It would need information as to the normal number of staff for an aircraft of that size and whether for this flight, the complement was complete or undermanned. It would also have been very helpful to have some evidence, possibly from a joint expert as to the duties to be carried out by cabin staff in an emergency crash of this kind. I think it would be surprising if good practice required there to be sufficient cabin staff for there to be one stationed at the top and another at the bottom of each of the chutes coming from the aircraft, but I make no finding as to that because there is simply no evidence. It is not sufficient ... to look at this on the basis of common sense. Common sense is all very well, but when dealing with safety precautions and manning in an aircraft, there must be some standard set either by the employer, or by authority or both and the Claimant has wholly failed to satisfy the burden which is on him, of proving his case in this regard.

Hone v Going Places Leisure Travel Ltd [2001] EWCA Civ 947 (13 June 2001)

LORD JUSTICE LONGMORE:

6. Mr Hone alleged in his claim form that there was a failure to perform, or improper performance of, the contract in that there were no trained personnel at the top or the bottom of the emergency chute and no instructions to passengers to remove their footwear or to use the chute only when it was clear of other passengers. The claim also alleged that there was a failure to prevent the accident; in the course of oral submissions it was put that the defendants (or those for whom they were responsible) failed to execute a safe evacuation. Mr Hone also alleged that the Regulations imposed an "absolute liability", subject to defences which the defendants could not show were available. The judge held that it was for the claimant to show that there was improper performance and that in the context of the present case that meant that he had to show that his injuries were attributable to the fault of someone supplying services in relation to the package tour. Liability was thus not absolute or strict, subject to exceptions. The judge held, further, that Mr Hone had wholly failed to establish that the accident was anyone's fault. There was no evidence about the number of cabin staff on board the aircraft, nor as to what the appropriate number of staff should be. Nor was there expert evidence on the duties of cabin staff in the kind of emergency that arose. He therefore dismissed the claim.

7. The judge refused to give Mr Hone permission to appeal on the question whether, if he had the burden of proving fault, he had discharged the burden of proving that fault. That application was renewed before us, but without enthusiasm, and we refused permission to argue that ground since the judge was plainly right for the reasons which he gave.

8. The judge did, however, give Mr Hone permission to appeal his decision that the Regulations did not impose strict liability and also his decision not to have regard to ministerial statements in **Hansard** to the effect that the Regulations were intended to impose a strict liability. In the course of the hearing we gave Mr Hone further permission (despite refusal by the judge) to appeal the judge's decision that the onus of proving fault was on the claimant rather than on the defendants to disprove any fault. We also gave him permission to appeal the sentence in the judgement which reads:

> "*Even if, contrary to my view, there was fault on the part of the airline staff, this was not an event which the Defendant, as the other party to the contract, could, with all due care, forestall.*"

9. This sentence of the judgment is a little difficult to interpret. If the judge is saying that fault on the part of the airline staff was due to an event which the defendants themselves could not forestall, that would be true but irrelevant if the onus were on the defendants to prove absence of negligence on the part of themselves and the airline staff. If, on the other hand, the words "the Defendant" are to be read as including the airline staff (as on this approach they should be read) it does not make much sense to hold that fault on the part of the airline staff was due to an event which the airline staff could not forestall. This only becomes relevant, however, if the appellant is correct on his main grounds of appeal.

10. In fact, the main three grounds of appeal are all linked to one another...

"(1) that, on their true construction, the Regulations of 1992 imposed an absolute or strict liability on the other party to the contract subject to defences, the onus of proving which was on that other party to the contract;

"(2) that the requirement of regulation 15(1) of "improper performance of the contract" was met because the expectation of the parties was that there would be safe carriage to and from the holiday and, if injury was sustained during that carriage, there was improper performance;

"(3) that the intention of the Regulations was to achieve a result comparable to that achieved by the unamended Warsaw Convention which, it was agreed, imposed liability for death and personal injury if the accident causing such death or personal injury took place on board (or in the course of embarking or disembarking from) an aircraft. That liability was a limited liability and was subject to the defence that the carrier was not to be liable if he were able to prove either that his servants and agents had taken all necessary measures to avoid the damage or that it was impossible to take such measures (Article 20), or that the damage was caused by the negligence of the injured person (Article 21);

"(4) that if the burden was on the claimant to prove improper performance in the sense of fault, the existence of the fault-based exceptions was otiose and made no sense;

"(5) that his submissions were supported by the statements of the relevant Ministers in the House of Commons and the House of Lords that liability was strict.

11. ... the respondent submitted:

(1) that a claimant had to prove either a failure of performance or improper performance of the contract;

(2) that the present case was not a case of failure to perform but, if anything, one of improper performance of the contract;

(3) that improper performance of the contract had to be a breach of the contract;

(4) that there was no breach of contract unless there was a failure to perform the contract with reasonable care and skill, and in that sense there had to be shown to be fault on the part of the other party to the contract or the supplier of the relevant service for whose fault he was responsible;

(5) that the Regulations were drafted differently from the Warsaw Convention and that such differences were significant;

(6) that the Ministers of the Crown in the course of parliamentary debates, by using the phrase "strict liability", did not intend to deny the effect of the requirement that there had to be improper performance of the contract.

12. The starting point must, in my view, be the contract which Mr Hone made with the defendants. Contracts for holidays are often made informally and it will often be

necessary to imply a term as to the standard of performance since the requirements will not be set out in any detail. In the absence of any contrary intention, the normal implication will be that the service contracted for will be rendered with reasonable skill and care. Of course, absolute obligations may be assumed. If the brochure or advertisement, on which the consumer relies, promises a swimming-pool, it will be a term of the contract that a swimming-pool will be provided. But, in the absence of express wording, there would not be an absolute obligation, for example, to ensure that the holiday-maker catches no infection while swimming in the swimming-pool. The obligation assumed will be that reasonable skill and care will be taken to ensure that the pool is free from infection. A similar term will be implied in relation to transportation in the absence of any express wording, viz that reasonable skill and care will be exercised. A travel agent or tour operator does not usually, for example, promise that the pilot of the aeroplane will not have a heart attack.

13. In the case of a travel agent it may, as a matter of common law, be controversial whether the travel agent himself assumes the relevant contractual responsibility or only agrees to put the customer into contractual relations with the actual provider of the service, whether tour operator, airline or other provider. This problem is now resolved by regulation 15(1) of the 1992 Regulations, which in terms provides for the party other than the consumer to be liable for the proper performance of the obligations, whether such obligations are to be actually performed by that party or by the supplier of the service. But regulation 15(1) gives no guidance as to the extent of the obligation. The decision of the Privy Council in *Wong Wee Wan v Kwan Kin Travel Services Ltd* [1996] 1 WLR 38 is a good example of the approach of the common law on both questions. It was there held, on the facts of that case, that the defendant travel agent had undertaken to provide all the tour services and not merely to arrange for their provision, even though many of the services were intended to be provided by other persons. It was also held that a term was to be implied into the contract that reasonable skill and care would be used in the rendering of the services which the travel agent had contracted to provide, whether they were carried out by the travel agent or by someone else.

14. In a case to which the 1992 Regulations apply, there will be no controversy on the first question and there is no such controversy in the present case. Going Places is the party liable on the contract and, for the purpose of regulation 15(1), it is liable for "the proper performance of the obligations under the contract". But regulation 15(1) says nothing about the content of that performance.

15. Regulation 15(2) provides for the other party to the contract to be liable for any damage caused to the consumer by failure to perform the contract or by the improper performance of the contract. The present case is not a case of failure to perform. It can only be a case of improper performance. It is only possible to determine whether it is a case of improper performance by reference to the terms of the contract which is being performed. To my mind, regulation 15(2) does not give the answer to the question, "What is improper performance?" Rather it is a requirement of the application of regulation 15(2) that there should be improper performance. That can only be determined by reference to the terms of the contract. There may be absolute obligations, e.g. as to the existence of a swimming-pool or any other matter, but, in the absence of the assumption of an absolute obligation, the implication will be that reasonable skill and care will be used in the rendering of the relevant service. There

will thus be no improper performance of the air carriage unless there is an absence of reasonable skill and care in the provision of that service. If, as here, it is the claimant who seeks to rely on regulation 15(2), then he has to show that there has been improper performance.

16. [The appellant] submits that there was improper performance because the parties expected that the air carriage would be safely executed. That would only be the position if there were a term of the contract that the air carriage would be safely executed. For my part, I do not consider that there was any such absolute term. In the absence of an express agreement, the implication was that the air carriage would be performed with skill and care.

17. There is a clear contrast with the terms of the Warsaw Convention. In that Convention, Article 17 imposes a liability for death or personal injury without any requirement of improper performance. Article 18 does the same for loss or damage to baggage and cargo, and Article 19 the same for delay to passengers, baggage and cargo. There are then specific provisions for exclusion or diminution of liability and for limitation. The 1992 Regulations could have adopted a similar scheme but, by the use of the term "improper performance", it is patent that they have not done so. The fact that it is open to the travel agent (or other party to the contract) to incorporate the limitation provisions of any applicable international convention, if they wish to do so, cannot make any difference to this conclusion.

18. I would not, for my part, accept that the existence of the fault-based exceptions in regulation 15(2) makes it otiose or nonsensical for the claimant to have to prove fault in an appropriate case. The exceptions will, in any event, come into play if the other party to the contract assumes obligations which are themselves not fault-based.

19. Nor do I obtain any assistance from the ministerial statements, recorded in *Hansard,* to the effect that regulation 15 makes the organiser or retailer strictly liable for the performance of the contract. The relevant Minister was not purporting to construe, let alone alter, the terms of the Directive requiring the Regulations to be enacted. It is significant that the terms of both the preamble and the body of the Directive itself refer to improper performance and must, therefore, envisage that the standard of performance is to be derived from the contract and not from the terms of the Directive itself. The contract will sometimes have terms which impose strict liability in any event and any breach of such terms will be a matter of strict liability, subject to any relevant qualifications. It is, moreover, not an abuse of the term "strict liability" for a non-lawyer to use it in the sense that the retailer or the tour organiser will be responsible for the acts of others who provide the relevant services.

Zoe Louise Jay V Tui Uk Ltd (Formerly Thomson Holidays Ltd) (2006) QBD (Bristol) (Adrian Palmer QC) 23/11/2006

A tour operator was not liable to pay contractual compensation to a holidaymaker who was injured through the accidental collapse of a defective boat mast because the accident was not foreseeable and the tour operator's contractual liability was not strict and did not extend to negligence by the boat manufacturer.

The claimant tourist (J) claimed damages for personal injuries that she sustained whilst on a holiday provided by the defendant travel tour operator (T). During the holiday J had gone on a boating excursion provided by a third party company which was a supplier of services to T. During the excursion, as the captain attempted to adjust the mainsail, the mast of the boat snapped and crashed onto the deck, injuring J. Under T's holiday contract with J, T agreed to pay compensation for personal injuries resulting from a failure by it or its suppliers to carry out their duties properly, except where such injuries were caused by an event which the relevant person could not have predicted or avoided even if they had taken all necessary and due care. J submitted (1) that the accident had been caused by the negligent seamanship of the boat's captain; (2) that T owed her a duty of care under the relevant terms of the contract and that it was liable for personal injuries occasioned during the boating excursion. T submitted, relying on *Hone v Going Places Leisure Travel Ltd* (2001) EWCA Civ 947, Times, August 6, 2001, that its exposure under the contract did not create an absolute liability unless there was a clear intention to that effect, which there had not been.

HELD: (1) The cause of the accident was a defect in the boat's mast that had been there since its manufacture. Moreover J's allegations of negligent seamanship on the part of the boat's captain were not supported by the evidence. (2) T had voluntarily extended its contractual liability to J so as to cover many events that might have occurred during J's holiday and the boat excursion, but T did not extend its liability as far back as negligence of the boat manufacturer. J had not alleged any lack of maintenance of the boat by the third party who undertook the boat excursion. There was no warrant for imposing an obligation to undertake a major inspection of the mast and no evidence that such an inspection would have detected the defect. The proper construction of the clause in the contract providing for personal injury compensation was that the "duties" in question were the duties of reasonable care in the provision of the services that constituted the boat excursion but such duties did not include strict contractual obligations, Hone considered. J's injuries were caused by an event, the breaking of the mast, that neither T nor its suppliers could have predicted or avoided by taking all necessary and due care. Accordingly, T was not liable to pay compensation under the contract for J's personal injuries.

Williams v *First Choice Holidays and Flights Ltd*, unreported, 2 April 2001, Warrington County Court (HHJ Hughes)

In June 1997, the claimant, Leanne Williams, who was then 18 went on a fortnight's holiday to Corfu with her friend, Donna Norris. It was a package holiday with a difference. Advertised as a twenties holiday, it was specially arranged for young people between 17 and 29 years of age. The flavour of what holidaymakers were to expect appears in the brochure. I read samples which are from the brochure ...

> *"High on fun and kicking as hell, Kavos is and continues to hold all the essential ingredients and flavour required for a truly mad twenties holidays. Still retaining much of its traditional Greek touch by day, you couldn't be blamed for thinking you were in a different place when the night scene charges up. Choose one of the 40 restaurants to get your energy levels going. As the clubs here are wild, funking and banging every night. Snobs Bar and Business always get you going whilst Whispers, Future and Venue mix the essential tunes for those sun kissed bodies that crave the party spirit."*

Elsewhere in the brochure:

> *"A direct connection to hedonism the twenties pleasure zone experience plugs your imagination on line in the selection of the best memories to be had on a twenties holiday."*

...the holiday was expected to be wild and exciting. Miss Williams arrived at her resort in Kavos on 16ᵗʰ June 1997. During the days that followed, excursions were arranged by the holiday company for its guests and she went on nearly all of them. She thinks there was one she missed but in evidence said that she could not remember which one it was. The calendar of excursions ... reveals that excursions were arranged every day of the week except Mondays although the claimant says there were about eight excursions available during her holiday.

Miss Williams bought all her excursion tickets in advance at the resort, on her first day there, during a welcome meeting held by the holiday representatives. One such excursion was called Greek Night. It was advertised as follows: "Food, wine, dancing plate smashing and much more. Go do the Zorba twenties style."

On 26ᵗʰ June therefore, some nine or 10 days into her fortnight's holiday, Miss Williams went on her Greek Night excursion. Two coaches took about 60 to 80 guests on a 25 minute journey to a taverna which opened on to a beach. They were accompanied by four holiday reps, including the head Rep, Miss Clare Last, who took her own car. At the tavern there was a bar where guests could pay for drinks before dinner. A three course meal was served with as much wine as the guests wanted, served in small jugs at the tables but watered down. After dinner there was dancing to Greek music on the open floor between the tables, and also the traditional plate smashing which was organised at the end of the evening in an area away from the tables and the dance floor, when guests were provided with the plaster plates specially for smashing.

As she stood watching the activities at a pillar which, according to a sketch prepared for the hearing was roughly between the tables and dance floor, and the area where the plaster plates were to be smashed, and while in a state which she herself described as "tipsy", she was injured. Another guest threw an ordinary plate from the table, not a special plaster plate, and it smashed and a chard of china but her right ankle, causing a bad injury involving the severance of her Achilles tendon, for which she needed immediate hospital treatment, including surgery under a general anaesthetic and the immobilisation of her leg in plaster.

Miss Williams blames the holiday company, the defendants, First Choice Holidays and Flights Limited, for her injury. The particulars of claim... alleges that the defendants were negligent and/or in breach of an implied term of their contract with Miss Williams that they would use all proper skill and care.

The particulars of negligence, as pleaded, and I summarise them, allege that before and during the holiday the defendants aided, abetted, encouraged and incited the holiday makers' wild and dangerous behaviour.

At the Greek Night excursion itself, the allegations are that the reps encouraged guests to drink excessively, by challenging each table to see which could drink the most, and by telling them how much guests on a previous holiday had drunk on the Greek Night and challenging them to drink more. It was also specifically pleaded in two separate places ... that during the Greek Night excursion, the reps themselves drank to excess, thus encouraging others to do likewise. It is alleged that the reps failed to control the party, to prevent a guest throwing real plates despite knowing that similar accidents involving real plates being smashed had happened before. The claimant also complains that at a time when so many young people had had so much to drink and at a party where plates were to be deliberately smashed as part of the fun of the evening, the defendants should have ensured that there were no ordinary plates left on tables which could also be picked up and smashed.

The defendants deny negligence and, for that matter, any breach of contract. They deny that their reps drank excessively on the Greek Night or that they aided, abetted, encouraged or incited wild and dangerous behaviour. Their defence also pleads contributory negligence against the claimant.

It seems to me that it is important to recognise that the kind of holiday offered was quite different from the usual package holiday. The claimant's evidence was, when she was asked in cross-examination what kind of holiday was being provided, "*It was a drink holiday, the wilder the better.*" She said that, at the beginning of the holiday, at the Welcome meeting, when it seems they were being given a briefing by the holiday reps about what to expect during their holiday, she said in her statement:

> "*We were told this holiday was all about having a good time, meeting people, getting drunk and other things which I will leave to your imagination.*"

She said that what they were told in the Welcome meeting was more of an encouragement to drink excessively rather than a warning not to do so... As she said she could not remember if anything was said about, firstly, the Greek Night excursion generally, and secondly, that special plaster plates would be provided for smashing. Nor did she remember whether anything was said which amounted to a warning that they should be careful of how much they drank.

There was evidence, however, from Clare Last, who was the head representative at the resort. She said that several warnings were given to guests at different stages, about the need to confine plate smashing to the special plaster plates. She said that such a warning was given at the Welcome meeting, that it would have been given on the coach on the way to the restaurant, and although Clare Last was not on the coach, the fact that such a warning was given on the coach was confirmed by the claimant herself, and finally, that such a warning was given in the restaurant by one of the reps, Courtney Simpson, who broadcasted it over the public address system.

Miss Last's evidence was that, while of course the guests were encouraged to have a good time, they were not encouraged to drink to excess although she realised on such an evening people would get drunk. She said that the average age was probably 21 to 22 years, and that they could not be patronised by being told they had had enough. Although she emphasised that they, the holiday representatives, did everything to maintain the safety of their guests.

She said that there were four reps on duty, for an excursion involving 60 to 80 guests... She said, in her experience, there had never been such an accident before, involving injury to a guest, by the smashing of the wrong sort of plate. She acknowledged that there was always a possibility that someone might throw a real plate if they were drunk and she recognised it might have been possible for the fruit to have been provided on paper or plastic plates. She said too that she knew too that the guests would probably get drunk and that most of them did.

One of the other reps, Courtney Simpson described how guests were warned both at the Welcome meeting and on the coach on the way to the restaurant about drinking too much. Apparently there is a need for the warning to be given, for a reason unconnected with what happened to the claimant: the coach drivers impose heavy financial penalties on those who make a mess by being sick on the bus. He also added, in evidence, that his warning on the coach had included telling the guests that only plaster plates were to be broken. This was a warning that the restaurant management required the reps to give each time.

Mr Simpson's statement asserts that the plate smashing took place only after the waiters had removed plates from the meal although it is clear, as I have said, that the fruit plates remained. He confirmed that he was on the microphone, and that he called up one table at a time to go to the designated area, away from the tables and the dancing, where they could smash the plaster plates distributed to them by other reps.

[The Claimant] said that she was watching the dancing and did not know if others were still finishing their meal and then someone threw a ceramic plate, in other words one of the real plates. She said she was not sure if the thrower was male or female, and she was not sure if the thrower was from her table or another table. ... I am quite satisfied that, on the night, Miss Williams did know who had thrown the plate but she chose not to divulge the culprit's identity to the head holiday rep. It seems she chose to take no further step to pursue any complaint against the plate thrower personally. ...Her statement therefore contains a misleading and exaggerated version of what was actually happening.

...The reliability of Miss Williams' evidence is, therefore, I am afraid open to question in several respects. While making allowances for the fact that it is now some three-and-a-half years or more since the incident and the effect that the passage of time no doubt has on her recollection, I am nevertheless satisfied that she was tipsy, as she put it herself, and was quite definitely affected by the amount that she had had to drink. I am also satisfied and find as a fact that the holiday reps were not so affected. The efficiency with which they dealt with the accident after it happened and arranged for Miss Williams to be taken to hospital (an efficiency which she herself acknowledges) confirms my conclusion that they were not affected by drink.

The consequence is that where their versions differ; I prefer the evidence of the holiday reps to that of the claimant. I am satisfied and find as a fact that warnings about excessive drink and the importance of using only plaster plates were given at the Welcome party, and on the coach on the way to the restaurant and at the restaurant yet another warning or instruction was given about the need to confine the plate smashing to the specially provided plaster plates. Furthermore, I find that the encouragement by the holiday reps, while no doubt enthusiastically given, was for the guests to enjoy themselves and to enter into the spirit of the lively energetic holiday which they had all bought. There may well have been stories about escapades during previous holidays. There may even have been an encouragement to drink, as Courtney Simpson accepted there was some limited encouragement to drink when at the very beginning of the meal at the Greek Night there was a toast. But what the reps were doing and what it is reasonable for them to have been doing, bearing in mind the very special nature of the holiday they were providing, is to encourage the guests to socialise, to dance, to join in the excursions, to join in the activities and the fun including the plate smashing. It was the holiday rep's job to make sure that everyone had a good time in accordance with the sort of good time which the holiday brochure had boasted would be provided. However, they had a responsibility to take care of their clients. I am satisfied that their encouragements to have a good time were adequately accompanied by such warnings as were necessary to ensure, so far as reasonably possible, that the guests also had a safe time.

The responsibilities of the defendants undertaken by their holiday reps and whether they were properly carried out, need to be assessed against the background of a number of authorities to which the court was referred during the closing submissions of both counsel. For example, the case of *Brannon v Airtours Plc* a 1999 case in the Court of Appeal, involved a holiday maker on a package holiday who, during a party night at a club, injured himself while leaving his table. The tables were so close together and the guests so tightly packed in, that from where he was sitting it was not easy for him to leave his place. He did so by climbing on to and along the table when he wanted to go to the toilet. He had been warned not to do so by a compere at the club, who had announced over the microphone that the fans, positioned directly above the table, would present a danger walking on them and that there had been injuries caused by the fans in such circumstances in the past. The holiday maker suffered injury to his face when he came into contact with the fan.

Like the Greek Night, in the present case, the occasion at the club, when the holiday maker was injured by the fan was one where everyone had drunk a great deal. There is, however, a significant difference between the case of *Brannon* and the present one. It is that in *Brannon* it was foreseeable that the holiday maker would climb onto the table and injure himself on the fan, because exactly the same thing had happened before. In the present case, as I find, that there had been no such incident before. It was not foreseeable, given the precautions that were taken that nevertheless somebody would pick up a real plate and throw it instead of a plaster one.

The precautions taken in the present case were extensive. In the *Brannon* case the elementary precaution of moving the tables away from the fans which could have been taken was found not have been taken.

The establishment of liability against the defendants in that case was based upon a finding that exactly the same mischief had occurred before and yet the defendants had not done enough to protect their guests from it.

In another case *Jepson v The Ministry of Defence*, in the Court of Appeal 1 WLR 2000 2055, the duty to take care, where soldiers returning from a night out and being transported in the back of an Army lorry, when it was foreseeable that they would have been drinking was a duty to ensure that a transport package was provided which was reasonably safe to avoid the possibility of injury from rowdy behaviour in the back.

The thrust of the authorities, it seems to me, is not that every conceivable step must be taken to avoid any risk at all, but that all reasonable steps must be taken to protect, in the present case, holidaymakers from risks that are foreseeable.

In the circumstances of the present case, I am not convinced that the risk of the wrong plate being thrown, so that injury would be caused, was foreseeable. It is not known who threw the plate. While the probability is that he or she was affected by drink, it is not known by how much they were affected. If it had been known there was a particular guest who had become very drunk, more drunk than the others, for example, and was not just tipsy, so it might be expected that there was a risk that he or she might act totally irresponsibly and completely ignore all warnings given then, if such a person then went on to create a danger, the defendants might have been justly criticised for not acting to protect their guests from what would be an obvious and foreseeable danger. But no such excessively drunken guest has been identified. The level of risk therefore was no higher than usual. As I find, there had never been such an incident before.

The standard of care, whether derived from contract or negligence, in the circumstances of the present case, is that the defendants owed a duty to take reasonable care of their clients' safety. There was, in this case, a system in place to provide for holidaymakers safety which, it seems to me, took into account, firstly, that the holiday was for young adults. Secondly, that it was a holiday which they had booked expecting to be given a wild time. Thirdly, that they were, on the Greek Night, likely to be affected by drink.

I am satisfied and find as a fact that warnings were given at three stages. The Welcome party, at the start of the holidays, on the coach to the Greek Night, about excessive drinking and about the importance of using plaster plates to thrown on the Greek Night, and thirdly, at the restaurant again, about the need to use only plaster plates.At the restaurant a substantial meal was served to offset the effect of alcohol. Free wine was provided only with the meal. No free drinks were provided before. The wine was served watered down, to make it less potent and soft drinks were also available for those who wanted them. The plate throwing was well organised. A special place was set aside for it, away from the dining tables and away from the dance floor. The plaster plates were distributed to the guests by the holiday representatives in an organised way. Plate throwing was supervised, in the sense that tables were called forward, in turn, one at a time, to go to the specified area where they could throw their plaster plates. All unnecessary crockery had been removed from the dining tables. All that were left were plates for the fruit dessert and glasses and jugs for the wine and soft drinks. There were four reps on duty to look after 60 to 80 guests and it was a relatively short evening between 7.30 and 10.30 p.m. In my judgment, it would be to go beyond the bounds of reasonableness to expect the defendants, when dealing with adults, to provide them with paper plates at the end of the meal as if it was a children's tea party. The expectation which the defendants had that their guests would become drunk, was not an expectation that they would become so drunk and then behave so irresponsibly so as to cause injury.

I am afraid I am not persuaded that the defendant could have reasonably done more than they did do to protect their clients in all the circumstances.

It follows, therefore, that the claim fails and there will be judgment for the defendants.

Unauthenticated Decisions

Joseph Logue v *Flying Colours Limited*, unreported, 7 March 2001, Central London County Court (HHJ Zucker QC)

Mr Joseph Logue was on holiday in Ibiza staying at the Hotel San Durat. He had been enjoying his time there and had become friends with the hotel manager. Ten days into his two week holiday, he had gone out "on the town" with the hotel manager and had returned at about 6am when he went to bed. Just before 9am he got up, and while doing so, he lost his balance and fell. He put his right hand out to arrest his fall and it went through the glass patio window of his bedroom. The window, which was normal annealed glass rather than toughened glass, shattered into large pieces which lacerated his right arm and brachial artery. He sustained serious injuries and was taken promptly to the local hospital.

The glass in the balcony door which shattered was established as being 5mm thick and made of annealed (normal) glass.

Expert evidence was that there were no regulations in Spain, or more locally in Ibiza, specifying the thickness of glass to be used in patio windows, but that 5mm was not in breach of the generally accepted standards in Spain. There was additional evidence that annealed glass, as opposed to toughened glass, of that thickness would not have complied with British Standards or the UK Building Regulations so far as hotels or public buildings were concerned.

The Claimant's claim was brought under Regulation 15 of the *Package Travel, Package Holidays and Package Tours Regulations 1992*.

It was submitted for the Claimant that Regulation 15(2) imposed strict liability for personal injury, subject to the specific exceptions in Regulation 15(2)(a)-(c).

It was argued in the Claimant's opening, though not pursued in closing submissions, that the 1992 Regulations imposed a *common* standard, that of the UK, in safety matters, and that the tour operator was liable if its suppliers failed to meet UK standards in their foreign hotels. Alternatively, it was argued that the EU Directive which led to the implementation of the 1992 Regulations was intended to create a common standard across the EU and that standard should require the provision of safety glass in hotel balcony and patio doors. It was further submitted for the Claimant that the Regulations created a free-standing cause of action.

The Defendant submitted that Regulation 15 concerned itself with the *proper performance of the holiday contract.* It was necessary, therefore, to consider what the obligations of the tour operator and the supplier of services were under the holiday contract. There could not be a failure to perform or an improper performance of the holiday contract when the supplier had complied with the standards applicable locally, whether those standards were to be found in local regulations or the general standard expected of accommodation locally. Reliance was placed by the Defendant on *Wilson v Best Travel* [1993] 1 All ER 353 and *Codd v Thomson Tour Operations Limited [CA]* TLR 20/10/2000.

The Defendant further argued that even if there was liability on these facts, there was substantial contributory negligence as the Claimant was drunk after his Ibizan "pub crawl".

The judge held that the construction of Regulation 15 was clear. It imposed liability on the tour operator *only* if the holiday contract was breached by a commission or omission by the tour operator or a supplier. The purpose of the Regulations was to make the tour operator liable for the acts of third parties in circumstances where it would not otherwise be so liable. There was no improper performance of the contract [that is no "breach"] where local standards were complied with. *Wilson v Best Travel* remained good law and survived the introduction of the Package Travel Regulations.

If the judge had found liability, he would have assessed contribution at 75% as the Claimant was considerably affected by drink at the time of the accident and this played a major part in the causation of the accident.

Permission to appeal to the Court of Appeal was refused on the grounds that the construction of Regulation 15 was clear.

Thompson v Thomson Holidays Ltd, unreported, 17 January 2005, Stoke on Trent County Court

The Claimant fell into a sunken footbath adjacent to a garden path at her package holiday Hotel in Cyprus on 19 May 2002 and claimed damages for her injuries (fractured foot). This was a classic PTR 1992 Regulation 15 case. The footbath, she claimed, was at the side of a narrow pathway and was a hazardous obstruction. There should have been a warning about it in the form of a clearly delineated boundary, fencing. Better still the footbath should have been moved to a safe place out of the way of pedestrians walking round the hotel gardens. The Claimant relied on the fact that the footbath was subsequently moved and also on the fact that at the time of the incident it was very sunny to the extent that the footbath and adjacent pavement appeared to be the same colour and one was not distinguishable from another.

The Claimant's case was supported by expert evidence from a Cypriot lawyer to the effect that the standard of care for hoteliers in Cyprus was the same as under the Occupier's Liability Act 1957 in England.

The Defendant contended that the sunken footbath had been in situ for many years without incident and the fact that the footbath had been moved as a result of the Claimant's accident such 20-20 hindsight did not render the hotel or the tour operator in breach of any duty to the Claimant. The Defendant will relied on the dicta of the CA in *Staples v West Dorset District Council* (1995) PIQR at P445 and Lord Pearce in *M'Glone v BRB* [quoted in *Ratcliffe v McConnell* (1999) 1 WLR at page 681] – to the effect that a responsible occupier is not to be criticised for taking action after an accident to avoid a recurrence.

The Defendant also relied on expert evidence from an engineer. The Engineer concluded that by Cypriot regulation the Hotel was obliged to have a footbath and that the one in question is consistent with others he had observed in Cyprus and that Cypriot Regulations in respect of such facilities did not impose any requirements on occupiers as to size, depth, configuration, colour or design of such a footbath or its positioning.

The judge concluded that the accident occurred because the Claimant was not looking where she was going - this had been an isolated incident. Furthermore, although it was correct to look at the general Occupiers' Liability standard of care that standard had to be approached in the context of what was both required and conventional in Cyprus by the regulations. As the regulations demanded that there be a footbath and the evidence was that this footbath was in keeping with local customs, neither its positioning nor construction constituted any breach of duty on the part of the Defendant or the Hotel. Finally, there was no obligation on the Hotel or the Defendant to issue warnings about such incidental property features that form part and parcel of many holiday resort hotels.

Judgment for the Defendant.

James v *Travelsphere Ltd*, unreported, 2 February 2005, Cardiff County Court (Recorder Hughes QC)

The Claimant took a package holiday to Sri Lanka in the course of the holiday on 14 February 2001 she visited the Pinnawela Elephant Sanctuary to watch the elephants bathe. She was escorted with the rest of her group to the water's edge where along with many others she stood on an apron of rocks to take photographs. She turned her back to return to the pathway just as the elephants left their bathing in the river to make their way back to the sanctuary; a person shouted "the elephants are coming"; the Claimant was taken by surprise and fell, breaking her ankle. The Claimant blamed the Defendant tour operator and claimed compensation.

Essentially the Claimant's allegations boiled down to this and that accordingly there had been "negligence" on the part of the guide responsible for the visit.

* She was allowed to stand where it was unsafe; and

* She was not warned that the elephants were leaving the river.

It also emerged that usually a handheld klaxon was sounded when the elephants were on the march to alert people to the need to get of the way – but that such a klaxon had not been used on the day in question – in breach of the sanctuary's usual system. In the original claim the Claimant had maintained that the sanctuary was a "supplier" of services within the meaning of regulation 15(1) of the PTR 1992, but somewhat surprisingly this basis for the claim was abandoned at trial and the Claimant accepted that the Defendant was no liable for any shortcomings on the part of the those who operated the sanctuary.

The judge concluded that indeed the sanctuary and its personnel had fallen short of their usual standards on the day of the accident and that had the klaxon been sounded the Claimant would have been alerted to the approaching elephants and the accident would have been avoided. However, as it was not alleged that the tour operator was liable for the negligence of this provider of a public facility the Defendant was not liable to the Claimant on this basis. Neither was the tour operator in breach of any duty through its own guide. The rocky apron was reasonably safe; many people used it for photographs; there had been no history of accidents and any warning to the effect that "elephants can move quickly" would not have made any difference to the outcome anyway because she had her back turned at the point when the elephants started to move.

Judgment for the Defendant.

Langton v *TUI UK Ltd*, unreported, 27 January 2005, Warrington County Court (HHJ Hale)

The Claimant took a package holiday in Corfu supplied by the Defendant. Unfortunately, during the course of his holiday, and on an occasion when he was in the shower at his hotel, there was a power cut. He reached out of the shower cubicle stretching for the door and had an accident. The Claimant blamed the Defendant tour operator and claimed compensation. The basis of the claim was either that the Hotel was responsible for the power cut because it had embarked on a deliberate campaign of cutting of the electricity in order to save overloading its system due to "overuse" of air-conditioning in guests' rooms. Alternatively, at trial the Claimant sought permission to amend the claim to assert that the Greek Electricity Board was a supplier of package holiday services pursuant to regulation 15(1) of the PTR for whose failure (the failure to warn of the impending power cut) the tour operator was responsible.

Permission to amend the claim at such a late stage was refused on the grounds that the claim based on the alleged negligence of the electricity board was not strong (since when did a British power supplier warn of impending power cuts?) and because it would have caused the trial to be adjourned for better evidence to be sought about whether the power cut had been foreseeable by the electricity board rather than arising out of a sudden emergency.

On the claim based in "negligence" against the Hotel the judge concluded that the hearsay evidence available from Corfu demonstrated that:

- The Hotel was concerned about misuse of air-conditioning units although more from an economic stand-point than anything else but their concern was not shown to be related to the power cut.

- Electrical failures were not so commonplace as to suggest the Hotel should have warned its guests about them.

- The electricity supply was checked regularly by maintenance staff and records were available to show this.

- What evidence there was suggested that the power failure was the result of an emergency arising in the village for which neither the Hotel nor the tour operator could be responsible.

This had been an unlucky accident for which liability could not be attached to the Defendant.

Grahame v JMC Holidays Ltd Current Law Cases: 02/2324

JMC appealed against an award of GBP 871 made to G and his family in respect of a package skiing holiday. On the outward journey there had been a delay of 22 hours and, on the return journey, an eight hour delay. JMC contended that (1) pursuant to its booking conditions and the Package Travel, Package Holidays and Package Tours Regulations 1992 Reg.15 it was not liable for loss or damage caused to G as the delay was not a typical technical delay, but had occurred as a result of a fault appearing whilst the plane was in flight. Accordingly JMC argued that the delay was therefore unforeseeable, unavoidable and beyond its control, and (2) the burden of proof was upon G, if alleging improper performance of the holiday contract, to provide evidence that the contract had been performed without reasonable care and skill and that G had not discharged this burden, *Hone v Going Places Leisure Travel Ltd* [2001] EWCA Civ 947, Times, August 6, 2001 cited. The judge at first instance had held that, since airline delays were common, it could not be argued that these were unforeseeable and unavoidable.

Held, allowing the appeal, that (1) in this case the delay was unforeseeable and unavoidable since it did not fall within the normal class of technical delays nor delays due to high volume of air traffic, and (2) the burden of proof was on G. G had adduced a copy of a league table in which the airline in question came bottom and had been ranked the worst of all the airlines reviewed in respect of every performance criterion. The judge rejected G's argument that the poor performance of the airline resulted from its failure to maintain its aircraft on a regular basis and that it had therefore been foreseeable that there would be delays if G used the airline. JMC had shown that the airline had an airworthiness certificate from the Civil Aviation Authority and had therefore established that the airline had been selected with reasonable care and skill, Hone considered.

McRae v Thomson Holidays Ltd Current Law Cases: 01/4291

M had booked a two week holiday to Gran Canaria through TH. His accommodation was in an apartment complex. Seven days into the holiday, M suffered an accident when one of the legs on a plastic poolside sunbed upon which he was lying face down, bent, causing him to "jolt". M did not fall from the bed, nor did he experience immediate pain. He got off the sunbed, straightened the leg by hand and continued to use the bed for a further hour. When he subsequently attempted to get off, he was unable to move. M contended that the incident had caused him to suffer a slipped disc. TH admitted the accident, but denied causation. Proceedings were issued, in which M pleaded breach of contract and breach of the Package Travel, Package Holidays and Package Tours Regulations 1992 Reg.15. TH maintained that (1) as a matter of contract, the imposition of liability for personal injury depended upon proof of fault, and (2) the standard of care applicable by contract was not an absolute guarantee of safety, but a duty to ensure that the consumer was reasonably safe, and, by extension, to keep furniture in a reasonable condition.

Held, dismissing the claim, that (1) strict liability was not applicable. TH had a duty to exercise reasonable care and skill; (2) as there had been no visible defect in the sunbed, it was difficult to accept that any non-scientific inspection prior to the accident could have detected the fault. Therefore, it could not be said that the sunbed had been unsafe at that time or that enforcement of a reasonable system of inspection would have avoided the accident, and (3) M had not established that the incident was causative of his injuries.

Martin v Thomson Tour Operations Ltd Current Law Cases: 99/3818

M brought an action against T, a tour operator, for damages for personal injuries suffered on a package holiday in Egypt. The holiday consisted of a full board seven day Nile cruise followed by a further seven days in Cairo and Luxor. On the sixth day of his holiday, M contracted diarrhoea and a stomach ache. M claimed that other passengers on the cruise boat had suffered from similar complaints. M believed that he had reported his condition to T's representative while on holiday, but it was common ground that T had no record of any formal complaint by M or his fellow passengers. M's condition continued throughout his holiday and, on his return to the UK, he attended a doctor who diagnosed dyspepsia. M was still suffering from the condition approximately a month and a half after his return to the UK. He attended his doctor who took a stool sample and a diagnosis of cryptosporidium, a reportable disease, was made. His condition resolved within a further 14 days. M alleged that the cryptosporidium condition had been contracted from the consumption of infected food while he was on the Nile cruise boat. M claimed that he had only consumed food provided on board the boat. M argued that the extent of T's contractual obligation to M went further than a duty to exercise reasonable care and skill in the provision of food fit for human consumption. Instead, it was argued that under the Package Travel, Package Holidays and Package Tour Regulations 1992 Reg.15, T and its suppliers had a strict duty to ensure that the food consumed on holiday was fit for human consumption and that liability could only be avoided if its default fell within Reg.15(2)(a), (b) or (c).

Held, that (1) M had failed to adduce any evidence as to the incubation period of cryptosporidium, or how the condition could be contracted, and had, therefore, failed to prove that his condition was caused by the consumption of infected food on the cruise boat, rather than general environmental factors; (2) in the absence of an express term, the contractual duty owed by T and its suppliers was to exercise reasonable care and skill to provide food fit for human consumption; (3) there was no evidence from M of any failure by T, or its suppliers, to exercise such reasonable care and skill; (4) in the circumstances, there was no evidence of any fault by T or its suppliers and such fault could not be inferred, and (5) there was nothing in the language of Reg.15(2) which required a finding that the contractual duty to provide food fit for human consumption was strict, rather than a duty to exercise reasonable care and skill.

Charlson v *Warner* Current Law Cases: 00/4043

C bought a skiing holiday from W and arrived at the resort in the late afternoon of the first day, being able to ski for a short time that day. The following day there was heavy rain and no ski lifts were open. Over the next three days there was heavy continuous snow and the holiday makers were advised by the local authority to stay in their hotels. Evening curfews were imposed. On the fifth day of the holiday W evacuated C from the resort. C sought damages from W for breach of contract on the basis that W ought to have been able to predict that the snow conditions would be such that it would not be possible for them to enjoy their holiday. W relied upon the defence of force majeure contained within its standard form booking conditions and the Package Travel, Package Holidays and Package Tours Regulations 1992 Reg.15.

Held, giving judgment for W, that (1) the holiday contracts between W and C were for the provision of flights, transfer and hotel accommodation. There was no guarantee within the contract that the holiday makers would be able to ski. The contract did not provide that W would supply skiing; (2) the weather conditions meant that the holiday as contracted for could not be provided in full as C had to be evacuated from the hotel; (3) all of the parties accepted that the weather during that week had been exceptional; (4) W had acted reasonably in obtaining information from the local authorities in the resort as to the weather and relying upon that information; (5) on the evidence, the court was not satisfied that W ought to have been able, even with all due care, to foresee the exceptional weather conditions. W was therefore entitled to rely upon the force majeure defence within its booking conditions and Reg.15(2)(c)(i) of the 1992 Regulations, and (6) C was not entitled to rely upon Reg.14, which provided holiday makers with a right to suitable alternative accommodation at no extra cost if it was not possible to perform the contract. Regulation 14 was dependent upon Reg.15 and had to be read conjunctively, as they were both subject to the same exclusions contained in Reg.15(2)(c).

SECTION 5

THE CONTRACTUAL STANDARDS OF CARE: LOCAL STANDARDS

THE CONTRACTUAL STANDARD OF CARE: LOCAL STANDARDS

Cases in this Section

Beever v *Hanson, Dale & Co* (1890) 25 LJNC 132 at 133 (Eng QBD)

Lord Coleridge CJ

Now a perfectly humane man naturally makes it physically impossible that a particular accident, which has once happened, can happen again, by fencing or covering, or, at any rate, making safe the particular thing from which it arose. That, however, is no evidence of, and I protest against its being put forward as evidence of, negligence. A place may be left for a hundred years unfenced when at last some one falls down it. The owner, like a sensible and humane man, then puts up a fence, and upon this the argument is that he has been guilty of negligence, and shows that he thought the fence was necessary, because he put it up. This is both unfair and unjust. It is making the good feeling and right principle of a man evidence against him. This is no evidence of negligence.

Hart v Lancashire & Yorkshire Railway Co 21 LT 261 at 263

Baron Bramwell

People do not furnish evidence against themselves simply by adopting a new plan in order to prevent the recurrence of an accident. I think that a proposition to the contrary would be barbarous. It would be as I have often had occasion to tell juries, to hold that because the world gets wiser as it gets older, therefore, it was foolish before.

Wilson v Best Travel Ltd [1993] 1 All ER 353

19 April 1991

PHILLIPS J: In 1986 Mrs Cheryl Bromley made a booking on behalf of a party of five with the defendants for a two-week holiday at the Vanninarchis Beach Hotel on the island of Kos. The defendants' brochure, from which Mrs Bromley selected the holiday, described the hotel as follows:

'C Class. This friendly family-run hotel is located right on the sea shore. The informal Vanninarchis Beach is close to several shops and tavernas and a short walk from the Kardomina Harbour. It has a reception/rustic style lounge with adjoining snack bar opening on to a terrace and a souvenir shop. All rooms have private bath/WC or shower/WC and balcony. Bed and breakfast.'

Mrs Bromley's party, in addition to herself, consisted of a gentleman friend, her 14-year-old daughter Cheryl, her elder daughter Yvonne, and Yvonne's fiancé, the plaintiff. Four of the party had never been out of England before and looked forward to the holiday with keen excitement.

The party flew to Kos on 13 August 1986 and arrived at the hotel in the evening. Yvonne and the plaintiff were allocated a room on the ground floor of the hotel and the other three members of the party were given the room next door. This room had a sliding glass door that led on to a patio. At about 10.30 am on 14 August, after exploring the beach, breakfast, and a short presentation by the defendants' local representative, the plaintiff and Yvonne joined the other three members of the party in the latter's bedroom. There, in circumstances to which I shall return, the plaintiff tripped and fell against the glass patio door. The door shattered and the plaintiff fell through it, sustaining lacerations from the broken glass to the right shoulder, elbow, hand and, in particular, multiple lacerations of the right leg. The plaintiff now claims from the defendants damages in respect of the consequences of this accident. Before dealing with the issue of liability, I propose to describe those consequences.

The Injuries

[His Lordship then considered the nature of the plaintiff's injuries and his consequential loss and concluded that if liability were to be established the plaintiff would be entitled to general damages of £12,500 for pain, suffering and loss of amenity and £30,000 for future loss of earnings. His Lordship continued:]

Liability

How did the accident occur? The accident happened quickly with a devastating shock to the plaintiff and the other members of the party in the room at the time and it is not surprising that the picture painted by their evidence is not entirely clear. The essence of the story is not, however, in doubt. The plaintiff had just closed the sliding door on to the patio and was standing with his back to it. A heavy pair of curtains was drawn open, flanking the door, but the curtain behind and to the right of the plaintiff as he faced into the room had become detached in part from the curtain rail and was trailing a little on the ground. In order to allow Cheryl Bromley access to a table close to which he was standing, the plaintiff took one or two steps back. His right foot caught in the sagging curtain and caused him to trip backwards. I think he must have fallen against the glass with his full weight, albeit not from a great distance, in order to cause the glass to break. Mr Burton, counsel for the defendants, urged me to reject this account of the accident, with which all the eye-witnesses concurred. He submitted that it is more probable that the accident resulted from the plaintiff falling against the window with greater momentum as a result of some high-spirited horseplay. The evidence provides no foundation for this submission, and I reject it. I do not find that the plaintiff was in any way responsible for his own misfortune. The immediate cause of his falling was the obstruction which resulted from the sagging curtain. The gravity of the consequences was attributable to the fact that the glass fractured into fragments of razor-edged sharpness.

The plaintiff's case

Mr Norris, counsel for the plaintiff, advanced his case in two alternative ways. The fundamental premise underlying each was that the characteristics of the glass fitted to the doors of the Vanninarchis Beach Hotel were such that the hotel was not reasonably safe for use by the defendants' customers. This constituted a breach of contract on the part of the defendants for two reasons. First, it was an implied term of the defendants' contract with the plaintiff that the structure of the hotel would be reasonably safe. Second, the defendants owed the plaintiff a duty to exercise reasonable skill and care to ensure that the hotel was reasonably safe. This duty required that the hotel should have been regularly and competently inspected. Such inspections should have disclosed the nature of the glass fitted in the sliding doors of the hotel and thus the fact that the hotel was not reasonably safe.

Implied warranty

In support of his first submission Mr Norris was able to point to no particular feature of the plaintiff's contract that gave rise to the implication of the term. Rather he contended that such a term fell to be implied in every contract for a package holiday of the kind with which this case is concerned. He submitted that if any bystander were to ask the parties whether it was an implied term of their contract that the hotel would be reasonably safe, they would both answer, 'Of course' (see *Shirlaw v Southern Foundries (1926) Ltd and Federated Foundries Ltd* [1939] 2 All ER 113 at 124, [1939] 2 KB 206 at 227). I do not agree. The defendants would not have considered it either obvious or reasonable that they should give a warranty of this kind. Mr Burton referred me to the transcript of a decision of Hodgson J in *Wall v Silver Wings Surface Arrangements Ltd* (18 November 1981, unreported), in which, in a case of very different facts, the plaintiff sought to establish a similar implied term in a contract for a package holiday. After a careful analysis of the relevant law, the judge rejected the term alleged on the ground that the implication of such a term was neither necessary 355 nor obvious nor reasonable. I share both his reasoning and his conclusion. Hodgson J observed:

> '*I think quite clearly that situations could arise in which the tour operator would be liable in negligence to his customers. If, for instance, a hotel included in a brochure had no fire precautions at all or was known to fail to reach the standards required by the law of the country, then the tour operator would, I apprehend, be in breach of duty.*'

This observation is germane to the alternative way in which Mr Norris advanced his case.

Duty of care

Section 13 of the Supply of Goods and Services Act 1982 provides:

> 'In a contract for the supply of a service where the supplier is acting in the course of a business, there is an implied term that the supplier will carry out the service with reasonable care and skill.'

The nature of the services provided by a travel agent when arranging a holiday can vary enormously, depending on the nature of the holiday. I am satisfied, having read their brochure, that the service provided by the defendants included the inspection of the properties offered in their brochure. Such service is implicit from a number of passages in their brochure ...

In my judgment, one of the characteristics of accommodation that the defendants owed a duty to consider when inspecting properties included in their brochure was safety. The defendants owe their customers, including the plaintiff, a duty to exercise reasonable care to exclude from the accommodation offered any hotel whose characteristics were such that guests could not spend a holiday there in reasonable safety. I believe that this case is about the standard to be applied in assessing reasonable safety. It is necessary at this stage to turn to the evidence in relation to the glass fitted in the doors of the Vanninarchis Beach Hotel.

Glass

Mr Vanninarchis, the manager and, with other members of his family, the owner of the Vanninarchis Beach Hotel, came to England from Kos to give evidence. He told me that the construction of his hotel was completed in 1980. The hotel had to comply with two sets of regulations, those imposed by the building authority and those imposed by the Greek tourist organisation, EOT. These regulations covered the specifications of the building, including the glass to be fitted to doors and windows. The glass for the doors of the hotel was 356 required to be 5 mm thick. The glass was also slightly tinted. At the time there was no one on the island of Kos who manufactured or supplied glass of that thickness so the aluminium frames for the doors had to be sent to Athens where a contractor made and fitted 5 mm thick glass. The doors were in due course inspected on behalf of the authorities and approved. Licences were duly issued and renewed by EOT, proving that the regulations were satisfied. Mr Vanninarchis brought three of the licences with him. Mr Norris for the plaintiff suggested to Mr Vanninarchis that the doors of his hotel should have been fitted with safety glass, which would fragment into innocuous small pieces if broken. Mr Vanninarchis's reaction to this was surprise and bewilderment which impressed me as genuine. He said that he was aware of such glass being fitted to motor cars but in Greece it was not the practice to fit it in hotels. The regulations did not require it and such glass was not used in building hotels. He did not accept that it was dangerous to fit ordinary glass in his hotel, observing that they had not had an accident such as that which befell the plaintiff either before or after his casualty.

Expert evidence

Mr Geoffrey Tibbs, a chemist with long experience of the glass industry, was called to give expert evidence for the plaintiff. He told me of a number of different types of glass. For present purposes, two are relevant. The first is annealed glass. This is the glass that is normally used for glazing. It is generally used in panes of 4 mm thickness, with 5 mm or 6 mm being used for larger panes and where increased strength is required. Annealed glass breaks into sharp and jagged pieces. The second type is toughened glass, sometimes known as tempered glass. Individual pieces of glass, already cut to size, are heated in a furnace and then cooled by jets of air so that the outside surface cools before the inside, resulting in a high compression in the surface of the glass and tension in the centre. A greater force is required to break toughened glass compared with ordinary annealed glass of the same thickness. Once it is broken it will immediately break into a very large number of small pieces which are relatively harmless. Toughened glass is used in many car windscreens. If broken by a flying stone it is usually necessary to push the glass out with a hand to restore visability. The characteristic small broken pieces will have been seen at the site of many road accidents. It cannot be cut to size after toughening, so that each piece has to be ordered specially. It is a true safety glass.

Mr Tibbs told me that there has been a growing awareness over recent years of the dangers of glass, particularly in respect of large panes of glass in doors. The present situation in this country with respect to the type of door through which the plaintiff fell, particularly in a hotel or similar public place, is that safety glass, either toughened or laminated, would always be used. Mr Tibbs referred me to the relevant British Standards. [The judge went on to consider the evidence about British standards and practice].

…It is apparent from this evidence that the standards currently applied in England in the interests of safety have yet to be adopted in Greece. It is at least arguable that, if the plaintiff's accident had occurred in England, the hotelier would be held to be in breach of the common duty of care imposed by s 2(2) of the Occupiers, Liability Act 1957.

What is the duty of a tour operator in a situation such as this? Must he refrain from sending holidaymakers to any hotel whose characteristics, in so far as safety is concerned, fail to satisfy the standards which apply in this country? I do not believe that his obligations in respect of the safety of his clients can extend this far. Save where uniform international regulations apply, there are bound to be differences in the safety standards applied in respect of the many hazards of modern life between one country and another. All civilised countries attempt to cater for these hazards by imposing mandatory regulations. The duty of care of a tour operator is likely to extend to checking that local safety regulations are complied with. Provided that they are, I do not consider that the tour operator owes a duty to boycott a hotel because of the absence of some safety feature which would be found in an English hotel unless the absence of such a feature might lead a reasonable holidaymaker to decline to take a holiday at the hotel in question. On the facts of this case I do not consider that the degree of danger posed by the absence of safety glass in the doors of the Vanninarchis Beach Hotel called for any action on the part of the defendants pursuant to their duty to exercise reasonable care to ensure the safety of their clients.

It is perhaps significant that Mr Norris did not expand on what action the defendants should have taken. It was not suggested that they had a duty to warn clients of this characteristic or that such a warning would have prevented the accident in this case. What was, I think, implicit in the plaintiff's case was that the defendants should not have permitted the Vanninarchis Beach Hotel to feature in their brochure. If that contention were valid, it would, on the evidence of Mr Vanninarchis, apply to many, if not the majority, of the other hotels, pensions and villas featured in the defendants' brochure and no doubt the brochures of the other tour operators who send their clients to Greece.

I have the greatest sympathy for the plaintiff for the horrifying accident he has suffered and its unhappy consequences but, for the reasons that I have given, it was an accident which involved no breach of contract or duty on the part of the defendants.

Codd v Thomson Tour Operations Ltd (9 November 2000) CA

1. LORD JUSTICE SWINTON THOMAS: This is an appeal, with permission given by this Court, against an order made by His Honour Judge Roach in the Torquay and Newton Abbot County Court on 21st May 1999, when he dismissed the claimant's claim...

2. The claimant's claim arose out of an accident which occurred on 28th October 1996, when he caught the middle finger of his right hand in the door of a lift. The claimant was born on 17th January 1986 and was 10 years and when the accident occurred. He brought these proceedings by his uncle, Mr Griffiths, who acts as his next friend and conducted the proceedings before the trial judge and has conducted this appeal before us.

3. The defendants, Thomsons, are well known holiday tour operator. On 3rd September 1996 the claimant's father booked his holiday for himself and on behalf of his wife and the claimant's two sisters at the Hotel Corfu at Cala D'or in Majorca. They went on holiday on 19th October 1996 for a period of ten days. By the terms of the agreement made between them the defendant agreed that they would be liable for injuries caused by the negligence of its suppliers, in this case the Hotel Corfu.

4. On the last day of the holiday, 28th October 1996, the claimant entered a lift in the hotel with his two sisters who were older than him. The lift was one of a fairly familiar type. There was an outer door which was hinged and an inner sliding door which close automatically when the outer door had been closed. The claimant and his sisters went in to the lift and neither of the doors shut. It appears that the outer door had, for some reason, jammed before it reached its proper resting place in the door frame. Gareth put his right hand round the door and pulled it towards him. The door then shut quickly and caught his right middle finger as a result of which he sustained a serious injury to it.

5. Judge Roach was trying the issue as to liability only. The defendants accepted that they would be liable to pay damages to the claimant if negligence was established against those who were responsible for running and managing the hotel.

6. The defendants initially alleged that the accident occurred because Gareth, the claimant, was playing about in the lift and was unaccompanied. They abandoned that suggestion and accepted that he had been in the lift with his sisters.

7. The claimant's father, Mr David Anthony Codd, gave evidence at the hearing. He said that on days prior to the accident he had noticed that the hinges on the outer door of the lift were worn and he thought the door was dropping and catching on the carpet underneath it. He said that he had noticed that the door on the lift where the accident occurred was heavier than the door on a second adjacent lift in the hotel. Mr Codd had not at any stage made that allegation prior to giving evidence at the hearing, despite the fact that he had met the tour representative and other representatives of the hotel immediately after the accident and had made a written statement through his son's solicitors. It was in those circumstances hardly surprising that judge did not accept that evidence.

...

9. The judge had before him documentation which showed that, in accordance with Spanish law, the lifts at the hotel were examined on a monthly basis by managers. ...

10. However, as I said a moment ago, there was clear evidence from Miss Stevenson (and the judge accepted it), that the lifts were working satisfactorily prior to and after the accident and, if they were inspected regularly by engineers in accordance with Spanish law, there was no reason why any inference should be drawn that the engineers or the hotel had failed in their duty to keep the lifts properly maintained.

...

12. On page 11 of if his judgment the judge said in relation to the documents:

> *"What do I make of those records? I think I can make this of them, that they show, according to Spanish law, because that is the certificate that is upon them, that this lift and this installation was looked at with a frequency of once a month, and that this lift and this system survived that inspection, and was found to be working, by record, adequately and safely."*

13. Then a little later on he said:

> *"I am driven to the conclusion, on the balance of probability, that there was a maintenance system in operation and an inspection system in operation, in accordance with Spanish law, as the certificates indicate."*

14. Those important conclusions were conclusions which, in my judgment, on the evidence before him that the judge was entitled to make.

15. The judge concluded that it was impossible to say why the door had closed in the way that it did. He said that there was no evidence to what caused the door to close that way. He said there was no evidence that it slammed shut as a result of poor maintenance or poor inspection by the engineers or the hotel staff. Mr Griffiths has submitted to us that the onus of proving that the accident did not result from the negligence of the hotel or Thomsons was upon them and not on the claimant.

16. In addition to alleging that the accident occurred as a result of the failure to maintain the lift properly, it was alleged on behalf of the claimant that there was no emergency equipment or proper advice in the lift as to what to do if the door did not close, or if the lift failed to operate correctly.

The judge said in his judgment that there were no regulations in Spain which required safety signs to be posted in lift or a requirement that there should be an emergency alarm or emergency procedure in the lift if the door did not close or the lift became stuck.

17. There is such a requirement in English law under current regulations governing the installation and use of lifts and we have those regulations with our documentation. The lift did not comply with those regulations but complied with Spanish legislation. In those circumstances the judge concluded that it could not be said that the managers of the hotel were negligent in failing to install alarm devices or instructions as to what to do in an emergency. The judge recorded that the lift performed as a standard unit to lifts throughout Spain. Accordingly he arrived at the

conclusion that negligence had not been established against the hotel owners or managers and, in consequence, it was not established against the tour operator.

18. Mr Griffiths on behalf of his nephew has put forward a number of proposed grounds of appeal. Those grounds are supported by what is described as an appendix for the revised grounds and by a skeleton argument. Mr Griffiths addressed us very fully in relation to each of his grounds. They are these:

(1) Defence evidence that both lifts were properly maintained prior to the accident was both insufficient and of an extremely unsatisfactory nature. As such it did not merit the weight given to it.

(2) Proper safety procedures were not followed by the defendant upon discovery of the accident.

20. I turn to the more substantive points taken by Mr Griffiths in the appeal. He criticises the quality of the evidence that was presented to the judge as to maintenance. He says that the originals of the inspection were not exhibited and their authenticity and completeness is much in doubt. He says that the copies that were provided were unsafe as evidence and should have been found to be admissible. He says that the inescapable conclusion is that the defendants were withholding evidence.

21. There is again, in my judgment, no evidence at all to support the submission that the defendants were in this case deliberately withholding material documents. Until very late in this case the claimant was represented by solicitors who were in a position to ask for further documentation if such was required. There is in my view some substance in the criticism as to the quality of the documents but there is nothing in the case which suggests to my mind that any documentation was deliberately withheld. The evidence which the judge accepted, particularly the evidence of Miss Stevenson tended to show that indeed the lifts were regularly inspected and maintained and were in good and proper working order at the time. As I indicated, Mr Griffiths makes stringent criticisms of Miss Stevenson's evidence and the judge's approach to it. The substance of the submission is that it is plain that she was lying and the judge should, in total, have rejected her evidence. In my view, the judge having heard her evidence was perfectly entitled to accept it if he accepted that she was by telling him the truth as she recollected it.

22. Mr Griffiths then submits that the judge was in error in not applying the British standards to this particular lift in the hotel in Cala D'or with the result that there was a breach of duty according to English law. That is not a correct approach to a case such as this where an accident occurred in a foreign country. The law of this country is applied to the case as to the establishing of negligence, but there is no requirement that a hotel for example, in Majorca is obliged to comply with British Safety Standards: see *Wilson v Best Travel Limited* [1993] 1 All ER at 353.

23. Mr Griffiths then goes on to criticise the safety procedures which were present in the lift at the time when this accident occurred. I have already dealt with the safety procedures so far as the lift itself is concerned, but Mr Griffiths relies upon the fact that there were no instructions in the lift as to what to do in the case of an emergency. In my judgment the judge was entitled to find as he did that there was no requirement by the regulations then in force in Spain to have in place any further instructions other than those which were present.

24. This is not a case in which, in my view, it is appropriate to say that the hotel or the tour operator is liable for this accident without proof of negligence. In order to succeed the claimant must prove that the hotel management was negligent either in relation to the maintenance of the lift or in relation to the safety procedures. In my view despite Mr Griffiths' submissions the judge approached that question in a proper manner. He was entitled to conclude on the evidence that it was not established that the hotel management was negligent in any of the facts alleged and I would accordingly and for those reasons dismiss this appeal.

James Evans v Kosmar Villa Holidays plc [2007] EWCA Civ 1003

Edited from the judgment of:

Lord Justice Richards.

1.　　　In August 2002, three weeks short of his eighteenth birthday, James Evans was on holiday with a group of friends at the Marina Beach Apartments in Kavos, Corfu. The holiday had been booked with a tour operator, Kosmar Villa Holidays plc ("Kosmar"). The apartment complex was under independent Greek ownership and management but was contracted exclusively to Kosmar and was featured in Kosmar's brochure. It included a small swimming pool. Towards the end of his stay, in the early hours of the morning, Mr Evans dived into the shallow end of the pool and hit his head on the bottom, sustaining serious injuries which resulted in incomplete tetraplegia. He brought a claim for personal injuries against Kosmar. His Honour Judge Thorn QC, sitting as a judge of the High Court, found Kosmar liable for the accident, subject to a finding of 50 per cent contributory negligence. Kosmar now appeals against that decision.

2.　　　It is clear that the claimant is a remarkable young man. The judge not only found him and his friends to be completely frank witnesses, unreservedly accepting their evidence as against any conflicting evidence for Kosmar, but also commented on how impressive the claimant had been at making the best of his disabilities after the accident and congratulated him on the triumphs he had achieved over his undoubted personal disaster. The warmth of the judge's remarks is a fine tribute to the claimant. As the judge himself made clear, however, that cannot affect the court's decision in the case, which must depend on the application of the relevant legal principles to the facts as found.

3.　　　By contrast, the judge found that Kosmar's lay witnesses had "variously committed themselves to an early and false joint account to save their backs" and on several issues was driven to the conclusion that "not only have they lied, but that they also put their heads together, probably at several stages, and conspired together to deceive" (para 15). Such conduct is a deeply troubling feature of the case and reflects very badly not only on the witnesses themselves but also on Kosmar. It will no doubt have added to the sympathy that the judge rightly felt for the claimant. Again, however, none of this can affect the legal analysis.

The facts

4.　　　The judge described Kavos as the sort of resort that was typically aimed at young single people holidaying without adult supervision, not infrequently in groups of already formed friends, and with ample opportunities to drink substantial quantities of alcohol for very substantial periods, or indeed all of the day and night, and generally for the traditional night to be turned into day. He said that the operation at the Marina Beach Apartments was particularly well set up to provide for the young and lively and to fit in with the commercial opportunities at the resort. It was generally free from any real rules, and relaxed to the point of permitting most things that kept the youngsters happy.

5.　　　The complex itself was next to the beach and consisted of a number of studios and apartments, a bar and the pool. A path ran from the accommodation block past the pool to the bar. The path was separated by a flowerbed from the paved area around the pool itself. The judge found that the bar might sometimes have closed by midnight, but more frequently it stayed open as long as there were guests wanting to drink. When the bar closed, the lights in the swimming pool and bar area were turned off, but the lights on the path remained lit. The judge rejected a defence contention that the pool was then closed. He found that its use by guests was continued and authorised.

6.　　　The pool was 11.2 metres long and 5.8 metres wide. At the deeper end, furthest away from the accommodation block, the maximum depth of the water was almost certainly no more than 1.5 metres, though there was a ledge under the water on which people could stand. At the shallow end, the depth of the water was probably only about 0.8 metres. There was a small depth marker at each end of the pool, though they were probably not visible at night.

7.　　　The experts agreed that the pool's dimensions made it unsuitable for diving. There were two small "no diving" signs in the general area of the pool at the material time. One was on the wall of the toilet block, on the other side of the path running between the accommodation block and the bar, though the judge found that there was shrubbery hanging partly over and adjacent to the sign. The other sign was on a tree on the far side of the pool, close to the bar area. Both signs were among a collection of other notices. Despite the existence of those signs, diving was in practice a regular occurrence. Indeed, the judge found that "the Defendant knew full well that not only was the pool regularly used when the bar was shut, but also that diving did take place, probably on a regular basis, and without any reproof or reprimand" (para 19(4)(e)).

8.　　　The judge accepted that the claimant had probably used the pool only once before the accident, on the Tuesday morning of his stay. In his witness statement, from which the judge quoted extensively, the claimant said that on that occasion he jumped into the deep end to cool off and stood on the ledge, leaning over the edge and talking to friends. He did not go into the shallow end. A little later he referred to his having seen people diving in from all sides and at all ends. He never thought that people would dive in like that to a shallow pool, and consequently he assumed that the pool was reasonably deep all around. He was not aware of there being a significant change in depth between the end he was using and the opposite end. He did not recall seeing any signs pointing out the depth of the pool or stating that there was to be no diving.

9.　　　On the Wednesday evening the claimant went out with his friends for a meal and stayed out late. When he returned with one of his room-mates, they stayed in their apartment talking until about 3.30 a.m. They had also woken up their other room-mate. It was very hot and they had the windows open. There was a lot of noise from the pool. They could not sleep, so they thought "if you can't beat them, join them" and went out to the pool. The claimant's witness statement continued:

"18. ... There were many other people using our pool and also the pool in the next door hotel. We couldn't see anyone else we knew there. The bar was shut and the light was poor as we were relying on light from next door and from the apartments.

People were diving in all over the place so I had no reason to think there would be a problem if I did the same. I had not seen any depth markings when it was light so none were apparent in the darkness. At the same time I also could not assess the depth of the pool before I entered but no-one else was having a problem so I assumed all would be fine if I dived in."

10.   The claimant went on to explain that he had learned to swim at about the age of 8 and had used pools in Turkey and Spain on family holidays as well as in the United Kingdom. He knew that you should not dive into water if you do not know how deep it is. However, he had assumed that this pool was safe. Because he was unaware of the depth of the pool and because he thought that it was perfectly safe to dive in, having seen other people doing it, he walked up and dived in. His was, as he recalled, "a very ordinary racing type of dive out into the water". The dive was in fact into the shallow end, close to the point where there are ladder-type steps into the pool. He hit his head on the bottom and, it seems, was fortunate to be rescued before he drowned.

....

14.   That leads on to the judge's specific findings about the accident itself. He found first that the claimant "should, and could, have known if he had really thought about it that the closest poolside into which he was to dive was the shallow end, and that his assumption that the pool was of the same depth at both ends might at least be inaccurate"   He then said that this could not be the end of his attempt to understand what happened and why the claimant dived in here having such knowledge that he previously had. The judge said that after careful consideration he made the following ten further findings of fact on the balance of probabilities:

"(1)   The Claimant was foreseeably tired. He had been living a fairly typical unstructured lifestyle compared with what he had been used to in the UK, which could only have been expected, and it was inevitable, and even offered as the nature of their holiday operation and the provision of a very late night bar and a swimming pool for which there was always open access.

(2)   The Claimant had had some alcoholic drink. It was almost certainly less than the defence might have expected of some of their young guests, especially amongst such a teenaged group as was this one.

(3)   He was in a holiday resort and location given to twenty-four hour hospitality with a purpose-built swimming pool facility that was available for use at all hours.

(4)   The Claimant not unreasonably thought, as I find, that the pool was available; it was in actual use; and that others were, and had previously been, diving in 'all around'.

(5)   Insofar as the Defendant had rules or advice to prevent either, they were inadequate by any objective standard, and for the Claimant there was nothing adequate to prevent what I find was then to happen in this accident.

(6)   Objectively, he knew that diving in here was unwise and potentially dangerous. In the ordinary event, he would never have done so, and he did not ordinarily need to be told that.

(7) That in the foreseeable exuberance of the youthful use of this pool, especially in the very late heat of the night, he copied what he had seen others doing on this occasion and others, both in deciding to go swimming this night when the bar was shut, and others were 'diving in from all sides'. In those circumstances he forgot his own good sense, but against which possibility properly and prominently displayed warning signs were surely designed to prevent, especially given the nature of this sort of holiday facility. I find that, on the balance of probability, such better placed and more prominent signs which were recommended would indeed have brought him to his better sense before he dived in.

(8) In the foreseeable spirit of the moment, lacking more mature years and experience, and lacking such precautions as the Defendant could, and should, have taken in reasonable foresight of such an accident, with such potentially disastrous consequences, the Claimant walked out of the accommodation block and simply dived in to join his mates and others, including a quite separate group from Liverpool in the pool.

(9) What previous knowledge of the dangers the Claimant had had, that deserted him on this occasion. With nothing in particular by way of adequate safeguards and warnings, not even as the defence alleged, to help bring him to his senses at this late hour, any prior and useful knowledge left him. He dived in at the nearest point to him. It happened to be the shallower end. He was thoughtless at the time – foreseeably so, as I find, in the circumstances and nature of this holiday venue run by the Defendant. I think they both share some blame here, but that might be another matter as to whether it amounts to legal culpability by the Defendant in this litigation, and, if so, how any liability might be apportioned.

(10) Finally, the Claimant knew beforehand that he should not have done as he did. He well knows now that he should not have done as he did. But, I find that the only explicable reason for what happened – as, indeed, the Claimant told me – was that actually at this particular time he was completely unaware and oblivious to the dangers he was courting. There was nothing then present that might adequately have deterred him from his brief state of inadvertence which the safety standards were designed to prevent, and thus briefly bring him to his senses on this occasion before he dived in. But for the simple and inexpensive precautions that have been canvassed here, this foreseeable accident could, and, on the balance of probabilities, would have been prevented in this case."

....

Other relevant matters

16.   I have already mentioned that the experts agreed that the pool was not safe for diving. The judge said that the significant disagreement between them was as to whether the "no diving" signs and the signage generally were adequate. The claimant's expert, Mr Boydell, criticised the positioning and size of the "no diving" signs and also said that the signage relating to closure should have been explicit and enforced. The defence expert, Mr Fowler, was less critical of the signage although he made a number of concessions helpful to the claimant's case. It is clear from the general tenor of his judgment that the judge preferred the evidence of Mr Boydell. In para 42 of his judgment, quoted above, he referred repeatedly to the absence of

adequate safeguards and warnings. In para 52 he found in relation to each of the "no diving" signs that the "the sign was visible, the message was not". He also found that the signage failed to comply with the guidance issued by the Federation of Tour Operators ("FTO"), which calls for fuller consideration.

17.   The FTO's Health and Safety Handbook contains a section headed "Suggestions for Swimming Pool Safety", which also appears to be available as a separate leaflet to be given to hoteliers and others. The judge referred in particular to the following paragraphs:

"4. Depth markings should be placed at regular intervals. Minimum 2m apart on small pools, 3m apart on large pools ....

5. Gradual changes in depths should be indicated at these regular intervals as indicated.

6. Sudden changes in depths should be clearly marked ....

...

8. No Diving signs should be displayed in a prominent position, especially in areas with depths of less than 1.5m.

9. Opening hours and emergency procedures should be clearly visible. "

....

17.   The judge did not deal with the status of the FTO guidance, but the issue featured in argument before us and it will be helpful to consider it here. We were informed that only about 30 per cent of tour operators are members of the FTO. The foreword to the handbook states that the handbook "*has been produced to help anyone who wishes to improve health and safety standards for holiday makers*", and that it is a tribute to the FTO's health and safety officers and others "*that significant improvements to safety standards have been achieved especially when, as they often do, these improvements are over and above the local regulations*". The foreword is followed by an "important notice" stating that "[t]he information and advice contained in this Handbook is designed to assist tour operators and their suppliers to develop their own safety systems. It should, however, be regarded as a starting point, and not as a definitive statement of the law or technical safety standards".

18.   There was evidence that the FTO guidance formed part of the documents used internally within Kosmar for the training of its representatives. There was, however, no evidence that it was regarded as laying down internationally recognised or uniform standards. Mr Fowler accepted in cross-examination that Mediterranean hotels conventionally have signs designating which end of the pool is the shallow end and which is the deep end, and also conventionally "comply with uniform standards about prominent diving prohibition signs", but did not cover the nature or detailed content of any such standards.

Breach of duty

19.   The claimant's case was based on the holiday contract between the claimant and Kosmar, with additional reliance on regulation 15 of the Package Travel, Package Holidays and Package Tours Regulations 1992 ("the 1992 Regulations").

20.   The amended particulars of claim pleaded implied terms of the contract that (i) the facilities at the apartments and in particular the swimming pool and its surrounds would comply with local regulations and safety standards applicable in Corfu in 2002, (ii) reasonable skill and care would be exercised in the provision of the facilities and services at the apartments and in particular at the swimming pool and its surrounds, and (iii) the facilities at the apartments would be of a reasonable standard by complying with recommended minimum standards laid down by the FTO. Breaches of each of those implied terms were pleaded.

21.   The amended particulars of claim also pleaded that there had been "improper performance" of the holiday contract within the meaning of regulation 15 of the 1992 Regulations. Regulation 15 covers the situation where services to which the contract relates are supplied by someone other than the contracting party. It therefore applied to the operation of the apartment complex in this case. Para (1) provides that "[t]he other party to the contract is liable to the consumer for the proper performance of the obligations under the contract, irrespective of whether such obligations are to be performed by the other party or by other suppliers of services ...". Para (2) provides that "[t]he other party to the contract is liable to the consumer for any damage caused to him by ... the improper performance of the contract ...". But the question whether there has been "improper performance" is to be determined by reference to the terms of the contract, which in this case takes one back to the implied terms as pleaded: see *Hone v Going Places Leisure Travel Limited* [2001] EWCA Civ 947, para 15.

22.   The first of the implied terms pleaded by the claimant may owe its formulation to *Wilson v Best Travel Ltd* [1993] 1 All ER 353. In Wilson the plaintiff, while staying in a hotel in Greece on a holiday booked through the defendant tour operator, sustained serious injuries on tripping and falling through glass patio doors at the hotel. The plaintiff's claim, which pre-dated the 1992 Regulations, was based on an implied warranty that the structure of the hotel would be reasonably safe, alternatively a duty of care arising out of the term implied by s.13 of the Supply of Goods and Services Act 1982. The judge, Phillips J (as he then was), found against a warranty but accepted the existence of a duty of care. He held that the service provided by the defendant included the inspection of properties offered in its brochure and that the defendant owed a duty to exercise reasonable care to exclude from the accommodation offered any hotel whose characteristics were such that guests could not spend a holiday there in reasonable safety (p.356d-h). The evidence was that it was the practice in England, but not yet in Greece, to fit safety glass to doors. In those circumstances the judge held that there was no breach of the defendant's duty, stating (at p.358b-d):

> "What is the duty of a tour operator in a situation such as this? Must he refrain from sending holidaymakers to any hotel whose characteristics, in so far as safety is concerned, fail to satisfy the standards which apply in this country? I do not believe that his obligations in respect of the safety of his clients can extend this far. Save where uniform international regulations apply, there are bound to be differences in the safety standards applied in respect of the many hazards of modern life between one country and another. All civilised countries attempt to cater for these hazards by imposing mandatory regulations. The duty of care of a tour operator is

> *likely to extend to checking that local safety regulations are complied with. Provided that they are, I do not consider that the tour operator owes a duty to boycott a hotel because of the absence of some safety feature which would be found in an English hotel unless the absence of such a feature might lead a reasonable holidaymaker to decline to take a holiday at the hotel in question."*

23.   A claim such as that in Wilson v Best Travel Ltd would no doubt be put differently under the 1992 Regulations: since the tour operator is directly liable under those regulations for improper performance of the contract by the hotel even if the hotel is under independent ownership and management, the focus can be on the exercise of reasonable care in the operation of the hotel itself rather than in the selection of the hotel and the offer of accommodation at it. But I do not think that this affects the principle laid down as to the standard to be applied to a hotel abroad, namely that the hotel is required to comply with local safety regulations rather than with British safety standards. That was the approach in *Codd v Thomson Tour Operators Limited* (Court of Appeal judgment of 7 July 2000), in which the claimant had been injured while travelling in a lift at a hotel in which he was staying in Majorca. The tour operator accepted that it would be liable (presumably under the 1992 Regulations) if negligence was established against those who were responsible for running and managing the hotel, but the judge found that liability was not established. The Court of Appeal dismissed the claimant's appeal, citing *Wilson v Best Travel Ltd* for the proposition that there was no requirement for the hotel to comply with British safety standards, and holding that there was no breach of local safety regulations and that there was no negligence by the hotel management either in relation to the maintenance of the lift or in relation to safety procedures.

24.   In the present case, there was no evidence to support the pleaded claim of non-compliance with local safety regulations, and that way of putting the case was not pursued at trial. In my view, however, it was still open to the claimant to pursue the claim on the other bases pleaded in the amended particulars of claim. What was said in *Wilson v Best Travel Ltd* did not purport to be an exhaustive statement of the duty of care, and it does not seem to me that compliance with local safety regulations is necessarily sufficient to fulfil that duty. That was evidently also the view taken in Codd, where the court found there to be compliance with local safety regulations but nevertheless went on to consider other possible breaches of the duty of care.

25.   I can deal briefly with the pleaded failure to comply with minimum standards laid down by the FTO. I have already described the FTO's Health and Safety Handbook and the "Suggestions for Swimming Pool Safety" contained within it. In my view the handbook is referred to correctly as guidance. It is advisory in character and has no legal force. It does not lay down standards with which Kosmar is required to comply. As I understood Mr Saggerson's submissions to us, he did not contend otherwise but relied on the handbook simply as "informing" the standard of care and as casting light on whether Kosmar had exercised reasonable care in this case.

26.   The case therefore comes down to the most general of the implied terms pleaded, that reasonable skill and care would be exercised in the provision of facilities and services at the apartment complex and in particular at the swimming pool and its

surrounds. It is common ground that such a term is to be implied. The dispute relates to the scope of the duty of care and whether there was in the particular circumstances a breach of that duty.

27.   If there was a duty to exercise reasonable care to guard against what the claimant did in this case, then in my view the judge was entitled to find a breach of duty. It was open to him accept the evidence of the claimant's expert, Mr Boydell, as to the deficiencies of the signage, and to find non-compliance with the FTO guidance; and his conclusion that there was a failure to exercise reasonable care, in particular as to the prominence of the "no diving" signage around the pool, is not one with which there is any reason to interfere.

28.   But did the duty of care extend that far? The essence of Kosmar's case is that there is no duty to guard against an obvious risk of the kind that existed here, namely that diving into shallow water (or into water of unknown depth) may cause injury. That risk was obvious to an ordinary able-bodied adult such as the claimant. The evidence shows that he knew of the risk and was able to assess it for himself. He took a deliberate decision to dive in. Kosmar was under no duty to warn him against such a course or to take other measures to prevent it. The fact that he dived in, as the judge found, in a brief state of inadvertence does not affect the position: that could be said of almost all accidents, and again there is no duty to guard against it. Nor is the position affected by the fact that a lot of people were taking the same obvious risk by diving in.

29.   The most important of the cases relied on by Mr Eklund is *Tomlinson v Congleton Borough Council* [2004] 1 AC 46. That case concerned a lake in a country park owned and occupied by the first defendant and managed by the second defendant. Swimming in the lake was prohibited and the defendants displayed prominent warning notices. The first defendant, aware that the notices were frequently ignored and that several accidents had resulted from swimming in the lake, intended planning vegetation around the shore to prevent people from going into the water but had not yet done so because of a shortage of financial resources. The claimant, aged 18, went into the lake and from a standing position in shallow water dived and struck his head on the sandy bottom, breaking his neck. He claimed damages, alleging that the accident had been caused by the defendants' breach of the duty of care they owed to him as a trespasser under s.1 of the Occupiers' Liability Act 1984, by which a duty is owed in respect of risks of injury by reason of any danger due to the state of the premises. His claim failed at first instance, succeeded by a majority in the Court of Appeal, but failed once more on a further appeal to the House of Lords.

30.   In his dissenting judgment in the Court of Appeal, Longmore LJ observed (p.62, para 47):

> "*One of the dangers of going for a swim in any stretch of water other than a dedicated swimming pool is that the swimmer may slip and injure himself. He may also quickly find himself out of his depth and be unable to cope; he may get cramp or be assailed by the coldness of the water and be unable to recover. All these are obvious dangers to anyone except a small and unaccompanied child. Another danger is that a swimmer may decide to dive into the water and hit his head on the bottom, if the water is too shallow; in*

> *my judgment that is an equally obvious danger and cannot provide a reason for saying that the owner or occupier of the water should be under any duty to take reasonable steps to prevent people swimming or diving in the relevant stretch of water."*

Mr Eklund submitted that that reasoning applies equally to an adult diving into a swimming pool, as occurred in this case.

....

31.   The leading speech in the House of Lords was given by Lord Hoffmann, with whom Lord Nicholls of Birkenhead and Lord Scott of Foscote agreed. Lord Hoffmann held that the only risk arose out of what the claimant chose to do and not out of the state of the premises, so that there was no risk of a kind which gave rise to a duty under the 1984 Act. But even on the assumption that there was such a risk, he held that there can have been no duty under the Act. An integral part of the reasoning that led to that conclusion was his consideration of what the position would have been if the claimant had been a lawful visitor owed the common duty of care under s.2(2) of the Occupiers' Liability Act 1957, namely "a duty to take such care as in all the circumstances of the case is reasonable to see that the visitor will be reasonably safe in using the premises for the purposes for which he is invited or permitted by the occupier to be there". Lord Hoffmann identified two important considerations. The first was the social value of the activities which would have to be prohibited in order to reduce or eliminate the risk from swimming, namely use of the beaches to sunbathe, paddle and play with children. The second consideration, examined under the heading "free will", was whether people should accept responsibility for the risks they choose to run. Lord Hoffmann said this:

> *"44. ... Mr Tomlinson was freely and voluntarily undertaking an activity which inherently involved some risk ....*
>
> *45. I think it will be extremely rare for an occupier of land to be under a duty to prevent people from taking risks which are inherent in the activities they freely choose to undertake upon the land. If people want to climb mountains, go hang-gliding or swim or dive in ponds or lakes, that is their affair ....*
>
> *46. My Lords, as will be clear from what I have just said, I think that there is an important question of freedom at stake. It is unjust that the harmless recreation of responsible parents and children with buckets and spades on the beaches should be prohibited in order to comply with what is thought to be a legal duty to safeguard irresponsible visitors against dangers which are perfectly obvious. The fact that such people take no notice of warnings cannot create a duty to take other steps to protect them. I find it difficult to express with appropriate moderation my disagreement with the proposition of Sedley LJ ... that it is 'only where the risk is so obvious that the occupier can safely assume that nobody will take it that there will be no liability'. A duty to protect against obvious risks or self-inflicted harm exists only in cases in which there is no genuine and informed choice, as in the case of employees whose work requires them to take the risk, or some lack of*

capacity, such as the inability of children to recognise danger ... or the despair of prisoners which may lead them to inflict injury on themselves ....

....

39.   The fundamental question, however, is whether the judge was right to distinguish the line of cases under the Occupiers' Liability Acts as he did and to treat them as having no relevance to the contractual context (and related statutory context) of the present case. There are of course factual differences between the cases. The judge was also right that the extent of the duty owed by occupiers of land to trespassers and even to lawful visitors may be affected by policy considerations that have no parallel in the context of a holiday contract. But the core of the reasoning in Tomlinson, as in earlier cases such as *Ratcliff v McConnell*, was that people should accept responsibility for the risks they choose to run and that there should be no duty to protect them against obvious risks (subject to Lord Hoffmann's qualification as to cases where there is no genuine and informed choice or there is some lack of capacity). That reasoning was held to apply in relation not only to trespassers but also to lawful visitors to whom there is owed the common duty of care under s.2(2) of the Occupiers' Liability Act 1957 – a duty which, by s.5 of the 1957 Act, can be owed to contractual as well as to non-contractual visitors. I do not see why the reasoning should not also apply to persons to whom there is owed a duty of care in similar terms under a contract of the kind that existed in this case.

40.   Mr Eklund drew our attention to the fact that in *Dean v Thomson Tour Operators Limited* (judgment of Silber J, 16 June 2000) it was agreed by the parties that where a tour operator was under a contractual duty to supply facilities to a reasonable standard, the principles to be applied were analogous to those in the Occupiers' Liability Act 1957. Mr Eklund was able to make forensic play of the fact that Mr Saggerson was on that occasion counsel for the defendant tour operator rather than the claimant, but I do not think that the case itself is of any real assistance, for the very reason that the point went by concession and, although implicitly accepted by the judge, was not the subject of any argument. For the reasons I have given, however, I think that the approach adopted in the case was the correct one.

41.   Applying that approach here, Kosmar's duty of care did not extend, in my judgment, to a duty to guard the claimant against the risk of his diving into the pool and injuring himself. That was an obvious risk, of which he was well aware. Although just under 18 years of age, he was of full capacity and was able to make a genuine and informed choice. He was not even seriously affected by drink.

42.   Mr Saggerson argued that, on the particular facts as found by the judge, the claimant was not aware of any risk. At the moment when he dived, he assessed it as safe for him to dive, as others were doing. As the judge said, any prior and useful knowledge left him and he acted in a brief state of inadvertence. Mr Saggerson submitted that this case should be about the need for prominent signage to reduce the risk of people in the claimant's position reaching a wrong conclusion as the claimant did. The point, in effect, was that it is not a matter of guarding against an obvious risk but of guarding against the possibility of a mistaken assessment of the risk. That is a clever way of seeking to meet the argument based on Tomlinson, but I would reject it. The risk in this case remained an obvious one of which the claimant himself

was previously aware and should have been aware at the moment he dived. The fact that at that moment he acted thoughtlessly, in a brief state of inadvertence, is not a good reason for holding Kosmar to have been under a duty that it would not otherwise have owed him.

43.   Accordingly I take the view that there was no duty to give the claimant any warning about the risk of diving into the pool, let alone to have better placed or more prominent signs than those actually displayed, or to take any other step to prevent or deter him from using the pool or from diving into it. His dive and its terrible consequences are matters for which he must take full personal responsibility.

44.   It follows that I would allow Kosmar's appeal against the judge's finding that Kosmar was in breach of its contractual duty of care and liable under regulation 15 of the 1992 Regulations for improper performance of the holiday contract.

Causation

45.   I will deal with this issue even though, because of the conclusion I have reached on the first issue, it is not strictly necessary for me to do so.

46.   The judge, having found breaches of contract and breach of statutory duty, continued (at para 60): "I find that on the balance of probabilities this accident would not have happened but for them, and that causation is established by the Claimant". More specifically, it seems that causation was established on the basis that the claimant acted in a brief state of inadvertence and that better placed and more prominent warning signs would have brought him to his senses before he dived in. It was the claimant's own belief, stated by him in evidence, that if he had seen signs he would not have dived in.

47.   The judge did not indicate the precise location or nature of the warning signs that in his view were required in order to fulfil the duty of care and have the requisite effect on the claimant's mind. The judge had before him, however, photographs of signage put up since the accident, which include a new "no diving" sign on the wall of the toilet block and an additional "no diving" sign on a post located on the paved area at the shallow end of the pool (but standing some distance away from the pool itself). He is likely to have had this material in mind when reaching his conclusions.

48.   This court will be slow to interfere with a finding of this kind. I have to say, however, that the finding in this case causes me considerable concern. It is striking that the claimant, on his own evidence, had not previously seen or taken in, even in daytime, any of the matters that indicated the existence of a shallow end, and did not see them on the occasion of the accident. He did not even see the ladder-type steps which were close to the point from which he dived in. Moreover the accident occurred in the hours of darkness, with the pool itself unlit, though the path lights were still on and would have cast some light onto the general area of the pool; and the claimant commented in his witness statement that the light was poor. In all the circumstances, if "no diving" signs of the kind that were put up after the accident had been present at the time of the accident, I think it improbable that they would have made any difference: it is unlikely that the claimant would have seen them or taken them in or that they would have operated to bring him to his senses and prevent the accident. Similar considerations apply in relation to any contention that there should

have been explicit signage prohibiting use of the pool after the bar had closed and the main lights had been turned off (though, as Mr Saggerson appeared to accept in argument, that was not the basis on which the judge found liability). It is also unlikely that additional signage would have stopped other people from using the pool and diving in, or therefore from setting the example which the claimant said he followed.

49.   In my view we are in as good a position as the judge to evaluate the relevant evidence and reach a conclusion on it; and, for the reasons given, I respectfully differ from the conclusion reached by the judge. In my judgment the claim should fail on causation even if a breach of duty were established. This provides an additional reason for allowing the appeal against the judge's finding of liability.

Contributory negligence

50.   Given the conclusion I have reached on liability, Kosmar's appeal against the judge's finding in relation to contributory negligence falls away. I shall do no more than outline the issue and express the conclusion I would have reached on it had it arisen for decision. Mr Eklund submitted that relevant causative responsibility for the accident lay almost wholly with the claimant, whose degree of responsibility was at least 80 per cent, and that the judge's conclusion defied rational analysis. Mr Saggerson submitted that this case had 50:50 stamped all over it. I would have accepted Mr Saggerson's submission. In my judgment, if the judge's approach to liability had been correct, there would have been no basis for interfering with his equal apportionment of responsibility.

Conclusion

51.   In conclusion, whilst sympathising greatly with the claimant's plight, I take the view that the judge's finding of liability was wrong, both as regards breach of duty and as regards causation. I would allow the appeal and dismiss the claimant's claim.

Singh v Libra Holidays [2003] EWHK 276 (Queen's Bench Division)

Mr Justice Holland:

Introduction

1.   On the 18ᵗʰ July 1998 the Claimant, Balram (otherwise Barry) Singh, sustained complete tetraplegia as a result of an accident sustained in the course of a package holiday supplied by the Defendants. He claims damages for this injury and for the very substantial consequential loss, alleging liability pursuant to the contract. Liability is strongly denied and it is alleged that the accident was wholly or substantially the fault of the Claimant. Having regard to the weight of the liability issue and the potential impact of the result in terms of costs, the parties have sensibly decided that this issue should be the subject of an initial preliminary trial. It is this that I have tried and my judgment follows.

Locus

2.   The venue for the holiday was the Christabelle Hotel and Apartments at Ayia Napa in Cyprus. The relevant part of the premises is well depicted in the agreed photographs and plan. Amongst the swimming pools available to the guests was that illustrated. Its width is 7.86 metres and its length is 17.82 metres. A gently sloping shallow end occupies 6.98 metres with the depth starting at 1.02 metres and deepening to 1.33 metres. Thereafter the pool can be categorised for present purposes as conventionally deep. There is no diving board and one corner of the shallow end is railed off from the rest of the pool to provide a children's pool.

3.   Immediately adjacent to the shallow end of this pool is a covered area containing tables and benches, in its turn abutting on to and servicing a bar, the Pool Bar. All around the pool are sun loungers.

4.   In the vicinity of the pool were certain notices. Material to this case were the following:

   a.   On the side of the horizontal truss that supported the roof over the covered area were two pictograms prohibiting diving. They could be seen when in or by the pool and facing the covered area.

   b.   On a wall to one side of and visible from the covered area was a notice prohibiting diving.

   c.   On a wall immediately adjacent to and visible from the covered area were two notices reading, respectively, "Own drinks, food or beverages strictly not allowed at the swimming pool" and "Warning. Use of the swimming pool is strictly prohibited after 22.00 hours".

   d.   A similar prohibition on using the pool after 10.0 p.m. was situate below notice b.

It is contended that at some point near the entrance to the pool there was a blackboard with the pool opening times specified as being between 9.0 a.m.

and 10.0 p.m. This contention is not admitted and no such blackboard is apparent on the photographs.

System of Work

5.   The Defendant's witnesses gave evidence as to the then operation of the pool and the pool bar and the resultant deployment of staff. This evidence was plainly credible and indeed not really in dispute: it amounted to the following:

    a.   The pool bar was staffed and open throughout the 24 hours. The staffing was on a shift system.

    b.   There was a shift change at 8.0 a.m.: the two male bar staff who had been on duty since midnight were replaced by Mrs. Lynne Ioannou. During the next ensuing hour, in the effective absence of customers, she cleaned and prepared the bar whilst cleaners similarly tackled the adjoining kitchen.

    c.   At 9.0 a.m. Mrs Ioannou was joined by another member of the bar staff and the chef started work in the kitchen, at this stage to prepare such breakfasts as were required.

    d.   At 11.0 a.m. a third person started work at the bar – the strength remained at three for the rest of the day.

    e.   Over the lunch time period two waiters came to work at the tables in the covered area.

The further deployment of bar staff need not be detailed. Suffice it to note that the bar staff did not remain behind the bar but from time to time went out and around the pool gathering up glasses and bottles.

6.   Amongst the cleaners coming into this area at 8.0 a.m. was Mrs Anastasia Georgiou. Her activities extending to cleaning in the covered area and around the pool. Further active at about this time, if not earlier was a male pool cleaner, Mr. Andreas Petrou, who routinely cleaned the pool and added chemicals as appeared appropriate.

7.   Adjacent to the pool area was the Reception. This was staffed on a 24-hour basis so that there were always one or two employees at that location. Finally, but importantly, the manager, Mr Michalis Poleos, was on daily duty from 9.0 a.m., on occasion leaving his office to visit the pool area.

The Clientele

8.   During July and August the clientele was substantial (up to 700 persons at a time) and dominated by young persons attracted by the clubs and ambience of Ayia Napa and determined to enjoy such, principally when under the influence of alcohol. Few guests got up before late morning; thereafter they were at the pool bar and the pool. In the course of the evening they migrated to the clubs and bars of the town, returning in the early hours to go to bed or to continue drinking in the obligingly ever open pool bar. The guests in

the area of the pool bar and the pool were commonly young, boisterous and to a greater or lesser extent under the influence of alcohol.

The Claimant's Case as to Fact

9. He was born on the 9th March 1971. Thus at the material time he was aged 27. He was holidaying at this resort as a member of an all male group of friends and relations, 12 or 13 in number. It is material to note that all save one (Mr Michael Green) were of Asian parentage. The holiday had started on the 12th July and was due to end on the 19th July. The group participated in a good deal of sustained drinking but up to the night in question the Claimant's drinking had been relatively moderate.

10. The Claimant was an experienced swimmer. During his stay he frequently used the pool, which use included shallow dives into the shallow end. In cross-examination he agreed that he knew which was the shallow end and that he was fully conversant with its depth. He agreed that it was not good practice to dive into the shallow end and that he did not need instruction by signs to that effect. That said, he had considered prior to the accident that he could dive safely into that end – as in the event had been the case. As to signs prohibiting diving, he was not aware of any such; as to supervision, no member of staff had said anything about his dives.

11. With respect to events leading up to and including the accident, he contends that he and other members of the group came back from a visit to the clubs at about 3.0 a.m. or 4.0 a.m. and settled down at a stable in the covered area. Whilst he had been drinking in the course of the evening he now stopped although the others continued. During the succeeding hours socialising continued, punctuated by periods in the pool. Entry to the pool on these occasions was by way of a dive or a jump. No member of staff offered any remonstration save that a female receptionist asked them to keep the noise down. seemingly to no avail. Eventually (he thinks between 7.0 a.m. and 8.0 a.m.) he walked to the nearby edge of the pool and dived in. On this occasion his outstretched hands slipped apart on contacting the tiled floor allowing his head to come violently into contact with it. Thereafter in addition to a wound to his lead there was the immediate loss of sensation from the neck downwards that signalled spinal damage and tetraplegia. Others in the group rescued him from the water.

12. This account was supported in evidence by other members of the group. Mr. Michael Green similarly contended that the Claimant and friends, him included, had been sitting in the covered area from about 3.0 a.m. to the accident (such happening, he thought, at about 8.0 a.m.) with no contemporaneous consumption of alcohol by the Claimant. He too had done shallow dives in the shallow end with impunity throughout the holiday – and was doing so in the period leading up to the accident. He had no recollection of any intervention by a receptionist. Mr Shilinder Singh was another of those then present with the Claimant. He too said that the latter did not drink following arrival in this area – he did however think that they had only arrived there at about 7.30 a.m. and his memory was of the Claimant running up to the pool's edge before diving.

The Defendants' Case as to Fact

13.   Oral evidence as to the events immediately preceding the accident was adduced from Mrs Lynne Ioannou and Mrs Anastasia Georgiou. A statement from Mr Andreas Petrou was admitted into evidence. Mrs Ioannou is a Welsh lady, married to a Cypriot and long resident in Cyprus. Her essential account appears in her witness statement and she sustained it in evidence. It relates to the period after the start of her shifty as one of the pool bar staff from 8.0 a.m:

> "On the day of the accident, I saw a group of Indian boys and one white boy, perhaps 5 or 6 of them all together, sat at a table under the canopy alongside the shallow end of swimming pool. They were rowdy, jumping in and out of the pool. They were all soaking wet and there was water everywhere. Judging from their appearance and conduct, I realised they were drunk.
>
> I noticed drinks on their table, which had been brought from a local supermarket. I knew this, as there were supermarket price stickers on the containers. I asked the boys to take their drinks to their rooms before the manager and owners arrived, as they were very strict in prohibiting shop-bought drinks by the bar. I* told them to go and get some sleep.
>
> One of the group, a tall boy with a ponytail, lost his temper. He pushed me, and told me to leave them alone. He told me to "fuck off grandma", and said that I could not tell them what to do. He was very threatening.
>
> Anastasia, the cleaner, was sweeping the floor nearby, and she came towards the table to back me up. The maintenance man, Andreas, was also present cleaning the swimming pools belonging to the Christabelle Apartments. Usually he would be cleaning the swimming pools when I arrived for work in the morning. He would tell everyone to keep out of the pools as there was chemicals in the water.
>
> I recall Mr Singh, the Claimant. He was not abusive in the way he spoke to me. I recall one of the group telling the others that they should leave me alone. It may have been him, but I cannot be sure. The other members of the group said I should join the party and have a drink with them. I repeatedly asked them to take their things to their rooms and go and get some sleep.
>
> I was walking from their table towards the bar area, and had just got inside the bar when I heard a splash. I turned around and saw several people at the edge of the shallow end of the pool lifting the Claimant out of the water. They laid him on the side of the pool outside the bar."

Mrs. Anastasia Georgiou similarly produced and sustained the account given in her witness statement:

"My shift started at 8 am and ended at 4 pm. At the start of my shift I would clean around the pool and bar area first, and then clean the bedrooms from approximately 10 am onwards.

On the day of the accident (18.7.98), I began cleaning around the pool, sweeping the surround and wiping tables. I started to clean near the shallow end adjacent to the bar. Every morning, Andreas, the pool maintenance man, would clean the pool. He was cleaning the pool when I started my shift.

I noticed a couple of Indian boys and one white boy with blond curly hair in the seating area beneath the canopy alongside the shallow end of the pool. They were very drunk, and some of them made derogatory remarks about women. I noticed various drinks in front of them on the table. These included large bottles of vodka, Cypriot brandy, Coca Cola and orange juice. The bar does not sell bottles of spirits, and I do not believe any of the drinks on the table had been purchased at the hotel bar.

I asked the group to leave the area and go to their rooms. They were rude to me, and when I spoke to them in English they started applauding me. The white boy told me to stop. However, the Claimant (who I now know was named Barry Singh) then announced that he was Indian, married with three kids, but he wanted to sleep with a Cypriot woman. I found this very embarrassing.

I asked them again to go to their rooms. I asked Barry Singh what his room number was, and started leading him toward the exit. However, he returned to the table where his friends were sitting. Two of his friends were in the shallow end of the pool. I again told him to go to bed, but he was shouting and swearing, and would not listen.

I was stood near the table with the Claimant's friends, when he ran from beneath the canopy to the edge of the pool (a distance of approximately 4 metres) and dived in headfirst into the shallow end of the pool. He was not wearing a t-shirt, but had on shorts or swimming trunks. I recall he was a bulky man.

The next thing I recall is that a number of the group were lifting the Claimant out of the swimming pool and placed him on the side outside the bar next to the shallow end".

In the witness box she insisted that the Claimant, normally 'a very good man' was drunk and offensive – so much so that it distressed her. She said that the two friends in the water were, respectively, white (presumably Mr Green) and Indian. The contribution made by the statement of Me Petrou amounted to a contention that he saw the Claimant's group whilst he was cleaning the pool and that they were making a lot of noise and seemed drunk. He thought that the accident must have happened at about 8.20 a.m. when he was in the reception area.

14.   Turning from the particular to the general, the hotel manager, Mr Poleos, told me that his functions included charge for and supervision over the pool. In the course of his working day he would visit the pool area from time to time. In the course of such visits he would if necessary deter guests from diving into the pool and he expected other hotel staff confronted by such activity to do the same. "Initially in a good manner we indicate the signs... in most cases they do not need another warning but if they continue to behave in this unbecoming way we asked them to leave.". He said that there were guests who objected to being subject to any such supervision.

15.   Mr Poleos pointed out that this hotel and its safety standards were subject to regular oversight by the Municipality of Ayia Napa (from which body an operating licence had to be obtained annually), by the Cyprus Tourism Organisation (from which body a certificate had to be obtained every two years) and by the Famagusta Public Health Inspectorate (from which body a certificate had to be obtained annually). None such had seen fit to withdraw certification or licensing because the hotel and its conduct failed to meet local standards. In support of this proposition evidence was given by, respectively, Mr. Michalis Papagorgis of the Cyprus Tourism Organisation and Mrs. Demetra Vraka-Karyou of the Famagusta Public Health Inspectorate as to their contemporaneous inspections, none such serving to find fault with the signage and the arrangements for pool supervision.

The Claimant's Case – Legal Basis

16.   Pursuant to Section 2(2) European Communities Act 1972 there were made the Package Travel, Package holidays and Package Tours Regulations 1991. Regulations 3(1) and (2) have the admitted effect of making the package holiday supplied by the Defendants to the Claimant subject to such Regulations. Regulation 15 provides so far as material:

> "(1) The other party is liable to the consumer for the proper performance of the obligations under the contract, irrespective of whether such obligations are to be performed by that other party or by other suppliers of services but this shall not affect any remedy or right of action which that other party may have against those other suppliers of services.

> (2) The other party to the contract is liable to the consumer for any damage caused to him by the failure to perform the contract or the improper performance of the contract unless the failure or the improper performance is due neither to any fault of that other party nor to that of another supplier of services..."

No doubt with this provision to mind certain terms of contract for this package holiday were such as to found pleading by way of paragraph 2 of the Particulars of Claim:

> "2.   There were express terms of contract by which the Defendant supplied the package holiday to the Claimant by reason of the Defendant's brochure which provided among other things that the Defendant:

2.1   accepted liability for any deficiency in the services it was contractually bound to provide in respect of the Claimant's holiday and for the failure of such services to reach a reasonable standard;

2.2   accepted liability in respect of bodily injury provided that it arose from the negligent acts/or omissions of the Defendant's employees, agents suppliers or subcontractors."

That paragraph is admitted by way of the Defence. In the overall result the case was conducted before me as a conventional action in negligence against the Defendants, their servants or agents – with the latter including the management and staff of the Christabelle Hotel. It is, of course, necessary to have to mind the foreign locus of this accident. Guidance as to the significance for the court comes from *Wilson v. Best Travel Ltd* (1993) All ER 353, 358 – a judgment of Phillips J. (as he then was):

"What is the duty of a tour operator in a situation such as this? Must he refrain from sending holidaymakers to any hotel whose characteristics, in so far as safety is concerned, fail to satisfy the standards which apply in this country? I do not believe that his obligations in respect of the safety of his clients can extend this far. Save where uniform international regulations apply, there are bound to be differences in safety standards applied in respect of the many hazards of a modern life between one countr7y and another. All civilised countries attempt to cater for these hazards by imposing mandatory regulations. The duty of care of a tour operator is likely to extend to checking that local safety regulations are complied with. Provided that they are, I do not consider that the operator owes a duty to boycott a hotel because of the absence of some safety feature which would be found in an English hotel unless the absence of such a feature might lead a reasonable holidaymaker to decline to take a holiday at the hotel in question."

17.   In the event there were in force in Cyprus at the material time certain plainly relevant regulations. The Public Swimming Pools Regulations of 1996. These specified certain mandatory requirements with respect to the operation of public swimming pools:

"Regulation 45(1) ... a person in charge of every pool must be appointed for the good operation and maintenance of the swimming pool in accordance to the provisions of these Regulations and in general cater for the pool facilities and for:

(b) The continuous presence of pool staff for the supervision of the bathers in accordance with the provisions of Regulation 47.

47(2) Trained supervisors ... shall be on duty during the entire time of operation of the swimming pool. Their number shall vary based on the size of the pool and the expected maximum number of bathers as provided herein below:

... at least one safety supervisor is required for small pools.

> 48(9) No bather is allowed to enter the swimming pool area without the presence of a supervisor or any other competent employee.
>
> 49(1) Signs with the ... rules for the proper use of the swimming pool shall be posted up at points which are clearly visible and are located near each swimming pool."

18.   Whilst the Claimant contended that there were in the event breaches of these Regulations, understandably he did not seek to use such as a cause of action. What he did contend – without opposition - is that the terms of these Regulations served to evidence the local safety standards, showing them to be no less than those prevailing within the jurisdiction. For his part, Mr Graham Eklund QC for the Defendants additionally invoked as evidence bearing upon the standard of care prevailing at the material time and place the inspections, findings and rulings of the various public authorities charged with oversight with respect to this hotel and its pool.

The Claimant's Case

19.   Mr. Saggerson put his client's case thus:

a.   Diving into this pool was dangerous inasmuch as such activity gave rise to a reasonably foreseeable risk of injury, whether to the diver through contact with the floor of the pool or to other users of the pool through collision. In advancing this proposition he has ready support from the fact of notices prohibiting diving and, with respect to diving into the shallow end, he can invoke the Health and Safety Handbook of the Federation of Tour Operators which predicates danger as and when the depth is less than 1.5 metres.

b.   The duty of care owed towards guests demanded a prohibition on diving by means of an appropriate number of suitability positioned notices supplemented by supervision of the use of the pool that was ever present as and when the pool was open for use. He contends that so much flows from the Regulations and from the Handbook.

c.   In the event there were only the three signs that prohibited diving as described in paragraph 4 above. Neither singly nor in conjunction did such serve adequately to communicate the prohibition. Those on the truss were useless; that on the wall was too removed from users of the pool to have any force; and in any event three notices were too few. His client was not aware through such notices of the prohibition and there was no good reason to criticise him in this regard.

d.   Again in the event there was, as he would contend, no supervision of this pool sufficient to supplement and complement the prohibition notices. His primary case is that the pool was at the material time in operation. His secondary case is that if it was not being operated as the Defendants contend (their case is that the pool opened at 9.0 a.m.), nonetheless guests were then permitted to use it so that there was the same continuing, contemporaneous need for supervision. As to this, he emphasises there was no prominent notice specifying the hours between which the pool was closed: the belief that such might have been specified on some blackboard at some uncertain location away from the pool effectively underlined the point. He drew my attention to the Handbook which advocates "Opening hours ... should be clearly visible" and suggests that such can helpfully be displayed on a freestanding notice positioned beside the pool when it is closed. Yet further, he points out that at the material time the manager, Mr. Poleos, was not on the premises (he started work at 9.0 a.m.) so that there was no one available who had any pretensions to being a trained supervisor.

e. Given these plain failures to take all reasonably practicable precautions appropriate for the safety of the Claimant as a guest, he contends that such failures made a material contribution to the accident. Had there been a properly promoted and maintained 'no diving' culture then his client would not have dived, alternatively he would have done so entirely at his own risk.

f. Realistically he concedes contributory negligence but contends that the apportioning should favour the Claimant.

The Defendants' Case

20. As deployed by Mr Eklund QC, their submissions can be summarised as follows:

a. The accident happened at about 8.30 a.m. but in any event before the pool was open for use by the guests. As to the timing of the accident, they rely upon Mrs Ioannou; as to the pool then being closed, they point to various sources of evidence. First, the evidence of all the Defence witnesses is to the effect that the pool did not open until 9.0 a.m., that is, until it was ready for use following cleaning and chemical enhancement – and until the dedicated supervisor, Mr Poleos, came on duty. Second, as they would contend, the pool was at the material time clearly not open to guests: an opening time was specified for the information of the latter on a blackboard and in any event the activities of the staff in and about the area of the pool were indicative that it was closed.

b. Given that the pool was closed to guests, the hotel's duty of care did not demand concurrent precautions to deter guests from diving into the pool. The Claimant dived wholly at his own risk as an effective trespasser.

c. If, contrary to these admissions, use of this pool at the material time was reasonably foreseeable (say, because it appeared to be open for use whether or no such was the case), then all reasonably practicable measures with a view to preventing diving had been taken. Thus there were prohibitory notices and – so the Defendants contend – they were adequate in number and suitably positioned. Yet further there was adequate supervision. Such would normally be provided by the manager; in his absence the bar staff similarly sought to control breaches of pool discipline – as was the case at the material time.

d. In assessing the standard of care appropriate to the locality (see Wilson v. Best Travel Ltd, op. cit.) I should have regard to the local certification and licensing process and the tacit approval of the hotel's measures for the safety of guests in terms of signage and supervision.

e. In assessing the efficacy of such measures and thus the standard of care, I should give weight to the fact that the Claimant's accident was and remains the only one of its kind notwithstanding a very substantial number of guests in the course of each year.

f. Events as described by Mrs. Ioannou and Mrs. Georgiou serve to challenge causation: what, if any, reasonably practicable precautions could have served to prevent or deter the Claimant from diving in this pool at that time in his then state?

g. In any event contributory negligence is manifest and any apportionment must be heavily in the Defendants' favour.

My Judgment

21. As to fact, in so far as there is conflict I prefer and accept the evidence advanced by the Defendants. Importantly, I unhesitatingly accept the evidence of Mrs. Ioannou and Mrs. Georgiou as to the events leading up to the accident. They were, respectively, good, palpably honest witnesses. Importantly, both were at the material time sober and engaged with the Claimant and his friends in trying to carry out their duties. I could discern no reason to discount their evidence: quite the contrary. In testing accuracy, I attached some weight in the case of Mrs Ioannou to the fact of near contemporaneous accounts given, respectively, to the police and the Defendants, and to the content of such, there being no marked contrast with her current evidence. I noted that Mrs. Georgiou had given no like accounts and, as urged by Mr. Saggerson, I sought to discern 0possible subsequent 'reconstruction' of events. I was unable to do so and I was indeed impressed by the graphic, almost emotional nature of her account, initially delivered in English and then repeated (at my instigation) in Greek. I am satisfied that I can rely upon her as a witness.

22. I should add that I do not think that the Claimant and his witnesses were seeking to mislead me. All presented well and over many matters the Claimant was admirably candid. Their evidential difficulties arose solely with respect to reliable recollection of events leading up to the account and, in my judgment, reflect the trauma of the accident itself (be it noted that the Claimant sustained a head injury additional to the tetraplegia), and, more importantly, prior consumption of alcohol to serious excess by the Claimant and those with him. As to this, it is not just the weight I attach to the

evidence of Mrs. Ioannou and Mrs. Georgiou; it is the inherent improbability of the Claimant giving up bed in order to spend hours as a non-drinking member of a group prepared for, and dedicated to drinking vodka – and it is the conspicuous lack of any sustained, consistent recollection of the material events provided by the Claimant and his witnesses. The essential problem is that all such were drunk.

23.   I turn to issues of liability. By way of premise I have reminded myself that the standard of care falls to be assessed in the light of the oft-cited guidance given by Lord Reid in *Morris v. West Hartlepool Steam Navigation Co Ltd* (1956) A.C. 552 at 574:

> "Apart from the cases where he maybe able to rely on an existing practice, it is the duty of an employer in considering whether some precaution should be taken against a foreseeable risk, to weigh, on the one hand, the magnitude of the risk, the likelihood of an accident happening and the possible seriousness of the consequences if an accident does happen and on the other hand, the difficulty and expense and any other disadvantage of taking the precaution."

Applying this guidance to assessment of the magnitude of the instant risk. I would hold that the hotel could reasonably regard the likelihood of an accident happening through a dive into this pool as modest to low but the possible consequences of any such accident as potentially very serious indeed. As to the possible consequences, I would regard the potential for serious spinal injury as notorious: what has happened to the Claimant is, alas, typical. As to the likelihood the facts speak for themselves. The Claimant and his witnesses spoke of frequent dives without consciously encountering danger, nor indeed anything to inhibit them from further dives – and they would find nothing surprising about the fact that there has been no other like accident on these premises. Mr Eklund QC seeks to argue that this accident free history reflects the adequacy of such precautions as were taken by the hotel. I think that it is easier to infer that shallow dives were not normally executed towards the shallow end but away from it. Turn to the dimensions of the pool and it therefore becomes reasonable to infer that most shallow end divers so propel themselves as to take advantage of the 1.33 metre depth, that is, the depth not far short of the 1.5 metre that is the key depth identified in the Handbook of the Federation of Tour Operators. It is to be noted that even on the instant occasion the Claimant thought that he would have been safe but for the fact that his outstretched hands slipped apart on contacting the tiled floor.

24.   With that assessment of the magnitude of risk to mind, I turn to the two areas of concern: the hotel's precautions in terms of signage and supervision. First, signage: I have no doubt but that the risk as identified called for provision and prominent positioning of signs prohibiting diving. Whatever the likelihood of a diving accident, the magnitude of the possible consequences justified a promulgated prohibition, as did the other problems potentially arising from dives into a relatively small, often crowded pool. Adverting to Lord Reid there was the identifiable risk on the one hand with,

in terms of signs, no difficulty and little expense in providing the precaution. In the event I uphold Mr. Saggerson's submission: the signs as provided were inadequate and did not serve to fulfil the hotel's standard of care. The signs on the roof truss were modest as to message and in an unsuitable place; the sign on the wall was adequate in itself but not well positioned being removed from the pool and not readily visible to guests. I am reluctant to find support for the Claimant's case from steps taken by the hotel in the light of the accident but the subsequent positioning of prohibited signs beside the shallow end demonstrates what could and, as I think, should have been done. With one or more signs so positioned every user of the shallow end of the pool could be forewarned of risk – or reminded of it, as the case may be. In the light of these findings I accept the Claimant's contention that he had not seen either of the signs relied upon by the hotel in partial fulfilment of this aspect of the duty of care.

25.　In reaching the foregoing judgment, I have not given weight to the contemporaneous assessments of the hotel by, for example, the Cyprus Tourism Organisation and the Famagusta Public Health Inspectorate. With every respect to Mr. Eklund's submission, I do not think that the standard of care as assessed by me requires any modification to reflect a Cypriot locus. There is no evidence to suggest that the Cypriot standard of care is materially less rigorous than that to be utilised within the jurisdiction – indeed, quite the contrary for the Public Swimming Pools Regulations of 1996 lay down standards that are seemingly mandatory. As I see it, having considered these local assessments I am entitled to differ if compelled so to do by the evidence put before me without risking the imposition of a 'foreign' and unrealistically high standard.

26.　The second area of concern is supervision, in general and at the material time. Adverting to sup0ervision in general I was initially less than impressed with the scope and potential of that to be exercised by Mr. Poleos during his visits to the pool. However upon reflection I became less censorious. This pool is not large; it tends to be surrounded by relatively short-term young holidaymakers, all potentially boisterous and many under influence of alcohol. Arguably, a permanent visible 'spoil sport' supervisor would be counterproductive and the low key, benign attendance by Mr. Poleos are all that promises effective support for a prohibition on diving that must initially stem from signage. In my judgment it is only the inadequacy of the signage that raises concerns about supervision but in any event the evidence does not permit me to condemn it as substandard.

27.　Moving from the general to the particular, two points arise as to supervision at the material time. First, what standard can appropriately be applied as at 8.30 a.m. (that is, when the accident happened, as I find) and before the pool officially opened? And second, was that standard met? As to the first point, I think that Mr Saggerson is right in his submission that the pool was then in operation, at least so that the duty of care towards guests had to encompass their safety when using the pool. I readily accept that the hotel did not intend the pool to open until 9.0 a.m. but they took no effective steps to communicate this fact to guests (I attach no significance to something chalked up on some obscurely placed blackboard) and absent such steps I think that guests were entitled to regard the pool as open at 8.30 a.m. on a summer morning. I note in passing the guidance given by the Handbook of the Federation of Tour Operators summarised earlier in this judgment; it reads so like common sense as fairly to set the standard.

28.   As to the second point, the irony (as I see it) is that at the material time there was supervision at a higher than usual level and certainly sufficient to meet the appropriate standard of care. I refer of course to that sought to be exercised, benignly and persistently by Mrs. Ioannou and Mrs. Georgiou. It may not have been directed to diving per se, but its effect, if heeded, would have amounted to the required prohibition.

29.   This leads to the key part of this judgment. It is incumbent upon the Claimant to prove a breach of duty with respect to his own care as at the material time and one that made a material contribution to his accident. At this juncture I have no option but to give weight to two matters. First, there is the Claimant's concession in cross-examination as noted by me "I do not need someone to tell me not to dive into the shallow end ... I did not need a sign to tell me not to dive into the shallow end". Second, there is the evidence of Mrs. Ioannou and Mrs Georgiou: jointly to the effect that immediately before the accident they were severally engaged in trying to persuade the Claimant to leave the pool area but that in the event he defined them with a drunken recklessness that may in turn help explain why this dive proved disastrous. With such matters to mind, I can see no basis for finding that the breach of duty with respect to signage made any material contribution to the accident. Granted that the Claimant never had sight of the material signs he clearly rejected signage as necessary for his safety given his state of knowledge as to risk. Further, at the material time the state of signage was wholly irrelevant: the presence or absence of signs had no bearing upon his reaction to the efforts of these two members of staff. In valiantly advancing his client's case, Mr. Saggerson surmised that a combination of proper signage and supervision would have promoted a 'no diving' culture that could have restrained the Claimant from the last dive. Such a submission might have weight in the context of standards in the work place but had no obvious relevance to conduct in and around this pool on the part of those in short term retreat from self-discipline. There was a role for prohibitory signs (say, in forcefully reminding the guest using the pool for the first time), but that role had expired with respect to the Claimant by 8.30 a.m. on the 18th July 1998. There was no breach vis a vis the Claimant; he was the author of his own misfortune.

Conclusion

30.   In the last paragraph I have signalled some regret at the findings forced upon me by the evidence. Of course, I am aware of the plight of the Claimant and the financial importance to him of even a modest apportionment of liability (and it could not have been more than, say 25%) but I cannot find the material wherein to found a judgment for him and his Claim must be dismissed.

Roberts v Iberotravel Limited (t/a Sunworld Limited)

Mr Justice Gibbs:

1.   This claim is brought on behalf of Kevin Roberts, now thirteen, son of Ray and Julie Roberts. Whilst the Roberts family was on holiday in Majorca in July 1993, Kevin suffered a terrible accident. He was then six. His date of birth was 16ᵗʰ May 1987. Whilst in a swimming pool at the Hotel complex where they were all staying, Kevin nearly drowned. His life was saved but he suffered catastrophic brain damage. The long term consequences of this are that he is gravely disabled, both mentally and physically, wheelchair bound and totally dependent on others for his everyday needs and care. The claim is brought by Kevin's litigation friend, his aunt, Caroline Axten. The defendant to the claim is the travel company through whom the holiday was organised, a limited company who is in the proceedings, has been referred to as 'Sunworld'.

2.   Kevin's father entered into a contract with Sunworld for the provision of the holiday on behalf of the members of the family, including Kevin. It is common ground that the benefit of the contract extended to Kevin. Kevin claims that his accident was caused by the breach of contract and negligence of the defendants. The contract provided that Sunworld was liable, not only for their own failures, but also those of the Majorcan suppliers, their servants or agents. These included the owners of the Hotel complex at which the Roberts family were staying and where the accident occurred.

3.   Sunworld whilst denying liability to Kevin have brought into the action the owners of the Hotel complex known as Triauno SL (formerly Triauno SA), owners/operators of Hotel Saturno, Hotel Marte and Hotel Jupiter (registered in the Pollensa Land Registry as the Reina del Mar, Reina de Alcudia and Reina Elisabeth) trading under the name "Hoteles Mac". Their part in the claim is as Part 20 defendants. They will be referred to in this judgment as in the proceedings themselves as 'the Hotel'. In the Part 20 proceedings Sunworld allege that the Hotel caused Kevin's accident by the breach of its contractual obligations to Sunworld and/or by negligence. Sunworld has also made a Part 20 claim against Kevin's parents, alleging that their failure to take reasonable care of their son caused or contributed to the accident. Liability is an issue in both aspects of Part 20 proceedings as it is in the main claim.

4.   *The evidence about the accident and its aftermath*

        I now set out a summary of the events leading to the accident and in its immediate aftermath. At this stage the summary will be as far as possible neutral. The Roberts wanted a family holiday abroad, not having taken one for several years. They wanted it to be suitable for the children. Mr and Mrs Roberts were attracted by a Sunworld brochure at a local travel agent. It provided a description of the Hotel complex in Majorca which was known as 'The Jupiter/Saturno Complex'. It was said that Sunworld offered facilities at two of the three Hotels; that these facilities included four outdoor swimming pools; that the accent was very much on holiday fun and activities for all the family; that there were superb amenities for young children. Mr Roberts booked the holiday in August 1992, well in advance. Contractual conditions of booking included the following, namely that Sunworld accepted full responsibility for ensuring that component parts of the holiday were provided as described in the brochure and were of a reasonable standard. (Condition 8(c)); that Sunworld accepted responsibility for any loss or damage suffered on holiday as a result of any negligence of their servants or agents (Condition 7(d)); that if any member of a party had suffered death or bodily injury arising from the negligence of Sunworld's suppliers, their sub-contractors, servants or agents, Sunworld would accept responsibility, (Condition 7(d)). The contract conditions also provided that the relevant parts of the brochure formed the basis of the agreement with Sunworld. The claimant contends that it was implied that the arrangements made and facilities provided by Sunworld at the Hotel complex were in particular suitable and safe for young children. Sunworld's contractual obligations are generally not in dispute, although the way in which their duties are to be interpreted in practice as regards the facts of the accident, are very much in issue.

5.   When the time came for the holiday, the family flew out together. Kevin has two brothers, Paul and John, and all five of the family went on the holiday. Paul was nine years old at the time and John, seven weeks short of his second birthday. The flight to Majorca was late at night and in the early morning of the 20th July 1993. There was a coach transfer from the airport and they got to the Hotel at about 4 a.m. It was the Jupiter Hotel, one of the three Hotels on the complex. After a few hours sleep they all went down to breakfast.

6.   It was the invariable practice of Sunworld's representative at the complex to hold a welcome meeting on the first morning for those holidaying with her company. The representative who held the meeting was Sally Mitchinson. It took place after breakfast. Mr Roberts said that from his family, only he attended the meeting. Mrs Roberts and the boys went back to the bedroom after breakfast. These facts are not seriously in issue. The content of the meeting – what was said or not said – and its significance, are in issue. When the meeting had finished Mr and Mrs. Roberts say that Mr Roberts rejoined the family and that they all went for a walk around the area surrounding the complex. This was known as Alcudia. They had a light lunch. They did not at that stage walk around or inspect the Hotel complex itself which included, amongst other pools, the outdoor swimming pool which this case concerns. After their excursion, they returned to their Hotel room. There is no evidence to contradict this account. There is no real cause to doubt it, though questions were raised on behalf of the other parties about whether the family may have at least inspected the facilities at the complex before the afternoon.

7.   What happened from then on is, at least in part, controversial. It is beyond doubt that in an adjacent apartment complex known as Bellevue, a young Spanish doctor called Dr Vita was just breaking off for lunch after his morning clinic. There is I think no evidence of the precise time at which this

happened. He was going to lunch when his secretary got a call from the Jupiter/Saturno Complex asking for a doctor to attend a person who had been injured in a swimming pool. There was nothing to indicate to him that it was an emergency, but still the doctor went across as quickly as he could. Because he was not told that there was an emergency or a drowning, he did not call the emergency ambulance unit known as 061. What he did was to hurry across to the nearby complex by car; his best estimate is that it took him some five to seven minutes before he got to Kevin, who by then had suffered the drowning incident. Kevin lay in a room next to the reception area of the middle Hotel in the complex known as The Hotel Marte. The normal time Dr Vita to get to the complex was four minutes. He has since timed himself during the short journey. However for the purpose of estimating the time taken on the day of the accident he added a minute or two onto that time since he did not get to Kevin at once. No one was there at the complex to meet the doctor. He had to ask the gardener in the area next to the Hotel where to go, and was directed by that person to where Kevin was.

8.   It is quite plain and there is no dispute about it, that some minutes before Dr Vita was called Kevin had suffered a near drowning accident in one of the pools in the complex. The evidence is that the pool in question was the Reina Beach pool. Again this fact is not in issue. The principal evidence on the claimant's behalf, that of his parents, is to the following effect. They had, following their return to the Jupiter Hotel after the family excursion, decided to go down to a pool. They put suntan lotion on the children in the Hotel room, then, as a family, they made their way with the children, taking towels and so on, together with a buggy for John, to the Reina Beach pool. There were lots of people, including families and children around and in the pool. It was crowded. They walked to a point on the edge of the pool, beside what is known as 'Lobe B'. The sun-beds were all occupied but just as they arrived at that point a family vacated theirs, thus allowing the Roberts to take their place by the pool.

9.   The intention was that they should all have a bathe in the pool. They were going to play together as a family. Paul at the age of nine was a capable swimmer. John, less than two, could not swim. Mr and Mrs Roberts brought with them for John's use a buoyancy aid shaped like a space shuttle. On their one previous holiday abroad, one of the elder boys had used this. Kevin was not a swimmer. He was able to do no more than a few strokes of dog paddle, but that was all. Back in England when he had been taken swimming, he sometimes wore armbands, sometimes not. His parents are uncertain whether they had brought any armbands for Kevin with them to the Hotel. If they had, they certainly did not take them to the pool on this ill fated visit.

10.   To return to the sequence of events according to Mr and Mrs Roberts. After the sun-bed became free Mr Roberts took Paul and Kevin to the shallow point of Lobe B. He said to them words to the effect "stay around here lads, I'll be with you shortly". He returned to the sun-bed which was at the eastern edge of Lobe B of the pool. He and his wife occupied themselves

sorting out the bathing towels and bags and taking John out of his buggy in order that they could join the two boys in the pool. According to Mr Roberts he asked his wife to look and see if the boys were all right. Mrs Roberts says that she saw the boys together in Lobe B of the pool. They were close to the side furthest from her, the western side. Shortly afterwards Mr and Mrs Roberts went to the shallow part of Lobe B with John to start using the pool themselves. According to the parents it was only a few minutes from the time the two boys entered the pool until they themselves went in with John, perhaps three minutes or so, although they do not claim to be precise. It was an even shorter time from the last sighting by Mrs Roberts of the two boys together. Mr Roberts thinks it could have been less than a minute.

.....

14.	...There is a difference between what each parent says that they then saw. Neither could see Kevin and both became concerned about it at that point. Mr Roberts says he saw Paul ahead of him at the far end of the deeper area of water and just by the peninsular. Mrs Roberts says she saw Paul still in Lobe B but as she and her husband entered the pool he began to swim over to the peninsular. At all events Mr Roberts says he swam over to Paul and swam back with him. Still not knowing where Kevin was Mr and Mrs Roberts took the other two boys back to the sun-beds and told Paul to stay there to look after John. They then walked around the whole pool, one clock-wise and one anti-clockwise, looking for Kevin. They believed he may have strayed away from the pool. They were calling out his name. Mr Roberts in particular admits to having a loud voice and shouting out, but without response. Mrs Roberts was upset because no-one seemed interested in their plight. She and her husband met at the far side of the pool and carried on round. They looked across the surface of the pool to see whether Kevin was there, but could not see him. It did not occur to them that he may have gone under the water and they did not make a search with this in mind, i.e. they did not peer into the water. They both got back to where the other two boys were waiting where they had been left. Paul had apparently not seen his brother.

......

16.	What had happened to Kevin between the time when Mr and Mrs Roberts say they last saw him and their undoubted arrival at the reception of the Hotel Marte? There is no oral evidence about this. There was to have been such evidence but for reasons unknown the sole available witness did not attend court. She is a German woman known as Fraud Germann, formally Galliard. ..... Her written statement, duly translated, is in evidence ...... She said:

> "We had been there for about three minutes and were in the process of unpacking. Suddenly my son who was about six at the time came running over and told me that there had been an accident. Robert was telling me that he had seen a girl with a young boy on her shoulder taking him to the Hotel. I shouted to

my husband Peter to do something. Later on my mother told me that she had heard the girl shouting for help, but no one was moving to help her. She shouted "No ass has moved". There were plenty of people around. No one helped. There were many people, but no one offered to help. I went over to the pool with Robert. The pools were packed with people. When I got to the edge of the pool I saw a girl on her way back to the Hotel with a young boy on her shoulders. After seeing the girl I followed her up to the Hotel. The girl was a couple of metres in front of me. We hurried to the Hotel reception. I would say that I spent approximately ten seconds arguing with my son when he told me that there had been an accident. I then spoke to my husband for a few seconds and then made my way to the pool. Having arrived at the pool we very quickly made our way to the Hotel. However, I cannot be precise as to how long it would have taken to get to the Hotel. Later on I spoke to the girl and she told me that she was in the pool and something touched her foot. She thought that somebody was playing around with her. She tried to push it away and then saw that it was an unconscious boy. She then pulled him out and shouted for help. When I arrived in the Hotel reception the young girl was standing in the Hotel reception, shouting "What shall I do". An employee of the Hotel was in the reception area. The girl was shouting for help and shouting for a blanket. The man did not understand her. I was surprised that even if he did not understand the girl (who was German) he should have seen the boy and realised that something serious had happened. At this point the boy was lying on the stone floor. It was very cold and he was unconscious. When my husband came into the Hotel lobby he tried to resuscitate the boy. My mother and father were there and they also shouted for help. However the Hotel receptionist simply stood there, not moving. The boy was on the floor on his back with his head to one side. When my husband pushed on his chest, water came flooding out of him. Eventually I ran and got a blanket because I saw that his body was too cold. After some time an older man (also an employee of the Hotel) came and shouted in Spanish. It was clear that he recognised the seriousness of the situation. It was only at this point that the other man then made a telephone call. The older man and my husband continued attempting to resuscitate the boy. I would estimate that it was about between three and five minutes before the older man appeared and the telephone call was made. It was then about another thirty minutes before the doctor arrived. Everyone was very stressed and panicked. When the old man arrived he pushed my husband away and took over the resuscitation. They carried on doing this until the doctor arrived. The boy was constantly given mouth-to-mouth resuscitation until the doctor arrived."

....

17.   *Findings of fact about how the accident happened*

......

20.   My judgment of Mr and Mrs Roberts' evidence is that it was honest and broadly accurate. ......

21.   ...There were many people in and around the pool. It was extensive in area and irregularly shaped. There were palm trees and bushes quite near. It was (according to Mr Roberts) quite noisy. It was a matter of chance whether or not Mr and Mrs Roberts would have seen Kevin taken from the pool, especially if they were up the other end of it at the time; and especially if the girl who rescued Kevin, once she realised the urgency, moved quickly with him to the Hotel Marte. I find that the girl did probably remove Kevin from the pool while his parents were on the far end of the pool. I find further that she probably did go quickly with him to seek help at the Hotel Marte. It is entirely credible that Paul may have missed it, being only nine years old and charged as he was with keeping an eye on his brother John.

....

25.   *Findings in relation to the pool layout and gradients*

        The layout and dimensions of the pool are at least potentially factors which are relevant to what caused Kevin to become immersed. I turn now therefore to this area of the case. ......

....

35.   In the event, I am quite satisfied that the base of the pool in the area between about half a metre and one and a half metres sloped at a gradient of about 16%. It was at least 14% along the western side. This was in the area of the pool in which a six to seven year old would get out of his depth. What are the consequences of this feature of the pool? First in terms of national standards for pools, the gradient substantially exceeds the advisory limit set by the Sports Council Health & Safety Commission in the United Kingdom (i.e. it amounts to a gradient of one in six rather than one in fifteen as advised). Further, it exceeds the minimum of 10% laid down by the Spanish authorities in regulations for covered pools and children's pools. As to the former, however, it is well established that the claimant cannot found a claim on any breach of English regulations. The authority for this comes from *Wilson v Best Travel* [1993] 1 All ER 353, and *Codd v Thomsons Tour Operators* unreported Court of Appeal 7ᵗʰ July 2000. As to the latter, the Spanish regulations, I am not satisfied that these regulations apply to the Reina Beach pool and I proceed on the basis that they do not. Mr Wingate-Saul on consideration did not pursue the allegation that there was a breach of the Spanish regulations in relation to the gradient of the pool. That was a correct decision since the Reina Beach is neither a covered pool, nor is it one specifically designed for children. However, certain consequences do flow from the gradient as I find it to have been.

36.   Mr Sanders described how within a pace or two, as a result of such a gradient, a child would be at risk of losing balance. This loss of balance

would be accentuated by the buoyancy of the water and the child would thus quickly become immersed out of his depth. Mr Robinson volunteered in his evidence in chief, that at about 80-85 centimetres a child of 1.1 metres in height would be left unstable and at risk of falling down. This would be aggravated by a crowded pool with choppy water and the glare of sun overhead. Those were matters which Mr Robinson very properly mentioned in his evidence and in the particular context of Kevin's accident.

37.   The nature and potential effect of the gradient was emphasised by the evidence of factual witnesses. Anthony Higham spent a holiday at Alcudia in 1995 and used the pool. He himself stepped backwards on the gradient in the relevant part of the Reina Beach pool. He then fell backwards and disappeared. His evidence was questioned on the basis that he had not included the incident in his earlier statement. But he insisted it was true. Indeed he said that after the experience, he ensured that his young sons were confined to a smaller children's pool. I accept his evidence. Whilst not in his written statement expressly mentioning the incident concerning him, which at the time he regarded as funny rather than serious, he had expressly mentioned the pool's 'unusually steep gradient' as he described it. Support is also gained for the sharpness of the gradient from the evidence of Jacqueline Smith. I found this evidence too to be credible.

38.   In my judgment the evidence concerning the layout and gradient of the pool operates in two ways. First it persuades me on the balance of probabilities that it was this feature of the pool which led to Kevin's accident. He was in the pool. I find, in the area of the Lobe affected by the gradient when last seen by his mother. Within a minute or so he had disappeared from view and was immersed in the water. It is possible that other things could have caused this to happen. He could for example have been accidentally knocked, although no evidence has emerged, either of such an incident or of any mark or injury consistent with it. It is just possible that he was trying to swim and got out of his depth. However in my judgment because of his position when last seen and the compelling features of the evidence already discussed, the probable cause of the accident was the unexpectedly steep gradient. The second effect or potential effect of the layout and gradient of the pool is as evidence of negligence on the part of the Hotel and/or Sunworld in providing such a pool for the use of children. I shall come to this issue next. At this stage, however, it is worth saying that the fact that Kevin's accident was caused by his loss of footing due to the gradient, cannot in itself mean that the Hotel and Sunworld are liable in relation to the gradient. That is an entirely separate issue.

39.   *Measures taken by Sunworld and the Hotel for safety in and around the swimming pools*

....

40.   It is clear that there were at the time of the accident no relevant depth markings around Lobe B of the pool. Thus is the only way in which anyone could work out the depth would be to try that part of the pool out for themselves. ....

....

42.   Controversy arose about the degree (if at all) to which Mr and Mrs Roberts
         were warned about the need for caution over pool safety. Sunworld's stated
         case was that considerable priority was given to questions of safety
         including pool safety. It was said that this priority was reflected both in the
         training courses for their representatives and in the written and oral advice
         given by their representatives to customers.

43.   I find that the facts do not support those contentions. The written material
         disclosed about the representatives' courses do not suggest that safety was
         given any great priority, rather the reverse. But it is more important in
         relation to this claim to assess what Mr and Mrs Roberts and other
         holidaymakers were actually told or shown. The main source of oral
         information was the welcome meeting already referred to. Mr Roberts does
         not recall any reference being made to pool safety. Nor does another witness
         who attended a similar meeting. Miss Mitchinson said that she ensured that
         pool safety featured prominently in the presentation. I find that she
         probably did say at that meeting that it was important for parents to
         accompany children when they were at the pool. I accept that Miss
         Mitchinson referred to safety to that extent. I find also that she probably
         indicated to those present including Mr Roberts, that further information
         could be found at the hotel desk and in the Hotel information book or
         booklet. It is, however, in my judgment, improbable that any further advice
         or warning was given beyond this.

44.   The Hotel information booklet as it stood in 1993 could not be produced.
         There is nothing sinister about that. It was no more than a collection of
         sheets in a ring binder; an example of a similar book was produced.
         Swimming pool safety features amongst 'other information'. There was a
         sketch of a pool within the book which Miss Mitchinson in evidence said
         she thought was the Reina Beach pool. The pool depicted in fact bore little
         resemblance to the Reina Beach.

45.   Realistically the book in question, insofar as it was presented as a safety
         warning, was of no use at all. There was only one in the Hotel and it was
         kept at the representatives' desk. In the unlikely event that each guest in turn
         was interested in going to the desk and reading it, most would not be able to
         do so until well into their holiday.

46.   Miss Mitchinson herself no doubt, in most respects, a competent and
         capable representative had not bathed in the Reina Beach pool. There is
         nothing to indicate that she had ever been instructed to familiarise herself
         with the sort of pool it was, with the gradients etc., nor indeed with any
         other pool. Indeed there is no evidence up to the time of Kevin's accident,
         that the Reina Beach pool had been assessed to see for example whether its
         depths were properly marked, or whether its gradients, dimensions and so
         on, made it suitable for use by children or non swimmers. The
         overwhelming inference is that it had not been so assessed. As a matter of
         fact, however, the senior management of Sunworld thought that such
         considerations were of great importance. This is made clear in a

memorandum from Simon Clark. His position was 'Overseas Director, Operations'. The memorandum is dated 1ˢᵗ July 1993, just under three weeks before the accident. An except from it reads as follows:

> "Pool Safety. Please ensure that your Hoteliers/apartment or villa owners have carried out instructions to mark pool depth clearly and accurately. Any sudden changes of depth must be clearly marked and any underwater obstacles or steps clearly pointed out to guests. Particular attention must be paid to diving boards and water slides, etc., making it quite clear where these facilities are not suitable for adults and older children and pointing out which areas of the pool are too shallow to dive into. Could I also please remind you that all Sunworld information books must contain a pool safety page pointing out any hidden dangers and a drawing of the pool showing the differing depths. Sunworld staff should continue to monitor the clarity of the pool water and should always advise guests not to use the pool if the water becomes so murky that the bottom of the pool is not visible."

Importantly he then concludes:

> "I realise that the above advice is all standard practice in this company, but it does not hurt to re-state and re-check".

.....

48.   At the time of the accident, there was a fixed notice at the entrance to the peninsular which jutted into the Reina Beach pool. This included warnings that people swam at their own risk and that children must be accompanied by an adult. Such a notice would not have been visible to, or have alerted people approaching the pool in the direction taken by the Roberts family.
....

49.   It should perhaps be observed that the extent of oral or written warnings about the use of the pools would not help the claimant unless there was any significant feature of the Reina Beach pool in relation to which warning was necessary. Conversely, if the specific criticisms of the pool's use by children are valid, it is not easy to see how advice as generalised as that which I have been discussing would assist the defendants or the hotel; or to put the matter another way, in the absence of any particular risk against which a warning is required, it seems to me that Hotels and tour operators are entitled to assume that parents will not cause or permit children of theirs who cannot swim to enter water which is obviously out of their depth. On the other hand if there is a hazard, a specific warning is likely to be appropriate. There was no specific warning relating to any of the hotels' pools in this case.

50.   Finally, there is the question of what, if any, provision existed for life-saving or resuscitation if a person got into difficulties in the pool. One provision was available: the telephone number of the medical practice of which Dr Vita was a member. That medical practice was not in the Jupiter/Saturno complex, but at a clinic a short distance away by car, as already stated.

51.   Beyond that there is really no evidence that any meaningful provision was available at all. There is no evidence that any staff member or other person connected with the hotel and who was in any way trained in life-saving or resuscitation responded to the emergency. The staff member who did respond was on the evidence of Dr Vita, untrained and unable to give effective resuscitation. His view which I accept is that resuscitation attempted before he arrived was of little or no effect. There was some evidence of a mask which could have been used for resuscitation, but this was suitable for an adult, not for a child. Dr Vita's evidence was that the Hotels have no oxygen or equipment suitable for the type of emergency experienced by Kevin. In the medical room at the Hotel Marte there was an oxygen bottle indicating that at some time somebody's mind may have focused on the need for oxygen to be available, but the bottle was empty.

52.   .... It is right in this context to mention that a distinction was drawn on behalf of the hotel and Sunworld between dedicated lifeguards (such as for example, are the subject of television programmes such as Baywatch) on the one hand; and on the other, employees working in the general area of the pool and sufficiently trained and skilled to administer resuscitation if called upon and close enough to be called upon in case of emergency.

53.   This distinction between dedicated lifeguards and suitably skilled and available employees appeared at the outset to be a significant one in terms of the legal duties owed by the Hotel under Spanish law and consequently in terms of the assessment of the contractual duty of and standard of care required of Sunworld to its customers. I shall return to that later. On the facts however, there is no evidence that *any* employee was on hand who fell into *either* category. In short there was, as I find, a complete absence of any significant staff, equipment or procedure to deal with any drowning emergency.

54.   *Liability*

        The issues on liability can be divided broadly into two headings. The first is concerned with the question of who (if anyone) was legally responsible for Kevin's accident. Submissions on Kevin's behalf are that Sunworld was responsible because of its breaches of contract and failure to take reasonable care for Kevin's safety. Sunworld denies responsibility but says that if it was responsible, it is entitled to contribution from both the other parties, the Part 20 defendants. It claims against the Hotel because it says that if there was something wrong with the pool, the way it was used or safety precautions relating to it, then the hotel must bear the blame or part of the blame, whether due to its breach of contract or as a joint tortfeasor. It claims against the parents on the simple basis that they owed Kevin a duty of care which must have been broken in the circumstances of Kevin's accident, and that therefore they must contribute as joint tortfeasors.

55.   The other heading of liability issues concerns the question of legal responsibility for any proven failure in lifesaving or resuscitation arrangements. Under this heading, the parents are not involved. The claimant alleges breach of contract and/or negligence against Sunworld,

which Sunworld denies. Alternatively Sunworld maintains that it is entitled to recover the full amount of loss and damage flowing from any breach of duty under this head by way of contractual indemnity against the hotel and/or by breach of contractual warranty by the hotel and/or that it is in any event entitled to contribution from the hotel as joint tortfeasor.

56. It is important to note that Sunworld concedes that it is contractually liable for any breach of duty proven against the hotel. The hotel is not and need not therefore be sued by the claimant.

57. It is also important to note that any breach of duty proven under the second heading would inevitably give rise to potentially difficult points on causation. These can be summarised in my judgment as follows:

   a)   To what extent did the failures under the second heading cause or aggravate Kevin's injuries and consequent loss and damage?

   b)   If there was no breach of contract or duty under the first heading, then the amount of damages would be defined by the answer to (a).

   c)   If there was a breach of contract and duty under the first heading, then Kevin would be entitled to the full amount of damages flowing from the accident (subject to one possible exception, mentioned at the end of the judgment). However it will still be necessary to answer (a) in order to decide the respective responsibilities of the parties to pay for or contribute to Kevin's loss. On any view this will be or would be a difficult exercise.

58. *The Pool*

   ...... It is no longer alleged that the pool itself as constructed was in breach of Spanish regulations. The relevant regulations relate to children's pools. Mr Wingate-Saul argued that had the pool been a children's pool, it would have been in breach of the regulations, but the way in the event in which he put Kevin's case, was that the pool was effectively only suitable and safe for the use of adults and competent swimmers, but that the terms of the Sunworld contract, the layout of the pool within the complex and the absence of warnings were such as to encourage its use by unaccompanied or inadequately supervised children. ....

59. Mr Brunner supported in this by Mr Turner relies on the absence of any breach of the Spanish regulations. All parties agree that in approaching questions of negligence, Spanish law is presumed to be the same as the law of England and Wales unless the contrary is proved. However, great reliance in this context is placed on the case of *Wilson v Best Travel* and *Codd v Thomson.* .....

.....

61. It is submitted that since the pool complied with Spanish regulations, it would be quite wrong to take into consideration that English regulations if applicable might have been broken. It is submitted therefore that the only other way in which the claim against Sunworld could be established would

be to show that they fell significantly below the reasonable standards regarded as common in the travel industry. It is argued that in the absence of expert evidence on that topic I should not make a finding adverse to Sunworld. Indeed, it is submitted that I am not entitled to do so. In support of this argument Mr Brunner relies on *Investors in Industry v South Bedford District Council* [1986] 2 WLR 937. Emphasis is also placed on the fact that there is no evidence that Sunworld received any complaints about the Reina Beach pool from the time that it was opened in the 1980's to the date of the accident; also on the fact that other tour operators organised holidays at the complex without relevant complaint or adverse incident.

62. I come now to my findings under the first heading of liability, (see paragraph 54). Under this heading I find at the outset without difficulty (since it is not disputed) that there was no breach of the Spanish regulations. It follows in accordance with the decision in *Wilson v Best Travel* as approved in *Codd v Thomson Tour Operators* that there can be no question of reliance upon any standards set by English regulations. Thus the claimant must rely on breach of contract by the defendants and/or breach of their duty of care towards Kevin on some other basis. If Mr Brunner is right, then the reasoning the *Investors in Industry* decision precludes the court from making any finding on the standard of care to be expected of tour operators, and whether the defendants fell short of it, without expert evidence.

63. This submission, however ingenious, must in my judgment be wrong. The factual matrix in the present case was very different from that in the case cited. Here the court is dealing not with abstruse technical matters, but with features of a swimming pool and its use which can readily be assessed. The court has the benefit of safety and pool experts as to the contours of the pool and the effect that they would have on people using it as well as the benefit of factual evidence from actual users. The court is also entitled to exercise a degree of judgment derived from everyday experience as to (for example) the effect on a non-swimmer of finding himself suddenly out of his depth because of the base of the pool shelving away. Additionally there is relevant background information about current legitimate concerns which have been debated on the subject of swimming pool safety and about standards recommended by interested bodies prior to Kevin's accident.

64. The material in question includes the FTO Guidelines 1990. Under the defined duties of care to clients of tour operators are included:

    (1)   regular inspections to identify potential hazards

    (2)   informing the proprietor of remedial action and

    (3)   warning the client if remedial action has not been taken and

    (4)   notice to senior management if safety improvement had not been implemented.

65. Sunworld at the time in question did not belong to the FTO. Thus I have described the standards mentioned above as 'background information'. However there is very specific and relevant evidence as to the standards

which Sunworld set itself at the material time. This is contained in the memorandum of Simon Clarke of 1ˢᵗ July 1993 (see paragraph 46 above). Based on those standards alone, Sunworld was in signal breach of its obligations as perceived by Mr Clark in a number of respects concerning the Reina Beach pool.

a)   no efforts had been made to ensure the hotel had carried out the instructions to mark pool depth clearly and accurately, indeed there were no pool depths in the relevant part of the pool and no instructions had been given. Sunworld's representatives had not addressed their mind to the point. It follows that no changes of depth, sudden or otherwise were marked.

b)   there is no or no sufficient evidence that any meaningful information book containing a pool information page showing the differing depths of the pool was available.

c)   it was asserted in the memorandum that these requirements were already standard practice in Sunworld and that the memorandum was no more than a reminder. On that basis the existing standard procedure was certainly not followed at the Jupiter/Saturno complex. It is I suppose possible that Simon Clark's memorandum reflected not simply a minimum duty owed by Sunworld but some optional higher standard which it had chosen to adopt. This is inconsistent both with the language used in it and with an objective judgment of all the other relevant circumstances.

....

68.   Had it carried out its duty, it would have looked at the Reina Beach pool. It would have found no significant depth markings. It would have found a 'banding' system which was virtually meaningless. It would and should have found that the gradient in Lobe B of the pool (and possible other lobes) was such as to be unsuitable and unsafe for recreational areas for children who could not swim. It would and should have appreciated that the pool including Lobe B was being used by and would be attractive to children who could not swim. The most cursory observation would have led to that conclusion. It would and should have told the Hotel to take the appropriate steps for safety of its clientele.

69.   Such steps should, as a minimum, have been

a)   To provide comprehensive depth markings around the lobe

b)   To put specific notices around the pool to say that it was unsuitable for children and non swimmers. (It would have been desirable to put a physical demarcation between the shallow and deeper parts of the pool as is illustrated in certain pictorial examples in the papers. However in my judgment the failure to do so cannot be characterised as negligent).

c)　　　　If the hotel failed to take such steps, then Sunworld should itself have ensured that their customers were specifically warned of the risks to children and non swimmers of using that particular pool.

70.　　In my judgment failure to take those steps unnecessarily exposed children using the pool to foreseeable danger. It therefore amounted to negligence. Further the state of the pool and the failure to take these steps had the result that the outdoor swimming pool as used was not of a reasonable standard consistent with the representations that there would be a family holiday with superb amenities for young children. Accordingly Sunworld was to that extent in breach of its contract.

．．．．．．．

73.　　*Lifeguards 'Baneros' and Resuscitation*

I have already found that the provision available for qualified people to be on hand to provide resuscitation and/or resuscitation equipment was virtually non existent. Thus on any view there was a breach of the Spanish regulation, however favourably that is interpreted towards the hotel.
．．．．．．．．．．．．．．

．．．．．．．．．．．．

75.　　....The order applicable to the Reina Beach pool was the ministerial order of 31st May 1960, Article 22. This provided that the pool must have pool attendants (who are) swimmers, trained in life saving and the practice of artificial respiration in cases of asphyxia from immersion in water. There should be a minimum of two attendants if the pool capacity does not exceed 200 bathers. If that is exceeded, there should be at least one more pool attendant per 200 or fraction thereof.

．．．．．．

77.　　...., the submissions of the hotel and Sunworld laid emphasis on the lose and unprescriptive nature of the requirements of this order. .... there was nothing laid down which prohibited these qualified attendants being employed in some other capacity provided they fulfilled the criteria laid down by the order. A wider impression was sought to be created by these submissions that Spanish law was essentially lax and permissive in this field and that it was neither surprising nor reprehensible that there was an absence of lifeguards as we might understand the term.

78.　　However, examination of the jurisprudence in question as interpreted with ......expert guidance leads to a very different conclusion. An important example of the jurisprudence was a civil claim for compensation brought in the High Provincial Court of Palma Majorca, Fifth Section in 1997. Date of judgment 16th May 1997, Ref Nos. 0279/97 and 0808/96. Here a young boy had been lost by his parents in a leisure complex and had become immersed in a pool. Tourists who had seen him removed him from the pool and tried to revive him with cardiopulmonary resuscitation. His family appeared. He was removed to hospital but subsequently died. The First Instance Court apportioned responsibility 50/50 between the parents and those administering the complex. The appellate court reduced the parents' responsibility to 30% and increased the owners' responsibility to 70%. The judgment reviews various factual issues as to how the boy came into the water and the parents' responsibility. Then it turns to the question of the owners of the complex and the lifeguard:

> "As far as the second aspect is concerned the family members emphatically deny that there was a lifeguard present and only agreed that the lady doctor, Mrs J was present, albeit in their opinion, belatedly. While on the contrary the co-defendant concerned has produced a witness Mr C who said that he was at the scene and he attended to the minor. As the trial judge rightly points out in either case whether the lifeguard was present or not, what is certain is that unfortunately the lifeguard whose presence is required under the current relevant administrative regulations – the Ministerial Order of 31ˢᵗ May 1960 – failed to notice the presence of the minor in difficulties in the pool. Nor did he take him out of the pool, something which was done by another person, a tourist bathing in the same pool, which implies scant diligence on the part of the individual whose task and raison d'étre is to avoid or prevent the occurrence of such situations as those which we are now considering and to be mindful at all times of the people using the pool and ready to provide prompt assistance should any bather be unable to swim or show external signs of drowning or of being in a situation of distress for whatever reason, be this because the individual cannot swim, a 'hydrocution', a fainting fit/dizzy spell, a trauma or any other reason. It is worth mentioning in this connection that in a case having marked similarities to the one with which we were concerned, the SYP of the 14ᵗʰ June 1984 attributed full liability to the owner of a private pool open to the public under the aforesaid ministerial order and on the ground of negligence in supervision or in election due to the absence of a lifeguard when the accident occurred. Therefore the circumstances of unforeseeable and inevitable result proper to an act of God (STS 13ᵗʰ March 1992 among others) are not present."

79. This case graphically illustrates that the lifeguard's duty under Spanish law is one of active supervision. This is so whether the individual concerned is at a fixed station or peripatetic (i.e. walking around the pool) and whether charged with other duties close to the pool or not. .....

80. ... there is the Spanish civil code. This provides for a general civil liability for wrong which is obviously akin to the English law of negligence. Indeed in at least one respect, the Spanish law appears to be stricter on the alleged tortfeasor. That is, where there is an obvious risk such as drowning established by a claimant, it seems that the burden of proof or at least the evidential burden shifts to a defendant whose duty is to guard against such a risk to prove that he did so. This illustrates the rigour of Spanish law. ....

81.   In summary, I am satisfied that the ministerial order if observed by the Hotel would have resulted in prompt and expert attention being provided to Kevin, once it became apparent to a reasonably competent and diligent lifeguard at the poolside that he was in difficulties. .....

82.   *Causation*

....

84.   On the basis of my conclusion as to the duties of lifeguards or pool attendants, one of them would probably have been giving Kevin expert resuscitation within a minute or two of his retrieval from the pool. It would, I think, have been too much to expect such a person to notice Kevin going under. That might have happened, but was less than probable. However, in the event there were two or three such attendants close to the pool, as Spanish law required, exercising safety supervision, one would probably have noticed very quickly the young unconscious child being removed from the pool. An attendant might possibly have missed him even when he was removed from the pool, but my conclusion on the point is based on probability.

....

87.   A joint medical report was prepared and agreed by all three experts. It is helpful and succinct and I propose to cite it here in full:

       "......

       1)   Kevin Roberts' current neurological impairment is attributable to the deprivation of blood supply and oxygen to the brain consequent upon the submersion episode.

       2)   If Kevin had been retrieved from the pool within three minutes of immersion, was in a state of cardiac arrest and effective cardiopulmonary resuscitation been applied immediately, it is probable that he would have survived without brain injury.

       3)   If submersion was between five and ten minutes, effective cardiopulmonary resuscitation could possibly have resulted in a return of a spontaneous circulation. Neurological impairment would be likely, although probably less than Kevin has suffered.

       4)   After more than ten minutes of submersion, it is possible that effective resuscitation would have resulted in a return of the spontaneous circulation, but his neurological impairment would be extensive and possibly similar to that which is seen in Kevin today in terms of residual functional disability.

       5)   Long term survival following longer periods of immersion (15-20 minutes) is occasionally reported if competent resuscitation including adrenaline (Epinephrine) is applied. However, unless submersion for this length of time occurs in icy water, profound brain damage is inevitable.

6) A lifeguard and the presence of other staff trained in delivering cardiopulmonary resuscitation (CPR) may have reduced the period of submersion and led to earlier initiation of defective CPR".

88. It now becomes necessary to apply to my findings about the sequence of events following Kevin's immersion these authoritative joint medical views. This is necessary in order to come to a probable judgment about what Kevin's state would have been as a consequence of the immersion, if the Hotel had complied with the Spanish Ministerial Order. My conclusions are:

a) It is extremely unlikely that Kevin would have suffered such severe injuries and disabilities as he did in fact.

b) There would have been a significant chance of him suffering no or no significant permanent effects from his accident, but this chance falls short of a probability.

c) The probability is that he would have suffered some permanent neurological damage but significantly less severe than that actually suffered.

89. The reasons for these conclusions may be summarised thus: the period of anoxia implied by my factual conclusions falls within the range of approximately four to seven minutes. ....

....

92. ...... it remains a feature of the case that Kevin's injuries flow from two distinct causes: his immersion, and the failure to provide lifeguards or resuscitation. The liability in relation to each of these causes and its apportionment (if appropriate) between the parties, is likely to differ. .....

....

95. The general conclusion upon all the evidence as to liability and causation is that Sunworld is liable to the claimant both in relation to his immersion in the pool and in relation to the failure to resuscitate. I come to matters of contribution and apportionment next.

96. *Claims against the Part 20 Defendants*

The parents

....

97. ... the court must take an objective view of the parents' legal duty and whether they were in breach of them. Mr Norton represented Mr and Mrs Roberts with considerable skill and discretion. He sought to meet criticisms of their care for Kevin at the time of the accident by submitting that its standard fell within that which ordinary loving and careful parents would give the children, given the rough and tumble of life. This formulation is based on that of the Vice Chancellor in the Court of Appeal decision in *Surtees v The Royal Borough of Kingston upon Thames* [1992] 1 PIQR 101 at 124. Mr Norton relied on the fact that Mr Roberts escorted Kevin to the

poolside. Mr and Mrs Roberts remained close by the pool. They kept an eye on him from time to time. They planned to join him in the pool in a very short time. He was with his nine year old brother who could swim. Any failure to use arm bands, submits Mr. Norton, should not be regarded as material since (according to Mr Sanders), arm bands in themselves should not be relied upon as safety equipment – rather as an educational aid to be used only under direct adult supervision.

98.   These are cogent arguments. However the fact remains that Kevin was permitted into the pool unaccompanied, save for his nine year old brother. If the pool was unsafe for use by a child who could not swim, it was not in my judgment a reasonably sufficient safeguard to leave him with a child of nine even one who could swim. Further despite Mr Sanders' no doubt technically correct view of arm bands, I do think that their absence as a matter of common sense and common experience has some significance. Kevin's parents had used arm bands for him previously. If he was to be left even temporarily unattended, then the use of arm bands though not a complete safeguard would have been a reasonable and sensible precaution.

99.   The reasonableness of the parents' actions has to be seen in the context that the depth and dimensions of the pool were completely unknown to them. It was a foreign country. It was their first visit to it. I regret that I am driven to the conclusion that to allow Kevin into the pool in those circumstances did fall short of the reasonable standard of care to be expected of them. I take into account that the pool must have looked attractive, tempting and family orientated and that there was little or nothing to alert them to its unsuitability for use by a child. In this context the presence or otherwise of a general warning as to the need to accompany or supervise children around pools adds little. Reasonable parents can be taken to know in general terms the importance of that. ....

100.   In my judgment therefore their negligence contributed towards Kevin's immersion. It did not however contribute towards to failure to provide properly for resuscitation or life-saving.

101.   In relation to immersion, I find in apportioning liability between the parents and Sunworld that there is nothing sensibly which enables me to distinguish between the degree of liability. I find their share of liability to be equal.

....

103.   *The Hotel: Kevin's Immersion*

....

105.   It was the Hotel who had the direct control over and responsibility for the physical aspects of the deficiencies mentioned, lack of depth marking, notices etc. On the other hand it was Sunworld who were the party bearing primary contractual responsibility towards Kevin to provide reasonably safe and suitable holiday facilities. Bearing in mind all the circumstances I find that the Hotel should bear an equal share of the blame with on the one hand

Sunworld and on the other hand the parents for the fact that Kevin became immersed.

The Hotel: Lifeguards and Resuscitation

106. The position here is on any view quite different. As already mentioned there is no question of the parents sharing liability for this important aspect of the case. The issues here are:-

    (a) Is Sunworld entitled to recover in full from the Hotel all losses attributable to the failure to provide proper life guards, resuscitation etc. by reason of the terms of the contract between the two parties.

    (b) If not, how should liability for this aspect of the case be apportioned between them.

107. The contractual provision relied upon Sunworld which it is not disputed is binding on the Hotel is as follows:-

> "The Hotel agrees that "the tourist establishment complies fully with national, local and trade regulations and codes of practice relating to hygiene, fire, safety and other standards for those using the tourist establishment in all respects and will hold Sunworld, its employees, agents, representatives, clients and all other third parties indemnified against any loss, expense and/or costs incurred by Sunworld or its said employees, agents, representatives and all other third parties in relation to any claims made by such persons aforesaid as a result of any failure on the part of the tourist establishment to comply with such regulations and codes".

    ....

108. Sunworld puts its case against the Hotel on the basis both of damages for breach of the express warranty and of indemnity. ....

....

116. It is I think important on this point to bear in mind that Sunworld owed a duty to Kevin to take reasonable steps to ensure that the facilities offered were of an acceptable standard. That duty in relation to lifeguards and resuscitation could not in my judgment be discharged simply by ensuring that an indemnity and warranty were inserted in its contract with the Hotel.

117. The evidence is that Sunworld's representative actually knew that there were no lifeguards. There is no evidence that she or anyone else employed by Sunworld checked on what, if any, resuscitation facilities there were. Inaction in the face of the relevant knowledge, and failure to check, were on the face of it breaches of Sunworld's direct duty to Kevin.

118. Construing the contract "contra preferentem", it cannot I think rightly be said that its words are wide enough to indemnify Sunworld against the consequences of the breaches of duty to Kevin as defined in the preceding paragraph; nor that the losses caused by those breaches of duty were

incurred "as a result of" the Hotel's failure to comply with the Spanish Regulations.

119.   Thus apportionment of liability under this heading is I find both permissible and appropriate. However the Hotel must in my judgment bear substantially the greater part of this liability. It was the party in breach of the regulations. It took on the evidence no step whatsoever to comply with them. It had the basic and primary responsibility to pool users to have suitable lifeguards and any necessary equipment available. It had warranted that the regulations were complied with and given an indemnity in relation to that. Under those circumstances I apportion under this head a relatively minor proportion of the blame to Sunworld: i.e. of the order of two to one to Sunworld's favour.

120.   I now come to deal with the apportionment of the liability globally on all aspects of liability. I adopt the approach to causation set out at paragraphs 88 to 94 above. Having regard to that and my findings in 96 to 119, I consider that the justice of this complex and difficult case is met by finding that Sunworld should be entitled to recover contribution to the damages for which it is liable to Kevin amounting to 17% for Mr and Mrs Roberts and 50% from the Hotel. The effect is to leave Sunworld liable for 33% of the damages without recourse against any third party. The basis of this apportionment is to attribute the cause of Kevin's injuries, or rather the loss flowing from them, equally to his original immersion on the one hand, and to the failure to resuscitate on the other. (The figures are rounded to the nearest decimal point.)

Moore v *Thomson Tour Operations Limited*, 2 May 2002, Stourbridge County Court (HHJ McKenna)

This is a claim for damages by Miss Elaine Moore against Thomson Holidays Limited (sued as Thomson Tour Operators Limited) in respect of an accident which took place when the claimant was on holiday in Rhodes, at the Hotel Oceanis, in May 1996. In the accident the claimant fell down some steps at the front of the hotel and in so doing sustained what Mr Bryan, a consultant orthopaedic surgeon, who saw the claimant and has prepared various reports in these proceedings, described as, "A fracture dislocation of her right ankle, which was initially treated conservatively in Rhodes by manipulation and application of a plaster-cast, but on her return to the United Kingdom was treated by way of open reduction and internal fixation with plates and screws".

This was, on any view, a serious injury which has caused (and indeed continues to cause) the claimant severe pain. The claimant has not recovered from it and, subject to liability and contribution, I am told that the general damages are agreed at £20,000.

The claim is made against the defendants under the Package Travel, Package Holidays, Package Tour Regulations 1992, which control the sale and performance of packages sold or offered for sale in the United Kingdom, and which it is accepted applied to the claimant's holiday. In particular, the claimant makes her claim pursuant to regulation 15, which concerns the civil liability of the contracting party (in this case the defendants) for the performance of obligations under the contract, both by itself and by other suppliers of services, such as in this case the hotelier in Rhodes. The regulations place on the contracting party an obligation to ensure the proper performance of the obligations owed to the consumer under the package contract, and the defendants are responsible not only for their own actions and omissions but also those of other suppliers involved in the contract.

The claimant, whose date of birth is 25th April 1955, says that the defendants are liable for alleged failures to ensure that the premises of the hotel were reasonably safe, in respect of which various matters are pleaded. Liability and quantum are both in issue and there is an allegation of contributory negligence.

Turning to the evidence, the claimant says that on the Wednesday morning, the fourth day of her one week's holiday at the hotel, she got up at about 8 o'clock and went down to breakfast in the dining room with her two sisters and brother-in-law at about 8.30 to 8.45. During breakfast she noticed that it was raining heavily. After breakfast she went back up to her room with the intention of subsequently going with her sisters and brother-in-law to visit a local zoo. This was a private visit and not an organised tour. Arrangements were made to meet up again downstairs in the hotel at about 10.30. She says that she remarked to her sister Linda, with whom she was sharing a room, that it had stopped raining, and her recollection was that this would have been between about 9.45 and 10 o'clock. She and Linda met up with their other sister and brother-in-law in the reception. For some reason they used a different exit to the hotel to Linda and the claimant, who proceeded to exit the hotel by the front entrance.

As she was about to leave the hotel, the claimant noticed that the chain she was wearing round her neck had broken, so she returned to reception to put the chain in a safety deposit box, while her sister carried on out of the hotel. The claimant then went back out through the main doors of the hotel, with the intention of joining Linda, her other sister and brother-in-law who were waiting for her outside. She said she was not in a hurry since the trip to the zoo was not an organised trip and they were simply going to catch a local bus. She was wearing open-toed flat heeled brown sandals. She stepped off the top step and, as she placed her lead (that is to say right) foot on the next step down, it slid forward and she landed on her bottom and, as she put it, bounced down the five or so stairs, hitting her foot on each step as she went down. Whilst she was lying there waiting for an ambulance, she noticed that the steps were wet. In her witness statement she refers to the steps being "waterlogged" and says that her clothes became damp. She recalls a maid or cleaner from the hotel mopping up the steps while she was still lying there waiting for the ambulance to arrive. The steps were, she says, made of a marble type material, and she contrasts these steps with two steps leading to the reception inside the hotel which she says had some form of runner on them, unlike these outer steps. She had used the outside steps on previous days and was therefore familiar with them.

She says that she was immediately aware of a very severe pain around the right foot and could see that there was considerable deformity of her foot and ankle. She was taken to a local hospital, where her ankle was x-rayed and it was confirmed that she had a fracture dislocation. Whilst in the local hospital her foot was repeatedly manipulated, without the benefit of anaesthetic, and she had what can only be described as an horrendous time in the hospital, and was fortunate to have her sister there to look after her. On her return to the UK, she was admitted to Birmingham Heartlands, where she had an operation, during the course of which the fracture was fixed with plates and screws, which plates and screws were subsequently removed in May 1998. She developed reflex sympathetic dystrophy syndrome, which has not responded to conservative treatment, and she has suffered psychological injury. She has been unable to return to work since the accident, her pre-accident employment being as a machine operator.

Mrs Walker did not in fact witness the fall itself, but did see the claimant lying at the bottom of the steps. She confirmed that it had been raining but had stopped some time before the accident, perhaps 20 or 30 minutes beforehand. She said that there was nothing obviously wrong with the steps as far as she could see, although she was not staying at the hotel and had not herself used the steps. They were obviously wet. She too recalled the maid or cleaner mopping up the steps as the claimant was lying there and waiting for an ambulance.

The court has also read a witness statement prepared by Mrs Walker's sister-in-law, Mrs Castell, who was unable to give evidence in person at the trial as she was ill. In her short witness statement, which was made in November 1996, Mrs Castell says that she was walking at the side of the hotel with Mrs Walker when she heard cries for help from the front of the hotel. She and her sister-in-law turned the corner and found Miss Moore on her back at the bottom of the steps, being assisted by two guests from the hotel. She confirmed that it had been raising and that the marble steps at the front of the hotel were wet. She expressed an opinion that they were extremely dangerous when they were wet because, she said, there were no mats or grips.

The defendants have served a Civil Evidence Act notice in respect of the evidence of the manager of the hotel, a Mr Christos Constantinou, whose witness statement, dated August 1999, the court has therefore read. In that statement he confirms that he is the manager of the hotel and that the hotel is covered by approved architectural and civil engineering codes which apply to all buildings erected in Greece, which must comply with government building codes which take into consideration public safety. He asserts that the hotel complies with such codes and would not be permitted to operate as a hotel if it did not comply with local standards. He says that the marble type flooring of the type found at the front of his hotel is extremely common throughout Greece and other Mediterranean countries, and that he has never had a claim of this nature against the hotel before. He says that it had been raining, and indeed he believed it was still spitting heavily at the time of the accident itself – an assertion which, of course, is at odds with the evidence of the claimant and indeed Mrs Walker. Her goes on to say that the hotel does take steps to remove water from the steps, and that the housekeeper or head cleaner instructs cleaners to mop the steps if they become waterlogged after rain, but he makes the point that here is little point in mopping steps whilst the rain is still falling.

For the sake of completeness, it is right that I also record that in the trial bundle there is a fax from Mr Constantinou dated 22nd May 2001 in which he says the following:

> *"We refer to your fax concerning the claim of Mrs Elaine Moore and the statement from NTO, and we like to inform you that the National Tourist Organisation cannot sign such a statement. They insist that, since we have got the certificates and the licence to operate as a hotel, we comply with all local building and health and safety standards."*

The claimant criticises the construction of the steps and says that they were unsafe because they were liable to become slippery in the rain. Furthermore, the claimant says that the defendants should have made inquiries with the hotel management as to what arrangements were in place to mop up water during inclement weather and should have required the management to put in place a suitable system and satisfied itself that that was done, or alternatively that clear warning notices were in place, or in the further alternative should have instructed local resort representatives to warn clients of the defendants of the risk of slipping.

The defendant puts its case on three alternative bases: one, the claimant has not proved that the accident happened in the way she describes; two, that there has been compliance with local standards; and, three, there was no negligence or breach of duty on the part of the defendant, or indeed of the hotelier.

So far as the first issue is concerned, the defendant points to the extreme deformity of the claimant's ankle and suggest that this is in some way inconsistent with the fall as described by the claimant, and may raise the possibility that the claimant was in a hurry to rejoin the rest of her party, so that she stumbled or tripped and was not herself taking sufficient care. They also criticise the claimant's evidence as to the extent of the water on the steps, pointing to what they regard as inconsistencies in the claimant's evidence on this aspect.

I do not accept those submissions. True it is that the use of the word "waterlogged" is inappropriate in connection with marble steps. Nevertheless, I am satisfied on the balance of probabilities that the steps were indeed significantly wet, accepting as I do the evidence of the claimant on this point, as corroborated by the evidence of Mrs Walker and Mrs Castell. I do not accept that there is anything in the mechanics of the injury which is inconsistent with the description put forward by the claimant, and I accept the claimant's description of the mechanism of the accident and find on the balance of probabilities that she slipped as she placed her right foot on the first step down as a result of the step being wet.

The duty of care owed by a tour operator to its customer is a duty to exercise reasonable care to exclude from the accommodation offered any hotel the characteristics of which were such that guests could not sped a holiday in reasonable safety. The obligation does not extend to ensuring that the standards to be complied with are those of the United Kingdom. As Phillips J put it in *Wilson v Best Travel Limited* [1993] 1 AE 353 at page 358:

> "*What is the duty of a tour operator in a situation such as this? Must he refrain from sending holiday-makers to any hotel whose characteristics in so far as safety is concerned fail to satisfy the standards which apply in this country? I do not believe that his obligations in respect of the safety of his client can extend this far.*"

He goes on:

> "*The duty of care of a tour operator is likely to extend to checking that local safety regulations are complied with. Provided they are, I do not consider that tour operators owe a duty to boycott a hotel unless the absence of such a feature might lead a reasonable holiday-maker to decline to take a holiday at the hotel in question*".

Furthermore, the defendant relies on clause 6 of its Fair Trading Charter, which is in these terms:

> "*We will arrange for you to have the services that make up the holiday that you choose and that we confirm that these services will be provided either directly by, or by independent suppliers contracted to us. We are responsible for making sure that each part of the holiday you have booked with us is provided to a reasonable standard and is described in this brochure and in any other amendments to it.*
>
> *If any part of your holiday is not provided as described and this spoils your holiday, we will pay you appropriate compensation – see the important note in section 4. Also, if you buy a local excursion or tour through a uniformed Thomson representative, we will pay you reasonable compensation if it is not as advertised on the Thomson notice-board or any information book or Thomson resort guide.*
>
> *We take all reasonable care to make sure that all the services which make up the holidays advertised in this brochure are provided by efficient, safe and reputable businesses and that they follow the local and national laws and regulations of the country where they are provided*".

In this case there is no expert evidence adduced on behalf of either party as to the condition of the steps. However, the claimant and Mrs Walker gave evidence that, so far as they could see, there was nothing wrong with the steps other than that they were slippery when wet. Looking at the photographs of the steps in question, they appear to be entirely typical of the sort of steps to be found in any number of hotels in mainland Greece, the Greek Islands and indeed across much of the Southern Mediterranean.

The claimant criticises the defendants' evidence as to compliance or otherwise with local standards and asserts that the defendants have failed to discharge the evidential burden on them to demonstrate that they did in fact take reasonable care. Whilst, in my judgment, the defendants' evidence on this aspect is in some respects unsatisfactory, and whilst I remind myself, of course, that it has not been tested in cross-examination, I cannot accept that submission. Whilst it would appear that Mr Constantinou is mistaken when he suggests that it was still raining when the claimant had her accident, nevertheless I accept the substance of his evidence that the hotel was built in accordance with local building codes and that the hotel would not have been allowed to operate as such had it not complied with local building and health and safety standards and, most importantly, that the steps thems3elves so complied. On the balance of probabilities, I conclude that there has been no breach of local standards so far as the construction of the steps is concerned. Furthermore, I infer that, in setting standards for the construction of steps, the Greek authorities must have taken into account the possibility of them becoming wet as a result of rainfall. To do otherwise would, in my judgment, be to fly in the face of common sense. It must be remembered that hat we are concerned with here is no special hazard, but merely rainwater.

Is that the end of the matter? The defendant says that it is, relying on clause 6 of the Fair Trading Charter. The claimant says that it is not; her case is put this way: the preponderance of the evidence is that the marble steps were wet at the time of the accident due to the presence of rainwater; rainwater is a potentially slippery medium, as is marble, and the steps were a foreseeable slipping hazard when wet. The risk was of such a magnitude that it should have been addressed and, applying the test of reasonableness, given the time that had elapsed between it having stopped raining and the accident itself, the hotelier was in breach of duty in not having mopped up the surface water prior to the accident occurring, such that in the circumstances the defendants are liable for the hotelier's failure.

The evidence is that it had been raining and that within 20 or 30 minutes of it having stopped raining the hotel had in fact mopped up the water, albeit that by that time it was too late to have prevented the accident to this claimant. In my judgment, it would be to impose too high an obligation on the hotelier to require them to mop up in any lesser period, if it indeed be right to impose any positive duty to operate a system of inspection at all in this regard, in respect of which I have grave doubts in circumstances where, as I have found, the steps were compliant with local standards, and in the light of the inference that I have drawn about the effects of rainwater having been taken into account in arriving at those standards, and in the light of the contents of clause 6 of the Fair Trading Charter, which applied to this contract.

In all the circumstances, therefore, in my judgment there has been no breach of duty by the hotelier and hence no breach of duty by the defendants. In the light of these findings on the issue of liability, there is no need for me to go on to deal with the issues of quantum, and I simply will dismiss this claim.

Serpell v *TUI (UK) Ltd*, 28 April 2003, Edmonton County Court (DJ Cohen)

This is a claim made by Nicholas Serpell against TUI UK in the sum of £300 for breach of contract. The basis of his claim is that he was not provided with seats of adequate quality and comfort during a nine hour flight to Jamaica.

I have heard evidence from Mr Serpell and from Geoff Atkinson [Group Lawyer for Monarch Airlines – LJ] on behalf of the Defendant. Mr Serpell has appeared in person and the Defendant is represented by Miss Johnson of Counsel.

Mr Serpell is six feet one inch tall and appears to be an experienced traveller. He booked his holiday having found information about it on a web site and paid £498 including flights and hotels. Although he found the information on a website he booked the holiday over the telephone. I am not quite sure when this was done, but some time early in 2002.

Mr Serpell's evidence is that he knew he was booking seats on a charter flight and he knew the difference between charter flights and scheduled flights. Mr Serpell also conceded that his holiday was a very good deal.

Mr Serpell asked to upgrade when he booked his holiday and was told he would have to speak to the airline. Nevertheless he continued with the booking. Subject to the Terms and Conditions it turned out that an upgrade was not available anyway. Mr Serpell never requested a copy of the Terms and Conditions, but accepted that he knew that some would exist.

Mr Serpell went ahead with the holiday but was told by the airline to arrive early to see if better seats were available.

Mr Serpell took a nine hour flight and gave vivid evidence about the conditions. A description of them is contained in his statement. He says that he felt like cattle in a crate. He could not move his arms or his legs and he could not stand up and move around. Mr Serpell did concede that he could do five out of six DVT exercises recommended by the airline.

He said that he could not move around because of trolleys and queues of people waiting for the toilets.

Some matters are not in dispute:

The seat pitch – the distance between the back of Mr Serpell's seat and the one in front - was 29 inches.

Mr Serpell also does not dispute that the Civil Aviation Authority recommendation is a pitch of 26 inches.

In effect what Mr Serpell is saying is that even though the Defendant did not breach the Civil Aviation Authority guidelines and he was not misled by the Defendant, the conditions were so appalling that he is entitled to damages.

The evidence of the Defendant is in Geoff Atkinson's statement. Annexed to it is the flight de-brief showing that even if Mr Serpell made a complaint it was not noted. It also shows a plan of the aircraft, the Terms and Conditions stating upgrades are not available and the Certificate of Airworthiness.

Mr Atkinson also said that Monatch Airlines have other aircraft with seat pitches of 28 inches. Both do transatlantic flights and there is no distinction between aircraft that fly transatlantic and aircraft that fly to European destinations.

Mr Atkinson conceded that the guidelines of the CAA relate to safety. It was said in submissions however that if seat were large enough for passengers to exit safely, passengers must be able to move in them.

Turning now to submissions.

Counsel for the Defendant submits that the test must be what is reasonable in the circumstances, not what is appropriate for this individual passenger. I agree. It was submitted that I must consider the circumstances and it was submitted that the relevant ones were the price, that the holiday was no frills and that the flight was charter not scheduled.

The Claimant says that the flight is part of a package and that the price is irrelevant. He says that the Defendant owes the same duty to ensure his comfort on the flight as in the hotel. He says that it is not good enough to be better than the minimum.

I am asked to make findings about the conditions on the flight.

It seems to me that if the pitch size was 29 inches it must be the case that Mr Serpell could have moved around in his seat. There might have been some discomfort because Mr Serpell is tall, but his height is not unusual.

Mr Serpell says that he could not walk around the aircraft. It seems to me that he could have done so. Pitch size and DVT were important considerations for Mr Serpell prior to the flight. I cannot see him sitting in his seat throughout the flight and grinning and bearing it. If he did so, it was his choice.

I find that he could, on the balance of probabilities, have done all six DVT exercises and walked around had he wished.

The Claimant may have had a stronger case had he been travelling on a scheduled flight or paid more for it. Price must be relevant to the degree of comfort.

I do have some sympathy with Mr Serpell. It is well known that charter flights have many more seats than scheduled flights. However when we choose a charter flight we are aware of the discomfort that it will involve.

I do not find that Mr Serpell has made his case either in fact or in law.

Brannan v *Airtours Plc,* 18 January 1999, CA (Civ)

LORD JUSTICE AULD: This is an appeal by the plaintiff, Alan Brannan, against a finding of 75 per cent contributory negligence by Mr Assistant Recorder Evans in the Norwich County Court on 19th March 1998, in awarding him damages against the defendant, Airtours Plc, for personal injuries caused by its negligence. There is no cross-appeal by Airtours on the finding of negligence and there is no dispute as to the primary facts found by the assistant recorder. They are as follows.

Mr Brannan went to Tunisia on a package holiday organised by Airtours. One of the holiday attractions arranged by the company was a party night at a club which it took over for the occasion. There was dinner, a cabaret performed by Airtours' staff, a discotheque and unlimited wine provided free of charge. It was clearly intended to be, and was, a jolly, relaxed and crowded evening at which at least some of those present could be expected to drink a good deal. I say "crowded" because, on Airtours's own evidence, the intention was to "pack "em in" - to pack the party-goers in.

The public area of the club consisted of a central stage surrounded by terraces separated by partitions, with rows of trestle tables and seating benches on each side of them at right angles to the stage. Each bench accommodated four or five people. The tables were placed very close together, with the ends towards the stage, against a partition separating them from the tables on the next lower level, or the stage itself.

The tables were so close together that when they were full, as they were on this night, it was not easy for those at the partition end or in the middle of the table to leave it. The alternatives seem to have been to ask the others on the same bench to move along and off it, out of the way; or to clamber along the benches between the backs of those at the same table and those on the adjoining table; or to ask both lots to move their respective benches forwards; or, as gave rise to the accident in this case, to clamber onto the table and walk along it to the free end. Mr Brannan was seated at the partition end of his table and thus in the least convenient position for leaving it, say to dance or to go to the lavatory.

Over the other end of the table leading on to the stage there was a revolving electric fan about seven feet six inches from the floor, or at about head height for someone standing on the table. It was one of about six operating fans in similar positions over other tables. They were clearly hazards to party-goers who, as the night developed and their inhibitions became loosened by drink, might use the tables as a convenient route from or to their seats rather than disturb their table companions. The fans were known by Airtours to be a hazard because one of its holidaymakers on a previous package had been injured by one.

A company employee who was acting as compere on this night thought that incident sufficiently important to warn Mr Brannan and the other party-goers about the risk of injury from the fans. He did so at the beginning of the evening and illustrated the hazard by mentioning tube incident. He asked them not to climb on the tables. However, as the evening wore on a number of the party-goers did climb onto and walk along the tables, either to get to the dance floor, to go to the lavatory or for some other reason; and some danced on the benches - all this without any further warning or any attempt by Airtours' representatives present to stop it.

Towards the end of the evening Mr Brannan, who by then was merry but not drunk, wanted to leave the table to go to the lavatory. There were three or four people on his bench blocking his exit. He did not want to trouble them by asking them to 1hove. He had done that more than once during the evening and he did not want to do so again. He had forgotten the compere's warning some three or so hours before and he had seen others on the tables. He climbed onto the table, walked along it and into the rotating fan at the end of it, injuring his face.

The assistant recorder found Airtours liable in negligence. In so doing, he relied on the following main matters. First, it was foreseeable that the Airtours' party-goers would get onto the benches and tables and injure themselves by contact with the fans. It had, to Airtours' knowledge, happened in the past. Second, the company could readily have taken steps to eliminate the risk by relocating the tables in the vicinity of the fans so that they were not sited immediately underneath them.

In concluding, nevertheless, that Mr Brennan bore the major responsibility for his injuries, the assistant recorder relied on two matters. The first was that his conduct in ignoring the compere's warning and walking into the plainly visible rotating fan should be considered independently of Airtours conduct in knowingly introducing him to a dangerous setting and intentionally putting him into a party mood. This is what the assistant recorder said at p.19 of the transcript of his judgment:

> "[it is submitted] there is no reason why the Plaintiff should not have had a lot to drink, and the Plaintiff could hardly be blamed for taking, as he called it, Route 1 and that that was unsurprising and contemplatable. I'm afraid that does not go to contributory fault. That goes to primary negligence. The test of contributory, fault, as I understand it, is whether the Plaintiff has taken reasonable care for his own safety. That is the simple test. I am bound to say, applying that simple test, this Plaintiff has not taken reasonable care for his own safety to a substantial degree."

[Mr. Brannan] has criticised that reasoning. He submitted that it was wrong of the assistant recorder to ignore the effect of Airtours' negligence on Mr Brannan when assessing his responsibility for what happened: in particular, the siting of the tables under the fans and so closely together as to impede free passage from them, the provision of free and unlimited quantities of drink in a crowded party atmosphere, and the failure to do anything to stop the party-goers climbing onto the tables as the evening wore on.

[regard should be had] to the requirement of section 1(1) of the Law Reform (Contributory, Negligence) Act 1945 to have regard to a plaintiff's "*share in the responsibility for the damage*". As Lord Reid said in *Stapley v Gypsum Mines Ltd* [1953] AC 663, HL, at 682, this involves consideration not only of the blameworthiness of each party but also of the relative importance of a plaintiffs acts in causing damage, apart from his blameworthiness. Applying that test, [it was] submitted that Mr Brannan's conduct was unwise but, as he aptly put it, it was contemplatable and, to an extent, fashioned by Airtours.

The assistant recorder's second main reason for finding a high degree of contributory negligence was that there was no necessity for Mr Brannan to climb onto the table to leave it. He could, as he had done earlier in the evening, have asked others on his bench to move and let him out.

... on behalf of Airtours, [it was] submitted in reply that the assistant recorder did in fact take into account both relative responsibility for Mr Brannan's injuries and relative blameworthiness. Such matters included, he submitted, not only the lack of need for Mr Brannan to climb onto the table or to walk along it, but also that he walked into a readily visible fan; he had forgotten or ignored the compere's warning at the start of the evening; and he had had a good deal to drink. ... the assistant recorder asked the proper question, namely whether Mr Brannan had taken reasonable care for his own safety. The answer to such a question, he suggested, was a matter of impression and essentially a factual one with which this court should not interfere unless it was plain that the assistant recorder had erred as a matter of principle in his assessment of the degree of relative responsibility for Mr Brannan's injuries.

[Reference was made to the case of *Barrett v Ministry of Defence* (1995) 1WLR 1217 in which Beldam LJ said at 1224:]

> "*I can see no reason why it should not be fair, just and reasonable for the law to leave a responsible adult to assume responsibility for his own actions in consuming alcoholic drink. No one is better placed to judge the amount that he can safely consume or to exercise control in his own interest as well as in the interest of others. To dilute self-responsibility and to blame one adult for another's lack of self-control is neither just nor reasonable and in the development of the law of negligence an increment too far.*"

That was a case where a serviceman drank himself insensible, albeit with alcohol dispensed at his base, but where no other hazard was created by those responsible for his conduct and safety. It was far removed from the party atmosphere in this case where, although it is implicit in the assistant recorder's finding that Mr Brannan had drunk to an extent that made him merry, there was no finding that he was drunk in the ordinary sense of that word.

In order to judge the relative responsibility of the parties for Mr. Brannan's injuries, it is important to remember that Airtours were in part responsible for the conduct of Mr Brannan constituting his contributory negligence. The respective responsibility of each party for his injuries cannot sensibly be considered in isolation one from the other. As to the lack of necessity for Mr Brannan's conduct, that is really much the same point as I have just made in relation to the relative responsibility of the parties for what occurred. It is not just and equitable, in the words of section 1(1) of the 1945 Act, to hold all or most of a plaintiffs conduct against him unless it was necessitated by the defendant's negligence. A defendant's negligence can be causative of injury where its effect fails short of necessitating self-injurious conduct by a plaintiff. Where it is such as to predispose a plaintiff or to influence him to act in a way contrary to his own safety, albeit negligently, it is clearly relevant to the assessment of the degree of that contributory negligence. It is part of the assessment of his relative responsibility for his injuries.

[There was] a third complaint about the assistant recorder's approach to the task of assessment of the degree of contributory negligence. It was that Airtours, having created and warned the party-goers of the danger, did nothing as the evening wore on to stop them ignoring its warning by climbing onto the tables. As against Mr Brannan's momentary lack of attention, its lack of judgment, he submitted, continued and became worse as the evening progressed.

But [it was] maintained that it was wrong to characterise Mr Brannan's failure as one of momentary inattention. He said that it was a deliberate decision not to do what he had done, apparently, without difficulty, before, namely ask his neighbors to move, and that it was very careless of him to walk along the table into a plainly visible rotating fan. [Our] attention [was drawn] again in this context to the amount of drink that Mr Brannan had taken, albeit not sufficient to make him drunk, sufficient to make him perhaps inattentive and to lose some of his normal inhibitions..

In any view, the key to the assessment of the degree of contributory negligence in this case is Airtours' conduct in exposing Mr Brannan to a risk which it could easily have avoided and in a party setting for which it was responsible. It organised a crowded, noisy party evening, in which it was plainly foreseeable that piney-goers might drink a bit too much and lose some of their normal inhibitions and close attention to their own safety. The Assistant Recorder's rejection, of the relativity of the respective conduct of the parties and his focus on the lack of necessity for Mr Brannan to do what he did led him, in my view, to assess too high a degree of responsibility by way of contributory negligence.

For those reasons, in my judgment, the assistant recorder's assessment of 75 per cent contributory negligence was outside the bounds of his proper margin of appreciation and was too high a proportion of responsibility and blameworthiness when compared with those of Airtours. I would substitute an assessment of 50 per cent and allow the appeal to vary the judgment to that extent.

Johnson v *First Choice Holidays and Flights Limited*, 22 August 2003, Northampton County Court (District Judge McHale)

The Claimant and his wife embarked on a 14 night package holiday at the RIU Ventura-Maxorata Hotel, Fuerteventura, Spain in September 2001. The cost of the holiday for the Claimant and his wife was £1,640. The Defendant was the tour operator. The index accident happened on 11 September 2001 when the Claimant slipped and fell while leaving the Hotel swimming pool. The Claimant slipped at a location close to the edge of the swimming pool. The Claimant commenced an action against the Defendant by reference to the Package Travel etc. Regulations 1992. The key allegations of s (4) negligence centred on four discrete matters. First, that the area adjacent to the swimming pool where the Claimant slipped was wet. Second, that there was no warning notice to the effect that the area adjacent to the swimming pool was wet. Third, that there was no hand rail. Fourth, the absence of non-slip material in the construction of the swimming pool surround. The Defendant relied on evidence from an employee of the relevant Hotel group (a specialist in matters of health and safety and the assessment of risks). It was her evidence that the relevant area was safe, constructed of a non-slip substance and complied with such local, Canarian, standards of health and safety as were relevant. The Claimant had no expert or other evidence as to the relevant local safety framework, nor as to the Hotelier's failure to comply with the same.

Held, dismissing the claim, (1) the standard of care and, therefore, breach of duty was to be assessed by reference to local, Spanish, rather than British safety standards (*Wilson* v *Best* [1993] 1 All ER 353 (QBD); *Codd* v *Thomson*, 7 July, 2000 (CA) and *Logue* v *Flying Colours Holidays Limited* [2001] 7 March (Central London County Court, HHJ Zucker QC) considered); (2) it was for the Claimant to adduce evidence of breach of local standards (see, *Codd* v *Thomson*); (3) the Claimant had failed to discharge the burden on him to prove that the Defendant had failed to comply with the relevant local standard insofar as any of the matters about which he complained were concerned; there was no evidence that there was excessive water in the vicinity of the swimming pool and there was no evidence that the Claimant would have made use of an handrail if one had been provided and there was no evidence that such a handrail was required in the Canary islands; (5) a warning notice would not have told the Claimant anything that he did not know already (*Staples* v *West Dorset District Council* [1995] (CA) considered).

Wren v *Unijet Holidays Ltd*, 17 December 2002, Guildford County Court (DJ Williams)

The essence of the claim was that the foyer of the Claimant's holiday hotel included a disguised step in the marble surface which was a hazard or a trap. This, it was alleged caused the accident and constituted a failure on the part of the Hotel to exercise reasonable care for which the tour operator was liable. The step was in fact a menace and had caused other accidents.

As the Claimant walked across the foyer on the first day of her package holiday, partially blinded by sunlight she had thought that the floor was flat. It was not – and over she went falling down the step and sustaining injuries.

The tour operator in its terms and conditions accepted liability for accidents caused by the provision of "deficient" services and, of course, regulation 15 of the Package Travel [Etc.] Regulations 1992 applied. In its Defence the tour operator maintained:

1.   That there was, in fact, a white stripe across the step to mark it out clearly from the rest of the dark floor.

2.   As the Claimant had failed to adduce any evidence to the effect that the hotel failed to comply with local standards, the claim was bound to fail.

Neither line of argument prevailed and the claim succeeded. It turned out that the white line had been placed across the top of the step after the Claimant's fall (as contemporaneous photographs clearly showed). Secondly, the judge accepted that the contractual obligation on hotel and tour operator was to supply facilities of a reasonable standard that were not deficient. Given previous accidents and the dangerous colouring of the floor, the facilities were not reasonable irrespective of any local standards. Furthermore, as the Hotel had put down a white line after the event this was good evidence that even by local standards it was considered reasonable to warn visitors that the step was there. There was no deduction for contributory negligence.

SECTION 6

IMPROPER PERFORMANCE: MISCELLANEOUS EXAMPLES

IMPROPER PERFORMANCE: MISCELLANEOUS EXAMPLES

Cases in this Section

7. *Jones* v *Airtours Holidays*   **Page 357**

Hotel's staff witnesses had mistakenly described a different incident to that in which the Claimant had her accident.

8. *Potter* v *TUI UK Limited*   **Page 359**

When providing a tennis court as part of the facilities available during a villa holiday the tour operator did not owe a duty to the consumer to ensure the tennis court was maintained to professional standards. A small amount of moss on the surface was reasonably to be expected.

9. *Prynn and Woolley (t/a "Romano Travel")*   **Page 360**

A staircase in a Spanish villa that was plainly unsafe and hazardous for children was nonetheless tolerably safe for any adult exercising reasonable care for their own safety. Thus, where an adult slipped and fell down a precipitous staircase, there was no causative breach of duty on the part of the company supplying the holiday villa.

10. *Stockman* v *First Choice Flights and Holidays Limited*   **Page 361**

Although the tour operator failed to provide the promised "min-bus" to transfer the Claimant from airport to hotel, there was no causative breach of duty because it had supplied a different sort of bus, and the step on which she had tripped proved to be lower than that which she would have encountered on a mini-bus.

11. *Bellinger* v *TUI UK Ltd*   **Page 364**

It is implicit in the contractual promise to provide a "half board" hotel regime that the main meal (be it lunch or dinner) would have 3 courses.

Improper Performance

Ouaret v *MyTravel*, 31 March 2005, Central London County Court (District Judge Taylor)

The Claimant was on holiday at the Sophia Hotel in Spain on 15th January 2002. Throughout the morning she had been confined to her bedroom because of a torrential downpour of rain. Approximately 30 to 45 minutes after the rain stopped she decided to visit the local pizzeria for lunch. She left the hotel through the fire exit and began to descend the five steps leading down to a partially covered patio area when she slipped and sustained injury. She stated that after she fell she looked up and noticed that the steps were wet with rainwater, and possibly also covered with a green slimy substance. The Claimant alleged that the Defendant was in breach of Regulation 15(1) of the Package (Travel etc) Regulations 1992 in failing to dry the steps or to warn of the presence of water having regard to the fact that the staircase was close to the reception area and was likely to be in frequent use. It was also alleged that the tiled surface of the steps was dangerous, and that handrails should have been installed, particularly since after the accident the Defendant had introduced a recommendation that all staircases with five steps or more should have handrails in place.

The Defendant's case was that it would have been obvious to the Claimant that an outside emergency exit would be slippery after heavy rainfall, and that no warning sign was required. The Defendant also argued that it would be absurd to require the hotel staff to clean the steps immediately every time that it rained, particularly bearing in mind that there were 13 external staircases on the site. The Defendant relied upon photographs from other hotels in the area which showed staircases in comparable or worse condition than the steps at Sophia Hotel.

The judge was satisfied that the Claimant had slipped on rainwater and not on any other substance. He held, however, that was no evidence to suggest that other hotels in the area would have mopped up the rainwater within a shorter time period of time, and this particular staircase did not require any greater attention than the others at the hotel:

> *"It seems to me on this matter that I can summarise the position quite shortly by saying that in terms of, as it were, an English case, applying the usual Occupiers Liability Act considerations and the usual common law criteria, that there is nothing to indicate that the defendant has breached its obligations, that even if it has a duty that it would be unreasonable to expect the defendant to have any spillage of heavy rainwater cleared from all parts of the building within 30 to 45 minutes of the rain stopping and in any event within one hour or so in circumstances where there are at least 13 or 14 staircases to deal with and the reception area in addition".*

The judge held that there was no evidence that the hotel did not comply with local standards in terms of its construction and design, and the steps it did not present a hazard to persons using them. There was no evidence from any other hotelier in the locality to suggest that their staircases had handrails, or that they used different materials or adopted a different design. Finally, relying upon *Staples v West Dorset* [1995] PIQR 439, the judge concluded that the fact that handrails were recommended after the accident could not, of itself, give rise to an inference of negligence.

The Claim was dismissed.

Brook v *Direct Holidays*, 16 January 2004, Bradford County Court (HHJ Finnerty)

Marion Brook, who was 63 years old, travelled with her sister to Gran Canaria on a package holiday provided by Direct Holidays. On the fifth day of the holiday the two women went on an excursion around the Island. The excursion consisted of a camel ride, lunch and a visit to the Cave of Ancite, a historically important open-ended cave set in a mountain. Access to and exit from the cave was by a rocky, mountain path. As the Claimant was descending the mountain, having visited the cave, she slipped and sustained a serious injury to her ankle. The accident was filmed by the tour operator, who had been making a video to sell to holidaymakers as a memento of the excursion. The Claimant stated that she had fallen on the top section of the path, which was very steep and covered with small loose stones, shale and rubble. In fact the video demonstrated, and the judge accepted, that the Claimant had fallen approximately three quarters of the way down the slope.

The Claimant alleged that the local operator of the excursion, for whose acts and omissions the Defendant accepted responsibility, was negligent in having failed to warn her that the egress from the cave was inherently more dangerous than the access, and for forcing her against her will to descend by this route. It was also alleged that the Defendant itself had failed adequately to monitor the excursion and its safety.

The Claim was dismissed. The judge held that the ground where the claimant fell was:

> "a typical mountain track such as one sees all over the world".

The path was not 'inherently dangerous' and there was not, the judge held, any significant difference between the access and egress from the cave. With regard to the allegation that the Claimant had been forced to walk down the mountain, the judge accepted the evidence of the tour guide that had any request been made to go back the way they had come, he would have acceded to it. Moreover, having viewed the video the judge could not see any discernible sign of fear or hesitation in the two women at the material time. In fact, he stated that:

> "it is apparent from the video that on their way down they were talking to one another and appeared smiling and happy. I do not find any of the allegations made against the tour operator to be established on the evidence".

The judge was also impressed with the fact that this excursion had been run for six or seven days per week for a number of years without any previous accidents or complaints. There was no evidence to suggest that the excursion was "anything other than a well run safe tour which gives pleasure to the customers who go on it". The judge concluded by commenting that:

> "This was an extremely unfortunate accident, which I have no doubt has caused her and her family a great deal of distress. However, in my judgement, it was an accident. Accidents do happen and that is what occurred on this particular day".

Grimshaw v *MyTravel*, 24 October 2005, Mayor's and City of London County Court (HHJ Cotran)

The Claimant went on a package holiday to Singapore in October 2002. The holiday itinerary included a tour provided by the Defendant's agents, Tour East, to the Thian Hock Keng Temple in Telok Ayer Street. At the entrance to the temple courtyard there was a red wooden board, approximately 18 inches high, spanning the entire width of the doorway. As the Claimant walked into the temple she caught her right leg on the edge of the board and sustained a laceration to her shin. The Claimant's husband filmed the accident on his video camera as he walked behind her.

The Claimant brought a claim pursuant to regulation 15(1) of the Package [Travel etc] Regulations 1992. She alleged that Tour East, for whom the Defendant accepted responsibility, should have been aware of the danger created by the board, either from previous visits to the temple or as a result of examining the site before the trip in question took place. The claimant alleged that although it was a sunny day the board was not visible because the entrance to the temple was in shadow. She claimed that brightly coloured warning steps should have been placed over the board, or alternatively that it should have been removed altogether.

The Defendant's case was that the temple was 150 years old and that there had not been any other accidents in the six years that the local agent had been taking holidaymakers there. The board was intended to represent the boundary between the religious and the secular. It was designed to encourage visitors to bow to the temple deities as they stepped over the threshold into the temple, and to act as a barrier against high tides. There were no warning signs because the Defendant did not have control over the temple and had no authority to interfere with its design. The Defendant also contended that had the Claimant waited for the tour guide's introduction or followed her into the courtyard of the temple, the significance of the entrance board would have been explained or become apparent to her. There was, it was argued, no duty to protect the Claimant against dangers or hazards which were perfectly obvious, even though the tour guide had, in fact, warned the tour group of its presence.

The judge was not persuaded by the Claimant's contention that the board was not visible. He stated that:

> "It is true that the sun was shining on the other side, but it is there for all to see. It cannot, in my judgement, be said that this was concealed in any way and anybody having traversed eight paces cannot help but see it if they are looking in front of them. This case really can be decided on the facts. The facts are there for all to see via the photographs".

He also placed weight on the Claimant's concession, under cross-examination, that the tour guide was some distance in front of her as she approached the temple, and that she could not tell whether the group had been warned about the board before they entered. The judge found as a fact that a warning had been given, but that it was not necessary in any event since the board did not represent an obstruction of any sort:

> "*I do not think that the Claimant has got anywhere near in this case of proving any negligence or breach of this regulation. The point is this: this was a visit not to any ordinary building but to a temple. It is all very well to say that one does not expect at the entrance a barrier 18 inches high, but we are dealing with a 150 year-old temple and it seems to me that this was a quick visit to the temple but, more importantly, this barrier, or whatever one wishes to call it, is so visible and so obvious that it would be wrong to say that it is necessary to give additional warnings*".

The board was, the judge concluded, "*a regular feature of temples which are regularly visited by tourists both in Singapore and throughout Southeast Asia*". The Claimant had failed to establish a breach of Regulation 15 and her claim was dismissed.

Hilton v *MyTravel*, 1 November 2005, (QBD) Manchester District Registry (Mr Recorder Hodge QC)

The Claimant and her husband were on a 14-night package holiday in Majorca. They were staying at the Palma Bay Club Hotel on an all-inclusive basis. On the sixth day of the holiday the Claimant was walking through the Acapulco self-service restaurant at the hotel when she slipped on a small pool of liquid on the ceramic clay tiled floor, suffering a serious knee injury.

The Claim was brought pursuant to Regulation 15(1) of the Package (Travel etc) Regulations 1992. The Defendant did not dispute that an accident had occurred, nor that it was caused by the presence of water or some other liquid on the floor of the restaurant. Both parties also accepted that this was a case to which the following passage from the judgment of Lord Justice Megaw in *Ward v Tesco Stores* [1976] 1 WLR 810, applied:

> "It is for the plaintiff to show that there has occurred an event which is unusual and which, in the absence of explanation, is more consistent with fault on the part of the defendants than the absence of fault; and to my mind the judge was right in taking that view of the presence of this slippery liquid on the floor of the supermarket in the circumstances of this case: that is, that the defendants knew or should have known that it was a not uncommon occurrence; and that if it should happen, and should not be promptly attended to, it created a serious risk that customers would fall and injure themselves. When the plaintiff has established that, the defendants can still escape from liability. They could escape from liability if they could show that the accident must have happened, or even on balance of probability would have been likely to have happened, even if there had been in existence a proper and adequate system, in relation to the circumstances, to provide for the safety of customers. But if the defendants wish to put forward such a case, it is for them to show that, on balance of probability, either by evidence or by inference from the evidence that is given or is not given, this accident would have been at least equally likely to have happened despite a proper system designed to give reasonable protection to customers."

The Claimant and her husband gave evidence that the restaurant was understaffed and that during the five days they had been on holiday they had not seen any member of staff carrying out cleaning duties whilst meals were in progress. They stated that they did not see any wet floor warning signs in place, and on a number of occasions they noticed spillages left on the floor for long periods of time without any attempt to clear them up.

The Defendant's evidence came from Miss McHugh, the Defendant's local representative at the time of the accident, and from a statement of Senor Figuera, the restaurant Maitre D. They both stated that the restaurant was capable of holding approximately 450 guests, with 10 waiting staff serving around 110 tables. The system in place when a spillage occurred was that one member of staff would stay on the spot whilst another went to fetch a warning sign and cleaning equipment. The spillage would then be cleaned away. The Defendant also claimed that during meal times the restaurant floor, and in particular the floor next to the central buffet counter, was constantly monitored. There was no history of any other accidents and there had been no previous complaints.

The Defendant argued that that the pool of liquid was small, and that if the Claimant could be excused for not seeing it, so could members of the restaurant staff. The hotel staff were required to take reasonable care to keep a proper look out for spillages, but they were not in the position of guarantors or insurers and could not be expected to react instantaneously. It followed, the Defendant stated, that one accident did not compromise the reasonableness of the system, but simply amounted to mere misfortune.

The judge preferred the evidence of the Claimant and her husband to that of the Defendant. He held that whilst Ms McHugh had given truthful evidence, she had only worked at the hotel for 4 to 5 months and was not well placed to give detailed evidence on the cleaning system. He also held that Senor Figuera clearly had an interest in asserting that there was an effective system in place and that his evidence was not persuasive. The judge stated that:

> "In light of all the evidence, and despite the fact that there is no established accident profile for this restaurant or restaurant floor, it does seem to me here that this is a case where, to paraphrase the language of Lord Justice Megaw, the Claimant and her husband have shown that there has occurred an event which is unusual and which, in the absence of explanation, is more consistent with fault on the part of the defendants than the absence of fault."

The judge went on to find that no trays were provided to restaurant guests, who were simply expected to carry their food on plates back to their tables. This, he said, made it particularly important to guard against the risk of spillages. Overall, he held that Defendant had failed to prove that they had a reasonable system of inspection in place:

> *"It does not seem to me, given the numbers of staff, tables and customers, that that is a system could that operate on a sensible basis (sic); and in any event, in the light of the evidence of Mr and Mrs Hilton, which I accept, it was clearly not a system that was in operation or operating effectively at the time of their holiday.*
>
> *[...]*
>
> *In my judgment on the meagre evidence put forward by Miss McHugh and the hearsay statement of Senor Figuera which is subject to the considerable reservations and qualifications I have already expressed, the burden has not been discharged on the balance of probability, bearing in mind the countervailing evidence from Mr and Mrs Hilton. I therefore find that liability has been established".*

The Claimant was awarded the sum of £20,321, plus costs.

Houghton v *Direct Holidays*, 25 November 2005, Preston County Court (HHJ Appleton)

Valerie Houghton was on a package holiday in Greece, which was provided by Direct Holidays, the Defendant. She and her husband were staying at the Icarus Hotel, on the Island of Zanti, for 14 nights. On the 8th day of the holiday, as she stepped out of the shower in her hotel bathroom, she slipped on the tiled floor and landed on her hand. Her injury was so serious that her little finger had to be amputated. The Claimant brought a claim alleging 'improper performance of the contract' pursuant to regulation 15(1) of the Package [Travel Etc] Regulations 1992.

The principal allegation related to the construction and layout of the bathroom, which consisted of a partially enclosed 'shower area', with a 'small' lip to contain excess water, and a shower curtain which hung down to the edge of the lip. Any water which spilled over into the centre of the bathroom would run into a further drain in the centre of the floor. The Claimant alleged that this construction was inadequate and unsafe, since it was not sufficient to prevent water running onto the bathroom floor, making it dangerously slippery, and the tiles were not slip-resistant. In particular, the Claimant relied upon the fact that after the accident the Defendant introduced certain alterations to the hotel bathrooms. The Defendant submitted that this was irrelevant to the question of breach of duty, and that the bathroom and shower were of a construction which was commonplace throughout resorts in Greece and that no other complaints had been received.

A further allegation related to bathmats. The Claimant's case was that at the 'welcome meeting' at the beginning of the holiday she had been told by the Defendant's representatives that there were no bath mats available, and that hotel guests were 'not allowed' to put towels down onto the floor. The Defendant argued that this was inaccurate, and that all that had been said was that the hotel management did not want towels to be used to mop up water from the floor. The Defendant further submitted that even if towels had been used, these would have created an additional tripping or slipping hazard.

The judge dismissed the claim. In relation to the allegation that the construction of the shower and bathroom was inadequate he found as a fact that the 'lip' at the bottom of the shower was *"perfectly generous and adequate for its purpose"* It was particularly significant, he said, that the Claimant had been at the hotel for seven days before the accident and had not experienced any difficulties. If there had been substantial water overflowing the lip on a daily basis, it would have gone into the bedroom. He was therefore driven to conclusion that it would not be the first time that somebody who has had a slipping accident has:

> *"possibly suffered a degree of over-enthusiasm in describing the slippiness or the volume of water involved"*.

The judge cited *Wilson v Best Travel* [1993] 1 All ER 353 and *Codd v Thomsons Tour Operators*, The Times, 20th October, 2000, and accepted the Defendant's submissions that the bathroom design complied with applicable local standards. He concluded that:

> *"There are obviously local and good reasons why the bathrooms are designed in this way. One of them maybe that, as opposed to us in this country, they have far better weather in Greece and bathrooms fully dry out rather more quickly than they would in this country if that arrangement was adopted. The use of tiling on the floors and walls is quite plainly a local tradition and custom"*

The judge was also impressed with the absence of any previous accidents or complaints, particularly bearing in mind the size of the hotel, which had 102 bedrooms, each with en suite facilities:

> *"...the fact that nobody has had an accident, nobody has complained, rather shows to me that there was not a foreseeable risk or any greater risk of somebody slipping in a bathroom than one would have to put up with in one's own home. After all, we all have to get out of the bath and our feet are wet when we do that and the bottom of the bath is wet. These are ordinary facets of everyday life"*

The judge agreed with the defendant that the fact that preventative measures had been taken after the accident could not be evidence of a breach of duty. He relied upon the 'ancient words' of Baron Bramwell in *Hart v Lancashire & Yorkshire Railway Company* 21 LT 261, at page 263, that:

> "People do not furnish evidence against themselves simply by adopting a new plan in order to prevent the recurrence of an accident. I think that a proposition to the contrary would be barbarous. It would be, as I have often had occasion to tell juries, to hold that, because the world gets wiser as it gets older, therefore it was foolish before".

Finally, the judge concluded that the additional allegation that holiday makers had been forbidden from placing towels on the floor *"did not really amount to anything"* since there had been no complaint by either the claimant or her husband to this effect during the first seven days of the holiday. He was again driving to find that this argument was *"thought up after the after the event"* and that towels on the floor would have introduced additional risks in any event.

Laurenson v MyTravel Plc, 10 November 2005, Central London County Court (District Judge Hasan)

The Claimant, along with his wife, son and a friend, were on a package holiday provided by the Defendant in Tunisia. On the third day of the holiday the Claimant returned from breakfast at around 9:15am, entered the bathroom adjoining his bedroom and slipped over, injuring his coccyx and right foot. He alleged that he had slipped on a 'thick film of water' on the tiled bathroom floor, which he said must have been left by one of the hotel cleaners. His evidence was that neither he nor his wife had had a shower or a bath in the morning, but had simply used the bathroom for brushing their teeth and going to the toilet. He could not recall seeing any cleaners' trolleys in the hallway outside his room, but assumed that the cleaner had been because the bed was made up and fresh towels had been left for them. The Claimant's wife also gave evidence that she had been wearing long trousers on the day of the accident, and the bottom of her trousers had become wet due to the amount of water on the floor.

The Defendant's evidence was that the hotel's cleaners would not start work until about 10am. The hotel manager gave evidence that when cleaners cleaned the bedrooms, they would start at the furthest point and work their way out of the room and into the corridor, so that no footsteps were left on the floor. Throughout this time, the trolley would remain in the corridor.

The judge held that the claimant had failed to establish that the cleaners had not adequately mopped up after cleaning the bathroom:

> "*I find the description of the amount of water that is alleged to have been left on the bathroom floor to be implausible. The whole of the room would have been cleaned and for their to have been an undue amount of water left in the bathroom is not made out by the Claimant*".

He also held that it was unlikely that the cleaners would have completed all their cleaning by 9:15am, since this was a holiday resort and cleaners would not start until holidaymakers had had breakfast and left their rooms for the day. The real cause of the accident, he concluded, was water left on the floor by the Claimant or his wife in the ordinary course of washing themselves in the morning:

> "*Bathrooms in strange places can be hazardous, particularly with flooring with which a person is unfamiliar and, in my view, the claimant cannot satisfy me that the defendants were responsible for the unfortunate accident which I am satisfied that he sustained*".

The Claim was dismissed.

Jones v *Airtours Holidays,* 26 October 2005, Liverpool County Court (Bennett J)

In April 2002 the Claimant, her partner, daughter and mother-in-law went on a package holiday to the Quinta Nova Sun Club in Alvor in the Algarve, Portugal. They stayed in two adjacent ground floor apartments. On the evening of the first day of the holiday, the Claimant and her partner went for a meal in the local village whilst her mother-in-law looked after her daughter. They each had two beers (in glasses which were larger than traditional English pint glasses) before walking back towards the club. The Claimant alleged that she tripped over on an undulating cobbled path leading through the grounds of the club, sustaining a fracture to her left arm. She stated that after the accident she pulled herself up and went back to her apartment where she was attended to by her mother-in-law.

The Defendant conceded that if the Claimant could prove that the accident occurred on the path, it would be liable under Regulation 15(1) of the Package [Travel etc] Regulations 1992 for failing to maintain the path, subject to any finding of contributory negligence. The Defendant, however, relied upon evidence from the head receptionist, Mr Ribeiro, who said that on the evening in question he and a maintenance man had witnessed the Claimant and her partner walking around the club grounds, and one apartment block in particular, as if they were lost. Mr Ribeiro lost sight of the claimant and when he went to look for her she and her partner were lying on an area of grass where there was no reason for her to have fallen. He stated that in his opinion the Claimant had been intoxicated and had been swaying from side to side prior to the accident. He also gave evidence that he accompanied the Claimant and her partner back to her apartment, which was otherwise empty.

The Judge preferred the Claimant's version of events. He drew attention to a number of inconsistencies in Mr Ribeiro's evidence, both as to the precise location where he came across the Claimant, and as to what exactly he had observed. Mr Ribeiro had given evidence that when he found Claimant on the grass she had referred to her partner as 'Mike Winn'. The Claimant's partner's name was in fact "Scott" and she had no reason to call him by any other name. It was also significant, the judge held, that the Claimant had been wearing trainers whereas Mr Ribeiro recalled carrying her 'sandles' back to her apartment. The judge also believed the Claimant's mother-in-law's evidence that when she attended to her daughter on the night of the accident there was nobody else present. Taking into account all the evidence the judge was driven to the conclusion that whilst Mr Ribeiro was not lying, he must have witnessed a different accident altogether:

> "*I find, having heard the witnesses, that the accident happened at the place and in the manner described by Maria and Scott. They were not drunk; they were not inebriated. They had had something to drink; that is perfectly right and perhaps it made them feel very relaxed, but it did not deprive them of their ability to behave in a normal way and to walk back from the village and up the path. I do not accept that they went round H6 twice. I think the real explanation for the confusion which Mr Ribeiro showed was that it probably was another couple whom he has confused with Maria and Scott*"

Bearing in mind the state of the path and the fact that it was late at night, the judge was not prepared to find that the Claimant should have been more careful as she walked back to her apartment. No deduction was made for contributory negligence and judgment was given for the Claimant in the sum of £8,000.

Potter v *TUI UK Limited*, 23 March 2006, Mayor's Court (HHJ Marr-Johnson)

The Claimant rented a villa with an attached tennis court from TUI in April 2004. On his first evening he and his friends went for a "knock-up". They played for about 20 minutes, after which when running for a wide forehand, the Claimant slipped (he alleged) on wet moss on the surface of the court. The "moss" was not of the green slimy variety, but he described it as a dark brown discolouration of the court. He fractured his wrist. He sued.

The basis of his claim was that any tennis court should be fit to be used for tennis and that meant it should be free from substances likely to cause someone to slip. Alternatively, he and his friends should have been warned that the surface was not free of hazards such as slippery moss.

Judgment for the Defendant.

The Judge was unable to conclude that the court was unfit for its purpose. He adopted reasoning in the Defendant's skeleton argument thus:

- This was a holiday villa tennis court, not Wimbledon or Roland Garros or even a David Lloyd centre – and what is reasonable should be judged in context.

- Photos taken by the Claimant were taken no doubt to *demonstrate* the condition of the court where the Claimant slipped – but it was far from obvious from those pictures why this court was said to be unreasonable.

- It may well be inevitable that an outdoor court will have modest imperfections – including the odd growth here and there, but that does not render its condition unreasonable.

- The Court was pressured washed annually in March (according to Civil Evidence Act evidence from the proprietor)

- It had been in situ for many years (22) without any other untoward incidents.

- There is a risk of slipping on any tennis court (particularly one of grass, or shale - & on shale players sometime deliberately slide around). This concrete surface was in *reasonable* condition even if affected by a dusting of moss here and there.

- It would be unreasonable to expect a court such as this to have a perfect or ideal surface, *not least of all* because such a standard would inevitably lead to the withdrawal of such facilities from holiday villas and hotel complexes in the face of potential legal action for rare accidents.

- Players (of the Claimant's experience) did not need to be warned.

Prynn v *Woolley (t/a "Romano Travel")*, 10 March 2006, Guildford County Court (HHJ Reid QC)

The Claimant sued for personal injury damages as a result of falling down the stairs at his holiday apartment at the Jardines Clubhouse (apartment 332) in Malaga on 14 August 2000. He and his family had arrived for their package holiday the evening before. On arrival the Claimant and his wife considered the (only) staircase at the apartment to be dangerous. Just after 7.00am on 14 August (first full day) the Claimant fell from about the fifth step down – fell all the way down and suffered a pneumothorax. [He was then 41].

The Claimant alleged an "improper performance" (i.e. breach of the implied term) of the holiday contract in two linked respects:

(a)   The staircase was dangerous – and not of a reasonable standard.

(b)   The Defendant had done nothing (and so much is common ground) to check-out (by means of local agents of course) the standard of the property he was selling as part of the package holiday.

There was no handrail at the material point of the stairs (the most dangerous being the sharp curve where the Claimant fell); the treads were of uneven size and there was no non-slip finish on the treads. All of these probably contributed to the Claimant's fall.

The Defendant (despite averring that local safety regulations applied) did not produced evidence to the effect that the Spanish safety regulations relied on by the Spanish safety expert did *not* apply although there were obvious and apparent doubts as to whether the regulations relied on were in force at the time the apartment was built.

However, it was alleged that apparent non-compliance with the Spanish regulations was good evidence that the premises were not of a reasonable standard. The pictures were enough to illustrate that the staircase was a menace – even for someone like the Claimant who had noted its problems when he first arrived the day before.

The Judge agreed that there was no meaningful handrail, and that the stairs were steep and narrow, and likely to be slippery. He felt that as regards children the safety measures were not good enough – and in that regard the staircase was not a reasonable standard. However, an adult aware of the limitations of the stairs, should have been able to cope with them and whilst they were far from ideal the stairs were not unlike many encountered in Spanish apartments and for that reason could not be described as "unreasonable". Accordingly, though less than ideal, the stairs did not represent any failure to perform the holiday contract to a reasonable standard and the claim was dismissed.

Stockman v *First Choice Flights and Holidays Limited*, 28 April 2006, Eastbourne County Court (District Judge Robinson)

1. Ms Stockman, a seasoned holidaymaker at 73 years of age, booked a package travel holiday to Tenerife in June 2004. When she arrived at Tenerfie Airport she was met by the Defendant's local representative, who in turn introduced her to a 'taxi driver', who would be transferring her to the hotel. Ms Stockman claims that she was 'marched' across the airport all the way to the Coach Station, whereupon a 25-seater 'coach' was waiting for her. In spite of her protestations that she was too old and too frail to climb up onto the step at the back of this vehicle, Ms Stockman attempted to do so and lacerated her leg.

2. Upon her arrival at the Hotel, Ms Stockman was attended by a foreign doctor who she says 'advised' her not to drink any alcohol. Contrary to this advice, and primarily because she had done so in the past in UK whilst taking similar medication, Ms Stockman continued to drink wine (and possibly vodka) with her evening meals, on a daily basis (the evidence from the Defendant's representative was that Ms Stockman was heavy drinker who had been known to drink up to a litre of sangria with her lunch on a regular basis!). The laceration to her leg became ulcerated and she had to fly home two days earlier than planned, at her own cost.

3. Ms Stockman, who was acting in person, had not properly particularised her claim. However, at the hearing the judge approved the Defendant's suggestion that were three discrete allegations begin made:

    a. The transfer should have been by taxi or minibus rather than by 'coach'.

    b. The 'coach' and/or the step on the back of the vehicle failed to comply with local or English safety standards because she had cut her leg on it.

    c. The bus/taxi driver had been negligent in encouraging Ms Stockman to take her time as she stepped on to the vehicle, when he should have known that she could not manage it at all.

4. With regard to the first allegation, the Defendant relied upon its Standard Terms and Condition of booking (which it was agreed did apply to this contract) which stated that *"the basic holiday cost as shown in the price panels includes: transfer to and from the resort airport, which will usually be by private taxi or shared mini-bus"*. The Defendant argued that:

    a. The word 'usually' expressly allowed for the possibility that an alternative form of transportation might be provided.

    b. In any event the vehicle provided to Ms Stockman was a 'micro-bus' which was, for all intents and purposes, a form of mini-bus.

    c. Since the access-step at the back of the 12-seater mini-bus was higher (46cm) than the step at the back of the 25-seater microbus

(38.5cm) Ms Stockman was in a better position than she would have been if she had been provided with the mini-bus.

5. The Second allegation was met with the familiar argument that Ms Stockman had failed to provide any evidence of how the bus or step failed to comply with local standards (in accordance with *Wilson v Best Travel* [1993] 1 All ER 353) and that the argument that the step 'must have been dangerous' because she cut her leg on it was at best circular, and at worst untenable.

6. Finally, the Defendant argued that that the bus driver had acted appropriately by encouraging Ms Stockman to take her time, had offered her assistance, and was not in any event contractually obliged to provide her with any other form of transportation.

7. Ms Stockman's claim was dismissed:

    a. The judge concluded that the transportation provided to Ms Stockman was not a mini-bus, since the Defendant itself did not label it as such. This was, according to the judge, a breach of contract (he did not address the Defendant's other arguments on this point). However, the fact that the step on the micro-bus was lower than the mini-bus meant that Ms Stockman had failed to establish that the provision of alternative transportation would have made any causative difference to her accident.

    b. In the course of evidence Ms Stockman appeared to claim that she should not have been 'marched' over to the Coach station and that a mini-bus or taxi should have been driven to the airport exit to pick her up. It was her 'fatigue' at the end of this trek which, according to her, had prevented her from stepping up onto the bus. The judge found that Ms Stockman's fatigue was 'singularly unfortunate', but that this was not something for which the Defendant should be held liable.

    c. There was no evidence whatsoever that the step was hazardous or dangerous. An elderly person who stumbled against a metal step was more likely to suffer injury than a younger person, but that was as much as Ms Stockman had been able to establish.

    d. The bus/taxi driver had not been negligent. He had encouraged Ms Stockman to take her time, and although there was a factual dispute about whether, and when, he had offered her assistance, she accepted under cross-examination that he was standing next to her throughout and she could have asked for his help at any time.

    e. The judge commented that if Ms Stockman had been regularly drinking against medical advice, this was a serious matter that would have had a significant impact upon her ability to recover substantial damages. However, since the Defendant was not liable he did not have to go on to consider that aspect of the claim.

8. A final aspect of this case that may be of some interest is that Ms Stockman had initially issued the Claim on the fast track, claiming damages for Pain, Suffering and Loss of Amenity in excess of £1,000. At a Case Management Conference a short time before the hearing, the judge had persuaded her (in the face of obvious objections from the Defendant) to reallocate the claim to small claims track, no doubt with one eye to the costs penalties that she was likely to otherwise incur. However, at the outcome of the final hearing the same judge agreed that whilst he had 'saved' Ms Stockman from costs after re-allocation, she was nonetheless liable to pay all of the Defendant's costs up to that date in accordance with CPR 44.11(2). She had entered into litigation fully aware of the risks involved and the fact that she was an elderly lady claiming a modest pension, he said, was irrelevant.

Bellinger v *TUI UK Ltd*, 21 August 2006, Central London County Court (District Judge Price)

C booked a package holiday over the telephone with D, a tour operator. At C's request D levied a half board supplement to the booking. D's brochure was silent as to the number of courses that would be provided under the supplement, stating only that breakfast along with lunch or dinner would be provided. On arrival C was informed by the hotel that she would be given just a main course for lunch or dinner. After D's representative intervened, the hotel offered to provide a starter in addition. C refused the offer, electing to eat only breakfast at the hotel. On the 3rd night of the holiday C sustained food poisoning from a local restaurant. C sued for breach of contract, claiming amongst other things damages for personal injury and the cost of her meals outside of the hotel.

Held: (i) as a matter of contractual construction, unless the contrary was stated in D's brochure, C was entitled under the half board supplement to a starter, a main course and a dessert for either lunch or dinner; (ii) in refusing the offer of a starter and a main course for either lunch or dinner C had failed to mitigate her loss; (iii) the measure of damages was what C would have been constrained to pay had she accepted the offer, i.e. the cost of 1 dessert per day in the hotel for the duration of the holiday; (iv) as a matter of law, D's breach of contract was not the cause of C sustaining food poising since the restaurant in question was entirely independent from D and the hotel.

SECTION 7

THE STATUTORY DEFENCES

THE STATUTORY DEFENCES

Franklyn v *Cosmosair Plc*, 25 July 2000, Huddersfield County Court

HHJ JUDGE COCKCROFT

On 17th August 1996 the Claimant and his extended family were enjoying a package holiday provided by the Defendants in the Atlantic Hotel in the Algarve in Portugal. It may well be that on this day was the first occasion the Defendant chose to sit on a white plastic chair by the swimming pool. He and his wife were ahead of the rest of the party and I accept their evidence that immediately he sat down, the chair collapsed. The 2 rear legs sheared off and the Claimant fell, striking his back on the concrete base whose purpose was as a support for a parasol. This was a very unpleasant accident and there were some painful consequences which lasted for 12 months, after which according to the agreed medical evidence the pre-existing condition in Mr Franklyn's spine would have produced his current genuine complaints in any event.

He brings this action against the Defendant company. Before the 1992 Package Travel, Package Tours & Package Holiday Regulations, in cases where there was local negligence abroad, Claimants were left to pursue their claims against hotels in the local courts. But the Regulations enable the Claimant to bring his action against the Tour Operator in this country, subject to common sense restraints. The relevant Regulation is Regulation 15 which says: "[here the Circuit Judge read out Regulation 15(1) and 15(2) of the Regulations]".

Until today it has been part of the Defendants case that the plastic chair collapsed because the Claimant was rocking back on it. There is some suggestion of this in the evidence but it is in the form of speculation and not from any eye witness. The evidence of the joint report from the engineer, Mr Magner says that the failure line was in the shape of inverted wine glasses, which may suggest a rocking movement. But Mr and Mrs Franklyn have given evidence today and I accept that the accident was not a result of him rocking back. So the Defendants allegation under Regulation 15(2)(a) cannot be relied on by them.

So the case turns on Regulation 15(2)(c), unusual and unforeseeable circumstances beyond the control of the Defendant and the hotel.

I proceed on the assumption that the chair collapsed because of some defect in it. The type of chair is used extensively world-wide. It is a MAKRO design, and there were about 40 of them round the swimming pool manufactured by a Spanish company, Resol. The design was approved in Germany when it was given a safety mark in 1993 ... It is a perfectly standard chair accepted world-wide. No criticisms could or should be made of the type of chair. The failure rate is very rare indeed.

So attention focuses on this particular chair. There is material provided from the hotel which the engineer in the course of his report relied on. The information does not have the status of evidence and is not agreed, but it is common sense that I should have regard to it. It is said that the chair was supplied on 14th August 1996. This is not agreed but if I proceed on the basis that the chair was provided new for the summer 1996 season, then the degradation risk can be eliminated. This was a new chair of an approved make and there is no evidence of similar collapses before or since the accident.

[The Defendant's expert reported] *"The probability is that failure would have centred on a foreign body inclusion trapped in the material during moulding or a crack starting either during manufacture or in subsequent handling and storage. The key effect of whatever physical feature may have been at the origin of the failure was to concentrate stress at that point. Whatever form this defect took, it may have been subsurface and of microscopic proportions. If it was, it would not have been discoverable on routine visual inspection."*

Even if the hotel had given the chair visual inspection, the defect therefore would not have been apparent. The report goes on: *"If there was any minor surface indication of such a defect, it is highly unlikely to have been seen on routine examination by a person not experienced in examining materials of this type. The only circumstances under which such a defect could have been rendered visible on routine examination by such a person would have been if it was a slowly developing failure which had grown to the stage of an obvious crack or cracks prior to collapse."*

The Claimant did not himself inspect the chair before sitting on it, apart from a brief assessment that there was no obvious defect with the chair. The Claimant's case must therefore depend on saying that on the balance of probabilities it is for the Defendants to bring themselves within Regulation 15(2)(c) and that in the absence of an examination of the chair, then on balance there is no evidence that the chair was not cracked.

I accept that I have to decide this case on a balance of probabilities, and if I was in the unusual position of feeling that it was just as likely as not that the chair was cracked, then the burden of proof would be relevant – but not in this case. In view of what I have heard ... I am satisfied on a clear balance of probabilities that there was no visible defect with the chair which the hotel, pursuant to its duties to exercise reasonable care, could have noticed and then taken the chair out of use.

So there was no negligence and no breach of contract.

... It is not properly understood in these days when people start actions more readily than they did in the past, that accidents still routinely happen which are not the fault of anyone.

I cannot conclude that the hotel was negligent and I am quite satisfied that this claim should be rejected. ...To hold the Defendant liable would stretch the current law beyond breaking point.

There will therefore be Judgment for the Defendant.

Unauthenticated Decisions

Hayes v *Airtours Holidays Ltd* Current Law Cases: 01/4283

H booked a 14-day package holiday in the Dominican Republic through A, a tour operator. Two days after their arrival at the resort, it was struck by a severe hurricane with the consequence that the resort was wrecked and H had to be moved to another resort in the north of the island. H brought an action for damages contending that A (1) had withheld hurricane forecast information on the predicted path of the hurricane and had thus put its commercial interest above the lives and safety of customers; (2) had failed in its duty of care to warn H of the risk of the hurricane striking the island, and (3) was in breach of contract with particular reference to the Package Travel, Package Holidays and Package Tours Regulations 1992 Reg.15(2) because it had failed to perform the contract to provide the holiday advertised in its brochure. A contended that at the time H flew to the Dominican Republic there was only at most a 20 per cent chance that the hurricane would come within 75 nautical miles of the eastern tip of the island. Accordingly, A was unable to justify cancellation of the holiday, as provided for in Reg.12 because it was not clearly forced or constrained to alter a significant term of or cancel the holiday contract. A could avail itself of the defence in Reg.15(2)(ii)(c) that the hurricane was an event that, even with all due care, it could neither foresee nor forestall.

Held, giving judgment for A, that A did not know or could not reasonably have known that before or at the time of H's departure from the UK, the hurricane was likely to strike the Dominican Republic. It was possible for hurricanes to change course and in any event the best prediction was that it would miss the island. It could not be said that A had been forced pursuant to Reg.12 to cancel holidays or the flight. The damage sustained by H could not have been forestalled even with the exercise of all due care even though hurricanes in the Caribbean were foreseeable. There had not been a duty to warn about poor weather conditions, and the courts should be slow to find a tour operator in breach of contract as a result of poor or extreme weather conditions.

Charlson v *Warner* Current Law Cases: 00/4043

C bought a skiing holiday from W and arrived at the resort in the late afternoon of the first day, being able to ski for a short time that day. The following day there was heavy rain and no ski lifts were open. Over the next three days there was heavy continuous snow and the holiday makers were advised by the local authority to stay in their hotels. Evening curfews were imposed. On the fifth day of the holiday W evacuated C from the resort. C sought damages from W for breach of contract on the basis that W ought to have been able to predict that the snow conditions would be such that it would not be possible for them to enjoy their holiday. W relied upon the defence of force majeure contained within its standard form booking conditions and the Package Travel, Package Holidays and Package Tours Regulations 1992 Reg.15.

Held, giving judgment for W, that (1) the holiday contracts between W and C were for the provision of flights, transfer and hotel accommodation. There was no guarantee within the contract that the holiday makers would be able to ski. The contract did not provide that W would supply skiing; (2) the weather conditions meant that the holiday as contracted for could not be provided in full as C had to be evacuated from the hotel; (3) all of the parties accepted that the weather during that week had been exceptional; (4) W had acted reasonably in obtaining information from the local authorities in the resort as to the weather and relying upon that information; (5) on the evidence, the court was not satisfied that W ought to have been able, even with all due care, to foresee the exceptional weather conditions. W was therefore entitled to rely upon the force majeure defence within its booking conditions and Reg.15(2)(c)(i) of the 1992 Regulations, and (6) C was not entitled to rely upon Reg.14, which provided holiday makers with a right to suitable alternative accommodation at no extra cost if it was not possible to perform the contract. Regulation 14 was dependent upon Reg.15 and had to be read conjunctively, as they were both subject to the same exclusions contained in Reg.15(2)(c).

Hibbs v *Thomas Cook Group Ltd* Current Law Cases: 99/3829

H travelled on a Canadian tour, advertised in T's brochure as the "Rocky Mountain Ranger". The length of the tour was 15 days and 17 nights. Until the tenth day, the tour followed the set itinerary. On day 11, the group were due to travel from Prince Rupert to Port Hardy by ferry. However, the ferry was suddenly withdrawn from service due to an entirely unforeseen mechanical fault. As a result, it became necessary to rearrange the itinerary at extremely short notice, which T did, rerouting the group via Whistler rather than Prince Rupert/Port Hardy, with the effect that the group rejoined the original itinerary in Victoria. H brought an action against T for damages, claiming that T's choice of alternative arrangements was inappropriate and that it effectively ruined the remainder of the holiday. H's claim was for GBP 900, which constituted a refund of one third of the original holiday cost.

Held, dismissing the claim, that the failure of the ferry was a force majeure event, which effectively released T from its obligation to perform the entire contract. T was not under any obligation to put alternative arrangements in place to reroute the tour, it could simply have flown H back to the UK.

Section 8

DAMAGES

Cases in this Section

General Principles

Jarvis v *Swan Tours Limited* [1972] 3 WLR 954 (CA)

LORD DENNING MR

Mr. Jarvis is a solicitor, employed by a local authority at Barking. In 1969 he was minded to go for Christmas to Switzerland. He was looking forward to a skiing holiday. It is his one fortnight's holiday in the year. He prefers it in the winter rather than in the summer. Mr. Jarvis read a brochure issued by Swans Tours Ltd. He was much attracted by the description of Morlialp, Giswil, Central Switzerland. I will not read the whole of it, but just pick out some of the principal attractions:

> "House Party Centre with special resident host. . . . Morlialp is a most wonderful little resort on a sunny plateau . . . Up there you will find yourself in the midst of beautiful alpine scenery, which in winter becomes a wonderland of sun, snow and ice, with a wide variety of fine ski-runs, a skating rink and exhilarating toboggan run . . . Why did we choose the Hotel Krone . . . mainly and most of all because of the 'Gemutlichkeit' and friendly welcome you will receive from Herr and Frau Weibel. . . . The Hotel Krone has its own Alphutte Bar which will be open several evenings a week. . . . No doubt you will be in for a great time, when you book this houseparty holiday . . . Mr. Weibel, the charming owner, speaks English."

Swans House Party in Morlialp. All these House Party arrangements are included in the price of your holiday. Welcome party on arrival. Afternoon tea and cake for 7 days. Swiss dinner by candlelight. Fondue party. Yodler evening. Chali farewell party in the 'Alphutte Bar'. Service of representative. Alongside on the same page there was a special note about ski-packs. "Hire of Skis, Sticks and Boots . . . Ski Tuition . . . 12 days £11.10."

In August 1969, on the faith of that brochure, Mr. Jarvis booked a 15-day holiday, with ski-pack. The total charge was £63.45, including Christmas supplement. He was to fly from Gatwick to Zurich on December 20, 1969, and return on January 3, 1970.

The plaintiff went on the holiday, but he was very disappointed. He was a man of about 35 and he expected to be one of a house party of some 30 or so people. Instead, he found there were only 13 during the first week. In the second week there was no house party at all. He was the only person there. Mr. Weibel could not speak English. So there was Mr. Jarvis, in the second week, in this hotel with no house party at all, and no one could speak English, except himself. He was very disappointed, too, with the ski-ing. It was some distance away at Giswil. There were no ordinary length skis. There were only mini-skis, about 3 ft. long So he did not get his skiing as he wanted to. In the second week he did get some longer skis for a couple of days, but then, because of the boots, his feet got rubbed and he could not continue even with the long skis. So his skiing holiday, from his point of view, was pretty well ruined.

There were many other matters, too. They appear trivial when they are set down in writing, but I have no doubt they loomed large in Mr. Jarvis's mind, when coupled with the other disappointments. He did not have the nice Swiss cakes which he was hoping for. The only cakes for tea were potato crisps and little dry nut cakes. The yodler evening consisted of one man from the locality who came in his working clothes for a little while, and sang four or five songs very quickly. The "Alphutte Bar" was an unoccupied annexe which was only open one evening. There was a representative, Mrs. Storr, there during the first week, but she was not there during the second week.

The matter was summed up by the judge:

> "During the first week he got a holiday in Switzerland which was to some extent inferior . . . and, as to the second week, he got a holiday which was very largely inferior"

What is the legal position? I think that the statements in the brochure were representations or warranties. The breaches of them give Mr. Jarvis a right to damages. It is not necessary to decide whether they were representations or warranties: because since the Misrepresentation Act 1967, there is a remedy in damages for misrepresentation as well as for breach of warranty.

The one question in the case is: What is the amount of damages? The judge seems to have taken the difference in value between what he paid for and what he got. He said that he intended to give "the difference between the two values and no other damages" under any other head. He thought that Mr. Jarvis had got half of what he paid for. So the judge gave him half the amount which he had paid, namely, £31.72. Mr. Jarvis appeals to this court. He says that the damages ought to have been much more.

What is the right way of assessing damages? It has often been said that on a breach of contract damages cannot be given for mental distress. Thus in *Hamlin v. Great Northern Railway Co.* (1856) 1 H. & N. 408, 411 Pollock C.B. said that damages cannot be given "for the disappointment of mind occasioned by the breach of contract." And in *Hobbs v. London & South Western Railway Co.* (1875) L.R. 10 Q.B. 111, 122, Mellor J. said that

> "for the mere inconvenience, such as annoyance and loss of temper, or vexation, or for being disappointed in a particular thing which you have set your mind upon, without real physical inconvenience resulting, you cannot recover damages."

The courts in those days only allowed the plaintiff to recover damages if he suffered physical inconvenience, such as having to walk five miles home, as in *Hobbs'* case; or to live in an over-crowded house, *Bailey v. Bullock* [1950] 2 All E.R. 1167. I think that those limitations are out of date. In a proper case damages for mental distress can be recovered in contract, just as damages for shock can be recovered in tort. One such case is a contract for a holiday, or any other contract to provide entertainment and enjoyment. If the contracting party breaks his contract, damages can be given for the disappointment, the distress, the upset and frustration caused by the breach. I know that it is difficult to assess in terms of money, but it is no more difficult than the assessment which the courts have to make every day in personal injury cases for loss of amenities. Take the present case. Mr. Jarvis has only a fortnight's holiday in the year. He books it far ahead, and looks forward to it all that time. He ought to be compensated for the loss of it.

I think the judge was in error in taking the sum paid for the holiday £63.45 and halving it. The right measure of damages is to compensate him for the loss of entertainment and enjoyment which he was promised, and which he did not get. Looking at the matter quite broadly, I think the damages in this case should be the sum of £125. I would allow the appeal, accordingly.

EDMUND DAVIES LJ:

...If in such circumstances travel agents fail to provide a holiday of the contracted quality, they are liable in damages. In assessing those damages the court is not, in my judgment, restricted by the £63.45 paid by the client for his holiday. Nor is it confined to matters of physical inconvenience and discomfort, or even to quantifying the difference between such items as the expected delicious Swiss cakes and the depressingly desiccated biscuits and crisps provided for tea, between the ski-pack ordered and the miniature skis supplied, nor between the "very good . . . houseparty arrangements" assured and the lone wolf second week of the unfortunate plaintiff's stay. The court is entitled, and indeed bound, to contrast the overall quality of the holiday so enticingly promised with that which the defendants in fact provided. When a man has paid for and properly expects an invigorating and amusing holiday and, through no fault of his, returns home dejected because his expectations have been lagely unfulfilled, in my judgment it would be quite wrong to say that his disappointment must find no reflection in the damages to be awarded. And it is right to add that, in the course of his helpful submissions, Mr. Thompson did not go so far as to submit anything of the kind. Judge Alun Pugh took that view in *Feldman v. Allways Travel Service* [1957] C.L.Y. 934. That, too, was a holiday case. The highly experienced senior county court judge there held that the correct measure of damages was the difference between the price paid and the value of the holiday in fact furnished, "taking into account the plaintiff's feelings of annoyance and frustration."

STEPHENSON LJ:

...The judge has, as I understand his judgment, held that the value of the plaintiff's loss was what he paid under the contract for his holiday; that as a result of the defendants' breaches of contract he has lost not the whole of what he has paid for, but broadly speaking a half of it; and what he has lost and what reduces its value by about one half includes such inconvenience as the plaintiff suffered from the holiday he got not being, by reason of the defendants' breaches, as valuable as the holiday he paid for.

...I further agree with my Lords that the judge was wrong in taking, as I think he must have taken, the amount the plaintiff paid the defendants for his holiday as the value of the holiday which they agreed to provide. They ought to have contemplated, and no doubt did contemplate, that he was accepting their offer of this holiday as an offer of something which would benefit him and which he would enjoy, and that if they broke their contract and provided him with a holiday lacking in some of the things which they contracted to include in it, they would thereby reduce his enjoyment of the holiday and the benefit he would derive from it.

I would add that I think the judge was right in rejecting the plaintiff's ingenious claim, however it is put, for a fortnight's salary. I agree that the appeal should be allowed and the plaintiff be awarded £125 damages.

Leitner v *TUI Deutschland GmbH and Co KG* ECJ C-168/00; [2002] ECR I-2631 (12 March 2002)

JUDGMENT

1. By order of 6 April 2000, received at the Court on 8 May 2000, the Landesgericht (Regional Court) Linz (Austria) referred to the Court for a preliminary ruling under Article 234 EC a question on the interpretation of Article 5 of Council Directive90/314/EEC of 13 June 1990 on package travel, package holidays and package tours (OJ 1990 L 158, p. 59, 'the Directive).

2. That question was raised in proceedings between Simone Leitner and TUI Deutschland GmbH & Co. KG ('TUI) concerning compensation for non-material damage sustained during a package holiday.

The relevant Community provisions

3. The second recital in the preamble to the Directive states that '... the national laws of Member States concerning package travel, package holidays and package tours, hereinafter referred to as packages, show many disparities and national practices in this field are markedly different, which gives rise to obstacles to the freedom to provide services in respect of packages and distortions of competition amongst operators established in different Member States. According to the third recital, 'the establishment of common rules on packages will contribute to the elimination of these obstacles and thereby to the achievement of a common market in services, thus enabling operators established in one Member State to offer their services in other Member States and Community consumers to benefit from comparable conditions when buying a package in any Member State.

4. According to the eighth and ninth recitals in the preamble to the Directive, 'disparities in the rules protecting consumers in different Member States are a disincentive to consumers in one Member State from buying packages in another Member State, and 'this disincentive is particularly effective in deterring consumers from buying packages outside their own Member State.

5. Article 1 provides that 'The purpose of [the] Directive is to approximate the laws, regulations and administrative provisions of the Member States relating to packages sold or offered for sale in the territory of the Community.

6. Article 5 provides that:

'1. Member States shall take the necessary steps to ensure that the organiser and/or retailer party to the contract is liable to the consumer for the proper performance of the obligations arising from the contract, irrespective of whether such obligations are to be performed by that organiser and/or retailer or by other suppliers of services without prejudice to the right of the organiser and/or retailer to pursue those other suppliers of services.

2. With regard to the damage resulting for the consumer from the failure to perform or the improper performance of the contract, Member States shall take the necessary steps to ensure that the organiser and/or retailer is/are liable unless such failure to perform or improper performance is attributable neither to any fault of theirs nor to that of another supplier of services...

...

In the matter of damages arising from the non-performance or improper performance of the services involved in the package, the Member States may allow compensation to be limited in accordance with the international conventions governing such services.

In the matter of damage other than personal injury resulting from the non-performance or improper performance of the services involved in the package, the Member States may allow compensation to be limited under the contract. Such limitation shall not be unreasonable.

(3) Without prejudice to the fourth subparagraph of paragraph 2, there may be no exclusion by means of a contractual clause from the provisions of paragraphs 1 and 2.'

...

The dispute in the main proceedings and the question referred

7. The family of Simone Leitner (who was born on 7 July 1987) booked a package holiday (all-inclusive stay) with TUI at the 'Pamfiliya Robinson club in Side, Turkey ('the club) for the period 4 to 18 July 1997.

8. On 4 July 1997 Simone Leitner and her parents arrived at the club. There they spent the entire holiday and there they took all their meals. About a week after the start of the holiday, Simone Leitner showed symptoms of salmonella poisoning. The poisoning was attributable to the food offered in the club. The illness, which lasted beyond the end of the holiday, manifested itself in a fever of up to 40 degrees over several days, circulatory difficulties, diarrhoea, vomiting and anxiety. Her parents had to look after her until the end of the holiday. Many other guests in the club also fell ill with the same illness and presented the same symptoms.

9. Two to three weeks after the end of the holiday a letter of complaint concerning Simone Leitner's illness was sent to TUI. Since no reply to that letter was received, Simone Leitner, through her parents, brought an action for damages in the sum of ATS 25 000.

10. The court of first instance awarded the claimant only ATS 13,000 for the physical pain and suffering ('Schmerzensgeld) caused by the food poisoning and dismissed the remainder of the application, which was for compensation for the non-material damage caused by loss of enjoyment of the holidays ('entgangene Urlaubsfreude). That court considered that, if the feelings of dissatisfaction and negative impressions caused by disappointment must be categorised, under Austrian law, as non-material damage, they cannot give rise to compensation because there is no express provision in any Austrian law for compensation for non-material damage of that kind.

11. The claimant appealed to the Landesgericht Linz, which concurs with the court of first instance so far as regards Austrian law, but considers that application of Article 5 of the Directive could lead to a different outcome. In that connection, the Landesgericht cites Case C-355/96 Silhouette International Schmied [1998] ECR I-4799, paragraph 36, where the Court ruled that, while a directive cannot of itself impose obligations on an individual and cannot therefore be relied upon as such

against an individual, a national court is required to interpret the provisions of national law in the light of the wording and the purpose of the directive so as to achieve the result it has in view.

12. The national court observes in addition that the German legislature has adopted legislation expressly concerning compensation for non-material damage where a journey is prevented or significantly interfered with and that in practice German courts do award such compensation.

13. Taking the view that the wording of Article 5 of the Directive is not precise enough for it to be possible to draw from it any definite conclusion as to non-material damage, the Landesgericht Linz decided to stay proceedings and to refer the following question to the Court for a preliminary ruling:

Is Article 5 of Council Directive 90/314/EEC of 13 June 1990 on package travel, package holidays and package tours to be interpreted as meaning that compensation is in principle payable in respect of claims for compensation for non-material damage?

The question

14. By its question the national court seeks to ascertain whether Article 5 of the Directive must be interpreted as conferring, in principle, on consumers a right to compensation for non-material damage resulting from failure to perform or the improper performance of the obligations inherent in the provision of package travel.

Arguments of the parties

15. According to Simone Leitner, the third recital in the preamble to the Directive makes it clear that operators must be able to offer packages in all the Member States on the same conditions. The fourth subparagraph of Article 5(2) of the Directive makes it possible to set contractual limits to liability incurred in the case of non-material damage resulting from the non-performance or improper performance of the services constituting a package holiday. That provision means that, according to the Directive, non-material damage must in principle be the subject of compensation.

16. TUI and the Austrian, French and Finnish Governments are, essentially, at one in arguing that the harmonisation of national laws sought by the Directive consists merely of defining a minimum level of protection for consumers of package holidays. In consequence, anything not expressly covered by the Directive in that field, and in particular the kind of damage to be compensated, remains within the competence of the national legislatures. The Directive does no more than set out a body of essential common rules concerning the content, conclusion and performance of package tour contracts without exhaustively regulating the entire subject, in particular, matters relating to civil liability. Accordingly, the existence of a right to compensation for non-material damage cannot be inferred from the absence of an express reference thereto in the Directive.

17. The Belgian Government submits that the general and unrestricted use of the term 'damage in the first subparagraph of Article 5(2) of the Directive implies that that term is to be construed broadly, with the result that damage of every kind must in principle be covered by the legislation implementing the Directive. In those Member States which recognise liability for non-material damage under the ordinary law, the

Directive provides the right to set limits to that liability in accordance with certain criteria. In those Member States in which liability for non-material damage depends on the existence of an express provision to that effect, the absence of such a provision must be deemed to exclude absolutely compensation for non-material damage, which is contrary to the Directive.

18. The Commission first points out that the term 'damage is used in the Directive without the least restriction, and that, specifically in the field of holiday travel, damage other than physical injury is a frequent occurrence. It then notes that liability for non-material damage is recognised in most Member States, over and above compensation for physical pain and suffering traditionally provided for in all legal systems, although the extent of that liability and the conditions under which it is incurred vary in detail. Lastly, all modern legal systems attach ever greater importance to annual leave. In those circumstances, the Commission maintains that it is not possible to interpret restrictively the general concept of damage used in the Directive and to exclude from it as a matter of principle non-material damage.

Findings of the Court

19. The first subparagraph of Article 5(2) of the Directive requires the Member States to take the necessary steps to ensure that the holiday organiser compensates 'the damage resulting for the consumer from the failure to perform or the improper performance of the contract.

20. In that regard, it is clear from the second and third recitals in the preamble to the Directive that it is the purpose of the Directive to eliminate the disparities between the national laws and practices of the various Member States in the area of package holidays which are liable to give rise to distortions of competition between operators established in different Member States.

21. It is not in dispute that, in the field of package holidays, the existence in some Member States but not in others of an obligation to provide compensation for non-material damage would cause significant distortions of competition, given that, as the Commission has pointed out, non-material damage is a frequent occurrence in that field.

22. Furthermore, the Directive, and in particular Article 5 thereof, is designed to offer protection to consumers and, in connection with tourist holidays, compensation for non-material damage arising from the loss of enjoyment of the holiday is of particular importance to consumers.

23. It is in light of those considerations that Article 5 of the Directive is to be interpreted. Although the first subparagraph of Article 5(2) merely refers in a general manner to the concept of damage, the fact that the fourth subparagraph of Article 5(2) provides that Member States may, in the matter of damage other than personal injury, allow compensation to be limited under the contract provided that such limitation is not unreasonable, means that the Directive implicitly recognises the existence of a right to compensation for damage other than personal injury, including non-material damage.

24. The answer to be given to the question referred must therefore be that Article 5 of the Directive is to be interpreted as conferring, in principle, on consumers a right to

compensation for non-material damage resulting from the non-performance or improper performance of the services constituting a package holiday.

Costs

25. The costs incurred by the Austrian, Belgian, French and Finnish Governments, and by the Commission, which have submitted observations to the Court, are not recoverable. Since these proceedings are, for the parties to the main proceedings, a step in the action pending before the national court, the decision on costs is a matter for that court.

On those grounds, THE COURT (Sixth Chamber), in answer to the question referred to it by the Landesgericht Linz by order of 6 April 2000, hereby rules:

Article 5 of Council Directive 90/314/EEC of 13 June 1990 on package travel, package holidays and package tours is to be interpreted as conferring, in principle, on consumers a right to compensation for non-material damage resulting from the non-performance or improper performance of the services constituting a package holiday.

Jackson v *Horizon Holidays Ltd* [1975] 1 WLR 1468 (CA)

Denning MR, Orr and James LJJ

The plaintiff booked a holiday at a named hotel in Ceylon for himself, his wife, and twin boys aged three, through the defendants, a travel company, after studying their holiday brochures, stating in a letter his precise requirements with regard to accommodation for the family, food, amenities and facilities, and receiving an assurance that they would be met. The price payable was £1,432. Shortly before the departure date, the defendants informed him that the hotel he had chosen would not be ready in time and they offered him for £1,200 a substitute which was also described in glowing terms in the brochure. He accepted it after being assured that it would be as good as his original choice. The accommodation, food, services, facilities and general standard of the hotel to which they were transported proved so unsatisfactory that the whole family suffered discomfort, vexation, inconvenience and distress and went home disappointed. The plaintiff brought an action against the travel company, claiming damages for misrepresentation and breaches of contract. The company, though initially denying all the allegations, later admitted liability. On the trial of the issue as to damages the trial judge awarded the plaintiff £1,100. He did not divide up that sum in any way; but he stated specifically that the damages were the plaintiff's and that though he could consider the effect on the plaintiff's mind of his wife's discomfort and the like, he could not award a sum which represented her own vexation.

Held, dismissing the appeal, (1) that the plaintiff had made a contract for a family holiday and though only he could sue for damages for breaches of that contract he could recover damages not only for his own discomfort and distress but also for the distress and discomfort suffered by his wife and children by reason of the defendants' breaches of the contract to provide them with the holiday for which the plaintiff had contracted. (2)That though the sum awarded would have been excessive if awarded only for the damage suffered by the plaintiff, it was a right and proper figure when extended to his wife and children.

Lord Denning M.R.: (at page 1472-3)

We have had an interesting discussion as to the legal position when one person makes a contract for the benefit of a party. In this case it was a husband making a contract for the benefit of himself, his wife and children. Other cases readily come to mind. A host makes a contract with a restaurant for dinner for himself and his friends. The vicar makes a contract for a coach trip for the choir. In all these cases there is only one person who makes the contract. It is the husband, the host or the vicar...

It would be a fiction to say that the contract was made by all the family, or all the guests, or all the choir... It would equally be a mistake to say that in any of these instances there was a trust. The transaction bears no resemblance to a trust.

What is the position when such a contract is broken? At present the law says that the only one who can sue is the one who made the contract. None of the rest of the party can sue, even though the contract was made for their benefit. But when that one does sue, what damages can he recover? Is he limited to his own loss? Or can he recover for the others? Suppose the holiday firm puts the family into a hotel that which is only half built and the visitors have to sleep on the floor? Or suppose the restaurant is fully booked and the guests have to go away, hungry and angry, having spent so much on fares to get there? Or suppose the coach leaves the choir stranded halfway and they have to hire cars to get home? None of them individually can sue. Only the father, the host or the vicar can sue. He can, of course, recover his own damages. But can not recover for the others? I think he can.

...It is the only way a just result can be achieved... Once (damages are) recovered, it will be money had and received to their use.

Farley v *Skinner* Case No: FC3 1999/7524/A2; QBENI 1999/0643/A2 (6 April 2000)

Stuart-Smith LJ

The Claimant's pleaded case
1. By his 'Re-amended Statement of Claim' the claimant pleaded the following matters:

> "1. The defendant is a chartered surveyor in practice at Hurstpierpoint in Sussex. In or about December 1990 he accepted the plaintiff's instructions to inspect and report on a private dwelling-house called Riverside House, Blackboys, East Sussex (`the property'). The plaintiff explained, as was the case, that he was considering the purchase and refurbishment of the property for his own use and occupation, especially for weekends and holidays. He specifically asked the defendant to advise whether the property might be affected by aircraft noise.
>
> 2. The defendant accepted those instructions and accordingly owed the plaintiff a duty to inspect and report on the said property with the skill and care to be expected of a reasonably competent chartered surveyor.
>
> 5. The defendant inspected the said property on Monday 10 December 1990. On Monday 17 December 1990 he reported to the plaintiff in writing. He did so knowing that the plaintiff would rely on his report in deciding whether to purchase and refurbish the property. But the defendant failed to inspect and report with reasonable skill and care. On
>
> page 35 of his report he wrote:
>
> > "You have also asked whether you [sic] felt the property might be affected by aircraft noise, but we were not conscious of this during the time of our inspection, and think it unlikely that the property will suffer greatly from such noise, although some planes will inevitably cross the area, depending on the direction of the wind and the positioning of the flight paths."
>
> 6. That advice was negligent. Had the defendant taken reasonable care he could have ascertained that the property was a short distance from a navigation beacon and that from time to time, especially at weekends, its use and enjoyment was badly affected by aircraft noise."

2. Paragraphs 6 and 7 plead the claimant's purchase and expenditure of substantial sums in refurbishment. Paragraph 8 alleges that it was not until early 1985 when the claimant took up residence that he discovered that the property was affected by aircraft noise. The date is wrong and should be June 1991.

3. Paragraph 9 claims the loss and damage as follows:

> "By reason of the defendant's negligence as aforesaid the plaintiff has
> incurred loss and suffered damage; and he claims damages on his own
> behalf and as trustee for himself and Mr David Parsons.
>
> Particulars
>
> (i)   The value of the property, had it been (in respect of aircraft noise)
>   as described by the defendant on page 35 of his report, would have
>   equated with the price paid by the plaintiff or thereabouts. Its true
>   value, affected as it is by aircraft noise, was and is substantially less
>
> (ii)   The plaintiff's use and enjoyment of the property has been
>   impaired by aircraft noise."

By amendment there was a claim for £63,000 - the cost of removal on the basis that
the claimant had decided to sell and move house because of the noise. He later
changed his mind and that claim was deleted. There was also a claim for the cost of
refurbishment; but that claim was also deleted by amendment. I have set out the
material part of the pleadings because it is of some importance in this case to see how
the case was pleaded and presented in the court below.

The Judge's findings
4. In his judgment, given on 27 May 1999, His Honour Judge Peter Baker QC, sitting
as a judge of the High Court, accepted the claimant's account of the conversation in
which the instructions were given to the defendant. As pleaded in the 'Further and
Better Particulars' it was said:

> "The plaintiff spoke to the defendant on the telephone at great length some
> weeks before the report was written. He cannot recall the precise words he
> used in the course of this conversation (which dealt with a number of
> matters) but they were to this effect: "I want you to check that there is no
> problem with aircraft noise, because the house is within a fifteen mile radius
> of Gatwick. I want you to make sure it is not on a flight path and is not
> affected by aircraft noise." "

In evidence he said:

> "I want you to check whether there is a problem with aircraft noise because
> the house is within 15 miles' radius of Gatwick. I want you to make sure it
> is not on a flightpath and that it is not affected by aircraft noise.
> Alternatively I asked him to check whether or not the property would be
> affected by aircraft noise particularly because of its relative proximity to
> Gatwick. I said I particularly did not want to be on a flightpath."

5. The problem with aircraft noise is that between about 6-8am and between 5.30-
7pm aircraft coming into land at Gatwick tend to stack up at what is called the
Mayfield Stack, if they cannot find a slot to land. The judge described it as follows:

> "The position is, with regard to aircraft noise, as is clear from the documentary evidence that has been obtained, that there is the Mayfield stack which is not far away which aeroplanes join at a certain height and maintain in a sort of spiral, as it were, until there is a slot ready for them to land at Gatwick. That means that one aircraft may pass and repass on more than one occasion."

and

> "It is fair to say that these aircraft are some miles away, and they are not below, I think, usually, about 6,000 feet although very occasionally there is one lower than that. Nobody claims that it is at Mr Farley's house, rather like having a house at the end of a B52 runway, but it is a question of degree, and Mr Atwood's evidence was called to help me on that matter."

Mr Atwood was a sound engineer called on the claimant's behalf. The house was nowhere near the flight path in and out of Gatwick, that being 20 miles to the north.

6. The judge held that the defendant was liable. It is not entirely clear to me in what respects the judge held Mr Skinner to have been negligent. All he says is, "It seems plain to me that Mr Skinner was not properly or adequately carrying out his instructions." But it seems to have been accepted by the defendant that if the instructions were as the claimant alleged, Mr Skinner should have made enquiries of the Civil Aviation Authority at Gatwick, and that if he had done so, he would have learnt of the Mayfield Stack. Be that as it may, and despite what might be thought somewhat imprecise instructions and a guarded answer given by Mr Skinner in his report (set out in paragraph 5 of the `Re-Amended Statement of Claim'), the judge's finding of negligence is not challenged by the

Appellant in this court.

7. The judge rejected the claimant's principal claim for diminution in value of the property in the sum of about £70,000. In so doing he preferred the evidence of the defendant's expert witness; there was also agreed evidence of three of the claimant's neighbours who said they were not in the least troubled by aircraft noise and that of a chartered surveyor who was familiar with properties in the neighbourhood who said that aircraft noise was not a factor raised in relation to property in the area and Blackboys was not materially affected by aircraft noise.

8. However, the judge awarded the claimant £10,000 for distress and inconvenience caused by the noise. The judge's findings with regard to the effect on the claimant were as follows:

> "Firstly he is particularly vulnerable because he has a habit, practice, of being an early riser and of wishing, when clement weather conditions prevail as even in this country occasionally do, to sit outside on his terrace, or whatever, and enjoy the delightful gardens, the pool and the other amenities which is made pretty intolerable, he says, and I accept from his point of view between say, the hours of 6 o'clock and 8 o'clock in the morning

which is the time when he would be minded to do this.

Likewise, pre-dinner drinks are not made the better for the evening activity in the sky not far away. That he is not a man, if I may say so, with excessive susceptibilities is shown by the fact that he did his best to grit his teeth and put up with it but, as he ultimately said, "Why should I when I had endeavoured to cover this particular point in the instructions that I had given to a professional man who I had paid to do this?" He finds it a confounded nuisance, and this is a matter that, of course, he will be stuck with. It is not a case of something like drains or dry rot or what have you that he can do anything about. Short of buying Gatwick and closing it down, this is a matter that will continue."

9. The judge referred to the case of *Watts v Morrow* [1991] 1 WLR 1421 and said, "It seems to me that the interference was very much less than the real discomfort that has been sustained by Mr Farley in this case." It is against the award of £10,000 that the defendant appeals to this court.

The Law

11. The law is succinctly stated in the much cited judgment of Bingham LJ in *Watts v Morrow* [1991] 1 WLR 1421. The main question in that case was whether on a claim for breach of contract against a surveyor on the grounds that he had negligently failed to report certain defects in the house which the claimant proposed to buy, the claimant could recover the cost of making good the defects or only the diminution in value of the house by reason of the existence of those defects. The court held that the latter was the proper measure of the damage. But the court also considered whether the claimant could recover damages for distress and inconvenience. At p1445 Bingham LJ said:

> "A contract breaker is not in general liable for any distress, frustration, anxiety, displeasure, vexation, tension or aggravation which his breach of contract may cause to the innocent party. This rule is not, I think, founded on the assumption that such reactions are not foreseeable, which they surely are or may be, but on considerations of policy.

> But the rule is not absolute. Where the very object of a contract is to provide pleasure, relaxation, peace of mind or freedom from molestation, damages will be awarded if the fruit of the contract is not provided or if the contrary result is procured instead. If the law did not cater for this exceptional category of case it would be defective. A contract to survey the condition of a house for a prospective purchaser does not, however, fall within this exceptional category.

> In cases not falling within this exceptional category, damages are in my view recoverable for physical inconvenience and discomfort caused by the breach and mental suffering directly related to that inconvenience and discomfort. If those effects are foreseeably suffered during a period when defects are repaired I am prepared to accept that they sound in damages even though the cost of the repairs is not recoverable as such."

The reference to cases in the exceptional category are exemplified by the cases of *Jarvis v Swan Tours Ltd* [1973] QB 233 and *Heywood v Wellers* [1976] QB 446.

21. Was this a contract to provide pleasure, relaxation or peace of mind, so that it comes within that exceptional class of contract for which damages for non-physical distress and annoyance can be awarded? The first point to make is that this was not the way the case was pleaded or presented in the court below; nor was the point raised in a respondent's notice. That does not necessarily prevent this court from entertaining it if it is a pure point of law.

> "*Addis v. Gramophone Co. Ltd.* established the general rule that in claims for breach of contract, the plaintiff cannot recover damages for his injured feelings. But the rule, like most rules, is subject to exceptions. One of the well established exceptions is when the object of the contract is to afford pleasure as, for example, where the plaintiff has booked a holiday with a tour operator. If the tour operator is in breach of contract by failing to provide what the contract called for, the plaintiff may recover damages for his disappointment: see *Jarvis v. Swan Tours Ltd.* [1973] Q.B. 233 and *Jackson v. Horizon Holidays Ltd.* [1975] 1 WLR 1468.
>
> This was, as I understand it, the principle which Judge Diamond applied in the present case. He took the view that the contract was one "for the provision of a pleasurable amenity." In the event, Mr. Forsyth's pleasure was not so great as it would have been if the swimming pool had been 7 feet 6 inches deep. This was a view which the judge was entitled to take. If it involves a further inroad on the rule in *Addis v. Gramophone Co. Ltd.* [1909] AC 488, then so be it. But I prefer to regard it as a logical application or adaptation of the existing exception to a new situation…"

29. I see no reason why it should be thought that these passages affect the decision in *Watts v Morrow* which was cited in argument, but not referred to in the speeches. It is not difficult to classify a contract to build a swimming pool as one of the *Jarvis v Swans Tours Ltd* category of contract. In the *Ruxley* case there was an express contractual obligation to achieve a result, not simply an obligation to exercise reasonable care and skill in giving information or advice; the nature of the contractual obligation is entirely different.

Mummery LJ
31. I agree with the judgment of Stuart-Smith LJ.

In view of the sharp division of judicial opinion on the first and second hearings of this appeal I shall add a few observations in favour of allowing the appeal.

(1) Policy Considerations.
32. The relevant legal principles were stated by Bingham LJ in *Watts -v- Morrow*. He mentioned, but did not discuss, the "considerations of policy " on which the courts base the **general** rule that compensation for intangible (i.e. non-pecuniary, non-physical) harm is not recoverable in an action for breach of contract. The policy factors are so patent that they do not require much elaboration, though they are

worth re-stating, as Mr Spencer contends that the general rule should be reconsidered in the light of *Ruxley Electronics -v- Forsyth* [1996] AC 344.

33. The policy considerations are discussed by Lord Justice Stuart-Smith in paragraphs 18 and 19 of his judgment. They were examined by the Law Commission in Part II of Consultation Paper No. 132 on Aggravated, Exemplary and Restitutionary Damages (1993) under the headings of incommensurability, subjectivity and difficulties of proof.

Paragraph 2.12 of the Consultation Paper stated that

> "Compensation involves the reparation of harm by the delivery of an equivalent or equivalent value. Compensation which takes the monetary form of compensatory damages therefore encounters peculiar difficulties when the harm is non-pecuniary. There is no exact equivalent and no standard measure of assessment by reference to which the harm can be converted into monetary form......This incommensurability gives rise to real danger of indeterminacy and of inconsistent awards."

I agree.

34. The incontrovertible fact is that the unobservable subjective nature and extent of intangible harm means that it is inherently difficult to prove (or to refute) ; that, even if properly proved, it is impossible to measure as there are no objective standards and no solid comparables ; that, even if "measured", the amount awarded is open to the trenchant criticisms that it is not truly or wholly compensatory, that it contains an impermissible punitive element and that it reflects the intrusion of an unacceptable level of subjectivity on the part of the judge ; and that the whole exercise fails to satisfy a fundamental requirement of a fair and workable litigation system that the outcome of a claim should be reasonably predictable, both as to liability and quantum, so that the parties and their advisers can negotiate satisfactory compromises and make informed decisions on Part 36 offers and payments and their acceptance. As to the last point see the speech of Lord

Steyn in *Wells -v- Wells* [1999] 1 AC 345 at 388D-E.

35. The significance of the policy considerations is demonstrated by the facts of this case and the history of these proceedings recounted in the judgment of Lord Justice Stuart-Smith. I shall comment on only two points: the nature of the harm and the nature of the contract.

(2) *The Nature of the Harm.*

36. What harm has Mr Farley suffered? He is upset by the noise of aircraft flying over the garden of Riverside House en route for Gatwick. The noise is "a confounded nuisance" in the early morning and early evening. Those are the times of day when he likes to relax in the garden.

37. In order to succeed in his claim for damages for professional negligence Mr Farley has to prove that he has suffered (a) pecuniary loss and/or (b) physical inconvenience or physical discomfort and directly related "mental suffering" caused by Mr Skinner's

breach of duty. Pecuniary loss was not established. Although the judge concluded that Mr Farley had suffered "real discomfort" there was no evidence that this amounted to anything more than upset and annoyance at hearing the sound of aircraft noise which diminished his enjoyment of the garden. That complaint was unrelated to any physical inconvenience or to any physical discomfort suffered by him and cannot reasonably be described as directly related "mental suffering."

38. I do not understand why Mr Farley should be legally entitled to recover from his surveyor any damages for hearing aircraft noise in his garden when Mr Addis was told by the House of Lords in *Addis -v- Gramophone Co Ltd* [1909] AC 486 that he was not entitled to recover any damages from his employer for injury to his feelings on hearing the news that he was dismissed, wrongfully and in a harsh and humiliating manner. That kind of harm is treated by the law as an uncompensatable risk of life, whether it be in employment or in the purchase and occupation of a home.

39. I appreciate the strength of Mr Farley's feelings: Mr Skinner negligently failed to check the position with the Civil Aviation Authority and the information supplied to him by Mr Skinner about aircraft noise affected his decision to buy a house which he would not otherwise have bought. But Mr Farley has not proved that he has suffered any pecuniary or physical harm in consequence of that negligence. The law binding on this court has been applied in many other cases and is reinforced by rational and pragmatic policy considerations. The law is that Mr Farley's perception that the tranquillity of his garden is spoilt by the presence of aircraft noise is not a recoverable head of damage against Mr Skinner.

40. Even if it was, the quantification of the claim exposes the judicial process to serious misgivings. I do not understand by what reasoning or on what evidence the compensation under this head was assessed at £10,000. Why not £5,000? Why not £20,000? The judge attempted to do his best on exiguous material to measure the unmeasurable and in the result awarded compensation for the uncompensatable. He was invited to participate in an exercise which was more like a lucky dip than a judicial process.

(3) *The Nature of the Contract*

41. It is impossible to regard the contract between Mr Skinner and Mr Farley as falling within the exceptional class of case in which the very object of the contract is to produce a particular pleasurable result, such as a relaxing holiday, a leisure amenity or a recreational activity. Mr Skinner was retained as a surveyor to inspect and report on Riverside House. It was not a contract for Mr Skinner to produce a result of rustic tranquillity. It was a contract for him to supply information, including information on the position as to aircraft noise, so that Mr Farley could decide whether or not to enter into another contract i.e for the purchase of Riverside.

42. If Mr Skinner's failure to perform his professional task with reasonable skill and care had resulted in the purchase of a property worth less than Mr Farley had paid for it or in Mr Farley incurring the expense of selling up and moving elsewhere, or in physical inconvenience or physical discomfort directly leading to mental suffering, then damages could be recovered by Mr Farley. But this is not such a case. Even if it

was in the contemplation of the parties that the level of aircraft noise would affect Mr Farley's pleasure in the use of the garden at Riverside, damages for his disappointment and diminished pleasure are not, for the policy reasons discussed above, recoverable for breach of this kind of contract.

Clarke LJ (Dissenting)

General Damages

44. The first question in this appeal is whether judge was right to award general damages to the claimant. I am bound to say that unassisted by authority I would unhesitatingly hold that he was. The defendant was in breach of contract and in breach of his duty of care owed to the claimant at law in failing to exercise reasonable care and skill in obtaining information about aircraft noise and passing it on to the claimant. As a result the claimant bought a property which he would not have bought but for the breach. Once he ascertained the extent of the noise he acted reasonably in not selling the property but in putting up with it. The noise was variously described by the judge as `pretty intolerable', `a confounded nuisance' and `a real discomfort'. If the claimant had sold the property and moved because of the noise it seems to me to be likely that it would have cost him significantly more than the £10,000 which he was awarded. In my judgment, he would in that event have been entitled to recover by way of damages from the defendant the reasonable cost of buying and selling the property and of moving to a new property. By not moving and putting up with the noise he thus saved the defendant money.

45. In all these circumstances, in my opinion, the claimant should in principle be entitled to recover general damages from the defendant and any analysis which leads to the conclusion that he is entitled to nothing should be exposed to detailed scrutiny. The argument that such damages are not recoverable depends upon the principles in *Watts v Morrow* and their application to the facts of this case. *Watts v Morrow* is one of a long line of cases which are not all easy to reconcile. It is I think important to note that it does not stand alone and must be considered in its context. Like many other cases it was concerned with the circumstances in which damages for non-pecuniary loss can be recovered for breach of contract.

46. The problem which the cases have sought to address is in what circumstances it is appropriate to permit a claimant to recover damages for breach of contract for non-pecuniary loss. It has long been recognised that it would not be appropriate to permit a claimant to recover damages for breach of a commercial contract in respect of disappointment or mental distress flowing, however directly, from the breach. Moreover, it has been so held notwithstanding the fact that the distress may have been within the reasonable contemplation of the parties when the contract was made. Leading cases include, in the employment context, *Addis v Gramophone Co Ltd* [1909] AC 488. The reason for the general principle is essentially one of policy. Thus, for example, in *Hayes v James & Charles Dodd* [1990] 2 All ER 815 Staughton LJ said (at page 823) that he would not view with enthusiasm the prospect that every shipowner who successfully claimed freight or demurrage could add a claim for general damages for mental distress suffered while he was waiting for his money. I agree.

47. The general principle is that damages for breach of an ordinary commercial contract cannot be recovered in order to compensate the claimant for disappointment or distress. *Watts v Morrow* is one of many cases which have explored the circumstances in which general damages can be recovered for non-pecuniary loss suffered as a result of a breach of contract. The principal judgment was given by Ralph Gibson LJ, but the relevant principles are concisely stated by Bingham LJ at page 1445 in what has become a much cited passage:

> "A contract-breaker is not in general liable for any distress, frustration, anxiety, displeasure, vexation, tension or aggravation which his breach of contract may cause to the innocent party. This rule is not, I think, founded on the assumption that such reactions are not foreseeable, which they surely are or may be, but on considerations of policy.

> But the rule is not absolute. Where the very object of a contract is to provide pleasure, relaxation, peace of mind or freedom from molestation, damages will be awarded if the fruit of the contract is not provided or if the contrary result is procured instead. If the law did not cater for this exceptional category of case it would be de defective. A contract to survey the condition of a house for a prospective purchaser does not, however, fall within this exceptional category.

> In cases not falling within this exceptional category, damages are in my view recoverable for physical inconvenience and discomfort caused by the breach and mental suffering directly related to that inconvenience and discomfort. If those effects are foreseeable suffered during a period when defects are repaired I am prepared to accept that they sound in damages even though the cost of the repairs is not recoverable as such. But I also agree that awards should be restrained, and that the awards in this case far exceeded a reasonable award for the injury shown to have been suffered. I agree with the figures which Ralph Gibson L.J. proposes to substitute."

48. It can be seen that there are potentially two bases upon which general damages may be recoverable in this class of case. The first is where the breach has caused physical inconvenience and discomfort or, perhaps, physical discomfort or inconvenience. Various different descriptions have been given in the cases to what has to be proved under this head, to which I now turn.

Physical Inconvenience and Discomfort

49. At the trial it was submitted on behalf of the claimant that the facts of this case fall into the exceptional category which Bingham LJ described as `physical inconvenience and discomfort' caused by the breach. As I read his judgment, the judge accepted that submission. If he had not done so, he could not have found for the claimant because no other basis of recoverability of general damages was advanced. Mr Simpson submitted on behalf of the defendant that the judge was wrong so to hold. In order to decide whether the judge was right or wrong it is I think helpful to consider what circumstances have been held to amount to physical inconvenience and discomfort in this context.

50. It is to my mind important to note that damages are recoverable under this head for physical inconvenience and that it is not necessary to establish any kind of

physical injury or loss, or indeed mental distress. Thus, for example, in an early case, *Hobbs v London and South Western Railway Co* (1874) LR 10 QB 111, the plaintiff his wife and two children took tickets on the defendant's railway from Wimbledon to Hampton Court by the midnight train. They were taken to Esher instead of Hampton Court and had to walk between four and five miles home. The jury awarded £8 general damages for the inconvenience of having to walk home. It was held by a Divisional Court of the Queen's Bench that those damages were recoverable. Cockburn CJ said (at page 111) that there was no authority that `personal inconvenience, where it is sufficiently serious, should not be the subject of damages' for breach of contract as being taken to be within the contemplation of the parties. Blackburn J put it in much the same way at page 121. Mellor J put the distinction between recoverable and irrecoverable damages thus (at page 122):

> "I quite agree with my brother Parry, that for the mere inconvenience, such as annoyance and loss of temper, or vexation, or for being disappointed in a particular thing which you have set your mind upon, without real physical inconvenience resulting, you cannot recover damages. That is purely sentimental, and not a case where the word inconvenience, as I here use it, would apply. But I must say, if it is a fact that you arrived at a place where you did not intend to go to, where you are placed, by reason of the breach of contract of the carriers, at a considerable distance from your destination, the case may be otherwise. It is admitted that if there be a carriage you may hire it and ride home and charge the expense to the defendants. The reason why you may hire a carriage and charge the expense to the company is with the view simply of mitigating the inconvenience to which you would otherwise be subject; so that where the inconvenience is real and substantial arising from being obliged to walk home, I cannot see why that should not be capable of being assessed as damages in respect of inconvenience."

His test was thus 'real and substantial physical inconvenience'.

51. That approach has been followed in a number of cases since 1874, to which it is necessary to refer to only a few. For example, in *Bailey v Bullock* [1950] 2 All ER 1167 the defendant failed, in breach of contract, to exercise reasonable care and skill as the plaintiff's solicitor. As a result the plaintiff did not obtain possession of a dwelling house which he had let and he and his wife had to live in cramped conditions with his parents in law. Bray J held that damages for inconvenience and discomfort were recoverable. In doing so he followed *Burton v Pinkerton* (1867) LR 2 Exch 340 and *Hobbs v London and South Western Railway*. He said (at page 1170) that there was a real difference between what he described as `mere annoyance and injury to feelings, on the one hand, and physical inconvenience, on the other'. He then quoted the part of the judgment of Mellor J in the *Hobbs* case which I have set out above, and referred to the judgments of the other members of the court, which he said decided that in a case based on a breach of contract alone damages could be awarded for `serious physical inconvenience and discomfort'. He added (at page 1171):

> "During the course of the argument before me, counsel for the defendants was disposed to admit that if in the present case the plaintiff had chosen to mitigate the discomfort to which he was subjected by taking rooms for

himself and his family at an hotel or making other arrangements for his accommodation, it would have been extremely difficult for the defendants to have resisted a claim for special damages based on the cost of such accommodation. It would indeed, be curious if, in the circumstances of this case, because the plaintiff suffered the inconvenience rather than incur expense to avoid it, he should be deprived of any remedy. Such, in my opinion, is not the law. I consider that *Hobbs'* case and *Burton v Pinkerton* clearly establish that in a proper case damages for personal inconvenience may be recoverable in an action of this kind. "

52. Those seem to me to be powerful considerations. They also show that no distinction is to be drawn for this purpose between a case like *Hobbs*, where the contractual obligation was to achieve a certain result, and a case like *Bailey*, where the contractual obligation was simply to exercise reasonable care and skill.

53. *Watts v Morrow* was itself a case in which the plaintiffs, who were a husband and wife, instructed the defendant to survey a property which they proposed to purchase as a second home. The defendant made a report which referred to a number of defects but failed to identify a number of other defects which were subsequently found to exist. The judge held that that failure amounted to a breach of the defendant's duty to exercise reasonable care and skill as a solicitor. If the plaintiffs had known of the defects, they would either not have bought the house at all or only at a much reduced price. A considerable amount of repair work was carried out during which the plaintiffs spent their week-ends at the house in what Mr Watts described (and I think the judge accepted) were deplorable conditions.

54. This court held that that the claimants were entitled to damages for the diminution in value of the property as a result of the defendant's breach of contract, that the contract was an ordinary surveyor's contract and that, in addition to the diminution in value, the claimants were entitled to recover general damages for what Bingham LJ described in the above passage as `physical discomfort and inconvenience'. Ralph Gibson LJ cited a number of cases including (apart from what may be called the holiday cases) *Hobbs v London and South Western Railway Co, Bailey v Bullock, Addis v Gramophone Co Ltd, Groom v Crocker* [1939] 1 KB 194, *Heywood v Wellers [1976] QB 446, Perry v Sidney Phillips & Son* [1982] 1 WLR 1297, *Bliss v South East Thames Regional Health Authority* [1987] ICR 700 and *Hayes v James & Charles Dodd.*

60. The question is on which side of the line the instant case falls on the facts. I have already set out the key conclusions reached by the judge. In short he held that the noise from the aeroplanes was pretty intolerable and a confounded nuisance and that it caused the claimant real discomfort. The judge concluded that that discomfort was greater than that found by this court in *Watts v Morrow*. In my judgment, he was entitled so to hold. The claimant's complaint was of noise, which of course affects one of the senses, namely hearing. It is, in my judgment, a physical inconvenience to have to put up with noise causing annoyance of the kind found by the judge. It has been held that it is a physical inconvenience to have to walk four to five miles at night or to live in cramped conditions for some months or to have to put up with inconvenience during repairs. I do not think that there can be any doubt that to have to put up with an evil-smelling cesspit of the kind referred to by Ralph Gibson LJ in

Watts v Morrow would involve physical inconvenience. In my opinion, the same is true of noise.

61. There was ample evidence to support the conclusion reached by the judge, who after all had the benefit of seeing the claimant give evidence. In the claimant's statement he said that the aircraft noise was a real source of annoyance and discomfort to him.

The defendant was expressly asked to investigate the noise. The claimant's object in asking him to do so was for his peace of mind. In these circumstances the law should afford the claimant a remedy.

79. Finally I quote one last passage from the judgment of Judge LJ. After referring to *Ruxley* and setting out the passages from it which have been quoted by Stuart-Smith LJ, he said:

> "The distinctions between *Ruxley Electronics* and the present case are obvious, but like the builder who failed to provide a swimming pool which did not conform with the householder's requirements, Mr Skinner failed to provided his client with accurate information which would have led him to avoid the specific problem which he wished to avoid, the purchase of a home with aircraft noise at levels which were unacceptable to him. The present damage to Mr Farley's amenity and enjoyment of his home was directly linked to and a foreseeable consequence of his surveyor's negligence. In these circumstances the claim against Mr Skinner is not defeated by the fact that he did not guarantee that there would be no significant aircraft noise, nor by Mr Farley's failure to establish any consequent diminution in the value of the property. If Mr Farley could not recover damages there would indeed, as Lord Mustill commented, be something wrong with the law."

Yet again, I entirely agree. In particular I agree that there is no relevant distinction in this regard between a case, like *Ruxley*, in which the defendant expressly promised to achieve a result, and the instant case, in which the defendant promised to use all reasonable care and skill to investigate the effect of aircraft noise at the property and tell the claimant

80. For these reasons, like Judge LJ, I would hold that if (contrary to my view) the claimant did not suffer any or any sufficient physical inconvenience such as to entitle him to general damages for breach of contract, he is entitled to general damages for breach of contract.

81. I would also hold that he was entitled to recover damages in tort. The defendant owed the claimant a common law duty to exercise reasonable care to investigate the effect of aircraft noise at the property and to tell the claimant. He had assumed the responsibility of doing so and knew that the claimant would be likely to rely upon what he was told, which indeed he did, with the result that the claimant bought the property and had to put up with the noise. I did not understand Mr Simpson to argue that the defendant was not in breach of a duty of care. In these circumstances I can see no policy reason why the claimant should not be entitled to recover general damages to compensate him for having to put up with the noise. On the contrary, it seems to me that ordinary members of the public would expect him to receive compensation, provided that it is assessed on a reasonable basis.

82. I recognise that it was held by this court in *Verderame v Commercial Union Assurance Co Plc* [1992] BCLC 793 that the policy considerations should be the same whether the claim is founded in contract or tort, but it seems to me that that too leads to the conclusion that, since there is no good policy reason for denying recovery in tort, there is no good reason for denying recovery in contract. I would therefore hold that, whether putting up with the aircraft noise is classified as physical inconvenience or not, the claimant should be compensated by an award of general damages. It follows that for the reasons which I have tried to give I have reached a different conclusion from Stuart-Smith and Mummery LJJ ... I would dismiss the appeal.

Miscellaneous Quantum Reports: Food Poisoning – Gastric Illness

Doree v *First Choice Holidays and Flights Limited*, 12 January 2005, Redditch County Court (Recorder Baker QC) Current Law Cases: 05/3216

D, female, aged 53 at the time of the incident and 57 at trial, suffered an acute gastrointestinal infection 3 days from the end of a package holiday. The acute phase of diarrhoea and stomach cramps lasted 3 days. Whilst visiting the bathroom she fainted and injured her face and knee. On her return to the UK she was off work for 6 weeks and was treated for worms in her stools as well as a campylobacter bacterium infection. She had existing depression which was worsened as a result of her symptoms. She recovered from her facial injury within 3 weeks and her knee within 2 months. Her condition developed into post infective irritable bowel syndrome which showed some improvement although at the date of trial she was suffering diarrhoea approximately every week, constipation every 2-3 weeks, swelling of the stomach every 2-4 weeks, and wind every 2-3 weeks. Once every 3 months she suffered acute symptoms of diarrhoea as well as severe stomach cramps. She was careful as to what she ate and her condition could be embarrassing in company, she was unable to pre-plan events as much as before and had to take medication. The prognosis was that she would have symptoms indefinitely but that they would improve with time. The judge awarded £15,000 by way of general damages for pain, suffering and loss of amenity which included loss of enjoyment of the holiday.

Ryan v *Thomas Cook Tour Operations*, 7 December 2004 (HHJ McDuff QC)

1.	The Claimant, aged 39, suffered a gastro-intestinal illness on the third day of a week's holiday to Turkey in October 2001. He initially developed a severe headache followed by the onset of severe diarrhoea with one episode of incontinence of faeces. The Claimant had acute symptoms throughout the holiday. Claimant attended his GP on return from holiday. Stool sample revealed no pathogen. Underwent colonoscopy on 9th February 2002 when haemorrhoids banded. Medical records revealed subsequent attendance at GP and hospital in 2002 and 2003 with symptoms. The Claimant had pre-holiday episodes of bleeding per rectum due to haemorrhoids.

2.	The Claimant claimed to suffer continuous left iliac fossa and loin pain, passing small amounts of blood per rectum on a weekly basis and urgency of defecation 2-3 times per day with frequent episodes of diarrhoea. He claimed to suffer a lot of flatus, persistent tiredness, abdominal bloating with intermittent episodes of constipation. He said symptoms affected concentration and performance at work. He was diagnosed as suffering infective irritable bowel syndrome with intermittent rectal bleeding due to haemorrhoids which were aggravated by increased bowel habits. Symptoms were expected to be permanent.

3.　　However, Court found Claimant had exaggerated symptoms as reported to Court and medical expert. Court satisfied that Claimant had suffered alteration of bowel habits on a permanent basis, that he suffered some urgency of defecation and stools were occasionally softer than in the past. That the Claimant did have continuing discomfort complained of but that symptoms were minimal.

4.　　Court awarded £6,000.00 general damages for PSLA. Judge indicated that if he had accepted the Claimant's case in full then the figure of £12,000.00 suggested to him by Claimant's Counsel was high but within the appropriate bracket. He also indicated that the case of Stanley v Thames Valley Police Authority (1988) was too old to form a reliable basis for assessment of damages. Parties had agreed special damages at £200.00, diminution of holiday value at £283.00 and loss of enjoyment of holiday at £360.00.

Morgan and Others v *Unijet Travel Limited*, 24 June 2006, Birmingham County Court (HHJ McKenna)

Morgan and others v Unijet Travel Ltd which was heard in the Birmingham County Court between 12th and 14th June 2006. The judge made no findings on the provision of flowers at Mr. and Mrs. Hallgarth's wedding (although the evidence was that some were provided) nor did he make any findings as to whether or not the marriage was legally binding in the U.K. (the claimants withdrew this allegation prior to trial). The photograph in the paper appears not to have been disclosed and less favourable photos appeared in the trial bundle. But of interest to readers of *this* august publication (whose contributors and reporters strive for accuracy) may well be the judge's judgment on quantum in this food poisoning claim.

The brief facts are that a wedding party of 15 went on a package holiday to the Dominican Republic. Mr. and Mrs. Hallgarth instigated the whole trip because they wanted to get married on a sandy beach in the Caribbean. Unfortunately on the first, second and third days of the holiday 14 of the wedding party developed acute gastroenteritis symptoms (history does not relate how the 15th member of the party escaped). Liability was admitted by Unijet and the judge was left to decide on the quantum of 11 of the claims.

The JSB Guidelines bracket 5(G)(b)(ii) states:

(ii) Serious but short-lived food poisoning, diarrhoea and vomiting diminishing over two to four weeks with some remaining discomfort and disturbance of bowel function and impact on sex life and enjoyment of food over a few years.　　**£5,250 to £10,500**

to bracket 5(G)(b)(i) which states:

(i) Severe toxicosis causing serious acute pain, vomiting, diarrhoea and fever, requiring hospital admission for some days or weeks and some continuing incontinence, haemorrhoids and irritable bowel syndrome, having a significant impact on ability **£21,000 to** to work and enjoyment of life.　　**£32,000**

Many claimants appear to suffer the sort of symptoms described in paragraph (ii) but the prognosis is that they will be permanent or, as the expert gastroenterologist Andrew Miller insists on describing them, "indefinite but gradually improving" (if he means "permanent" then why does he not say so?). The £10,500 to £21,000 range of awards has become a bracket with no guidelines.

The case of Morgan should assist practitioners in a number of ways: it provides quantum judgments for pain, suffering and loss of amenity ("PSLA") in 11 claims ranging from £5,500 to £13,000; it includes awards for PSLA which are below £10,500 where the symptoms have been found by the judge to be permanent; it provides a further quantum judgment in a holiday/wedding claim for loss of enjoyment. A full report has been submitted to *Kemp & Kemp* but I have summarised the cases in the table below.

Claimant	Chronology	Symptoms	PSLA	LOE	DIV
Dawn Morgan (36 at date of holiday)	Acute Symptoms	14 days of Colicky abdominal pain, diarrhoea, nausea and vomiting.			
	Thereafter	Diarrhoea every 1 to 2 weeks, abdominal distension and flatulence. 4 yrs after holiday symptoms every 4-6 weeks.			
	Prognosis	Symptoms indefinite but gradual improvement over time.	£10,500	£1000	£600
Kimberley Morgan (6 at date of holiday)	Acute Symptoms	2 weeks of severe diarrhoea, faecal incontinence and weight loss.			
	Thereafter	Pain, diarrhoea, incontinence and constipation every 1 to 2 weeks. After 3 years improvement but faecal incontinence every 1-2 weeks causing embarrassment.			

	Prognosis	Symptom free 5 to 6 years post holiday.	£7,500	£1,000	£287
Christopher Morgan (9 at date of holiday)	Acute Symptoms	14 days of diarrhoea.			
	Thereafter	32 months later still suffering episodes of intermittent diarrhoea, abdominal pain and urgency.			
	Prognosis	Symptoms resolved 2 yrs 11 months post holiday.	£5,500	£1,000	£287
Kate Vance (78 at date of holiday)	Acute Symptoms	Severe diarrhoea, abdominal pain and vomiting. Diarrhoea constant for 2 weeks. Urgency and incontinence.			
	Thereafter	Bowels opening 2 to 3 times per day with mild gripes in the abdomen which improved on bowel evacuation. More significant diarrhoea twice a week. Once a month severe enough to prevent her from leaving her home.			
	Prognosis	Symptoms continue for rest of life. She had unrelated terminal illness.	£13,000	£1,000	£677
Joyce Yeates (52 at date of holiday)	Acute symptoms	Severe diarrhoea and abdominal pain. Vomiting for 24 hours. Acute phase lasted for almost 5 weeks.			

	Thereafter	16 months post holiday urgent attacks of pain and diarrhoea every 6 or 7 weeks. Spicy foods also led to a recurrence of symptoms. 41 months post holiday her symptoms had improved to attacks once every 2 months with abdominal pains.			
	Prognosis	Symptoms to continue indefinitely although they would improve with time.	£10,000	£1,000	£677
Adrian Hallgarth (28 at date of holiday) Groom	Acute Symptoms	Intially sweats and shivers. Diarrhoea lasting 5 to 6 weeks.			
	Thereafter	Intermittent bowel symptoms every 6 or 8 weeks with urgency and some sense of incomplete evacuation. 41 months post holiday he was suffering diarrhoea and urgency once per month with abdominal pain which went with the opening of bowels. At trial symptoms 6-10 weeks.			
	Prognosis	Indefinite but might be expected to improve with time.	£9,000	£4,000	£677
Sheena Hallgarth (aged 33 at the date of holiday). Bride.	Acute Symptoms	Severe diarrhoea, pains and weight loss lasting 5 weeks.			
	Thereafter	Symptoms became intermittent with bouts			

		of diarrhoea every 2 weeks. She was reluctant to eat out. 3 ½ years post holiday symptoms intermittent with bouts lasting 1-2 days every 4-6 weeks. By trial symptoms every 6-10 weeks.			
	Prognosis	Symptoms to continue indefinitely but becoming gradually less with time.	£9,000	£4,000	£677
Tori Hallgarth (aged 3 at the date of holiday)	Acute Symptoms	Developed severe diarrhoea and abdominal pain and vomited during first 34 hours. Acute phase settled within 21 days.			
	Thereafter	By 1 year 4 months post holiday suffering diarrhoea about once a month lasting for less than 1 day. Almost 3 ½ years after holiday bouts of diarrhoea once every 2-3 months although some relapse prior to trial.			
	Prognosis	Complete resolution of symptoms within 2-3 years.	£5,500	£1,000	£287
Keavy Hallgarth (2 years old at date of holiday)	Acute Symptoms	Severe diarrhoea and abdominal pain. Had to go back to wearing nappies. Acute phase lasted 18 days.			
	Thereafter	1 year 4 months post holiday she continued to have diarrhoea and abdominal pain lasting			

		2-3 days every 1-2 weeks. Improvement by 3 years 4 months post holiday but semi-formed stools every 2-3 weeks, urgency of defaecation and some abdominal pain relieved on defaecation.			
	Prognosis	Complete resolution of symptoms within 2-3 years.	£6,500	£1,000	£287
David Banks (aged 55 at the date of holiday)	Acute Symptoms	Severe diarrhoea and abdominal pain, nausea and lethargy. Acute phase lasted 4 weeks.			
	Thereafter	1 year 9 months post holiday he was experiencing recurrent attacks of acute abdominal pain and diarrhoea every 1-2 weeks. Exacerbated by spicy foods. Some improvement 3 years 5 months post holiday: attacks of diarrhoea, marked urgency and colicky pain every 2-3 weeks lasting for 1-2 days. At trial attacks every 5-6 weeks.			
	Prognosis	Ongoing improvement with resolution 4½ - 5½ years post holiday.	£6,500	£1,000	£677
Kathleen Banks (aged 55 at the date of holiday)	Acute Symptoms	Severe diarrhoea and abdominal pain lasting 22 days.			
	Thereafter	At 1 year 9 months post accident: attacks			

of diarrhoea and
abdominal pain 3-4
times per week
exacerbated by certain
types of food. She had
some colicky
abdominal pain, soft
motions, bloating and
distension.

| Prognosis | Recovery within 4½-5½ years of holiday. | £6,500 | £1,000 | £677 |

Miscellaneous Quantum Reports: Quality Complaints

Unauthenticated Decisions

Cherry v *Malta Bargain Ltd*, 5 May 2005, Gravesend County Court (District Judge Gore) Current Law Cases: 05/1978

The claimant holidaymaker (C) brought an action against the defendant travel agent (M) under the Package Travel, Package Holidays and Package Tours Regulations 1992. C had booked a seven day holiday for her, her husband and their four children at a three star hotel in Malta for GBP 1,848. She found the bedrooms and bathroom assigned to the family dirty, the bedding being stained. She was offered an upgrade to a four star hotel in return for GBP 546. In making the move in the midday heat, she incurred taxi fares of GBP 10 and paid GBP 3 for drinks. The new hotel was clean but unsuitable for her family. On the third day of the holiday, she was allowed to move to another hotel, which proved satisfactory. C alleged that the first three days of the family's holiday had been ruined.

Held, giving judgment for C, that M was responsible for the standard of the hotel, where cleanliness was a basic requirement. The standard of cleanliness in Malta should be the same as it was in England, and the star rating of the hotel was irrelevant. M was accordingly liable to C. Damages were awarded in the sum of GBP 1,207, which comprised: GBP 546, being the sum paid to upgrade hotel; the sum of GBP 13 incurred in moving hotel on the first occasion; GBP 198 for the diminution in the value of the holiday, the accommodation, according to standard custom, being 25 per cent of the cost of the holiday; and GBP 450 for loss of enjoyment, calculated at the rate of GBP 25 per person per day.

Dixon v *Direct Holidays Plc*, 29 June 2004, Sunderland County Court (District Judge Arkless) Current Law Cases: 06/Feb/265

The claimant holidaymakers (D) brought an action against the defendant tour operator (H) alleging breaches of the Package Travel, Package Holidays and Package Tours Regulations 1992. D had paid GBP 1,025 to H for a 14 night self catering holiday for themselves and their three children at an apartment complex in Tenerife. After arriving, D discovered that the apartment and the complex suffered from a number of serious defects: there were problems with the electricity supply; there was an overpowering stench of sewage coming from a drain in a storage area; there was severe damp in the bathroom and children's bedroom; dirt had accumulated throughout the apartment; the hot water supply was inadequate; raw sewage bubbled up in the bath; the staff were hostile; there was more extensive maintenance work on the swimming pool than they had been warned about; and heavy duty construction work was being carried out on the concrete stairs near their apartment. As a result of the smell and damp, the children slept with their mother in the second bedroom, while the father slept on a couch. D chose to eat out for all their meals. They complained frequently until on the fifth day of the holiday they were offered alternative accommodation. That would cost an extra GBP 165, it was not self catering and there was no guarantee that the rooms offered would be on the same floor. D rejected the offer and asked to be taken home, but H refused.

Held, giving judgment for D, that H had breached Reg.15 of the Regulations by failing to properly perform the obligations under the contract. H had also breached Reg.14(2) and Reg.14(3): it had failed to provide a significant proportion of the holiday services; it had failed to offer suitable alternative accommodation; and it had refused to repatriate D. Damages of GBP 1,615 were awarded, comprising GBP 615 for difference in value, GBP 400 in respect of the expenses incurred in eating out, GBP 200 to compensate D for having to sleep separately and GBP 400 for distress and disappointment. D's refusal to accept the alternative accommodation offered was not an unreasonable failure to mitigate their loss.

Stainsby v *Balkan Holidays Ltd*, 29 September 2005, Middlesbrough County Court (District Judge Cuth) Current Law Cases: 06/Mar/152

The claimant holidaymaker (S) sought damages from the defendant tour operator (B) arising from a spoilt holiday. S had booked a package holiday in Bulgaria for two weeks at a cost of GBP 718. The holiday was S's honeymoon. On arrival at the two star hotel, which had no lift, S was allocated a room on the fourth floor, despite having requested, on the ground of her pregnancy, a room on the lower floors. The room allocated to her was dirty and damp. S was offered an upgrade to three star accommodation at an additional cost of GBP 600. She declined the offer, as she was unable to afford the upgrade. She was eventually given a room on the lower floors. However, the room was incredibly noisy, and S and her husband were unable to sleep or relax. B offered S an alternative hotel at an additional cost of GBP 422, which S accepted. However, construction works, which had not been mentioned to S, were being carried out at this alternative hotel; S found the works very noisy and disruptive. Further, the food was of a poor standard, causing S to incur extra expenses in eating out.

Held, giving judgment for S, that having regard to the matters complained of, S would be awarded damages of GBP 1,000 for loss of bargain and loss of enjoyment.

Samuels v *My Travel Tour Operations Ltd (t/a Cresta Holidays)*, 27 February 2004, Barnet County Court (District Judge Karet) Current Law Cases: 05/1979

The claimant (S) sought damages for breach of contract against the defendant (M), a tour operator. S had booked a luxury holiday in Mauritius for two weeks for his honeymoon at a cost of GBP 3,778. The hotel was rated as an all inclusive four star. Upon arrival at the hotel S found construction work taking place. S was woken early every morning because of the noise and found that the construction work continued all day, with the workmen working late into the evening, using floodlights once it became dark. Since S received no help from M's representatives he had spent many hours trying to rectify the situation. When M's representatives told him that no alternative accommodation could be found, S found some on his own and moved there at his own cost.

Held, giving judgment for S, that S would be awarded damages of GBP 3,778 representing the full cost of the holiday, GBP 1,000 to compensate him for loss of enjoyment, and GBP 135 to compensate him for unnecessary expenses including taxi fares and telephone calls.

Richards v *Goldtrail Travel Ltd*, 15 September 2003, Bromley County Court (Deputy District Judge Sullivan) Current Law Cases: 04/1880

R claimed damages from G for loss of enjoyment and the diminution in value of her holiday. R and her four travelling companions had booked a 14-night holiday with G to apartments in Turkey on an all inclusive basis for a total cost of GBP 2,195. When the party arrived at the apartments they were informed that no room was available as the apartments were overbooked. They were taken to another hotel, 10 minutes from the apartments, for the first night of their holiday. The following day the party were taken back to the apartments and were given a small room that was used by staff and were told that there was no alternative room available. Although R had been told, when making the booking, that English food was provided at the apartments, the food was only suited to Turkish tastes and in addition R had concerns over food hygiene. There had been no hot water available during the evenings, the apartments experienced frequent power cuts and the telephone in R's room did not work.

Held, giving judgment for R, that total damages would be awarded of GBP 4,917, being GBP 1,317 in respect of diminution in value of the holiday, GBP 3,400 loss of enjoyment and GBP 200 food expenses. G would also be ordered to pay costs in the sum of GBP 2,145 on the ground of their unreasonable behaviour pursuant to the Civil Procedure Rules 1998 Part 27 r.27.14(2)(d).

Dickinson v *Thomson Holidays*, 20 October 2003, Leeds County Court (District Judge Taylor) Current Law Cases: 04/1877

D brought an action against T for breach of the Package Travel, Package Holidays and Package Tours Regulations 1992 Reg.14 and Reg.15, seeking damages for the diminution in the value of her holiday and loss of enjoyment. D had booked a holiday with T to a hotel in La Pineda, Spain for herself, her husband and their 10-year-old son. They were attracted to the particular hotel by the fact that it was advertised in the brochure as being directly on the beach and particularly suitable for families. The brochure depicted a pool at the front of the hotel with the beach immediately across the road. D claimed that shortly before departure she received two telephone calls and two letters from T about building works in the resort. The first call and letter informed D that there were works going on behind the hotel which might cause a disturbance. The second call and letter informed D that the works would after consideration cause no disturbance as they were actually being carried out some distance from the hotel. However, on arrival at the hotel, D discovered that the beach opposite the hotel was like a building site as a consequence of ongoing sand works. D had not been informed of these works. The beach was unusable. The works caused a disturbance in terms of noise and dust, both during the day and during the night. D's view was obscured by lorries and machines on the beach, and she was unable to use the balcony to her hotel room, which was at the front of the hotel, or open the patio doors due to the noise and the dust. D was unable to use the pool, which was also situated at the front of the hotel, or use the hotel's eating facilities situated by the pool without being disturbed. D and her family avoided the disturbance by taking additional day trips and walking 15 minutes to a usable beach. T sought to defend the claim by relying on Reg.13(3) and contending that the works being undertaken were necessary as an unforeseeable consequence of April storms.

Held, giving judgment for D, that (1) for D's family, the holiday would have been a disappointment; (2) there had been a breach of contract and of the Regulations; (3) breach was foreseeable and avoidable; (4) measures should have been in place to deal with such storms as did occur in holiday resorts, and (5) in the particular instance there was sufficient time before D departed to alert the family to the works and give them the opportunity to make alternative arrangements. General Damages of GBP 660 were awarded amounting to two thirds of the cost of the holiday and GBP 750 for loss of enjoyment, representing GBP 250 for each family member.

Dale v *Golden Sun Holidays Ltd,* 12 February 2003, Ipswich County Court (Deputy District Judge Hamilton) Current Law Cases: 04/1875

D sought damages for breach of contract from G under the Package Travel, Package Holidays and Package Tour Regulations 1992 Reg.15. D had booked a 14- day package holiday to Greece for himself and his family with G at a total cost of GBP 1,300. The two studio apartments allocated to them were completely unsuitable. Both were below ground, dark, dirty and infested with ants and cockroaches. The door handle on the entrance door to one studio was broken, cooking facilities were inadequate and the only cooking utensils provided were rusty and unusable. The swimming pool and showers around the pool were dirty. Although G had provided alternative accommodation for D's wife and daughter that accommodation was just as dirty, and D and his son were not moved. D and his family came home early, leaving after only one week.

Held, giving judgment for D that the problems that D had experienced were sufficient to give rise to a breach of contract and it had been reasonable for D and his family to return home early. D could not recover the full cost of the holiday as his family had stayed in the accommodation for a week and would have had some enjoyment of the holiday. D was awarded GBP 975 for the cost of the holiday, GBP 310 for the cost of the return flights home and GBP 750 for loss of enjoyment.

Buhus-Orwin v *Costa Smeralda Holidays Ltd,* 16 August 2001, Mayor's and City of London Court (District Judge Trent) Current Law Cases: 01/4279

B brought a claim against a tour operator, C, with whom he had booked a two week holiday in Sardinia promised by C in its brochure to be "opulent luxury in a dramatic landscape and a beautiful villa with private garden and swimming pool". On arrival, B and his family found that the villa was infested with rats. B complained to C, who eventually offered smaller alternative accommodation with only a communal pool and no private garden. No compensation was offered. B declined the alternative accommodation and returned home. B contended that C was in breach of (1) an implied contractual term to exercise reasonable care and skill in the provision of holiday services, and (2) the terms of the Package Travel, Package Holidays and

Package Tours Regulations 1992. C argued that the rodent infestation was mice rather than rats and was unavoidable in that area. Further, that B, by declining the alternative accommodation, had failed to mitigate his loss.

Held, finding in favour of B, that (1) Reg.6, Reg.14, and Reg.15 of the 1992 Regulations applied to the holiday contract; (2) C had failed to provide luxury, rat-free accommodation in breach of the implied warranties in the descriptive material in its brochure and had failed to comply with its duties under Reg.14(2) and Reg.14(3); (3) C had failed to exercise reasonable care and skill in the provision of contractual services, and (4) B's refusal of the alternative accommodation had to be judged by reference to the luxury holiday that he had booked. In the circumstances, he had acted reasonably and mitigated his loss, particularly as C's offer had not included an offer of compensation. B was awarded a sum representing the whole of the holiday lost and consequential losses, together with the sum of GBP 2,000 for loss of enjoyment.

Forsdyke v *Panorama Holiday Group Ltd*, 13 November 2001, Kingston upon Thames (District Judge Sturdy) Current Law Cases: 02/2321

F, who had booked a last minute one week package holiday at a named hotel for himself and his wife, sought damages from a tour operator, P. At the time of booking, F had specifically requested a hotel with a heated swimming pool because his wife was about to have a hip operation and wished to exercise in warm water. In addition, F's wife was able to enjoy only a restricted range of holiday activities because of her arthritic hip. It was accepted by P that it was a term of the contract that the pool be heated, notwithstanding that P's brochure did not advertise the hotel as having a heated pool. The pool in fact was cold. F complained and was offered three alternatives, namely (1) move to another hotel A; (2) upgrade to hotel B at a cost of GBP 150, or (3) use the pool at hotel B at no extra cost. F rejected the first offer because hotel A was built into the side of a hill and unsuitable for people with walking difficulties. He rejected hotel B because, on visiting, he found the pool temperature to be only 20 degrees celsius which he considered too cold to use.

Held, giving judgment for F, that hotel A was clearly not a viable alternative and the pool at hotel B, whether heated or not, was too cold to swim in comfortably. The principal purpose of the holiday was to swim in a heated pool and that was made clear to P at the time of booking. In the circumstances, F was entitled to damages for diminution in the value of the holiday assessed at GBP 450, equivalent to approximately two thirds of the value of the holiday, and GBP 75 for distress suffered.

Thomson v *RCI Europe*, 14 February 2001, Manchester County Court (Deputy District Judge Hugman) Current Law Cases: 01/4275

T claimed accommodation costs and also sought to recover damages for disappointment, distress and inconvenience. T had paid a fee to RCI to exchange the use of an apartment which she owned in Portugal for an apartment in the US for the duration of a holiday for herself and members of her family. T alleged that the accommodation in the US was totally unacceptable, principally because the apartment could only be reached by climbing 87 open wooded steps. The steps were covered in leaves and, as such, were totally inappropriate for the party, which included a two year old child and T herself, aged 69. T immediately made it clear to RCI that the apartment was unsatisfactory and unsuitable and she was informed that no alternative accommodation was available. T initially found a motel for three nights and, thereafter, a house where the party stayed for the remainder of their holiday. RCI submitted, inter alia, that it merely offered an accommodation exchange service and that the case was not analogous to a package holiday claim.

Held, giving judgment for the claimant, that the case was analogous to a package holiday claim. T was awarded GBP 1,030 for the cost of the alternative accommodation and GBP 1,000 by way of general damages for upset, distress and inconvenience, Jarvis v Swans Tours Ltd [1973] Q.B. 233 and Jackson v Horizon Holidays Ltd [1975] 1 W.L.R. 1468 applied.

Coughlan v *Thomson Holidays Ltd*, 20 March 2001, Romford County Court (District Judge White) Current Law Cases: 01/4276

C sought to recover damages for breach of contract and loss of enjoyment. C and his wife booked a 14 day "gold" package holiday in Majorca with T for a total cost of GBP 1,320. The outward flight was delayed by more than 23 hours due to severe problems with air traffic control and technical problems with the aircraft, as a result of which the crew ran out of flight hours. C was not informed until 11.45 pm, some 10 and a half hours after their flight had been due to depart, that there would be no available flight that night. C was offered a hotel for the night which involved a wait for a taxi, a one hour drive and a return to the airport by 7.30 am the next morning. C refused the hotel and was offered blankets which never materialised; accordingly C and his wife spent the night in freezing and uncomfortable conditions and the first two days of the holiday were ruined. T denied liability and argued that (1) liability for loss caused by technical problems with aircraft was expressly excluded under the contract by virtue of the section entitled "events beyond our control"; (2) the technical fault could not reasonably have been foreseen or guarded against and hence there was no liability under the Package Travel, Package Holidays and Package Tours Regulations 1992 Reg.15(2)(c), and (3) any loss was not a consequence of a significant failure on its part, T having made satisfactory arrangements for the period of delay.

Held, giving judgment for the claimant, that there was no evidence that the brochure relied upon by T was applicable. It was implied that a "gold" holiday must have been of a quality above the ordinary and therefore T should have given prompt assistance to C. The circumstances of the delay were foreseeable and C did not unreasonably refuse the offer of a hotel. Accordingly, C was awarded a total of GBP 550 for a three day period of frustration, disappointment, tiredness and irritability, the sum of GBP 40 which was paid from a separate insurance policy having been taken into account.

Westerman v Travel Promotions Ltd, 26 November 26 1999, Stafford County Court (District Judge Ilsey) Current Law Cases: 00/4042

W brought an action for damages against a tour operator, T, after he and his wife returned from a package holiday in Switzerland, Italy and the Mediterranean. The holiday consisted of a sightseeing programme with transport between locations to be provided by rail, bus and boat. The cost of the holiday was GBP 795 per person. The holiday brochure promised that part of the travel arrangements on days 3 and 10 of the holiday would be on a "unique" 1939 built train, "the Red Arrow". W's evidence was that himself and his wife were rail enthusiasts and would not have booked the holiday but for the attraction of the Red Arrow and the rail travel thereon. Days before the tour commenced W was informed by letter that the Red Arrow had been withdrawn from service. T provided an alternative itinerary which provided instead for first class travel on Swiss Rail and for a significantly longer period to be spent travelling by train than would have been provided on the Red Arrow as originally scheduled. T also made provision for a flight in place of a stretch of the journey that was scheduled to be covered by bus and the Red Arrow. W and his wife embarked on the holiday and upon their return, sought compensation for the failure to provide the Red Arrow train journeys. T provided a GBP 50 per person refund and argued that, given only three hours in total would have been spent on the Red Arrow and that more than adequate alternative arrangements had been made, that satisfied their liability to compensate W under the Package Travel, Package Holidays and Package Tours Regulations 1992 Reg.13 and Reg.14. T relied upon Reg.14(2) in support of its refusal to make any further payment to W.

Held, giving judgment for the claimants, that (1) the primary reason why W and his wife had booked the package holiday was the Red Arrow element of the package; (2) the changes to the Red Arrow element of the package, which also formed a major part of T's brochure advertising for the holiday, constituted a significant alteration to the itinerary and/or a failure to provide a significant proportion of the package holiday services; (3) while T had made alternative arrangements and had paid GBP 50 per person in compensation, that did not amount to adequate compensation in accordance with T's duty under Reg.14(2) of the 1992 Regulations, and (4) in the circumstances, W and his wife would be awarded GBP 100 each for the diminution of the value of their holiday and a further GBP 100 each for their distress and disappointment.

Crossley v *Thomson Holidays Ltd*, North Shields County Court (18th January 2001) [2001] ITLJ 72

Comment: This is a report of an action in the small claims court. It is of interest because it appears to be the only reported case where it was held that there is an implied term in a package holiday contract that a tour operator's employees and agents will treat clients with reasonable politeness and courtesy and a failure to do so will render the tour operator liable. In terms of legal principle this seems unexceptionable, as is the application of the case of *Jarvis v Swan Tours* [1973] 1 QB 233 to award damages for the ensuing distress and disappointment. In terms of where it fits into the mainstream of package holiday law it is analogous to other cases where the tour operator found itself liable for the defaults of its front line staff. Cases such as *Glover v Kuoni* [1987] CLY 1151 where the tour operator's representative did nothing to ameliorate the position of clients who were stranded on a small island in the Maldives without luggage for three weeks and *Richmond v Airtours* (1991, Leeds County Ct, unreported) where passengers were stranded at Stansted Airport for 24 hours without information or assistance.

District Judge Powell: By his claim form Mr Crossley seeks damages for breach of contract by the defendant company arising out of a package holiday that he booked with them. It is not the usual claim that one sees in package tour holiday disputes. This is a claim more akin to what one sees in the law of tort for defamation. However, this claim is not brought as a defamation claim under the law of tort. It is fought purely and simply under the law of contract.

The particulars of claim state:

> 'In May 2000 my wife and I had a 14 day holiday in Egypt organised by the defendant for which I paid £1,316.40. The holiday itself was satisfactory but while waiting in the crowded departure lounge at Luxor Airport an employee or agent of the company asked loudly if anyone was from Room 639 of the Sheraton Hotel. I replied that I was and he then said, in a loud voice, 'You owe the hotel £157 for your bill. You haven't paid your bill'. My wife and I were deeply embarrassed. I had paid my bill and obtained a receipt.
>
> In my contract with the defendant I believe there is an implied term that the defendant's employees and agents will treat me and my wife with reasonable politeness and courtesy. This they have failed to do. I have attempted on two occasions to reach a friendly settlement with the defendants but they will not consider my claim and I claim interest at the rate of £1.10 per day.'

That is what he says his claim amounts to.

There are a number of issues but it is conceded by counsel for the defendant firstly that there was a contract, and secondly that Regulation 15 of the Package Travel Regulations 1992 apply.

That regulation makes it clear that the package tour company is liable to the consumer for the proper performance of the obligations under the contract irrespective of whether such obligations are to be performed by that other party or by other suppliers of services. Thirdly, that an employee of Thomson's passed on a message to the claimants that Room 639 had an outstanding bill. What is in dispute is the volume or tone in which the allegation of an outstanding bill was passed on.

Counsel for the defendant says that the issues are: was there an implied term that the defendants and their employees, agents or representatives would treat their customers with reasonable politeness and courtesy? That is something which I have to answer as a basic question because, unless I answer it in the affirmative the claim fails.

I believe what the claimant is saying when he alleges that there is an implied term that the defendants would treat their customers with reasonable politeness and courtesy amounts to an implied term that they would provide peace of mind or freedom from distress during the course of the holiday. It is well documented that there is such an implied term and the authority goes back as far as *Jarvis v Swans Tours* [1973] QB

233 and [1973] 1 All ER 71 (Court of Appeal) in which case damages were awarded for disappointment, distress, annoyance and frustration and they were assessed at that time at £125; not as submitted to me this morning by the claimant in a much greater figure.

It has been said in the Court of Appeal that the test of whether there is an implied term is whether, if it is posed, one would unhesitatingly say immediately 'Of course'. I have no doubt in this case that there was such a term.

The evidence in the main is the evidence of the claimants. The defendant has chosen, for reasons that are perfectly understandable and having regard to proportionality, to only put in a written statement by Mr Mahmood Nasr. They have not produced any oral evidence and there has, therefore, not been any cross-examination of Mr Nasr. Mr Nasr says in his statement:

> 'The only time I shouted was to ask for the following room numbers from the Sheraton Hotel to make themselves known to me as it is busy and noisy in the departure area.'

In fact, the particulars of claim by the claimant do not allege that there was any shouting at all.

The particulars of claim say, 'He then said in a loud voice...'

When Mr and Mrs Crossley gave evidence, Mr Crossley, going first, confirmed what he said in his particulars of claim and clarified it by saying this, 'Having completed our tour of Luxor and the Nile we were in the departure Lounge at Luxor Airport at about 3.15 on 24th May awaiting departure. The Thomson employee came into the lounge and shouted, "Room 639". I put my hand up in acknowledgement and he then said, in a loud voice, in the presence of other departing passengers, about 200 in number, "You owe the hotel £157 for your bill. You haven't paid your bill". He said that in a loud voice. He was about 20 yards from me and I was very embarrassed. I had paid my bill and obtained a receipt the night before.

He then approached me and repeated that I hadn't paid my bill. I explained that I'd paid it and that I had a receipt. It was in my suitcase which was being loaded onto the plane and couldn't get to it.

He then said, as if I was a pupil being addressed by a headmaster, "Wait there". He walked a few paces away, spoke on his mobile phone in Arabic and returned to us. He asked if we had been to a particular pizzeria. I explained that my wife and I had not travelled to Egypt to visit such a place.

He spoke again on his mobile phone and said, "Okay, you can go". The other people standing round us knew us. We had met them on holiday and that's why we were so embarrassed. To be branded a fraud and cheat I found particularly embarrassing'. That was his examination-in-chief with which Mrs Crossley agreed.

In cross-examination he confirmed that the holiday was satisfactory and he says so in his particulars of claim. He went as far as saying it was enjoyable. He said he had no objection whatsoever to an employee shouting his room number to get his attention but what he objected to was the accusation in a loud voice for all to hear that he had not paid his bill. He emphasised that the employee was not speaking in his natural voice. He was loud. That continued until he came closer to them when he addressed them in more measured volume and tone.

Counsel put it to him that he had been spoken to in measured tones all along save that when the representative came into the departure lounge he might have said in a loud voice or enquired for the occupier of the room 639 to identify themselves.

The defendant denies and denied through counsel today that any words were spoken in a loud voice and shouted other than the request for the occupiers of Room 639 to identify themselves.

I accept the evidence of Mr and Mrs Crossley, and I accept that the defendant's employee, who it is conceded was an Egyptian national, used the words that amount to an allegation of dishonesty.

The whole event, it is accepted, took no longer than five minutes but Mr and Mrs Crossley say that it took the shine off the holiday and I can well understand that, particularly bearing in mind that the claimant and his wife are people of obvious integrity. Mr Crossley told me in his submissions that he is a Chief Trading Standards Officer and a Justice of the Peace. However, I can make no award for loss of reputation in these proceedings because the claim is founded in damages for breach of contract. This is not a defamation claim founded in tort. However, the claim does succeed for injury to feelings and distress.

The question that finally has to be decided is how much should be awarded under that head of damage, for the injury to feelings and distress. I have had the benefit of considering a number of cases starting with *Jarvis v Swans Tours* none of which are on similar facts. As I have stated at the beginning of this judgment this is an unusual claim. I end by perhaps also looking at wedding day cases. I have considered two cases there which were for distress and disappointment. The first is *Deisen v Samson* [1971] SLT 49 where a bride was awarded £30 for distress and disappointment when a photographer failed to attend her wedding and a later case of *Cole v Rana* [1993] CLY 13645 CL 114, a case where a fleet of four wedding cars failed to arrive at the wedding was largely spoiled because of that. General damages of £2,500 were awarded. It is the other end of the spectrum to the *Deisen v Samson* case but there is a considerable time lapse between the two cases. One is 1971 and the other is 1993 but that by itself cannot account for the difference being so large.

Taking all matters into account I award £850 to each.

Damages for Distress and Disappointment – Why Us?

Stephen Mason (Stephen Mason Solicitors & co-editor of the International Travel Law Journal) [2001] ITLJ 9

A tour operator describes a hotel as being 'in a peaceful location'. On arrival at the hotel, consumers find that it is in a location above which aeroplanes stack while waiting to land at the local airport. The tour operator will find himself not only having to rebate a substantial part of the price of the holiday, but also a large sum by way of compensation for the distress, disappointment and loss of enjoyment suffered by the consumers.

Contrast the scenario above with this situation: in purchasing a house a consumer instructs a surveyor. The consumer is aware that the house is 15 miles from Gatwick airport, and therefore specifically asks the surveyor to establish whether the property is affected by aircraft noise.

Negligently the surveyor gives the house the 'all clear'. In fact the property is precisely below the position where aircraft stack whilst flying round in a spiral while waiting for a landing slot. The consumer, who has proceeded to purchase the house based on the surveyor's advice, sues the surveyor. He receives not a penny by way of compensation.

What is the justification which the law applies in reaching this apparently contrary position? – especially bearing in mind that the house buyer has paid a great deal more than the holiday makers and the noise is now a permanent feature of the purchaser's domestic lifer, not a temporary inconvenience whilst on holiday.

The leading textbook on damages, *McGregor on Damages*, has discerned a distinct trend away from the award of damages for distress and disappointment.

Certainly, that view received a strong endorsement from the case of *Farley v Skinner (No. 2)* (Lawtel), which was decided by the Court of Appeal on 6th April 2000. This is the case, referred to above, of the surveyor who negligently advised on the subject of aircraft noise. It appeared that the house which the claimant bought was not reduced in value as a result of the aircraft noise. Accordingly, the only loss which the claimant could identify, which he had suffered as a result of the surveyor's negligence, was the distress and disappointment – 'confounded nuisance' as it is put by the judges – of not being able to have a peaceful breakfast or a pre-dinner drink, on his terrace enjoying his delightful gardens. For this, the trial judge awarded the sum of £10,000. The defendant surveyor appealed.

The Court of Appeal found in favour of the surveyor, but not unanimously. Of the three judges, Stuart-Smith LJ and Mummery LJ were in favour of the surveyor, and Clarke LJ gave a dissenting judgment in favour of the consumer. (The case has an interesting history as this was in fact the second appeal hearing – the first appeal was before a two man Court of Appeal and the judges were split!).

The two majority judges reached their conclusions in slightly different ways, Stuart-Smith LJ preferring a careful legalistic approach, whilst Mummery LJ mounts a scathing attack upon the concept of damages for distress and disappointment.

The origin of the rule, that such damages cannot be recovered for breach of contract is a case called *Addis v Gramophone Co Limited* [1909] AC 488 where it was held that an employee was not entitled to recover any damages from his employer for injury to his feelings on hearing the news that he was dismissed, wrongfully and in a harsh and humiliating manner. That kind of harm is treated by the law as an uncompensatable risk of life.

More recently was the case of *Watts v Morrow* [1991] 1 WLR 1421. This was another case concerning a negligent surveyor. In that case, in the Court of Appeal, Bingham LJ said:

> 'A contract breaker is not in general liable for any distress, frustration, anxiety, displeasure, vexation, tension or aggravation which this breach of contract may cause to the innocent party. This rule is not, I think, founded on the assumption that such reactions are not foreseeable, which they surely are or may be, but on considerations of policy. But the rule is not absolute. Where the very object of a contract is to provide pleasure, relaxation, peace of mind or freedom from molestation, damages will be awarded if the fruit of the contract is not provided or if the contrary result is procured instead'.

Probably the most famous example of a contract to provide pleasure, relaxation etc, was found in the case of *Jarvis v Swans Tours* [1973] QB 233. This case, where a solicitor booked a skiing houseparty in Switzerland, only to find that he was the only guest and there was no skiing, is generally credited with creating the entire subject of holiday law. (See Grant and Mason 'Holiday Law' 2nd Edition, p.256 and [1994] TLJ 4 for a commentary on the case).

Let me examine in greater detail the reasoning of the judges for maintaining this distinction.

Stuart-Smith LJ confirmed that as well as actual injury, physical inconvenience and discomfort can result in an award of damages. But he says;

> '...nor can I accept the argument that because the claimant hears the noise through his ears and therefore experiences it through his senses, this amounts to physical discomfort.

> Persistent high levels of noise can cause physical discomfort, indeed this is a well known form of torture. But there is nothing approaching that here ... All distress, annoyance, frustration, vexation and so on is a reaction to things perceived through the senses, usually of sight or hearing. But that does not make the distress physical'.

Referring to the words already set out from the judgment of Bingham LJ in *Watts v Morrow*, he confirmed that the law takes this approach for purely policy reasons, and not as a matter of legal principle. He says:

> 'The reasons are understandable. In an action for damages for personal injury, the claimant must prove either physical injury or a recognised psychiatric injury. Distress and annoyance will not do. Annoyance, vexation etc, is entirely subjective; moreover as this case illustrates, I find it difficult to see how it can be assessed'.

The judge then turned to deal with this question: Why is a surveying contract unlike a holiday contract? In other words, why cannot it be said that it is a contract for pleasure, peace of mind etc. This time he quotes from a different judgment, the case of *Knott v Bolton* (1995) 45 Con LR 127, also from the Court of Appeal. In that case, the following analysis is given by Russell LJ:

> '*In my judgment the words "the very object of the contract" are crucial within the context of the instant case. The very object of the contracts entered into by Mr Terence Bolton was to design for the Knotts their house. As an ancillary of that of course it was in the contemplation of Mr Bolton and of the Knotts that pleasure would be provided, but the provision of pleasure to the occupiers of the house was not the very object of the contract... [The claimant] has endeavoured to persuade us that the true nature of the contract entered into by Mr Bolton...was to provide pleasure for Mr and Mrs Knott. I disagree...the true nature of the contract was to design the home. It was not to provide pleasure for Mr and Mrs Knott, although that was a necessary ancillary of what Mr Bolton did'.*

The Dissenting Judgment

It is only fair to point out that, in his dissenting judgment, Clarke LJ makes a heartfelt and strong plea for the idea that damages for distress and disappointment should be extended to many, if not all, breach of contract cases.

Perhaps the key point which he makes is this: claimants are under a duty to take reasonable steps to mitigate their loss. In the well known old case of *Bailey v Bullock* (1950) 66 TLR (Pt. 2) 791, in which the defendant was a solicitor who negligently failed to obtain possession of a dwelling house for the plaintiff and his wife, it was said:

> '*During the course of the argument before me counsel for the defendants was disposed to admit that if in the present case the plaintiff had chosen to mitigate the discomfort to which he was subject by taking rooms for himself and his family at a hotel or making other arrangements for his accommodation, it would have been extremely difficult for the defendants to have resisted a claim for special damages based on the cost of such accommodation. It would indeed be curious if, in the circumstances of this case, because the plaintiff suffered the inconvenience rather than incur expense to avoid it, he should be deprived of any remedy. Such in my opinion is not the law'.*

Clarke LJ was also unimpressed with the argument about the difficulty of assessing the correct amount of compensation in such cases, saying it was no more difficult than many exercises which judges have to carry out.

Scottish Dimension

Having said that, clearly the law is as stated by the two majority judges in Farley. To emphasise that, on 11th July 2000, the Scottish Court of Session, in a case brought by an employee, (*Fraser v State Hospitals Board for Scotland*) decided that, whilst the duty of care owed by an employer to take reasonable care to avoid exposing his employees to unnecessary risk of injury extended to psychiatric damage and was not limited to physical injury, nonetheless there was no duty to protect the employee from unpleasant emotions such as grief, anger, resentment or normal human conditions such as anxiety or stress, 'those did not involve any form of injury at all'.

Holiday cases are different

It can be seen that the courts are well aware that damages for distress and disappointment have no real justification either in logic, policy or tradition.

Nonetheless there is clearly no appetite for overturning *Jarvis v Swans Tours.* Tour operators must bite the bullet and recognise that they enjoy 'least favoured nation status' in the courts.

Tour operators often feel hard done by that high awards for compensation are made against them; so that any breach of contract by them results in a higher penalty than it does for most traders. Feeling aggrieved, they might read the above citation and think: 'the very object of a holiday contract is not the providing of pleasure.

The true nature of the contract is to transport people to and from their destination, and book them into the accommodation of their choice. It was not to provide pleasure, although pleasure is a necessary ancillary of what we do'.

Indeed one is reminded of the naivete of Swans Tours in the *Jarvis* case, whose brochure actually stated: 'You will be in for a great time when you book this house party holiday'.

Certainly, in that case, Swans Tours appear to have represented, if not promised as a term of the contract, pleasure. But most tour operators these days would be far too sensible to promise consumers that they were bound to have a good time! Indeed, what contracts as their 'very object', do have the provision of pleasure?

Judgment of Mummery LJ

Mummery LJ quotes from a Law Commission report from 1993 which is critical of compensation where the loss is non-pecuniary. The report says 'there is no exact equivalent and no standard measure of assessment by reference to which the harm can be converted into monetary form..... this incommensurability gives rise to a real danger of indeterminacy and of inconsistent awards'.

In a startlingly strong passage Mummery LJ goes on:

> *'The incontrovertible fact is that the unobservable subjective nature and extent of intangible harm means that it is inherently difficult to prove (or to refute); that even if properly proved it is impossible to measure as there are no objective standards and no solid comparables; that even if 'measured' the amount awarded is open to the trenchant criticisms that it is not truly or wholly compensatory, that it contains an impermissible punitive element and that it reflects the intrusion of an unacceptable level of subjectivity on the part of the judge; and that the whole exercise fails to satisfy a fundamental requirement of a fair and workable litigation system that the outcome of a claim should be reasonably predictable both as to liability and quantum, so that the parties and their advisers can negotiate satisfactory*

> compromises and make informed decisions on Part 36 offers and payments
> and their acceptance'.

He goes on, turning to Mr Farley's claim:

> 'The quantification of the claim exposes the judicial process to serious
> misgivings. I do not understand by what reasoning or on what evidence the
> compensation under this head was assessed at £10,000. Why not £5,000?
> Why not £20,000? The judge attempted to do his best on exiguous material
> to measure the unmeasurable and in the result awarded compensation for
> the uncompensatable. He was invited to participate in an exercise which was
> more like a lucky dip than a judicial process'.

Tour operators may jump for joy to read these words. Exactly so! They will say
'that's what we have been complaining about for years'. And yet there is no
awareness from the judges that these criticisms can equally be made of the *Jarvis v
Swan Tours* type of case.

Last One Left at the Luggage Carousel? Tour Operators' Liability for Luggage Delays

Jackie Hewitt (Solicitor - Consumers' Association) [1999] ITLJ 193

When luggage goes missing on the outward flight at the start of a holiday, it can be nothing short of disastrous. If you find yourself the only one left at the luggage carousel, you might console yourself with the fact that the airline will have to pay you some compensation designed to cover the loss, delay or damage to your luggage. But you could also be bitterly disappointed when you find out how much (or little) that is. On the other hand, if you take a package holiday, surely the tour operator will step in and take responsibility? Again you could be disappointed.

For the most part holiday companies want little to do with luggage delays on flights. This attitude appears to be backed up by the legal advice they receive that assumes holiday companies enjoy exactly the same limitations on liability for delayed baggage as that enjoyed by airlines. But a recent small claims case makes clear what most consumers would assume – holiday companies do have a responsibility to their customers in this situation, even if it is the airline's fault. And that this responsibility can extend further than that imposed on the airline.

If companies ignore this responsibility, they could find themselves liable in court.

The claim

This case involved a Caribbean cruise in March last year with Royal Caribbean International. The claimants, Mr and Mrs Holmes, had taken the cruise to celebrate their 25th wedding anniversary.

Travel to the ship involved flights to Miami via Chicago. It was during these flights that the Holmes' entire luggage went missing, meaning they had to join their cruise at Miami without it. And they remained without it for all but the final two days of their thirteen-day holiday, despite the fact that the luggage had been located at its ticketed destination in Miami the day after it went missing.

Mr and Mrs Holmes' luggage contained many specially purchased holiday clothes and they spent much of their holiday trying to replace these and to adjust to the inconvenience of being without their luggage. To make matters worse, on the ship they were charged for the hire of a tuxedo and for special laundry services at a 50% surcharge.

The Holmes were also very disappointed at the lack of action taken by Royal Caribbean (through the onboard purser or anyone else) to reunite them with their luggage. They made their own efforts to track down their luggage by contacting the onshore information desk and speaking with the purser daily, but to no avail. Essentially, the Holmes' were left to their own devices, with no real help being given to reunite them with their luggage until towards the very end of their holiday. All this time the luggage had been waiting in Miami. Apart from Royal Caribbean making no real efforts to locate the luggage, the other problem was that Royal Caribbean had given their customers instructions to label luggage with the airport destination only rather than the cruise ship, making it more difficult to identify the final destination of delayed luggage.

So, what remedy did Mr and Mrs Holmes have and against whom? They were told about the airlines' limited liability for lost or delayed luggage under the Warsaw Convention and they duly claimed the 250 francs per kilo from the airline under Article 19 of the Convention. This they received, but it did not cover all their expenses and did not take into account the loss of enjoyment of a special holiday costing £2,932, so the Holmes' looked to Royal Caribbean for help. Royal Caribbean refused to offer any compensation, as their terms and conditions entitled them to limit their liability for delayed luggage to the limits set out in the Warsaw Convention just as the airline had been able to do. Therefore they said the Holmes' had already been compensated for their loss and there could be no other remedy. The line from the lawyers was simply that damages were restricted to the limits set out in the Warsaw Convention and so there could be no other liability on Royal Caribbean in connection with the luggage. The Holmes' disagreed and it was this issue that was tested at Middlesbrough county court.

The Warsaw Convention and the Package

Travel Regulations

Mr and Mrs Holmes accepted that the Warsaw Convention applied to the situation where luggage is delayed during air travel. Article 19 of the Convention, incorporated into English law by the Carriage by Air Act 1961, states that:

The carrier is liable for damage occasioned by delay in the carriage by air of passengers, baggage or cargo.

Article 22 (2) of the Convention provides the monetary limit on compensation payable in this situation based on the weight of the luggage. Mr and Mrs Holmes accepted that this limit applied to the liability of the airline for the delay of the luggage during the carriage by air. Further, while there was some argument over incorporation of terms and conditions, the claimants accepted that the Package Travel, Package Holidays and Package Tours Regulations 1992 entitled Royal Caribbean to limit their own liability in respect of the delayed luggage to those limits enjoyed by airlines under the Warsaw Convention. 15(3) of the Package Travel Regulations states:

In the case of damage arising from the nonperformance or improper performance of the services involved in the package, the contract may provide for compensation to be limited in accordance with the international conventions which govern such services.

Nor were Mr and Mrs Holmes arguing that the Convention limits should not apply to delay of baggage during carriage by air just because the services provided were part of a package. They accepted that the Convention at Article 24(1) limits remedies for damage occurring during carriage by air to those set out in the Convention when it says:

In the case of passengers and baggage, any action for damages, however founded, can only be brought subject to the conditions and limits set out in this Convention, without prejudice to the question as to who are the persons who have the right to bring suit and what are their respective rights.

Therefore Article 24 of the Convention (and indeed the case of *Sidhu v British Airways* [1997] 1 All ER 193 confirming the lack of other remedies in Warsaw Convention cases) combined with 15(3) of the Package Travel Regulations make it clear that Royal Caribbean could rely on Convention limits in respect of the delay to the luggage during the carriage by air. All this was not in issue as far as the claimants were concerned.

Wider obligations

Instead Mr and Mrs Holmes argued that the situation was not just a question of delay in carriage by air as Royal Caribbean assumed. They argued that Royal Caribbean was under a duty to provide the holiday in accordance with its brochure promises and its obligations under the Package Travel Regulations 1992. They accepted that they had been compensated by the airline for the delay to their luggage caused by carriage by air and were claiming instead for breaches of the holiday contract over and above this delay.

The Holmes' claimed that Royal Caribbean's failure to provide proper labelling instructions had contributed to the failure to reunite them with their luggage once it had turned up in Miami. They also claimed that the failure to take action to locate the luggage in Miami and to alleviate the inconvenience on board ship was a breach of their obligations according to Regulation 15(8) of the Package Travel Regulations. This states:

If the consumer complains about a defect in the performance of the contract, the other party to the contract, or his local representative, if there is one, will make prompt efforts to find appropriate solutions.

The actual claim for damages being made against Royal Caribbean was therefore for the expenses, disappointment, distress, anxiety and loss of enjoyment caused by the delay in reuniting Mr and Mrs Holmes with their luggage after it had been located in Miami. This period between location and return was not part of the carriage of baggage by air. By the second day of the holiday the luggage had been found and had arrived safely at its ticketed airport – the carriage by air was over.

As such the Warsaw Convention ceased to apply to the situation because from then on it did not involve carriage of baggage by air within the meaning of the Convention. The period before this had been compensated by way of Warsaw Convention damages from the airline. The problems experienced after this date were all down to the failure of Royal Caribbean to exercise reasonable care to reunite the claimants with their luggage. While 15(2) of the Package Travel Regulations provides that holiday companies can take advantage of the limitations afforded to airlines in the Warsaw Convention, it does not entitle Royal Caribbean to claim a wider limitation than that afforded to the airline. Therefore, it was argued that the period following the location of the luggage in Miami until the Holmes' were reunited with it, was not subject to the limits of the Warsaw Convention and compensation could be awarded if Royal Caribbean was found to be in breach of the holiday contract.

The decision

The District Judge agreed with the argument put forward by the claimants and found Royal Caribbean in breach of its obligations. He decided that he was not constrained by the limits of the Warsaw Convention and was entitled to award the Holmes' damages for assorted expenses and loss of enjoyment of a special holiday. He awarded the full amount claimed.

It is perhaps obvious that a holiday company must take some responsibility for problems its customers face on holiday rather than assume someone else will pick up the tab. Even if there is little that can be done (in this case things may have been different if the luggage remained lost in transit), surely it is not too much to expect a tour operator to step in and try to make the situation as bearable as possible?

It is also worrying to see that in some cases tour operators are seeking to limit their liability inappropriately, and are prepared to argue the case all the way to court and beyond. Royal Caribbean appealed this small claims decision and Mr and Mrs Holmes faced the unenviable prospect of defending the appeal, with all its costs implications. Fortunately they were able to defend what was a very strong case and, at the last minute, the set aside application due to be heard in September this year was abandoned. So finally, albeit seven months after the original decision, Mr and Mrs Holmes are properly compensated for their lost luggage let-down.

SECTION 9

THE 1992 REGULATIONS

PACKAGE TRAVEL, PACKAGE HOLIDAYS AND PACKAGE TOURS REGULATIONS 1992

Made --- 22nd December 1992

Whereas the Secretary of State is a Minister designated for the purposes of section 2(2) of the European Communities Act 1972 in relation to measures relating to consumer protection as regards package travel, package holidays and package tours;

And whereas a draft of these Regulations has been approved by a resolution of each House of Parliament pursuant to section 2(2) of and paragraph 2(2) of Schedule 2 to that Act;

Now, therefore the Secretary of State in exercise of the powers conferred on him by section 2(2) of that Act hereby makes the following Regulations

1 CITATION AND COMMENCEMENT

These Regulations may be cited as the Package Travel, Package Holidays and Package Tours Regulations 1992 and shall come into force on the day after the day on which they are made.

2 INTERPRETATION

(1) In these Regulations—

"brochure" means any brochure in which packages are offered for sale;

"contract" means the agreement linking the consumer to the organiser or to the retailer, or to both, as the case may be;

"the Directive" means Council Directive 90/314/EEC on package travel, package holidays and package tours;

["member State" means a member State of the European Community or another State in the European Economic Area;]

"offer" includes an invitation to treat whether by means of advertising or otherwise, and cognate expressions shall be construed accordingly;

"organiser" means the person who, otherwise than occasionally, organises packages and sells or offers them for sale, whether directly or through a retailer;

"the other party to the contract" means the party, other than the consumer, to the contract, that is, the organiser or the retailer, or both, as the case may be;

"package" means the pre-arranged combination of at least two of the following components when sold or offered for sale at an inclusive price and when the service covers a period of more than twenty-four hours or includes overnight accommodation:—

> (a) transport;

> (b) accommodation;

> (c) other tourist services not ancillary to transport or accommodation and accounting for a significant proportion of the package,

> > and

> > (i)   the submission of separate accounts for different components shall not cause the arrangements to be other than a package;

> > (ii)   the fact that a combination is arranged at the request of the consumer and in accordance with his specific instructions (whether modified or not) shall not of itself cause it to be treated as other than pre-arranged;

and

"retailer" means the person who sells or offers for sale the package put together by the organiser.

(2)   In the definition of "contract" in paragraph (1) above, "consumer" means the person who takes or agrees to take the package ("the principal contractor") and elsewhere in these Regulations "consumer" means, as the context requires, the principal contractor, any person on whose behalf the principal contractor agrees to purchase the package ("the other beneficiaries") or any person to whom the principal contractor or any of the other beneficiaries transfers the package ("the transferee").

NOTES
Amendment
Para (1): definition "member State" inserted by SI 1995/1648, reg 2(a).

3 APPLICATION OF REGULATIONS

(1)   These Regulations apply to packages sold or offered for sale in the territory of the United Kingdom.

(2)   Regulations 4 to 15 apply to packages so sold or offered for sale on or after 31st December 1992.

(3)   Regulations 16 to 22 apply to contracts which, in whole or part, remain to be performed on 31st December 1992.

4 DESCRIPTIVE MATTER RELATING TO PACKAGES MUST NOT BE MISLEADING

(1)   No organiser or retailer shall supply to a consumer any descriptive matter concerning a package, the price of a package or any other conditions applying to the contract which contains any misleading information.

(2)   If an organiser or retailer is in breach of paragraph (1) he shall be liable to compensate the consumer for any loss which the consumer suffers in consequence.

5 REQUIREMENTS AS TO BROCHURES

(1)   Subject to paragraph (4) below, no organiser shall make available a brochure to a possible consumer unless it indicates in a legible, comprehensible and accurate manner the price and adequate information about the matters specified in Schedule 1 to these Regulations in respect of the packages offered for sale in the brochure to the extent that those matters are relevant to the packages so offered.

(2)   Subject to paragraph (4) below, no retailer shall make available to a possible consumer a brochure which he knows or has reasonable cause to believe does not comply with the requirements of paragraph (1).

(3)   An organiser who contravenes paragraph (1) of this regulation and a retailer who contravenes paragraph (2) thereof shall be guilty of an offence and liable:—

(a)   on summary conviction, to a fine not exceeding level 5 on the standard scale; and

(b)   on conviction on indictment, to a fine.

(4)   Where a brochure was first made available to consumers generally before 31st December 1992 no liability shall arise under this regulation in respect of an identical brochure being made available to a consumer at any time.

6 CIRCUMSTANCES IN WHICH PARTICULARS IN BROCHURE ARE TO BE BINDING

(1)   Subject to paragraphs (2) and (3) of this regulation, the particulars in the brochure (whether or not they are required by regulation 5(1) above to be included in the brochure) shall constitute implied warranties (or, as regards Scotland, implied terms) for the purposes of any contract to which the particulars relate.

(2)   Paragraph (1) of this regulation does not apply—

> (a)   in relation to information required to be included by virtue of paragraph 9 of Schedule 1 to these Regulations; or

> (b)   where the brochure contains an express statement that changes may be made in the particulars contained in it before a contract is concluded and changes in the particulars so contained are clearly communicated to the consumer before a contract is concluded.

(3)   Paragraph (1) of this regulation does not apply when the consumer and the other party to the contract agree after the contract has been made that the particulars in the brochure, or some of those particulars, should not form part of the contract.

7 INFORMATION TO BE PROVIDED BEFORE CONTRACT IS CONCLUDED

(1)   Before a contract is concluded, the other party to the contract shall provide the intending consumer with the information specified in paragraph (2) below in writing or in some other appropriate form.

(2)   The information referred to in paragraph (1) is:—

> (a)   general information about passport and visa requirements which apply to [nationals of the member State or States concerned] who purchase the package in question, including information about the length of time it is likely to take to obtain the appropriate passports and visas;

> (b)   information about health formalities required for the journey and the stay; and

> (c)   the arrangements for security for the money paid over and (where applicable) for the repatriation of the consumer in the event of insolvency.

(3)   If the intending consumer is not provided with the information required by paragraph (1) in accordance with that paragraph the other party to the contract shall be guilty of an offence and liable:—

(a)   on summary conviction, to a fine not exceeding level 5 on the standard scale; and

(b)   on conviction on indictment, to a fine.

NOTES
Amendment
Para (2): in sub-para (a) words "nationals of the member State or States concerned" in square brackets substituted by SI 1998/1208, reg 5.
Date in force: 30 June 1998: see SI 1998/1208, reg 1.

8 INFORMATION TO BE PROVIDED IN GOOD TIME

(1) The other party to the contract shall in good time before the start of the journey provide the consumer with the information specified in paragraph (2) below in writing or in some other appropriate form.

(2) The information referred to in paragraph (1) is the following:—

(a)   the times and places of intermediate stops and transport connections and particulars of the place to be occupied by the traveller (for example, cabin or berth on ship, sleeper compartment on train);

(b)   the name, address and telephone number—

(i) of the representative of the other party to the contract in the locality where the consumer is to stay,

or, if there is no such representative,

(ii) of an agency in that locality on whose assistance a consumer in difficulty would be able to call,

or, if there is no such representative or agency, a telephone number or other information which will enable the consumer to contact the other party to the contract during the stay; and

(c)   in the case of a journey or stay abroad by a child under the age of 16 on the day when the journey or stay is due to start, information enabling direct contact to be made with the child or the person responsible at the place where he is to stay; and

(d)   except where the consumer is required as a term of the contract to take out an insurance policy in order to cover the cost of cancellation by the consumer or the cost of assistance, including repatriation, in the event of accident or illness, information about an insurance policy which the consumer may, if he wishes, take out in respect of the risk of those costs being incurred.

(3) If the consumer is not provided with the information required by paragraph (1) in accordance with that paragraph the other party to the contract shall be guilty of an offence and liable:—

(a)   on summary conviction, to a fine not exceeding level 5 on the standard scale; and

(b)   on conviction on indictment, to a fine.

9 CONTENTS AND FORM OF CONTRACT

(1) The other party to the contract shall ensure that—

(a)   depending on the nature of the package being purchased, the contract contains at least the elements specified in Schedule 2 to these Regulations;

(b)   subject to paragraph (2) below, all the terms of the contract are set out in writing or such other form as is comprehensible and accessible to the consumer and are communicated to the consumer before the contract is made; and

(c)   a written copy of these terms is supplied to the consumer.

(2) Paragraph (1)(b) above does not apply when the interval between the time when the consumer approaches the other party to the contract with a view to entering into a contract and the time of departure under the proposed contract is so short that it is impracticable to comply with the sub-paragraph.

(3) It is an implied condition (or, as regards Scotland, an implied term) of the contract that the other party to the contract complies with the provisions of paragraph (1).

(4) In Scotland, any breach of the condition implied by paragraph (3) above shall be deemed to be a material breach justifying rescission of the contract.

10 TRANSFER OF BOOKINGS

(1) In every contract there is an implied term that where the consumer is prevented from proceeding with the package the consumer may transfer his booking to a person who satisfies all the conditions applicable to the package, provided that the consumer gives reasonable notice to the other party to the contract of his intention to transfer before the date when departure is due to take place.

(2) Where a transfer is made in accordance with the implied term set out in paragraph (1) above, the transferor and the transferee shall be jointly and severally liable to the other party to the contract for payment of the price of the package (or, if part of the price has been paid, for payment of the balance) and for any additional costs arising from such transfer.

11 PRICE REVISION

(1) Any term in a contract to the effect that the prices laid down in the contract may be revised shall be void and of no effect unless the contract provides for the possibility of upward or downward revision and satisfies the conditions laid down in paragraph (2) below.

(2) The conditions mentioned in paragraph (1) are that—

(a)   the contract states precisely how the revised price is to be calculated;

(b)	the contract provides that price revisions are to be made solely to allow for variations in:—

(i)	transportation costs, including the cost of fuel,

(ii)	dues, taxes or fees chargeable for services such as landing taxes or embarkation or disembarkation fees at ports and airports, or

(iii)	the exchange rates applied to the particular package; and

(3)	Notwithstanding any terms of a contract,

(i)	no price increase may be made in a specified period which may not be less than 30 days before the departure date stipulated; and

(ii)	as against an individual consumer liable under the contract, no price increase may be made in respect of variations which would produce an increase of less than 2 per cent, or such greater percentage as the contract may specify,("non-eligible variations") and that the non-eligible variations shall be left out of account in the calculation.

12 SIGNIFICANT ALTERATIONS TO ESSENTIAL TERMS

In every contract there are implied terms to the effect that—

(a)	where the organiser is constrained before the departure to alter significantly an essential term of the contract, such as the price (so far as regulation 11 permits him to do so), he will notify the consumer as quickly as possible in order to enable him to take appropriate decisions and in particular to withdraw from the contract without penalty or to accept a rider to the contract specifying the alterations made and their impact on the price; and

(b)	the consumer will inform the organiser or the retailer of his decision as soon as possible.

13 WITHDRAWAL BY CONSUMER PURSUANT TO REGULATION 12 AND CANCELLATION BY ORGANISER

(1)	The terms set out in paragraphs (2) and (3) below are implied in every contract and apply where the consumer withdraws from the contract pursuant to the term in it implied by virtue of regulation 12(a), or where the organiser, for any reason other than the fault of the consumer, cancels the package before the agreed date of departure.

(2)	The consumer is entitled—

(a)   to take a substitute package of equivalent or superior quality if the other party to the contract is able to offer him such a substitute; or

(b)   to take a substitute package of lower quality if the other party to the contract is able to offer him one and to recover from the organiser the difference in price between the price of the package purchased and that of the substitute package; or

(c)   to have repaid to him as soon as possible all the monies paid by him under the contract.

(3) The consumer is entitled, if appropriate, to be compensated by the organiser for non-performance of the contract except where—

(a)   the package is cancelled because the number of persons who agree to take it is less than the minimum number required and the consumer is informed of the cancellation, in writing, within the period indicated in the description of the package; or

(b)   the package is cancelled by reason of unusual and unforeseeable circumstances beyond the control of the party by whom this exception is pleaded, the consequences of which could not have been avoided even if all due care had been exercised.

(4) Overbooking shall not be regarded as a circumstance falling within the provisions of sub-paragraph (b) of paragraph (3) above.

14 SIGNIFICANT PROPORTION OF SERVICES NOT PROVIDED

(1) The terms set out in paragraphs (2) and (3) below are implied in every contract and apply where, after departure, a significant proportion of the services contracted for is not provided or the organiser becomes aware that he will be unable to procure a significant proportion of the services to be provided.

(2) The organiser will make suitable alternative arrangements, at no extra cost to the consumer, for the continuation of the package and will, where appropriate, compensate the consumer for the difference between the services to be supplied under the contract and those supplied.

(3) If it is impossible to make arrangements as described in paragraph (2), or these are not accepted by the consumer for good reasons, the organiser will, where appropriate, provide the consumer with equivalent transport back to the place of departure or to another place to which the consumer has agreed and will, where appropriate, compensate the consumer.

15 LIABILITY OF OTHER PARTY TO THE CONTRACT FOR PROPER PERFORMANCE OF OBLIGATIONS UNDER CONTRACT

(1) The other party to the contract is liable to the consumer for the proper performance of the obligations under the contract, irrespective of whether such obligations are to be performed by that other party or by other suppliers of services but this shall not affect any remedy or right of action which that other party may have against those other suppliers of services.

(2) The other party to the contract is liable to the consumer for any damage caused to him by the failure to perform the contract or the improper performance of the contract unless the failure or the improper performance is due neither to any fault of that other party nor to that of another supplier of services, because—

> (a)   the failures which occur in the performance of the contract are attributable to the consumer;

> (b)   such failures are attributable to a third party unconnected with the provision of the services contracted for, and are unforeseeable or unavoidable; or

> (c)   such failures are due to—

>> (i) unusual and unforeseeable circumstances beyond the control of the party by whom this exception is pleaded, the consequences of which could not have been avoided even if all due care had been exercised; or

>> (ii) an event which the other party to the contract or the supplier of services, even with all due care, could not foresee or forestall.

(3) In the case of damage arising from the non-performance or improper performance of the services involved in the package, the contract may provide for compensation to be limited in accordance with the international conventions which govern such services.

(4) In the case of damage other than personal injury resulting from the non-performance or improper performance of the services involved in the package, the contract may include a term limiting the amount of compensation which will be paid to the consumer, provided that the limitation is not unreasonable.

(5) Without prejudice to paragraph (3) and paragraph (4) above, liability under paragraphs (1) and (2) above cannot be excluded by any contractual term.

(6) The terms set out in paragraphs (7) and (8) below are implied in every contract.

(7) In the circumstances described in paragraph (2)(b) and (c) of this regulation, the other party to the contract will give prompt assistance to a consumer in difficulty.

(8)   If the consumer complains about a defect in the performance of the contract, the other party to the contract, or his local representative, if there is one, will make prompt efforts to find appropriate solutions.

(9)   The contract must clearly and explicitly oblige the consumer to communicate at the earliest opportunity, in writing or any other appropriate form, to the supplier of the services concerned and to the other party to the contract any failure which he perceives at the place where the services concerned are supplied.

16 SECURITY IN EVENT OF INSOLVENCY—REQUIREMENTS AND OFFENCES

(1)   The other party to the contract shall at all times be able to provide sufficient evidence of security for the refund of money paid over and for the repatriation of the consumer in the event of insolvency.

(2)   Without prejudice to paragraph (1) above, and subject to paragraph (4) below, save to the extent that—

> (a)   the package is covered by measures adopted or retained by the member State where he is established for the purpose of implementing Article 7 of the Directive; or
>
> (b)   the package is one in respect of which he is required to hold a licence under the Civil Aviation (Air Travel Organisers' Licensing) Regulations 1972 or the package is one that is covered by the arrangements he has entered into for the purposes of those Regulations,

the other party to the contract shall at least ensure that there are in force arrangements as described in regulations 17,18, 19 or 20 or, if that party is acting otherwise than in the course of business, as described in any of those regulations or in regulation 21.

(3)   Any person who contravenes paragraph (1) or (2) of this regulation shall be guilty of an offence and liable:—

> (a)   on summary conviction to a fine not exceeding level 5 on the standard scale; and
>
> (b)   on conviction on indictment, to a fine.

(4)   A person shall not be guilty of an offence under paragraph (3) above by reason only of the fact that arrangements such as are mentioned in paragraph (2) above are not in force in respect of any period before 1 April 1993 unless money paid over is not refunded when it is due or the consumer is not repatriated in the event of insolvency.

(5)   For the purposes of regulations 17 to 21 below a contract shall be treated as having been fully performed if the package or, as the case may be, the part of the package has been completed irrespective of whether the obligations under the contract have been properly performed for the purposes of regulation 15.

17 BONDING

(1) The other party to the contract shall ensure that a bond is entered into by an authorised institution under which the institution binds itself to pay to an approved body of which that other party is a member a sum calculated in accordance with paragraph (3) below in the event of the insolvency of that other party.

(2) Any bond entered into pursuant to paragraph (1) above shall not be expressed to be in force for a period exceeding eighteen months.

(3) The sum referred to in paragraph (1) above shall be such sum as may reasonably be expected to enable all monies paid over by consumers under or in contemplation of contracts for relevant packages which have not been fully performed to be repaid and shall not in any event be a sum which is less than the minimum sum calculated in accordance with paragraph (4) below.

(4) The minimum sum for the purposes of paragraph (3) above shall be a sum which represents:—

> (a)   not less than 25 per cent of all the payments which the other party to the contract estimates that he will receive under or in contemplation of contracts for relevant packages in the twelve month period from the date of entry into force of the bond referred to in paragraph (1) above; or

> (b)   the maximum amount of all the payments which the other party to the contract expects to hold at any one time, in respect of contracts which have not been fully performed,

whichever sum is the smaller.

(5) Before a bond is entered into pursuant to paragraph (1) above, the other party to the contract shall inform the approved body of which he is a member of the minimum sum which he proposes for the purposes of paragraphs (3) and (4) above and it shall be the duty of the approved body to consider whether such sum is sufficient for the purpose mentioned in paragraph (3) and, if it does not consider that this is the case, it shall be the duty of the approved body so to inform the other party to the contract and to inform him of the sum which, in the opinion of the approved body, is sufficient for that purpose.

(6) Where an approved body has informed the other party to the contract of a sum pursuant to paragraph (5) above, the minimum sum for the purposes of paragraphs (3) and (4) above shall be that sum.

(7) In this regulation—

"approved body" means a body which is for the time being approved by the Secretary of State for the purposes of this regulation;

"authorised institution" means a person authorised under the law of a member State[, of the Channel Islands or of the Isle of Man] to carry on the business of entering into bonds of the kind required by this regulation.

NOTES
Amendment
Para (7): in definition "authorised institution" words in square brackets inserted by SI 1995/1648, reg 2(b).

18 BONDING WHERE APPROVED BODY HAS RESERVE FUND OR INSURANCE

(1)   The other party to the contract shall ensure that a bond is entered into by an authorised institution, under which the institution agrees to pay to an approved body of which that other party is a member a sum calculated in accordance with paragraph (3) below in the event of the insolvency of that other party.

(2)   Any bond entered into pursuant to paragraph (1) above shall not be expressed to be in force for a period exceeding eighteen months.

(3)   The sum referred to in paragraph (1) above shall be such sum as may be specified by the approved body as representing the lesser of—

> (a)   the maximum amount of all the payments which the other party to the contract expects to hold at any one time in respect of contracts which have not been fully performed; or

> (b)   the minimum sum calculated in accordance with paragraph (4) below.

(4)   The minimum sum for the purposes of paragraph (3) above shall be a sum which represents not less than 10 per cent of all the payments which the other party to the contract estimates that he will receive under or in contemplation of contracts for relevant packages in the twelve month period from the date of entry referred to in paragraph (1) above.

(5)   In this regulation "approved body" means a body which is for the time being approved by the Secretary of State for the purposes of this regulation and no such approval shall be given unless the conditions mentioned in paragraph (6) below are satisfied in relation to it.

(6)   A body may not be approved for the purposes of this regulation unless—

> (a)   it has a reserve fund or insurance cover with an insurer authorised in respect of such business in a member State[, the Channel Islands or the Isle of Man] of an amount in each case which is designed to enable all monies paid over to a member of the body of consumers under or in contemplation of contracts for relevant packages which have not been fully performed to be repaid to those consumers in the event of the insolvency of the member; and

(b)   where it has a reserve fund, it agrees that the fund will be held by persons and in a manner approved by the Secretary of State.

(7)   In this regulation, authorised institution has the meaning given to that expression by paragraph (7) of regulation 17.

NOTES
Amendment
Para (6): in sub-para (a) words in square brackets inserted by SI 1995/1648, reg 2(c).

19 INSURANCE

(1)   The other party to the contract shall have insurance under one or more appropriate policies with an insurer authorised in respect of such business in a member State under which the insurer agrees to indemnify consumers, who shall be insured persons under the policy, against the loss of money paid over by them under or in contemplation of contracts for packages in the event of the insolvency of the contractor.

(2)   The other party to the contract shall ensure that it is a term of every contract with a consumer that the consumer acquires the benefit of a policy of a kind mentioned in paragraph (1) above in the event of the insolvency of the other party to the contract.

(3)   In this regulation:

"appropriate policy" means one which does not contain a condition which provides (in whatever terms) that no liability shall arise under the policy, or that any liability so arising shall cease:—

(i)   in the event of some specified thing being done or omitted to be done after the happening of the event giving rise to a claim under the policy;

(ii)   in the event of the policy holder not making payments under or in connection with other policies; or

(iii)   unless the policy holder keeps specified records or provides the insurer with or makes available to him information therefrom.

20 MONIES IN TRUST

(1)   The other party to the contract shall ensure that all monies paid over by a consumer under or in contemplation of a contract for a relevant package are held in the United Kingdom by a person as trustee for the consumer until the contract has been fully performed or any sum of money paid by the consumer in respect of the contract has been repaid to him or has been forfeited on cancellation by the consumer.

(2)   The costs of administering the trust mentioned in paragraph (1) above shall be paid for by the other party to the contract.

(3)   Any interest which is earned on the monies held by the trustee pursuant to paragraph (1) shall be held for the other party to the contract and shall be payable to him on demand.

(4)   Where there is produced to the trustee a statement signed by the other party to the contract to the effect that—

> (a)   a contract for a package the price of which is specified in that statement has been fully performed;

> (b)   the other party to the contract has repaid to the consumer a sum of money specified in that statement which the consumer had paid in respect of a contract for a package; or

> (c)   the consumer has on cancellation forfeited a sum of money specified in that statement which he had paid in respect of a contract for a relevant package,

the trustee shall (subject to paragraph (5) below) release to the other party to the contract the sum specified in the statement.

(5)   Where the trustee considers it appropriate to do so, he may require the other party to the contract to provide further information or evidence of the matters mentioned in sub-paragraph (a),(b) or (c) of paragraph (4) above before he releases any sum to that other party pursuant to that paragraph.

(6)   Subject to paragraph (7) below, in the event of the insolvency of the other party to the contract the monies held in trust by the trustee pursuant to paragraph (1) of this regulation shall be applied to meet the claims of consumers who are creditors of that other party in respect of contracts for packages in respect of which the arrangements were established and which have not been fully performed and, if there is a surplus after those claims have been met, it shall form part of the estate of that insolvent other party for the purposes of insolvency law.

(7)   If the monies held in trust by the trustee pursuant to paragraph (1) of this regulation are insufficient to meet the claims of consumers as described in paragraph (6), payments to those consumers shall be made by the trustee on a pari passu basis.

21 MONIES IN TRUST WHERE OTHER PARTY TO CONTRACT IS ACTING OTHERWISE THAN IN THE COURSE OF BUSINESS

(1)   The other party to the contract shall ensure that all monies paid over by a consumer under or in contemplation of a contract for a relevant package are held in the United Kingdom by a person as trustee for the consumer for the purpose of paying for the consumer's package.

(2) The costs of administering the trust mentioned in paragraph (1) shall be paid for out of the monies held in trust and the interest earned on those monies.

(3) Where there is produced to the trustee a statement signed by the other party to the contract to the effect that—

(a) the consumer has previously paid over a sum of money specified in that statement in respect of a contract for a package and that sum is required for the purpose of paying for a component (or part of a component) of the package;

(b) the consumer has previously paid over a sum of money specified in that statement in respect of a contract for a package and the other party to the contract has paid that sum in respect of a component (or part of a component) of the package;

(c) the consumer requires the repayment to him of a sum of money specified in that statement which was previously paid over by the consumer in respect of a contract for a package; or

(d) the consumer has on cancellation forfeited a sum of money specified in that statement which he had paid in respect of a contract for a package,

the trustee shall (subject to paragraph (4) below) release to the other party to the contract the sum specified in the statement.

(4) Where the trustee considers it appropriate to do so, he may require the other party to the contract to provide further information or evidence of the matters mentioned in sub-paragraph (a),(b),(c) or (d) of paragraph (3) above before he releases to that other party any sum from the monies held in trust for the consumer.

(5) Subject to paragraph (6) below, in the event of the insolvency of the other party to the contract and of contracts for packages not being fully performed (whether before or after the insolvency) the monies held in trust by the trustee pursuant to paragraph (1) of this regulation shall be applied to meet the claims of consumers who are creditors of that other party in respect of amounts paid over by them and remaining in the trust fund after deductions have been made in respect of amounts released to that other party pursuant to paragraph (3) and, if there is a surplus after those claims have been met, it shall be divided amongst those consumers pro rata.

(6) If the monies held in trust by the trustee pursuant to paragraph (1) of this regulation are insufficient to meet the claims of consumers as described in paragraph (5) above, payments to those consumers shall be made by the trustee on a pari passu basis.

(7) Any sums remaining after all the packages in respect of which the arrangements were established have been fully performed shall be dealt with as provided in the arrangements or, in default of such provision, may be paid to the other party to the contract.

22 OFFENCES ARISING FROM BREACH OF REGULATIONS 20 AND 21

(1)   If the other party to the contract makes a false statement under paragraph (4) of regulation 20 or paragraph (3) of regulation 21 he shall be guilty of an offence.

(2)   If the other party to the contract applies monies released to him on the basis of a statement made by him under regulation 21(3)(a) or (c) for a purpose other than that mentioned in the statement he shall be guilty of an offence.

(3)   If the other party to the contract is guilty of an offence under paragraph (1) or (2) of this regulation shall be liable—

>   (a)   on summary conviction to a fine not exceeding level 5 on the standard scale; and

>   (b)   on conviction on indictment, to a fine.

23 ENFORCEMENT

Schedule 3 to these Regulations (which makes provision about the enforcement of regulations 5, 7, 8, 16 and 22 of these Regulations) shall have effect.

24 DUE DILIGENCE DEFENCE

(1)   Subject to the following provisions of this regulation, in proceedings against any person for an offence under regulation 5, 7, 8, 16 or 22 of these Regulations, it shall be a defence for that person to show that he took all reasonable steps and exercised all due diligence to avoid committing the offence.

(2)   Where in any proceedings against any person for such an offence the defence provided by paragraph (1) above involves an allegation that the commission of the offence was due—

>   (a)   to the act or default of another; or

>   (b)   to reliance on information given by another,

that person shall not, without the leave of the court, be entitled to rely on the defence unless, not less than seven clear days before the hearing of the proceedings, or, in Scotland, the trial diet, he has served a notice under paragraph (3) below on the person bringing the proceedings.

(3)   A notice under this paragraph shall give such information identifying or assisting in the identification of the person who committed the act or default or gave the information as is in the possession of the person serving the notice at the time he serves it.

(4)   It is hereby declared that a person shall not be entitled to rely on the defence provided by paragraph (1) above by reason of his reliance on information supplied by another, unless he shows that it was reasonable in all the circumstances for him to have relied on the information, having regard in particular—

(a)   to the steps which he took, and those which might reasonably have been taken, for the purpose of verifying the information; and

(b)   to whether he had any reason to disbelieve the information.

25 LIABILITY OF PERSONS OTHER THAN PRINCIPAL OFFENDER

(1)   Where the commission by any person of an offence under regulation 5, 7, 8, 16 or 22 of these Regulations is due to an act or default committed by some other person in the course of any business of his, the other person shall be guilty of the offence and may be proceeded against and punished by virtue of this paragraph whether or not proceedings are taken against the first-mentioned person.

(2)   Where a body corporate is guilty of an offence under any of the provisions mentioned in paragraph (1) above (including where it is so guilty by virtue of the said paragraph (1)) in respect of any act or default which is shown to have been committed with the consent or connivance of, or to be attributable to any neglect on the part of, any director, manager, secretary or other similar officer of the body corporate or any person who was purporting to act in any such capacity he, as well as the body corporate, shall be guilty of that offence and shall be liable to be proceeded against and punished accordingly.

(3)   Where the affairs of a body corporate are managed by its members, paragraph (2) above shall apply in relation to the acts and defaults of a member in connection with his functions of management as if he were a director of the body corporate.

(4)   Where an offence under any of the provisions mentioned in paragraph (1) above committed in Scotland by a Scottish partnership is proved to have been committed with the consent or connivance of, or to be attributable to neglect on the part of, a partner, he (as well as the partnership) is guilty of the offence and liable to be proceeded against and punished accordingly.

(5)   On proceedings for an offence under regulation 5 by virtue of paragraph (1) above committed by the making available of a brochure it shall be a defence for the person charged to prove that he is a person whose business it is to publish or arrange for the publication of brochures and that he received the brochure for publication in the ordinary course of business and did not know and had no reason to suspect that its publication would amount to an offence under these Regulations.

26 PROSECUTION TIME LIMIT

(1)   No proceedings for an offence under regulation 5, 7, 8, 16 or 22 of these Regulations or under paragraphs 5(3), 6 or 7 of Schedule 3 thereto shall be commenced after—

(a)   the end of the period of three years beginning within the date of the commission of the offence; or

(b)   the end of the period of one year beginning with the date of the discovery of the offence by the prosecutor,

whichever is the earlier.

(2)   For the purposes of this regulation a certificate signed by or on behalf of the prosecutor and stating the date on which the offence was discovered by him shall be conclusive evidence of that fact; and a certificate stating that matter and purporting to be so signed shall be treated as so signed unless the contrary is proved.

(3)   In relation to proceedings in Scotland, subsection (3) of section 331 of the Criminal Procedure (Scotland) Act 1975 (date of commencement of proceedings) shall apply for the purposes of this regulation as it applies for the purposes of that section.

27 SAVING FOR CIVIL CONSEQUENCES

No contract shall be void or unenforceable, and no right of action in civil proceedings in respect of any loss shall arise, by reason only of the commission of an offence under regulations 5, 7, 8, 16 or 22 of these Regulations.

28 TERMS IMPLIED IN CONTRACT

Where it is provided in these Regulations that a term (whether so described or whether described as a condition or warranty) is implied in the contract it is so implied irrespective of the law which governs the contract.

SCHEDULE 1INFORMATION TO BE INCLUDED (IN ADDITION TO THE PRICE) IN BROCHURES WHERE RELEVANT TO PACKAGES OFFERED

Regulation 5

1 The destination and the means, characteristics and categories of transport used.

2 The type of accommodation, its location, category or degree of comfort and its main features and, where the accommodation is to be provided in a member State, its approval or tourist classification under the rules of that member State.

3 The meals which are included in the package.

4 The itinerary.

5 General information about passport and visa requirements which apply for [nationals of the member State or States in which the brochure is made available] and health formalities required for the journey and the stay.

6 Either the monetary amount or the percentage of the price which is to be paid on account and the timetable for payment of the balance.

7 Whether a minimum number of persons is required for the package to take place and, if so, the deadline for informing the consumer in the event of cancellation.

8 The arrangements (if any) which apply if consumers are delayed at the outward or homeward points of departure.

9 The arrangements for security for money paid over and for the repatriation of the consumer in the event of insolvency.

NOTES
Amendment
Para 5: words "nationals of the member State or States in which the brochure is made available" in square brackets substituted by SI 1998/1208, reg 4.
Date in force: 30 June 1998: see SI 1998/1208, reg 1.

SCHEDULE 2 ELEMENTS TO BE INCLUDED IN THE CONTRACT IF RELEVANT TO THE PARTICULAR PACKAGE

REGULATION 9

1 The travel destination(s) and, where periods of stay are involved, the relevant periods, with dates.

2 The means, characteristics and categories of transport to be used and the dates, times and points of departure and return.

3 Where the package includes accommodation, its location, its tourist category or degree of comfort, its main features and, where the accommodation is to be provided in a member State, its compliance with the rules of that member State.

4 The meals which are included in the package.

5 Whether a minimum number of persons is required for the package to take place and, if so, the deadline for informing the consumer in the event of cancellation.

6 The itinerary.

7 Visits, excursions or other services which are included in the total price agreed for the package.

8 The name and address of the organiser, the retailer and, where appropriate, the insurer.

9 The price of the package, if the price may be revised in accordance with the term which may be included in the contract under regulation 11, an indication of the possibility of such price revisions, and an indication of any dues, taxes or fees chargeable for certain services (landing, embarkation or disembarkation fees at ports and airports and tourist taxes) where such costs are not included in the package.

10 The payment schedule and method of payment.

11 Special requirements which the consumer has communicated to the organiser or retailer when making the booking and which both have accepted.

12 The periods within which the consumer must make any complaint about the failure to perform or the inadequate performance of the contract.

SCHEDULE 3 ENFORCEMENT

REGULATION 23

ENFORCEMENT AUTHORITY

1(1)   Every local weights and measures authority in Great Britain shall be an enforcement authority for the purposes of regulations 5, 7, 8, 16 and 22 of these Regulations ("the relevant regulations"), and it shall be the duty of each such authority to enforce those provisions within their area.

(2)   The Department of Economic Development in Northern Ireland shall be an enforcement authority for the purposes of the relevant regulations, and it shall be the duty of the Department to enforce those provisions within Northern Ireland.

PROSECUTIONS

2(1)   Where an enforcement authority in England or Wales proposes to institute proceedings for an offence under any of the relevant regulations, it shall as between the enforcement authority and the Director General of Fair Trading be the duty of the enforcement authority to give to the Director General of Fair Trading notice of the intended proceedings, together with a summary of the facts on which the charges are to be founded, and to postpone institution of the proceedings until either—

(a)   twenty-eight days have elapsed since the giving of that notice; or

(b)   the Director General of Fair Trading has notified the enforcement authority that he has received the notice and the summary of the facts.

(2) Nothing in paragraph 1 above shall authorise a local weights and measures authority to bring proceedings in Scotland for an offence.

POWERS OF OFFICERS OF ENFORCEMENT AUTHORITY

3(1) If a duly authorised officer of an enforcement authority has reasonable grounds for suspecting that an offence has been committed under any of the relevant regulations, he may—

(a) require a person whom he believes on reasonable grounds to be engaged in the organisation or retailing of packages to produce any book or document relating to the activity and take copies of it or any entry in it, or

(b) require such a person to produce in a visible and legible documentary form any information so relating which is contained in a computer, and take copies of it,

for the purpose of ascertaining whether such an offence has been committed.

(2) Such an officer may inspect any goods for the purpose of ascertaining whether such an offence has been committed.

(3) If such an officer has reasonable grounds for believing that any documents or goods may be required as evidence in proceedings for such an offence, he may seize and detain them.

(4) An officer seizing any documents or goods in the exercise of his power under sub-paragraph (3) above shall inform the person from whom they are seized.

(5) The powers of an officer under this paragraph may be exercised by him only at a reasonable hour and on production (if required) of his credentials.

(6) Nothing in this paragraph—

(a) requires a person to produce a document if he would be entitled to refuse to produce it in proceedings in a court on the ground that it is the subject of legal professional privilege or, in Scotland, that it contains a confidential communication made by or to an advocate or a solicitor in that capacity; or

(b) authorises the taking possession of a document which is in the possession of a person who would be so entitled.

4(1) A duly authorised officer of an enforcement authority may, at a reasonable hour and on production (if required) of his credentials, enter any premises for the purpose of ascertaining whether an offence under any of the relevant regulations has been committed.

(2) If a justice of the peace, or in Scotland a justice of the peace or a sheriff, is satisfied—

> (a)   that any relevant books, documents or goods are on, or that any relevant information contained in a computer is available from, any premises, and that production or inspection is likely to disclose the commission of an offence under the relevant regulations; or

> (b)   that any such an offence has been, is being or is about to be committed on any premises.

and that any of the conditions specified in sub-paragraph (3) below is met, he may by warrant under his hand authorise an officer of an enforcement authority to enter the premises, if need be by force.

(3) The conditions referred to in sub-paragraph (2) above are—

> (a)   that admission to the premises has been or is likely to be refused and that notice of intention to apply for a warrant under that sub-paragraph has been given to the occupier;

> (b)   that an application for admission, or the giving of such a notice, would defeat the object of the entry;

> (c)   that the premises are unoccupied; and

> (d)   that the occupier is temporarily absent and it might defeat the object of the entry to await his return.

(4) In sub-paragraph (2) above "relevant", in relation to books, documents, goods or information, means books, documents, goods or information which, under paragraph 3 above, a duly authorised officer may require to be produced or may inspect.

(5) A warrant under sub-paragraph (2) above may be issued only if—

> (a)   in England and Wales, the justice of the peace is satisfied as required by that sub-paragraph by written information on oath;

> (b)   in Scotland, the justice of the peace or sheriff is so satisfied by evidence on oath; or

> (c)   in Northern Ireland, the justice of the peace is so satisfied by complaint on oath.

(6) A warrant under sub-paragraph (2) above shall continue in force for a period of one month.

(7) An officer entering any premises by virtue of this paragraph may take with him such other persons as may appear to him necessary.

(8) On leaving premises which he has entered by virtue of a warrant under sub-paragraph (2) above, an officer shall, if the premises are unoccupied or the occupier is temporarily absent, leave the premises as effectively secured against trespassers as he found them.

(9) In this paragraph "premises" includes any place (including any vehicle, ship or aircraft) except premises used only as a dwelling.

OBSTRUCTION OF OFFICERS

5(1) A person who—

(a) intentionally obstructs an officer of an enforcement authority acting in pursuance of this Schedule;

(b) without reasonable excuse fails to comply with a requirement made of him by such an officer under paragraph 3(1) above; or

(c) without reasonable excuse fails to give an officer of an enforcement authority acting in pursuance of this Schedule any other assistance or information which the officer may reasonably require of him for the purpose of the performance of the officer's functions under this Schedule,

shall be guilty of an offence.

(2) A person guilty of an offence under sub-paragraph (1) above shall be liable on summary conviction to a fine not exceeding level 5 on the standard scale.

(3) If a person, in giving any such information as is mentioned in sub-paragraph (1)(c) above,—

(a) makes a statement which he knows is false in a material particular; or

(b) recklessly makes a statement which is false in a material particular,

he shall be guilty of an offence.

(4) A person guilty of an offence under sub-paragraph (3) above shall be liable—

(a)   on summary conviction, to a fine not exceeding level 5 on the standard scale; and

(b)   on conviction on indictment, to a fine.

IMPERSONATION OF OFFICERS

6(1)   If a person who is not a duly authorised officer of an enforcement authority purports to act as such under this Schedule he shall be guilty of an offence.

(2)   A person guilty of an offence under sub-paragraph (1) above shall be liable—

(a)   on summary conviction, to a fine not exceeding level 5 on the standard scale; and

(b)   on conviction on indictment, to a fine.

DISCLOSURE OF INFORMATION

7(1)   If a person discloses to another any information obtained by him by virtue of this Schedule he shall be guilty of an offence unless the disclosure was made—

(a)   in or for the purpose of the performance by him or any other person of any function under the relevant regulations; or

(b)   for a purpose specified in section 38(2)(a),(b) or (c) of the Consumer Protection Act 1987.

(2)   A person guilty of an offence under sub-paragraph (1) above shall be liable—

(a)   on summary conviction, to a fine not exceeding level 5 on the standard scale; and

(b)   on conviction on indictment, to a fine.

PRIVILEGE AGAINST SELF-INCRIMINATION

8 Nothing in this Schedule requires a person to answer any question or give any information if to do so might incriminate him.

Lightning Source UK Ltd.
Milton Keynes UK
19 August 2010
158657UK00001B/2/P